The American People

The American People

Stories,
Legends,
Tales,
Traditions,
and
Songs

B. A. Botkin

With a new introduction by
Louis Filler

Transaction Publishers
New Brunswick (U.S.A.) and London (U.K.)

This book is printed on acid-free paper that meets the American National Standard for Permanence of Paper for Printed Library Materials.

Library of Congress Catalog Number: 97–27086
ISBN: 1–56000–984–5
Printed in the United States of America

Library of Congress Cataloging-in-Publication Data

Botkin, Benjamin Albert, 1901–1975.
    The American people : stories, legends, tales, traditions and songs / B.A. Botkin ; with a new introduction by Louis Filler.
        p. cm.
    Originally published: London : Pilot Press, 1946.
    Includes bibliographical references.
    ISBN 1–56000–984–5 (pbk. : alk. paper)
    1. Folklore—United States. 2. Tales—United States. 3. Legends—United States. 4. Folk songs, American. 5. United States—Social life and customs. I. Title.
GR105.B56   1997
398'.0973—dc21   97–27086
                                                                                CIP

Contents

Miracle Men

Patron Saints

PART TWO: BOOSTERS AND KNOCKERS

Tall Talk

Local Cracks and Slams

PART THREE: JESTERS

Pranks and Tricks

Humorous Anecdotes and Jests

PART FOUR: LIARS

PART FIVE: FOLK TALES AND LEGENDS

Witches, Devils and Ghosts

PART SIX: SONGS AND RHYMES

Rhymes, Catches and Songs

Ballads and Songs

Introduction to the Transaction Edition

Ben Botkin:
Much More Than Folklore

I first met Ben Botkin in 1944 in a government warehouse in Washington, D.C. The national records of the Federal Art Project of the Works' Progress Administration had been stored or stacked there while arrangements were being made to move them into the National Archives. Those stacks covered Federal Project Number One, familiarly known as Federal One, including the Federal Art Project, the Federal Writers' Project, the Federal Music Project, the Federal Theater Project, and one project that included the social arts, of which the Index of American Design—native concepts in architecture, costume, houseware, and whatever—became famous and is still culled through by design experts today.

A Rockefeller grant to the American Council of Learned Societies had called for scholars to prepare studies from those records. A Columbia University Fellow and Ph.D., I had been brought in with several others to serve those records. My background was unusual. I had published my then-named *Crusaders for American Liberalism*—later better known as *The Muckrakers*—before entering graduate school. Allen Nevins had welcomed me there and showed me what an historian was and ought to be about. And now here I was, immersed in papers of and about the Federal Art Project and Federal Writers' Project and the others as well, and enriching myself with subjects I had scarcely known existed: individual writers and artists, some later famous, murals, new techniques, like silk screen prints—actually developed on the Federal Art Project—and much more.

And here now was this solid, medium-sized man who came in and informed me that he had been hired to be a consultant on the projected study of the Federal Writers' Project. It had been closed down along with all the other projects—closed down from coast to coast as the federal government gave its full attention and all its resources to World War II. Ben made himself at home opposite me at another desk and we discussed drawers and folders. Both were in disarray and wanted rearrangement and coding for best results. Meanwhile we had to work with them as they were, and to work our way through national memos and big city functionaries and national operations to circulating exhibitions, art centers, personnel, historic tours, and many other Project themes.

Ben had many of these matters in his head, and as we pulled drawers he would notice and call to my attention this writer and that artist whom he knew personally, some of whom were still in Washington at one job and another. I got to know Merle Colby, for instance, who had written a well-esteemed novel, and who good-naturedly told me how his publisher had walked him through his enormous library of published books; by the end of the walk Colby had wondered whether his own book's writing had been worthwhile. He had become a troubleshooter for the Federal Writers' Project, called in when a unit of the Project had shown difficulties in Production, quality, working together, budget.

I somehow got to mention to Ben Mark Twain's searing essay on James Fenimore Cooper's *Deer-Slayer* novels, in which that legendary rifleman struck imbedded bullets *on the head* at unnaturally long distances, and in which ships moved improbably in narrow waters. To my surprise Ben took me up on the point of exaggeration. What of Achilles and his incredible feats of strength and accuracy in Homer? What of the inordinate feats' of lifting and throwing in Mike Fink and John Henry songs and stories in our own legends? So I learned that he was *the* Ben Botkin, formerly of the University of Oklahoma, where he had collected the folklore of living and dead men and women. He had invented the idea of "Folk-Say" which he had put into books, and drawn the lore of growing masters of their own people, in poems, songs, stories, and reminiscences. Great names came readily into our conversation: then still-young Carl Sandburg, J. Frank Dobie, master of cowboy stories and exploits, such blacks as Sterling Brown and Alain Locke, Ben was a unique pioneer in the gathering of black cultural voices and individual talents as a natural outgrowth of native thinking and feeling.

The sheer sweep of Ben's grasp of and receptivity to older and new voices—of Mary Austin, Percy MacKay ("Noble Illiteracy"), Stanley Vestel ("Cacique and Koshare"), Sterling Brown ("The Blues as Folk Poetry"), Handicraft, Chain Gang Songs, localism in literature, and Ben's own probes of "onetime Religion," of songs and dances, and Paul Bunyan—I had not known that he was a made-up thing of folk-lore, in 1912 as I recall—took and still takes my breath away every time I open one of Ben's books. But then it was all new to me. I heard him with full receptivity.

I did not then note his resemblance to George Gershwin. It was only later when I saw repeated views of Gershwin's jaw and the forward thrust of his lower face and knew they were cousins that their resemblances struck me. But as our conversations increased did I not hear regularly from Ben something astonishing that I did not know before.

Why had he left the University of Oklahoma? Today, his rich mix-ture of birth and upbringing abroad in a Jewish Russian ghetto is easier appreciated than it was then, especially as intermixed with his Boston growth. All his later life Ben wrote his mother in Yiddish for her comfort, while he absorbed the Boston of Puritans and Catholics and other Boston immigrants. He made a brilliant record in the schools, and topped it off by being an early Jewish entry in Harvard. It was a fact that was sensational at home and in the Brooklyn family of the Gershwins. Ben's fine record at Harvard, where he received his B.A., and then at Columbia where he took his M.A. seemed of a piece, ensuring his ready rise in his chosen field of literature and folklore. It was no mere coincidence that he shifted his studies from Harvard to Columbia, conscious as he was of the rising fortunes in new music of cousins Ira and George.

Ben's rapid accumulations of folklore and folk friendships had taken place in changing times and in the decade of the volatile Twenties. It did not arouse enthusiasm in those who still taught American culture the old way, as engrossing Cotton Mather-Benjamin (not "Ben") Franklin-Ralph Waldo Emerson, as idealist and leader and Thoreau as nature lover. And Longfellow, soon to become a symbol of vapid American culture. T.S. Eliot was soon, with publication of a few hun-dred copies of what were called the "Prufrock" poems, to launch an overwhelming attack on what he called "Waldo" and "Matthew"—none other than Ralph Waldo Emerson and Matthew Arnold.

Times were better in the popular market and Broadway, where Irving Berlin for music and Jed Harris for plays were leading the pack. Critics were not yet ready to say that Berlin was more than a musician—that he *was* American music—and Harris proved too eccentric to do more than burn a path through the brush of Broadway trivia. Ben was aware and regardful of these developments in the big cities and especially New York. Later he would tutor George Gershwin in the black lore which would be reflected in Gershwin's *Porgy and Bess*. But meanwhile, he was expected to teach American literature at the University of Oklahoma, where he had received his opportunity to grow, though not without skepticism on many sides. And after all, he *was* of Jewish descent.

He took his Ph.D. degree at the University of Nebraska, with Louise Pound, who was not wholly in folklore but enough so to guide him to his degree. She also encouraged and supported his efforts to advance folklore and dialect, and often against others who were willing to let it grow but not too aggressively. A sample of the kind of resistance that Ben had to work his way through in helping folklore become established in university curricula he was later to cite in a whole edition of *Folk-Say*, published after his success with *A Treasury of American Folklore*. The ill-natured comment was by Carey McWilliams:

> In times so strenuous as ours, it is rather annoying to discover intelligent men devoting their talents to such tasks as listing the animals and plants in Oklahoma folk-cures and noting, with infantile delight, the eroticisms in the folk-speech of taxi-drivers.[1]

The long University of Oklahoma years, in which Ben was an academic professor, on one hand, and, on the other, an overworked pioneer in folklore—in which he drew together numerous friends and associates, mostly in the wider world—fed the neurotic side of his personality. Now a married man, he had academic anxieties, despite tenure and despite his status with a variety of people. When he relaxed, his wit flowed freely, as in his mention of an associate as "friend, philosopher, and guide," the actual attributes being the reverse. Tensed, he could be formal and over-careful in speech.

---

1. B.A. Botkin, ed., Folk-Say, 1929–1930 (New York, 1970), xiii.

He was overjoyed to be offered the Folklore editorship of the Federal Writers' Project. It says something about the academic career he gave up, that he should have been not concerned about the security it contained. He did not foresee that times could change and close down his Project. Despite his numerous friends, jobs did not come readily to one of his vast experiences, that is, experiences of the mind. For example, his black associations and knowledge did not then open wide fields for augmenting his income. He enjoyed his status and work with the Federal Writers' Project, but when it was abruptly dissolved, he was a man with a family and without a job. The Rockefeller grant gave him a small salary, but he did not know how long it would last.

A Godsend arrived in the form of his acquaintanceship with Archibald MacLeish, then at the peak of his remarkable career as poet, government official, and now Librarian of Congress. I heard him query Ben on the phone. Was he interested in a Library job? Ben put it carefully that he was always interested in his personal advancement. MacLeish, miraculously, needed a Folklore—more precisely a music—department head. Ben kept his voice steady as he suggested that he visit the Library at MacLeish's convenience and discuss the matter. The next time I heard from him, by phone, was from his Library office.

How happily placed Ben was now quickly became evident. His FWP editorship had not cramped his style. He had pushed boldly the expansion of black experience in past and present. FWP had attracted talented writers of the quality of Richard Wright, but also would-be writers who were unemployed and needed to be given something to do. Ben had sent them into strategic southern places to search out still-living former slaves whose reminiscences could serve as folklore as well as add nuances to understanding of the slavery experience on individuals. Ben did his best to prepare those subordinates for what they could expect, what they could derive from their oral interviews. Nevertheless, they were not experts in the field and liable to errors of several sorts. Ben, however, was the expert and able to separate dross from reality to considerable extent.

At the Library, he was surrounded by its folklore findings of many years, especially rich in native and foreign music of native and foreign origin. He could continue to work over the former-slave narratives he had amassed. But, in addition, the Library drew music masters from everywhere. I recall a Peruvian visitor who was seeking recordings from his native land. Yes, the Library had some. Ben put on a record to which the Peruvian master listened with intense interest. There was a bleak passage reflecting the coldness of the air of the Peruvian heights. He pointed this out to us in pure delight.

Ben also let friends from the Federal Projects or from his Oklahoma connections learn of his new position. Among others this brought Charles Seeger to his office, Seeger being a recognized authority in musical folklore. He was also the brother of Alan Seeger, who had been well regarded as a poet of the younger generation, whose poem, "I Have a Rendezvous With Death" had been made as famous as Rupert Brooke's "If I Should Die, Think Only This Of Me." Both poets had underscored their commitment in blood during the First World War. Had Seeger lived, he would have been uncle to the later radical musician Pete Seeger.

All such experiences, plus others on the way, should have put a quietus to the nervousness Ben had endured because of the collapse of Federal One. Some of it, unfortunately, had become ingrained. At luncheon meetings, he checked his watch. When I met him, he pointed out that I was ten minutes "late." When I tried my sometimes jest, that he felt his honor was as "st(e)ake," he did not smile. On another occasion, to which he brought a friend, the subject of tips came up. Salaries were low at the time, but his was better than it had recently been. He and his friend actually added up an average of luncheons, and, barring special occasions, concluded that they could not afford tips generally.

Ben's home was run peacefully by his wife Gertrude, who industriously typed Ben's manuscripts and also reared their two children. He was less defensive at home, especially when he hosted some of his colleagues of the Federal Art Project who were still in Washington. Notable was Harold Rosenberg, if only for his height, which was in the area of six-foot-three or four, set off with the baby in his arms. He was good natured and patently intellectual, though I did not foresee him as the artistic guru he became following his return to New York. Regrettably, to me, was his loss of humor as he pursued new ways at looking, not so much at art as at parts of art, such as "seeing" ambiance not evident to the mere duffer. In Washington, he was more fun.

I was less impressed at the time, to my regret, by Harold Courlander who was then a friendly folklorist studying black culture in the Caribbean. I recall him arguing mildly against the over-naturalism being practiced by new writers especially as in sexual matters. After all, he suggested, we do not think it necessary to go into detail with respect to bathroom practices. I missed the steel under his easy deportment. Courlander was a specialist in black music and gathered tunes he could explicate in terms of folk meaning.

A less talented writer blatantly lifted some of his findings. Courlander was not then well to do, but he committed himself to court procedures. Had he lost, it would have put him in ill condition. But he demonstrated to the court's satisfaction that certain lilts and tremulos had been unknown before his researches, and won. The victory and funds freed him of his modest workings. He undertook African research and became a master of the field, producing a wide series of fiction and non-fiction folktales as well as oral materials. He was said to have inspired the direction of Haley's *Roots*.

For Ben, good fortune continued, though always involving heavier duties. He completed his review of the oral interviews and sent his manuscript of *Lay My Burden Down: a Folk History of Slavery* to the University of Chicago Press; it was issued with all due regard for its distinction. But, in addition, he was offered the job of preparing a full "Treasury of American Folklore," by a New York publisher. It was a heavy burden, and Ben often looked tired. Still, he was at the Library of Congress, and had his own accumulations at home. His work, therefore, became less of a delight than it should have been. Ben was anxious. "I keep sending them materials, and asking them for advice—and they keep sending me checks," he said. The work went faster than I would have expected, possibly at the expense of his Library duties, to a degree. The publishers kept pressuring for more copy, and Ben labored to oblige. He did get in a happy suggestion. Carl Sandburg had been moving to the height of his career in his Lincoln volumes and he was an old friend of Ben's. Ben urged that he be brought in to provide the book's preface.

Even before the book was released, it seemed destined for success. Reviewers faced with its formidable size were grateful for Sandburg's warm praise and its memorable phrases. Reviewing was then in excellent order, drawing in educated editors who, in turn, stimulated felicitous academics and others to write effectively on new books. Sandburg's preface achieved a certain fame of its own, editors agreeing that Ben's book was "a big shot." Ben was now as visible in the literary market as he ever was to be.

Gertrude had dreamed—and Ben, too, possibly—of his being offered a name professorship at a great university, though folklore then
was not yet at full accord with literature on campuses. It is not wholly
clear how he arrived at his second largest decision since Oklahoma.
He resigned his Library position and—with promises of more "Treasuries" on hand—moved to Croton on Hudson, a liberal community
which such famous names as Max Eastman's had adorned and continued to adorn, sitting high over the Hudson River and promising interesting associates.

Was Ben wrong to give up his solid Washington base and modest
salary to depend on his production of more folklore anthologies? Be it
noted that his *Treasury of American Folklore* did not make him rich.
His royalty, though still substantial, was only a royalty, and he had
eaten up much of its substance in making up the book.

Yet, had he stayed on in Washington, could he have continued to
gather up the fine materials which were in prospect? It is difficult to
say. There may have been politics at the Library of Congress of which
I did not know. MacLeish was gone, and the cultural temper of the
times was changing. It was an era of "explication," featuring Henry
James as an icon. J.D. Salinger had literary academics swooning. There
was endless babble about "Ernest and Scott." None of this should have
influenced doings at the Library.

A thought I had at the time which I was and still am reluctant to
pursue: Was it possible that Ben had developed a compulsion to create
conditions which might embarrass him and feed his insecurity? There
were the Oklahoma disappointments. There was anti-semitism. There
could have been factors of which I was unaware.

We were in good touch by mail, and occasionally by telephone. We
discussed a book we could do together. Writers' Project authors had
produced short stories and novels. Federal Theater playwrights had
written plays which might be adapted to new conditions. Ben had piles
of manuscript which we could read with an eye to edited editions or
other work.

But meanwhile there was a living for him to further. Ben was
orderly in many ways. He set up his researched materials for ready
use. He made schedules for reading at the main library in New York.
He kept up his connections, folklore and otherwise. In time, and in
regular time, with introductions and thoughtful notes, his treasuries
matured. They became treasuries of *Railroad Folklore, Southern Folk-*

lore (prefaced by Douglas Southall Freeman), the delightful *Sidewalks of New York, Western Folklore*, and others.

He had also made a modestly useful connection with a reprint corporation of the time. It endowed him with the title of Editor in Chief for a series of reprints entitled *Rediscovering America*. The pamphlet he produced for this strictly reprint firm was masterly, but in the overflow of reprinting of the time, it made little impact, and less money. It coincided with the rise of the Youth movement, which was fated to shake the campuses of the nation and to diminish the impact of scholarship in all humanistic disciplines. The hope of an endowed professorship faded from sight. Although Ben's friends in folklore and academe remained loyal, an apparently formidable foe came over the horizon: Richard Dorson, who directed a Folklore Institute at Indiana University. Dorson held that the true folklorist should concern himself with accounts of tales which could be traced in origin, and probably in variant versions. They could thus be controlled accounts, and of little if any value. Ben's accounts strove for interest and entertainment. They added nothing to the growth of folklore as a discipline. They were "fake lore." In fact, in producing his doctorate, Ben had served his apprenticeship in such method as Dorson touted and Dorson missed the richness which so often came from Ben's matchless "secondary" sources—if Carl Sandburg could be considered a secondary source.

It worried Ben more than was necessary. The humanities as a whole were coming on dire days: this was a more worrisome fact of life. None of the *treasuries* attained the success of his first one, and he found himself requesting foundation funds to supplement his income. Friends in folklore, notably Bruce Jackson, took time and collected the money necessary for a *festschrift* honoring Ben. It appeared as *Folklore & Society* (1966) and was filled with good things, as well as an account of Ben's labors and results and a handsome photograph of himself. Charles Seeger, now long in academe, was represented from the old days. Ben took genuine pleasure in the event. Such were the tight politics of his associates, working within the larger bodies of literature and history, that the *festschrift* even included an essay by Dorson!

That Ben should have written me anxiously for a recommendation to be included in a foundation application merely reflected his inner struggle to do the correct thing. He knew I would help any way I could. But he could not refrain from following up with precise and detailed instructions about what I should and should not say. And all because I was technically in academe.

I visited him in Croton and all was well. He was charming and witty, and we even discussed the collaboration which would never take place. We walked all over Croton. He was his usual authentic guide to all its details—where John Reed had stayed, and where the talented black playwright, Lorraine Hansberry, was sadly buried. But the sight of sights for me was the dam and water purifier high over the Hudson, built beautifully early in the century to supply water for New York City. Ben had somewhere learned that the workers on the dam had been Italian immigrants. He always noticed things like that.

The purifier was later placed as a monument on the campus of City College. So much that is forgotten. . . . The celebration marking the opening of the plant, the lovely markers set up there by the Union, and other human elements which contributed to the work. I was doing a turn of teaching on City College campus, when strikers and arsonists permitted, and I pointed to the mementos while walking by with a 25-year professor and told him of the Croton connection. He had never noticed the display.

Ben visited me in New York. We had another fine exchange. We looked in at the City Museum, which was having a Gershwin exhibition. We stopped in at his brother Henry's apartment. I knew his paintings in several museums. It was a less joyous occasion. His wife had passed away, and his mind was elsewhere. We stopped into the Greenwich Village Police Station, where I could contribute a morsel of information. Built sturdily, it still retained its 1890s tone, when such journalists as Stephen Crane and David Graham Phillips began their careers with sordid accounts of prostitutes and con men brought to justice or injustice.

All our meetings were good, and I felt cheered by his evident pleasure in the trip.

He visited me in my Ohio home on his way to a conference. His first words were: "How do I look?" I said fine, and meant it. He did not look very different from how he had looked when I first saw him years before in Washington. A little grayer, with a very light show of wrinkles on his cheeks. We walked over the Antioch College campus, commenting on many things. We had some light refreshment before my fireplace, with talk of folklore and its potential in agitated times.

Several years passed. I was unprepared when I learned that he had suffered a stroke, so severe that he had been hospitalized. This proved insufficient for the nature of his stroke. He could not write. His active life was over. He spent his last period in a home not his own.

When he died, the *New York Times* gave a dignified report. Ben had been a pioneer in folklore. His *Treasury of American Folklore* had been highly successful. He had followed it with numerous others. In the meantime, as it happens, the Youth uprising had settled down. Bookstores reorganized to serve a new generation of customers with not a few new categories which had not been evident before.

And then, wonderful to be told, his books began to come out, not sporadically, but as all but permanent elements of the book world. The final judgment on Ben was not in academic discourse but in sales. He was at last a patent success, read not for his distinction, but simply because his collections were interesting, fun to read. I like to think there was something intrinsically American in Ben's saga. Gertrude wisely gave his papers to the University of Nebraska, where he had spent pleasant and profitable time. There will be a biography of Ben by an industrious and talented academic. As Meyer Levin once had said in his democratic way: So long as we go on talking, it will all turn out all right.

Louis Filler
July 1997

Preface

When I began to think of a book of American folklore, I thought of all the good songs and stories and all the good talk that would go into it, and of what a richly human and entertaining book it would be. A book of American folklore, I thought, should be as American as Davy Crockett and as universal as Brer Rabbit. For when one thinks of American folklore one thinks not only of the folklore of American life—the traditions that have sprung up on American soil—but also of the literature of folklore—the migratory traditions that have found a home here.

Because folklore is so elemental and folk songs and stories are such good neighbours and pleasant companions, it is hard to understand why American folklore is not more widely known and appreciated. For this the word "folklore" is partly responsible. Folklore is the scholar's word for something that is as simple and natural as singing songs and spinning yarns among the folk who know the nature and the meaning but not the name—and certainly not the scholarship—of folklore. Because the word denotes both the material and its study, and has come to stand more for the study of the thing than for the thing itself, folklore, in fact, seems to have become the possession of the few who study it rather than of the many who make or use it.

The essence of folklore, however, is something that cannot be contained in a definition but that grows upon one with folklore experience. Old songs, old stories, old sayings, old beliefs, customs, and practices—the mindskills and handskills that have been handed down so long that they seem to have a life of their own, a life that cannot be destroyed by print but that constantly has to get back to the spoken word to be renewed; patterned by common experience; varied by individual repetition, inventive or forgetful; and cherished because somehow characteristic or expressive: all this, for want of a better word, is folklore.

Complementary of the "Stop me if you've heard this" aspect of folklore is the trait implied in the comeback: "That's not the way I heard it." For what makes a thing folklore is not only that you have heard it before yet want to hear it again, because it is different, but also that you want to tell it again in your own way, because it is anybody's property. On the one hand, repeated retelling establishes confidence in the rightness of what is said and how it is said. On the other hand, the beauty of a folk lyric, tune, story, or saying is that, if you don't like it, you can always change it, and, if *you* don't, someone else will.

But if folklore is old wine in new bottles, it is also new wine in old bottles. It says not only, "Back where I come from", but also, "Where do we go from here?" If this book is intended to bring the reader back to anything, it is not to the "good old days" but to an enjoyment and understanding of living American folklore for what it is and what it is worth. This is an experience in which Americans as compared with other peoples are sadly deficient. Perhaps it is because we are not one people but many peoples in one, and a young people, who have grown up too close to the machine age. The industrial folk tales and songs in this book are evidence enough that machinery does not destroy folklore. Rather, in our rapid development from a rural and agricultural to an urban and industrial folk, we have become estranged from the folklore of the past, which we cannot help feeling a little self-conscious or antiquarian about, without yet being able to recognize or appreciate the folklore of the present.

Perhaps the best way to understand the songs and stories in this book is in terms of a species of living literature which has no fixed form (in this respect differing from the classics, which it resembles in permanence and universality of appeal) and which is constantly shifting back and forth between written and unwritten tradition. Since print tends to freeze a song or a story, folklore is most alive or at home out of print, and in its purest form is associated with the "grapevine" and the bookless world. But that does not make it synonymous with illiteracy or ignorance, nor is it true that the educated do not also have their lore, or that lore ceases to be lore as soon as it is written down or published. Folk literature differs from the rest of literature only in its history: its author is the original "forgotten man".

Not only does folklore shift, but it changes as it shifts, between the top and bottom layers of culture. As it gets nearer to the world of professional poets and story-tellers, it tends to shape about itself a formal "literary" tradition of its own, as in the great collections of legends and folk tales that have come down to us from ancient and medieval times and have been pored over by scholars. But alongside this more classic folk literature, which has acquired scholarly prestige and which gives and takes erudition, is the humbler and homelier folk literature of everyday life and the common man—today's people's literature which the older folk literature may once have been.

This range of variation within the folklore field is a source of both strength and weakness. For while it enables folklore perpetually to rebuild itself from the ground up, it creates a kind of class-consciousness among folklorists. Thus the British folk-song and folk-dance expert, Cecil J. Sharp, while very much taken with the vigour and beauty of our mountain songs and dances, was unable to see in our cowboy songs anything but the fact that the "cowboy has been despoiled of his inheritance of traditional song" and has "nothing behind him" and nothing but "himself and his daily occupations to sing about, and that in a self-centred, self-conscious way, e.g., 'The cowboy's life is a dreadful life'; 'I'm a poor lonesome cowboy'; 'I'm a lonely bull-whacker', and so forth".

Further complicating and diversifying the picture is a third quantity, midway between "folk" and "academic"—the "popular". The latter is distinguished by its wider and more passing acceptance, the result of transmission through such "timely" media as stage, press, radio, and films. Yet the so-called lively arts—jazz, vaudeville, burlesque, comic strips, animated cartoons, pulps—often have a folk basis or give rise to new folk creations, such as Mickey Mouse and Donald Duck. Many of the innovations of popular lore are associated with new inventions: e.g., the Ford joke and the gremlins. At the same time many of our modern gags have an ancient and honourable, if somewhat wheezy, lineage.

Also close to folk sources but to be distinguished from folk literature proper is literature about the folk. This ranges from oldtimers' reminiscences (one of the best examples of which in this book is Martha L. Smith's "Going to God's Country") and homespun humour and verse to local colour and regional stories and sketches, all of which throw light on the folk and folklore backgrounds, culminating in that small body of masterpieces of "folk art" mined out of the collective experience and imagination by writers, known and unknown, who have succeeded in identifying themselves with their folk tradition.

Although for the most part I have preferred to let American folklore speak for itself, in one respect it is necessary to distinguish between folklore as we find it and folklore as we believe it ought to be. Folklore as we find it perpetuates human ignorance, perversity, and depravity along with human wisdom and goodness. Historically we cannot deny or condone this baser side of folklore—and yet we may understand and condemn it as we condemn other manifestations of human error.

Folklore, like life itself, in Santayana's phrase, is animal in its origins and spiritual in its possible fruit. Much of the animalism, of course, does not appear here except by implication because of the taboos surrounding print. What does come through, however, often in violent contradiction of our modern social standards, is the essential viciousness of many of our folk heroes, stories, and expressions, especially in their treatment of minorities—Indians, Negroes, Mexicans, Chinese, etc.

In stories of anti-social humour and "necktie justice" the narrator inevitably reflects the prejudices belonging to his and his hero's race and class. Such stories stick because they have the tang of life and are a historical comment. They should be preserved not to perpetuate but to reveal and correct the errors and evils they narrate. With this perspective the whole of folklore may become an instrument for understanding and good will.

Grateful acknowledgements are due to the many authors and publishers, selections from whose publications are included in this book, and to Paul R. ("Febold Feboldson") Beath, Gertrude Botkin, Hugo V. Buonagurio who made the music drawings; Crown Publishers, Edmund Fuller, Bertha Krantz and Charles Seeger.

Finally, without the collections of the Library of Congress, with which my work as Fellow in Folklore as well as folk-song archivist has brought me in close contact, this book would not have been possible.

B. A. Botkin

Washington, D.C.

March, 1944

PART ONE

HEROES AND BOASTERS

The history of any public character involves not only the facts about him but what the public has taken to be facts. —J FRANK DOBIE

The heroic spirit, as seen in heroic poetry, we are told, is the outcome of a society cut loose from its roots, of a time of migrations, of the shifting of populations. —JOHN G. NEIHARDT

Braggin' saves advertisin' —SAM SLICK

Introduction to Part One

BACKWOODS BOASTERS

> *The Backwoodsman is a soldier from neces-*
> *sity. Mind and body have been disciplined in*
> *a practical warfare. He belongs to this conti-*
> *nent and to no other. He is an original. He*
> *thinks "big"; he talks "big"; arid when it is*
> *necessary to toe the mark, he acts "big". He*
> *is the genius of the New World.*
> —James K. Paulding

> *These are the untamable. America has always*
> *been fecund in the production of roughs.*
> —Bernard DeVoto

Hero tales tell us more about a people than perhaps any other tales. For, as admirable or exceptional men, heroes embody the qualities that we most admire or desire in ourselves. So we begin with the heroes as our most potent folk symbols and most reliable touchstones of a people's "choice".

In every age heroes arise from a people's dream of greatness or from homage to the great and near-great. In other tunes and places heroes received their sanction from religion or mythology as they derived their being or their powers from a world other than our own. Lacking a body of true myth and ritual, Americans conceive of their heroes, save for vague demigods of the Paul Bunyan type, as strictly of this world, however much they may take us out of it.

In modern times, especially in a democracy, hero myths and hero worship have become inextricably mixed. From a universal need of models larger than life or "desire to be ruled by strength and ability", Americans choose or create heroes in their own image. In a complex industrial society, hero-making goes on at various levels, so that every walk of life and almost every occupation have their heroes. Essentially, however, American heroes are of three main types: the poor boy who makes good, the good boy gone wrong, and the kind that is too good or too bad to be true. Thus, on the one hand, the schoolbooks and popular literature of edification draw upon the ranks of leaders—explorers, pioneers, soldiers, statesmen, inventors, and industrialists—for patron saints and tutelary geniuses, to inspire love of country or teach the ethics of success. On the other hand, the dime-novel concealed behind the geography book glorifies the gentlemen on horseback and the demons with the six-shooter. Midway between these two extremes is an American fairyland of strong men and giants who perform the impossible.

A composite picture of the American hero would show him to be a plain, tough, practical fellow, equally good at a bargain or a fight, a star-performer on the job and a hell-raiser off it, and something of a salesman and a showman, with a flair for prodigious stories, jokes, and stunts and a general capacity for putting himself over. Our nearest approach to a national myth, explaining and justifying the many contradictions in our heroes, is the frontier or pioneer myth. This reconciles the primitive virtues of brute strength, courage, and cunning with the economic virtues of thrift, hard work, and perseverance.

The backwoodsman was the first of our tall men, whose words were tall talk and whose deeds were tall tales. Romantic fiction has made much of his fierce, wild courage and independence and his "rough diamond" chivalry as well as of his skill with the rifle. "That murderous weapon", wrote Audubon of the Kentucky hunters, "is the means of procuring them subsistence during all their wild and extensive rambles, and is the source of their principal sports and pleasures". It also brought them into national prominence in the Battle of New Orleans, January 8, 1815. "Tough as a hickory", these "coonskin voters" helped put "Old Hickory" in the White House thirteen years later.

By this period, it should be noted, the backwoodsman had emerged into his later phases. Like Mike Fink, the hunter had become a riverman; and beyond the Mississippi, following his free, wild way of living, he was to revert once more, like Mike Fink, to hunting and trapping.

In pursuit of game, skins, scalps, land, or adventure, the backwoodsman followed the shifting fringe of settlement, marching ahead of civilization or running away from it. As a picaresque type, the footloose adventurer, he illustrates what Lucy Lockwood Hazard calls the "dwindling of the hero", from the godlike or kinglike to the average human and subhuman level.

More and more, as the country was settled, the backwoodsman's motto became, in the words of the picaresque Simon Suggs, "It is good for a man to be shifty in a new country." To be shifty in a new country meant beating the other fellow to it. For a society that cannot support a large population puts a premium on outdoing—out-running, out-licking, and out-hollering—one's neighbour.

Boasting—the epic brag—has always been part of the trappings of the hero. The strong man would gird himself for combat and inspire confidence in his followers by rehearsing his exploits in big talk. In his "paradise of puffers", however, the backwoods boaster tended to boast in terms of the future rather than of the past, and seemed more interested in making claims than in living up to them. Moreover, since boasting, like bombast, contains in itself the seeds of its own travesty, it became hard to distinguish bragging from windy laughing at bragging and serious from mock or burlesque boasts.

From his noise the boaster became known as a roarer or screamer. Because the qualities of the horse and the alligator seemed most fitting to the animal antics and noises of the ring-tailed roarer, the alligator horse or half-horse, half-alligator became his emblem. "It is an old remark", writes Washington Irving, "that persons of Indian mixture are half civilized, half savage, and half devil—a third half being provided for their particular convenience. It is for similar reasons, and probably with equal truth, that the backwoodsmen of Kentucky are styled half man, half horse, and half alligator, by the settlers on the Mississippi, and held accordingly in great respect and abhorrence."[1]

Like the first successful Yankee character—Jonathan, in Royall Tyler's *The Contrast* (1787)—the first full-length portrait of the ring-tailed roarer was a stage creation. This was Colonel Nimrod Wildfire, the hero of James K. Paulding's lost prize-play, *The Lion of the West,*[2] which was produced at the Park Theatre, New York City, on April 25, 1831. The role of Colonel Wildfire, "a raw Kentuckian recently elected to Congress", was created by James J. Hackett, the "rising young comedian" and donor of the prize, who was also responsible for the names of the play and the hero. Wildfire was acclaimed as a contribution to the gallery of native American types (along with Hackett's Solomon Swap), and, through two rewritings of the play over a period of twenty years, remained one of the most successful roles of the actor's career.

The one surviving speech of the play appears in several newspaper, almanac, and jokebook versions, attributed now to Colonel Wildfire and now to the meteoric Davy Crockett, who in 1831 was nearing the end of his second term in Congress. According to Paulding's son and biographer, the playwright disclaimed any intention of a take-off of that "well-known personage",[3] eliciting from him the following reply: Whatever Paulding's intentions, the actor's interpretation and the acceptance of Wildfire must have profited by the resemblance between

> Washington City, 22nd Decr. 1830.
> Sir your letter of the 15 Inst was handed to me this day by my friend Mr. Wilde—the newspaper publications to which you refer I have never seen; and if I had I should not have taken the reference to myself in exclusion of many who fill offices and who are as untaught as I am. I thank you however for your civility in assuring me that you had no reference to my peculiarities. The frankness of your letter induces me to say a declaration from you to that effect was not necessary to convince me that you were incapable of wounding the feelings of a strainger and unlettered man who had never injured you—your charecter for letters and as a gentlemen is not altogether unknown to me.
> I have the honor with
> great respects &c—
> David Crockett[4]

the two lions of the West, even to Crockett's taking a bow at a performance of the play. Thus the wood-engraving of Crockett on the cover of the 1837 almanac is virtually indistinguishable from the cut of Hackett in the role of Wildfire.[5] Following the Crockett version of the Wildfire speech, the author of the *Sketches and Eccentricities of Col. David Crockett, of West Tennessee* (1833), has this to say of the play:

> This scene, with some slight alteration, has been attributed I understand to an imaginary character, Colonel Wildfire. This I have not seen. But I am unwilling that the hard earnings of Crockett should be given to another.

Such curious coincidences and correspondences illustrate the way in which folklore becomes mixed with life and literature, and also point to the fact that many Crockett stories may have had their source in current anecdotes and been identified with other characters.

If the prevailing rusticity of American folk heroes may be said to constitute one of their chief attractions, then none of them is more attractive than Davy Crockett, the prime example of the country boy who made good. "Crockett was rude and uncouth", writes one of his admirers, "but honest and heroic. To the homely sense of the backwoodsman, he joined a spirit as brave and chivalrous as any that followed the banner of the Black Prince against the infidel."[6] His rise to fame serves as a peg on which to hang the moral, "You can't keep a good man down."

> It is certainly a very curious phase of American and especially of western character, which is exhibited in the ease and promptness with which the colonel passes from one act of the singular drama of his life to another. Yesterday, a rough bear-hunter, to-day, a member of the legislature, tomorrow about to become a member of Congress, and the fearless opponent of his old commander, General Jackson.
>
> Such sudden and successful advances in life are scarcely seen except in our own country, where perfect freedom opens a boundless field to enterprise and perseverance.[7]

Although in his own day Crockett's name was a household word for his jokes as well as his achievements, the image of the "Colonel" that endures to-day is not that of a national political figure or the martyr of the Alamo but that of the comic backwoodsman. While historians of the American epic may, with Frank Norris, deplore the fact that "Crockett is the hero only of a 'funny story' about a sagacious coon",[8] the epic's loss is humour's gain. The transformation of this prototype of the folks-of-the-creek philosopher and grass-roots politician into the archetype of the protean, wandering, legendary, American hero of the Munchausen-Eulenspiegel breed is an important and fascinating chapter in the annals of American hero-making.

In the "gentleman from the cane" the ring-tailed roarer is superimposed upon the comic backwoodsman, who is essentially the droll Yankee with more guts and gusto and less guile, to become the "gamecock of the wilderness". Because of his many-sidedness, his lively, humorous, homespun figure has supplanted the romantic frontiersman of the Daniel Boone type as the "heroic version of the poor-white", and rivals many another American hero. Thus, in his gumption he outdoes his older contemporary, Mike Fink, whom he resembles as game-hog and Indian-fighter but to whose tough guy he plays the smart aleck among backwoods boasters. In his role of cracker-box philosopher and story-telling politician, the coonskin Congressman anticipates Lincoln, although with Crockett story-telling was a business rather than an art—the business of being a wag and a good fellow.

> While electioneering, the colonel always conciliates every crowd into which he may be thrown by the narration of some anecdote. It is his manner, more than the anecdote, which delights you. . . .
>
> Pursuing this course, he laughs away any prejudice which may exist against him; and having created a favourable impression, enforces his claims by local arguments, showing the bearing which great national questions have upon the interests of the persons whom he wishes to represent. This mode, together with the faculty of being a boon companion to every one he meets, generally enables him to accomplish his object.[9]

The anecdotes of Crockett's Washington adventures show the "irrepressible backwoodsman" playing up to the accepted notion of himself as the rustic wag and wisecracker, a role in which he seems to have been the victim partly of his own ambition and good nature and partly of the designs of political friends and foes. Yet in his speeches in Congress, where he served three terms between 1827 and 1835, he is a sincere, plain-spoken champion of the people, with an occasional stroke of hard-hitting sarcasm:

> Sirs, I do not consider it good sense to be sitting here passing laws for Andrew Jackson to laugh at; it is not even good nonsense . . . out of those that the President has got about him, I have never seen but one honest countenance since I have been here, and he has just resigned.[10]

In the autobiographical comic prose epics ascribed to him (1833–1836), he becomes "our first Southern humorist". From now on, laughter gains the ascendancy, and horse sense gives way to horseplay Posthumously, he plays the buffoon in the "Crockett" almanacs (1835–1856), where his heroics are swallowed up in slapstick and hokum. Hoax, legend, myth, and caricature, he thus runs the gamut from the poor but honest farmer who made good by his own wits and go-aheadativeness ("Be sure you are always right, then go ahead") to the demigod who "totes the thunder in his fist and flings the lightning from his fingers". Somewhere between these two extremes the real Crockett has been lost. Even the stock figure of the backwoods bully and boaster yields to the rip-roaring superman of the jokebooks, whose tedium is relieved by an occasional flash of vernacular prose poetry and comic sublimity, as in "Crockett's Morning Hunt". Folk memories of Crockett linger in occasional hunting yarns of the South.[11]

Throughout the following sketches Crockett is essentially the hunter in pursuit of ever bigger and better game, from varmints and politicians to the challenging elements. Nowhere is backwoods mythology more alive than in Crockett's encounters with his animal friends and foes, in which Crockett is half-varmint and every varmint is half-Crockett.

The feats of marksmanship, which figure so prominently in backwoods mythology, are in the true Mike Fink tradition, which ranged from driving nails with bullets to shooting tin cups and scalp locks from heads. Mike's unique claim to fame among deadshots lay in the fact that most of his shooting wagers were sadistic pranks. For as a bully and cut-up, hell-bent for fun, Mike had more in common with the pseudo-bad men of the West than he had with the river pirates and common ruffians among whom he moved. Unlike the frontier rascals who thought that "even a crime might take on the aspect of a good joke", Mike was one to carry a joke to the point of being a crime. He was quite impartial in his choice of victims, shooting off a Negro's heel because he disliked its shape or forcing his woman to lie down in a pile of leaves to which he set fire, to cure her of looking at other men.

Born of Scotch-Irish parents at old Fort Pitt in 1770, Mike Fink in his youth acquired a reputation as an Indian scout and the best shot in Pittsburgh. As the country filled up and the Indians were pushed across the Lakes and beyond the Mississippi, wrote Morgan Neville, in "The Last of the Boatmen" (1829), many of the scouts, "from a strong attachment to their erratic mode of life, joined the boatmen, then just becoming a distinct class". It was the perpetual fight of these boatmen with the river that made them "reckless savages". Among the various types of river craft the keelboat offered the greatest challenge to the boatman's strength, skill, and endurance.

In the same year that Noah Ludlow introduced "The Hunters of Kentucky" to the people of New Orleans, Mike Fink became one of Ashley's men in the service of the Mountain Fur Company. For, as the supremacy of the steamboat was established, the flatboatmen and keelboatmen turned to other fields. Some went to work on the steamboats, others became raftsmen, and still others like Mike Fink joined the trapping and trading expeditions that crossed the Rockies. At Fort Henry in Montana this champion marksman, fighter, drinker, lover, boaster, and jester was "killed in a scrimmage", in which his various types of prowess were called into play.

PSEUDO BAD MEN

*I'm a two-gun man and a very bad man and
won't do to monkey with.*

—COWBOY YELL

With the passing of the keelboat many of Mike Fink's tribe became raftsmen, joining the new crew of hardy adventurers that brought the forests down to the towns in the form of rafts, put together in "cribs" of logs or boards and then taken apart to be sold.

"The typical raftsmen", writes Charles Edward Russell, in *A-Rafting on the Mississip'* (1928), "was reckless, dissolute, daring and all that, but he was more; he was humorous with a style of humour all his own and largely his own language in which to frame it; emotional at bottom, sophisticated on the surface; a singer, a dancer, an improviser of wild yarns, ready with fist, dagger, or pistol; something of a poet, curiously responsive to charitable appeals, something of a Lothario, something of a pirate, something of a blackguard, and in profanity equipped with resources incomparable for richness of invention and competence of authority."

Lumber rafting on the Upper Mississippi lasted roughly from 1840 to 1915; but the old-time raftsman began to disappear when the raft-boat, or steamboat used to tow or push rafts, came in, about 1865. The hardihood of the raftsman of the floating days tended to be measured by the strength of his whisky, which was so powerful that it would take the hair off a buffalo robe. Or, to cite another school of thought on the buffalo robe test, Mike Fink "drank so much whisky that he destroyed the coating of his stomach, and the doctor told him that before he could get well, he would need a new coat for it. Mike thought the thing over, and said, when he had a new coat for his stomach, he would have one that would stand the whisky; and he made up his mind that a buffalo robe with the hair on it was just the thing, and so he sat down, and swallowed it. He could drink any amount of whisky after that, and never so much as wink."[12]

But when a buffalo robe failed as a stomach lining, oqueejum did the trick. Something of the toughness of the raftsman and the humour of his invention may be gleaned from the following advice of one raftsman to another:

"Hey! Don't let that stuff drop like that on your boots !" I heard one raftsman say to another that was passing him a bottle. "I spilt some on my new shore shoes last week and it ate the uppers clean off down to the soles."

"Was them shoes tanned with oqueejum?" asked the other in a quietly interested way, as if he were seeking scientific knowledge.

"No, sir. That there leather was tanned with the best hemlock bark, and the shoes cost me 3 in Red Wing."

"Now, say, my friend"—gently remonstrative—"don't you know better than to buy leather tanned with hemlock? What you want is leather tanned with oqueejum and then whisky can't eat it. You see, whisky and hemlock, they get together on social terms, same's you and me, and then the whisky does its deadly work and swallers the leather. But whisky and oqueejum's enemies, and when they meet whisky gets licked every time. That's why I keep my stomach lined with it. Oqueejum's made from the bamjam tree which grows in India to a height of more than a thousand feet. Its wood is so hard they have to cut it with a cold chisel. It stands to reason that it's stronger than hemlock. Try some on your stomach and then your liquor won't get to your head like this."[13]

The hardihood of the raftsman tended also to be measured by his boasting. In the famous raft scene in *Life on the Mississippi* (1874), which gives us our first glimpse of Huck Finn, Mark Twain has immortalized the "screamer". The "screamer" is the ring-tailed roarer grown maudlin, who boasts out of his weakness rather than his strength. He is the bogus bad man, who has already been glimpsed in the canebrake cockalorum and in the cock-of-the-walk pose of Mike Fink.

West of the Mississippi the scream of the backwoods boaster and bully passed into the howl of the pseudo or mock bad man, who, in his boasting chants and yells, proclaimed his intestinal fortitude with more and more weird anatomical details. In addition to the usual animal traits he claimed a mythical animal nurse and a more than usual endowment of teeth and other hard substance in his make-up. Crockett, too, it will be recalled, boasted of being "half chicken hawk and steeltrap" and of his wilderness birthplace—"born in a cane brake, cradled in a sap trough, and clouted with coon skins".

No one liked to play bad man more than the cowboy on a spree; and from his favourite interjection, "Whoopee!", originally a call to animals, "making whoopee" has become a general term for carousing. But if a would-be desperado announced that it was his time to howl, this was chiefly for the benefit of the uninitiated. For the rest knew that with the true bad man or killer the rule was: "Shoot first and talk afterward."[14]

On the frontier, however, "apparent rage" and "vigorous language" had their uses in bluffing or blustering one's way out of a tight place as well as in letting off steam. By such devices an Iowa squatter is reported to have got rid of a prospective settler from Illinois "who casually remonstrated against any one holding more than one claim and not even that 'unless he lived on it'":

> "My name, Sir, is Simeon Cragin. I own *fourteen* claims, and if any man jumps one of them I will shoot him down at once, Sir. I am a gentleman, Sir, and a scholar. I was educated in Bangor, have been in the United States army and served my country faithfully—am the discoverer of the Wopsey—can ride a grizzly bear, or whip any *human* that ever crossed the Mississippi; and if you dare jump one of my claims, die you must."[15]

KILLERS

> *He gained this recognition not because he was bad but rather because he was a man of swift and decisive action.*
> —Capt. John R. Hughes

The line of western heroes is an unbroken one. one of the most famous American "bad men" was James Butler Hickok, born the year after Crockett died.

Although no seasoned trouper like Buffalo Bill, with whom he appeared briefly in Ned Buntline's melodrama, *The Scouts of the Prairie*, in 1873, Wild Bill displayed considerable showmanship in living up to his early-acquired reputation as a "bad man to fool with". Throughout his varied career as stage-coach driver, Civil War sharpshooter and spy, Indian fighter, scout, guide, and peace officer, Wild Bill helped create his own legend by combining a certain amount of pose with a sense of his own mission. Thus do heroes both during and after their lifetime make it easier for the folklorist and harder for the historian.

Wild Bill's reputation as a bad man to fool with rested on his reputation as a gunfighter and this in turn on his use of all those tricks of gunplay which old-timers attribute to the pseudo bad man and the fancy shooter, such as carrying two guns, shooting from the hip, and "fanning" (firing a revolver by brushing back the hammer with the palm of the left hand). Whether this show of daredeviltry and flashiness were due to courage or the lack of it, Wild Bill made the most of it, while at the same time taking no chances. The result was such myths as the "McCanles massacre" and such stunts as simultaneously killing two assailants who had entered by opposite doors of a restaurant. He could do this not because he "had eyes in the back of his head, or some sixth sense", but because he "drew his pistols, both of them, with a movement almost quicker than the eye could perceive, and with one he killed the man in front of him, and at the same time with the other gun hand resting on the opposite shoulder he killed the man behind him, looking through the mirror" over the front door.[16]

Wild Bill's good looks and gallantry, plus his taste for fancy clothes, also gained for him the reputation of a lady-killer. Mrs. Cody was entranced at the actuality, as she had been terrified at the prospect of meeting him.

There was no end of miracles among his exploits. Many of his hair-raising exploits during the war involved his well-trained horse, Black Nell (reminiscent of the marvelous steeds of earlier heroes), whose "trick of dropping quick" saved his life time and again. With the warriors and tribal chieftains of other heroic ages this "prince of pistoleers" was linked not only by his saga of daring challenges, thrilling combats, and miraculous escapes but also by his tragic doom. In fact, the fairies presided at his death as well as at his birth. Even his remains, as evidenced at the time of their exhumation for reburial underwent the Coracle of natural embalming.

The superman among killers was Billy the Kid, whose golden legend has grown out of all proportion to the few sordid facts of his short, lightning-swift career. Born as William H. Bonney in New York City in 1859, he was brought to Kansas at the age of three; at twelve killed his first man in Silver City, New Mexico, for insulting his mother; after a series of wanderings and crimes in Arizona, Mexico, Texas and New Mexico, joined the Murphy-Dolan faction in the Lincoln County war; made a sensational escape from his captors at Lincoln; and while visiting his sweetheart at Fort Sumner was shot in the dark by Sheriff Pat Garrett. This bare outline has been filled in by old-timers, journalists, and dime novelists with some of the most lurid and fantastic traditions and fictions that the popular imagination has ever concocted. Both the hero-worshippers and the debunkers have had a field day with the apocrypha of the "Southwest's most famous desperado" and "best-loved hero in the state's history"—the "darling of the common people". The list of twenty-one killings in twenty-one years which was the Kid's boast has been repeatedly revised downward, conservative estimates ranging from twelve to three. And the reputedly handsome, generous daredevil stands unmasked by his only authentic photograph, according to one unsympathetic critic, as "a nondescript, adenoidal, weasel-eyed, narrow-chested, stoop-shouldered, repulsive looking creature with all the outward appearance of a cretin".[17]

His dual personality has made him something of an enigma, which has fascinated his biographers. According to Pat Garrett:

> The Kid had a lurking devil in him. It was a good-humoured, jovial imp, or a cruel and blood-thirsty fiend, as circumstances prompted. Circumstances favoured the worser angel, and the Kid fell.

Like many another Western gun fighter—Wild Bill, Jesse James—Billy the Kid was killed without a chance to fight for his life. An extra touch of tragic irony is added to the Kid's fate by the fact that his slayer was, up to the time of his appointment as sheriff, a good friend.

By writing his *Authentic Life of Billy the Kid*, Pat Garrett also tried to kill the monstrous lies that sprang up after Billy the Kid's death. But as late as 1926 the rumour persisted that the Kid was still alive, as reported in an El Paso paper for June 24:

> Leland V. Gardiner . . . believes Billy the Kid, notorious outlaw of pioneer days, still lives, and has thought so for the past ten years, he said. He is not the El Pasoan, however, who communicated his belief to the New Mexico Historical Society. That informant said he had seen the Kid about ten years ago (in an eastern City).
> "I am not certain, but believe I have seen the Kid", said Mr. Gardiner. "I am told that he is on an isolated ranch within 500 miles of El Paso. When strangers come to the Erich he disappears until they are gone. . . . He can't take chances on being detected."[18]

Similar rumours have dogged the memory of Jesse James, and no less than seventeen persons, according to his granddaughter, have claimed to be the "original Jesse James". As Billy the Kid was the child of the cattle rustling wars, so Jesse James was the product of the bloody border warfare of Western Missouri and Eastern Kansas, beginning with the conflict over the Free Soil issue, passing into Civil War bushwhacking, and culminating in postbellum outlawry. As a boy on a Missouri farm, Jesse played at shooting or hanging Jim Lane or John Brown. In his youth Wild Bill Hickok was a member of Jim Lane's Red Legs and had his cabin burned down in retaliation by Missouri border ruffians; and-Buffalo Bill's father, Isaac Cody, was likewise involved in the free-state cause. In 1863 what had been a game became for Jesse a life-and-death affair. While ploughing in a cornfield, he was seized and lashed with a rope by a squad of Federal militia, who nearly hanged his step-father and subsequently arrested and jailed his mother and sister. Joining the guerillas under "Bloody Bill" Anderson, he was outlawed at the close of the war. Whether or not they were "driven" to crime by "persecution", he and his brother Frank and their cousins, the four Younger boys, all ex-guerillas, turned to robbing banks and trains for a livelihood.

This background in sectional conflict and civil strife perhaps helped to make Jesse James stand out in the popular imagination as a symbol of revolt and protest against the forces of tyranny and injustice. For most Americans he represents the Robin Hood tradition of the "good bad man", certain aspects of which are seen in Billy the Kid. In his bland, quixotic humour and impish wiliness, however, the Kid, like Wild Bill Hickok, has more in common with the tradition of the "cheerful rogue", which has given us "bad boys" and "bad good men" from Robin Hood and Tyl Eulenspiegel to Huckleberry Finn. Jesse James, on the other hand,

> robbed from the rich and he gave to the poor,
> He'd a hand and a heart and a brain.

And he all but achieved martyrdom through death by treachery. These lines, reminiscent of the refrain of the ballad, were inscribed on his monument at his mother's request:

> Murdered by a Traitor and Coward Whose
> Name Is Not Worthy to Appear Here

The classic instance of Jesse James' chivalry is the episode in which he paid off the mortgage for a poor widow and then stole the money back from the mortgage owner. The same story is told of Sam Bass, the "Texas Robin Hood", who was also a victim of the treachery of one of his own men—the best example of the good boy gone wrong.

FREE LANCES

Less well known to English readers is Stackalee, coloured gambler, killer and bad man, about whom many highly coloured stories and ballads have grown up. He is essentially a comic figure, as that other fantastic hero, Roy Bean, the judge who specialized in finable cases and kept most of the fines himself—a type not uncommon in the West and of which Roy Bean is the classic example. A Kentuckian by birth, he counted the art of bluff as part of his backwoods heritage; and in his late fifties, after knocking about California, New Mexico, and Texas, playing for small stakes as adventurer and jack-of-all-trades—saloon-keeper, ranger, bull-whacker, blockade-runner, wood merchant—he gave up fortune-hunting and sought the limelight. In the lawless waste of the Trans-Pecos country he followed the construction of a new line on the Southern Pacific Railroad as camp saloonkeeper, first at Vinegarroon and then at Langtry, where in 1883 the tracks were joined and Bean moved in as a squatter on the railroad right of way. With some 8,000 workers on their hands, the railroad contractors learned the truth of the saying that "West of the Pecos there is no law" and called in the Texas Rangers to help counteract crime. On August 2, 1882, Roy Bean got himself appointed justice of the peace, on a hunch that it might be doubly profitable to preside over both the bar-room and the bar of justice. From then until his death in 1903, he held court in the "Jersey Lily" saloon, named, like the town, for the English actress, whom Bean never met but who visited the place after his death.

There was plenty of precedent for Roy Bean in the usual Western "Law" or sheriff, who was "judge, jury, and executioner" all in one, and in frontier vigilantism. In fact, he had had first-hand knowledge of the latter when he narrowly escaped from hanging for killing a rival in a love affair in California. And the many anecdotes of his shady business dealings before he became the "Law West of the Pecos" testify to the native shrewdness and bluster which enabled him to dispose of cases in his own way. At any rate, the red rope-burn that he wore about his permanently stiff neck, usually hidden by a bandana, was his only diploma, and his only law book was the *Revised Statutes of Texas* for 1876. But he inspired respect for the law with his two six-shooters and such bizarre punishments as the use of the bear-and-stake method for sobering up drunks, while the stories of his weird decisions and judgments entertained the newspaper public and have become classics of the Southwest bench and bar. In his comic rôle of fining-judge Roy Bean rivals the famous "hanging judge" of Fort Smith, Arkansas, Isaac C. Parker.

"Hear ye! Hear ye! This honourable court is now in session, and if anybody wants a snort before we start step up to the bar and name your poison."

"It is the judgment of this court that you are hereby tried and convicted of illegally and unlawfully committing certain grave offenses against the peace and dignity of the State of Texas, particularly in my bailiwick, to wit: drunk and disorderly, and being Law West of the Pecos, I fine you two dollars; then get the hell out of here and never show yourself in this court again."[19]

In the same year that Roy Bean was appointed justice of the peace, another masterpiece: of showmanship was being created. This was the Wild West, Rocky Mountain, and Prairie Exhibition, which opened at Omaha, Nebraska, on May 17, 1883, and its star, Buffalo Bill. Of all the types of showman produced by the "histrionic West", none was more characteristic than the "professional Westerner", in long hair and fringed buckskins. For this role no one was more perfectly cast than William F. Cody, born on a farm in Scott County, Iowa, in 1846, who was endowed by nature and experience to be the epitome of all that was "high, wide, and handsome" in the Old West. Having lived all his life on the plains, in almost every capacity—"herder, hunter, pony express rider, stage driver, wagon master in the quartermaster's department, and scout of the army", to quote his press agent—and finding all Indian wars fought and himself out of a job in 1869, at the age- of 26 Buffalo Bill discovered his true mission. As a buffalo hunter employed by the Kansas Pacific to supply meat to construction crews, he had won his name, killing 4,280 buffalo in one year. Always something of a show-off, he now took to performing stunts of horsemanship and marksmanship and fell in with the promotion schemes of James Gordon Bennett, editor of the New York *Herald*, who had employed him as a guide on a hunting trip, and Ned Buntline (E. Z. C. Judson), the author.

In February, 1872, Buffalo Bill came to New York at Bennett's expense for the opening of Fred G. Maeder's play, inspired by Buntline, *Buffalo Bill, the King of Bordermen*, taking a bow before the audience; and in December of the same year he made his first stage appearance in Chicago in Buntline's *The Scouts of the Prairie*. Ned Buntline, from whom Buffalo Bill parted after his first theatrical success, was only the first of the four creators of Buffalo Bill. The second was Major John M. Burke, the world's greatest press agent, who publicized Buffalo Bill's duel with Yellow Hand in 1876 and was publicity man of his "Wild West", which Nat Salsbury, who was Number Three, suggested. The fourth was Prentiss Ingraham, author of over two hundred dime novels about Buffalo Bill. In this way, "Unlike those popular heroes who grow in folklore fortuitously, Buffalo Bill was the subject of the deliberate and infinitely skilful use of publicity."[20]

Although Buffalo Bill lived to see himself and the Wild West show outmoded, as he had once seen the passing of the Old West, the legend of the West, which was partly his creation as he in turn was its creature, still lives in Western pulp-paper magazines and movies and in the hearts of Americans.

MIRACLE MEN

The American genius for invention has produced its hero in Paul Bunyan. Although he handles nature like a toy and accounts for the bigness of certain American geographical features, such as Puget Sound, he is primarily a work giant whose job is to invent logging. By reason of his having to start from scratch, there is something primordial about him; but unlike most Titans, he combines brain with brawn, and employs both for the good of mankind. He has gone a long way from the giant of nursery tales whose chief purpose was to scare little children and be slain by the hero.

Tales of the Paul Bunyan type originated as separate anecdotes or "gags" exchanged in competitive bragging or lying contests and involving "sells" and the pranking of greenhorns. "The best authorities", writes W. B. Laughead (and in this the experts all agree), "never recounted Paul Bunyan's exploits in narrative form. They made their statements more impressive by dropping them casually, in an offhand way, as if in reference to actual events of common knowledge". Such remarks often began with a phrase of reminiscence or reminder: "Time I was with Paul up in the Big Onion country———"; "That happened the year I went up for Paul Bunyan"; "Did you ever hear of the——— that Paul Bunyan———?"

James Stevens traces the mythical Paul Bunyan to a French-Canadian logger named Paul Bunyan, who won a reputation as a prodigious fighter in the Papineau Rebellion against the Queen in 1837, and later became famous as the boss of a logging camp—"he fight like hell, he work like hell, and he pack like hell."[21] But whatever his historical origins, if any, Paul Bunyan—the superman in a world of super-gadgets—has become an American symbol of bigness and a proverbial character on which to tack an extravagant anecdote. Although the tradition has spread to many other occupations—the oil fields, the wheat fields, and construction jobs, Paul Bunyan tales are told popularly, outside of the industry more than within it, and depend for their effect upon pure exaggeration rather than upon occupational colouring.

The first appearance of Paul Bunyan in print seems to have been an advertising man's idea. In 1914 the Red River Lumber Company issued a booklet of tales which has since gone through twelve editions, gradually incorporating more and more advertising matter along with the original stories. To-day Paul Bunyan is the company's trademark and "stands for the quality and service you have the right to expect from Paul Bunyan".

The author and illustrator of these booklets, W. B. Laughead, who claims to have invented many of the names of characters and who is given credit for initiating the preservation of the Paul Bunyan stories, has never made clear whether Paul Bunyan dreamed up the lumber business or *vice versa*.[22]

How much of Paul Bunyan is folklore and how much of it is literature is still an open question. But in the absence of authentic oral versions, scholars give credence to the view that he is, if not actually a hoax, at least the product of downward transmission.[23]

Although American legendary heroes like Paul Bunyan and the other work giants are occupational heroes, they are industrial pioneers rather than industrialists. Thus Paul Bunyan represents the days before the timber beast became a timber mechanic and Old Stormalong, the days of wooden ships and iron men. Under the influence of the machine the hero undergoes a change. The work boss is supplanted by the ordinary worker, who distinguishes himself not so much for innovations as for doing a good job of whatever he is doing. He is a strong man or a star performer with tragic and social rather than comic significance. The tragedy usually results from his being overcome by a superior force—the machine. Thus John Henry dies in a contest with a steam drill and Casey Jones in a train wreck with one hand on the whistle cord and the other on the airbrake lever; while Joe Magarac offers himself up as a sacrifice to make better steel.

Originally a flesh-and-blood hero of the rock-tunnel gangs, the great steel-driver who died with his hammer in his hand while competing with a steam-drill at Big Bend Tunnel on the Chesapeake and Ohio Railroad in West Virginia in 1870, John Henry has become a legendary and mythical figure with various symbolic significances. In folk song tradition the "tiny epic of man's last stand against the machine" has produced a work song (the hammer song), a ballad, and a social song or blues, in which the central theme of the drilling contest has attracted to itself double meaning stanzas and conventional ballad lines and motifs. The few John Henry tales that have been recovered are of the Paul Bunyan type, elaborating the hero's size, strength, skill, and prowess with food, women, etc. As the tradition moved west, other kinds of labour were substituted for tunnel construction, until in Roark Bradford's version John Henry becomes the champion cotton picker, roustabout, and railroad man with more than a touch of the bad man and boaster or "big mouth".

The supreme symbol of industrial strength is Joe Magarac, who comments thus on his name and nature: "Sure! Magarac. Joe. Dat's me. All I do is eatit and workit same lak jackass donkey." He symbolizes not only the power of steel but the power of the men behind the steel, the human basis of our basic industry.

> There is no glory comparable to poured iron or poured steel. The gushing out of fiery metal from a great wheel-like container seems like the beginning of Creation. This black container of molten iron is twenty feet high. A ladle advances on an overhead railway. It travels to the container of molten iron. It moves forward on its track and then laterally and then down. The black container swings around slowly on its axle as a man presses a lever.
>
> Then follows the sudden magnificence of poured metal. Like giant fireworks, a thousand sparks fly from it, a river of white fire throwing off cascades of stars, a fiery shower on all sides. On a greasy platform above the ladle are the men who operate it. They look down with indifference into its seething deadly brightness.
>
> My guide said: "A man fell into that once, and they buried him and all the tons of metal. Right here they held the burial service."
>
> The story of the man who fell into the vat of molten metal and became part of it obsesses the men's minds. I have heard it told in different ways.
>
> They tell you of a man made into iron rails, of another who went into the structure of great buildings.
>
> This story is as old as time. There was a great bell once which was cast and re-cast and would not ring true until a human being was sacrificed to it.[24]

PATRON SAINTS

The hero is a man who has fought impressively for a cause of which we approve.
—DUMAS MALONE

On the purely patriotic level our heroes are apt to be too good to be true. Such is the case with that "typically good man", Washington, whose integrity is traditionally taught by means of what the Doubter in the Sazerac-Lying Club characterizes as the "doggonedest biggest lie as was ever told in this here Club".

As human being and folk hero, as American image and symbol, Lincoln is more satisfying. His genius as a folk story-teller helped in the making of his own legend; and he suffered the martyrdom which is the hero's apotheosis. Rather than too good to be true, Lincoln was great because he was not afraid to be common.

That saints are not far from cranks is seen in the fanatic Johnny Appleseed, whose resemblance to Saint Francis is balanced by his likeness to a Yankee peddler. His "benevolent monomania" of "planting appleseeds in remote places" has overshadowed his less beneficent fixation of sowing the seed of dog-fennel, from a belief that it possessed valuable anti-malarial virtues.

Part One

BACKWOODS BOASTERS

THE BALLAD OF DAVY CROCKETT[25]

Now, don't you want to know something concernin'
Where it was I come from and where I got my learnin'?
Oh, the world is made of mud out o' the Mississippi River!
The sun's a ball of foxfire, as well you may disciver.

Chorus:
    Take the ladies out at night. They shine so bright
    They make the world light when the moon is out of sight.

And so one day as I was goin' a-spoonin'
I met Colonel Davy, and he was goin' a-coonin'.
Says I, "Where's your gun?" "I ain' got none."
"How you goin' kill a coon when you haven't got a gun?[26]

Says he, "Pompcalf, just follow after Davy,
And he'll soon show you how to grin a coon crazy."
I followed on a piece and thar sot a squirrel,
A-settin' on a log and a-eatin' sheep sorrel.

When Davy did that see, he looked around at me,
Saying, "All I want now is a brace agin your knee."
And thar I braced a great big sinner.
He grinned six times hard enough to git his dinner!

The critter on the log didn't seem to mind him—
Jest kep' a settin' thar and wouldn't look behind him.
Then it was he said, "The critter must be dead.
See the bark a-flyin' all around the critter's head?"

I walked right up the truth to disciver.
Drot! It was a pine knot so hard it made me shiver.
Says he, "Pompcalf, don't you begin to laugh—
I'll pin back your ears, and bite you half in half!"

I flung down my gun and all my ammunition.
Says I, "Davy Crockett, I can cool your ambition!"
He throwed back his head and he blowed like a steamer.
Says he, "Pompcalf, I'm a Tennessee screamer!"

Then we locked horns and we wallered in the thorns.
I never had such a fight since the hour I was born.
We fought a day and a night and then agreed to drop it.
I was purty badly whipped—and so was Davy Crockett.

I looked all around and found my head a-missin'—
He'd bit off my head and I had swallered his'n!
Then we did agree to let each other be;
I was too much for him, and he was too much for me.

TREEING A WOLF[27]

Once thar war a deep snow on the ground, and I sot out to make a call on my friend Luke Twig, as it war a leisure day, and I war goin' to be idle. Luke lived next door to me, only about fifteen mile off, and so I war goin' to foot it. Jest as I got up by Brush Hollow, the snow war as deep as my middle, the wind blowed so hard that I went into a hollow tree to warm myself. I hung kill-devil up and begun to thrash my hands, when a wolf cum along, and looked in. He stared right up in my face, as much as to ax leave to pick a breakfast off of any part of me he wanted. I war so astonished at his imperdence that I stood right still a minit. Then the wolf turned about, and war going off, when the end of his tail stuck through a big knot hole in the tree. I ketched hold and pulled his tail through. He jumped and twitched and tried to get away, and screeched like a dying hawk. I tied his tail into a big knot and fastened it with a strap, so that he couldn't haul it out, and left him thar to amuse himself. I could hear him holler all the way till I got to Luke Twig's house.

SKINNING A BEAR[28]

One day when Oak Wing's sister war going to a baptizing, and had her feed in a bag under her arm, she seed a big bear that had come out from a holler tree, and he looked first at her, then at the feed, as if he didn't know which to eat fust. He kinder poked out his nose, and smelt of the dinner which war sassengers maid of bear's meat and crocodile's liver. She stood a minute an looked at him, in hopes he would feel ashamed of himself an go off; but he then cum up and smelt of her, and then she thort twar time to be stirring. So she threw the dinner down before him, an when he put his nose to it, to take a bite, she threw herself on him, an caught the scuff of his neck in her teeth; an the bear shot ahead, for it felt beautiful, as her teeth war as long an sharp as nales. He tried to run, an she held on with her teeth, and it strips the skin clear off of him, an left him as naked as he was born, she held on with her teeth till it cum clear off the tale. The bear was seen a week arterwards up in Muskrat Hollow, running without his skin. She made herself a good warm petticoat out of the pesky varmint's hide.

THE DEATH HUG[29]

We are all smashen huggers in our parts, an arter we once git a reglar natral embrace, it takes us a day to git apart agin, but the all smashinest huggin I ever knowed, was the one that I give a great he barr that squeezed me out of a nap once, as I laid at the root of a big holler black oak. You see the tarnal cowardly crittur had put both his great fore paws around me, and clinched 'em behind my back, and begun huggen me up-to him to take a taste o' my Kentucky taller, an the way he curled his tail an wiped his red tongue about was elegantifferously greedy, and his mouth watered for it, like a fresh medder ditch in the spring o' the year, but he war most pressenly disappointed, for he jist woke up about half o' me, and left t'other half still asleep. I snored a leetle tantalization at him, then grabbed him by the ear with my finger flesh vice, put an arm around his tarnal fat body, and with jist a single squeeze I hugged him in a bar jelly, corked it up in his skin, and took it home for presarves.

A SENSIBLE VARMINT[30]

Almost every boddy that knows the forest, understands perfectly well that Davy Crockett never loses powder and ball, havin' teen brort up to blieve it a sin to throw away amminition, and that is the bennefit of a vartuous eddikation. I war out in the forrest won arternoon, and had jist got to a plaice called the grate gap, when I seed a rakkoon setting all alone upon a tree. I klapped the breech of Brown Betty to my sholder, and war jist a going to put a piece of led between his sholders, when he lifted one paw, and sez he, "Is your name Crockett ?"

Sez I, "You are rite for wonst, my name is Davy Crockett."

"Then", sez he, "you needn't take no further trubble, for I may as well cum down without another word"; and the cretur wauked rite down from the tree, for he considered himself shot.

I stoops down and pats him on the head, and sez I, "I hope I may be shot myself before I hurt a hare of your head, for I never had sich a kompliment in my life."

"Seeing as how you say that", sez he, "I'll jist walk off for the present, not doubting your word a bit, d'ye see, but lest you should kinder happen to change your mind."

CROCKETT'S MORNING HUNT[31]

One January morning it was so all-screwen-up cold that the forest trees war so stiff that they couldn't shake, and the very day-break froze fast as it war tryin' to dawn. The tinder-box in my cabin would no more ketch fire than a sunk raft at the bottom o' the sea. Seein' that daylight war so far behind time, I thought creation war in a fair way for freezin' fast.

"So", thinks I, "I must strike a leetle fire from my fingers, light my pipe, travel out a few leagues, and see about it."

Then I brought my knuckles together like two thunder clouds, but the sparks froze up afore I could begin to collect 'em—so out I walked, and endeavored to keep myself unfriz by goin' at a hop, step and jump gait, and whistlin' the tune of "fire in the mountains!" as I went along in three double quick time. Well, arter I had walked about twenty-five miles up the peak o' Daybreak Hill, I soon discovered what war the matter. The airth had actually friz fast in her axis, and couldn't turn round; the sun had got jammed between two cakes o' ice under the wheels, an' thar he had bin shinin' and workin' to get loose, till he friz fast in his cold sweat.

"C-r-e-a-t-i-o-n!" thought I, "this are the toughest sort o' suspension, and it mustn't be endured somethin' must be done, or human creation is done for."

It war then so antedeluvian and premature cold that upper and lower teeth an' tongue war all collapsed together as tight as a friz oyster. I took a fresh twenty pound bear off o' my back that I'd picked up on the road, an' beat the animal agin the ice till the hot ile began to walk out on him at all sides. I then took an' held him over the airth's axes, an' squeezed him till I thaw'd 'em loose, poured about a ton on it over the sun's face, give the airth's cog-wheel one kick backward, till I got the sun loose—whistled "Push along, keep movin'!" an' in about fifteen seconds the airth gin a grunt, and begun movin'—the sun walked up beautiful, salutin' me with sich a wind o' gratitude that it made me sneeze. I lit my pipe by the blaze o' his top-knot, shouldered my bear, an' walked home, introducin' the people to fresh daylight with a piece of sunrise in my pocket, with which I cooked my bear steaks, an' enjoyed one o' the best breakfasts I had tasted for some time. If I didn't, jist wake some mornin' and go with me to the office o' sunrise!

LIFE AND DEATH OF MIKE FINK

THE DISGRACED SCALP-LOCK[32]

. . . Among the flat-boatmen there were none that gained the notoriety of *Mike Fink*. His name is still remembered along the whole of the Ohio as a man who excelled his fellows in every thing,—particularly in his rifle-shot, which was acknowledged to be unsurpassed. Probably no man ever lived who could compete with Mike Fink in the latter accomplishment. Strong as Hercules, free from all nervous excitement, possessed of perfect health, and familiar with his weapon from childhood, he raised the rifle to his eye, and, having once taken sight, it was as firmly fixed as if buried in rock. It was Mike's pride, and he rejoiced on all occasions where he could bring it into use, whether it was turned against the beast of prey or the more savage Indian; and in his day these last named were the common foe with whom Mike Fink and his associates had to contend. On the occasion that we would particularly introduce Mike to the reader, he had bound himself for a while to the pursuits of trade, until a voyage from the head-waters of the Ohio, and down the Mississippi, could be completed. Heretofore he had kept himself exclusively to the Ohio, but a liberal reward, and some curiosity, prompted him to extend his business character beyond his ordinary habits and inclinations. In accomplishment of this object, he was lolling carelessly over the big "sweep" that guided the "flat" on which he officiated; the current of the river bore the boat swiftly along, and made his labour light; his eye glanced around him, and he broke forth in ecstasies at what he saw and felt. If there is a river in the world that merits the name of beautiful, it is the Ohio, when its channel is

"Without o'erflowing, full."

The scenery is everywhere soft; there are no jutting rocks, no steep banks, no high hills; but the clear and swift current raves beautiful and undulating shores, that descend gradually to the water's edge. The foliage is rich and luxuriant, and its outlines in the water are no less distinct than when it is relieved against the sky. Interspersed along its route are islands, as beautiful as ever figured in poetry as the land of the fairies; enchanted spots indeed, that seem to sit so lightly on the water that you almost expect them, as you approach, to vanish into dreams. So late as when Mike Fink disturbed the solitude of the Ohio with his rifle, the canoe of the Indian was hidden in the little recesses along the shore; they moved about in their frail barks like spirits; and clung, in spite of the constant encroachments of civilization, to places which tradition had designated as the happy places of a favoured people.

Wild and uncultivated as Mike appeared, he loved nature, and had a soul that sometimes felt, while admiring it, an exalted enthusiasm. The Ohio was his favourite stream. From where it runs no stronger than a gentle rivulet, to where it mixes with the muddy Mississippi, Mike was as familiar with its meanderings as a child could be with those of a flower-garden. He could not help noticing with sorrow the desecrating hand of improvement as he passed along, and half soliloquizing, and half addressing his companions, he broke forth:—"I knew these parts afore a squatter's axe had blazed a tree; 't wasn't then pulling a————sweep to get a living; but pulling the triggers the business. Those were times to see; a man might call himself lucky. What's the use of improvements? When did cutting down trees make deer more plenty? Who ever found wild buffalo or a brave Indian in a city? Where's the fun, the frolicking, the fighting? Gone! Gone! The rifle won't make a man a living now—he must turn nigger and work. If forests continue to be used up, I may yet be smothered in a settlement. Boys, this 'ere life won't do. I'll stick to the broadhorn 'cordin' to contract; but once done with it, I'm off for a frolic. If the Choctaws or Cherokees on the Massassip don't give us a brush as we pass along, I shall grow as poor as a starved wolf in a pitfall. I must, to live peaceably, point my rifle at something more dangerous than varmint. Six months and no fight would spire me worse than a dead horse on a prairie."

Mike ceased speaking. The then beautiful village of Louisville appeared in sight; the labour of landing the boat occupied his attention—the bustle and confusion that followed such an incident ensued, and Mike was his own master by law until his employers ceased trafficking, and again required his services.

At the time we write of, there were a great many renegade Indians who lived about the settlements, and which is still the case in the extreme south-west. These Indians generally are the most degraded of their tribe—outcasts, who, for crime or dissipation, are no longer allowed to associate with their people; they live by hunting or stealing,

and spend their precarious gains in intoxication. Among the throng
that crowded on the flat-boat on his arrival, were a number of these
unfortunate beings; they were influenced by no other motive than that
of loitering round in idle speculation at what was going on. Mike was
attracted towards them at sight; and as he too was in the situation that
is deemed most favourable to mischief, it struck him that it was a good
opportunity to have a little sport at the Indians' expense. Without
ceremony, he gave a terrific war-whoop; and then mixing the language
of the aborigines and his own together, he went on in savage fashion
and bragged of his triumphs and victories on the warpath, with all the
seeming earnestness of a real "brave". Nor were taunting words spared
to exasperate the poor creatures, who, perfectly helpless, listened to
the tales of their own greatness, and their own shame, until wound up
to the highest pitch of impotent exasperation. Mike's companions joined
in; thoughtless boys caught the spirit of the affair; and the Indians
were goaded until they in turn made battle with their tongues. Then
commenced a system of running against them, pulling off their blankets, together with a thousand other indignities; finally they made a
precipitate retreat ashore, amid the hooting and jeering of an unfeeling
crowd, who considered them poor devils destitute of feeling and humanity. Among this crowd of outcasts was a Cherokee, who bore the
name of Proud Joe; what his real cognomen was, no one knew, for he
was taciturn, haughty—and, in spite of his poverty and his manner of
life won the name we have mentioned. His face was expressive of
talent, but it was furrowed by the most terrible habits of drunkenness.
That he was a superior Indian was admitted; and it was also understood that he was banished from his mountain home, his tribe being
then numerous and powerful, for some great crime. He was always
looked up to by his companions, and managed, however intoxicated
he might be, to sustain a singularly proud bearing, which did not even
depart from him while prostrated on the ground. Joe was filthy in his
person and habits—in this respect he was behind his fellows; but one
ornament of his person was attended to with a care which would have
done honour to him if surrounded by his people, and in his native
woods. Joe still wore with Indian dignity his scalp-lock; he ornamented it with taste, and cherished it, as report said, that some Indian
messenger of vengeance might tear it from his head, as expiatory of
his numerous crimes. Mike noticed this peculiarity; and reaching out
his hand, plucked from it a hawk's feather, which was attached to the

scalp-lock. The Indian glared horribly on Mike as he consummated the insult, snatched the feather from his hand, then shaking his clenched fist in the air, as if calling on Heaven for revenge, retreated with his friends. Mike saw that he had roused the savage's soul, and he marvelled wonderfully that so much resentment should be exhibited; and as an earnest to Proud Joe that the wrong he had done him should not rest unrevenged, he swore that he would cut the scalp-lock off close to his head the first convenient opportunity he got, and then he thought no more about it.

The morning following the arrival of the boat at Louisville was occupied in making preparations to pursue the voyage down the river. Nearly every thing was completed, and Mike had taken his favourite place at the sweep, when looking up the river-bank, he beheld at some distance Joe and his companions, and perceived from their gesticulations that they were making him the subject of conversation.

Mike thought instantly of several ways in which he could show them altogether a fair fight, and then whip them with ease; he also reflected with what extreme satisfaction he would enter into the spirit of the arrangement, and other matters to him equally pleasing, when all the Indians disappeared, save Joe himself, who stood at times reviewing him in moody silence, and then staring round at passing objects. From the peculiarity of Joe's position to Mike, who was below him, his head and upper part of his body relieved boldly against the sky, and in one of his movements he brought his profile face to view. The prominent scalp-lock and its adornments seemed to be more striking than ever, and it again roused the pugnacity of Mike Fink; in an instant he raised his rifle, always loaded and at command, brought it to his eye, and, before he could be prevented, drew sight upon Proud Joe and fired. The ball whistled loud and shrill, and Joe, springing his whole length into the air, fell upon the ground. The cold-blooded murder was noticed by fifty persons at least, and there arose from the crowd a universal cry of horror and indignation at the bloody deed. Mike himself seemed to be much astonished, and in an instant reloaded his rifle, and as a number of white persons rushed towards the boat, Mike threw aside his coat, and, taking his powder horn between his teeth, leaped, rifle in hand, into the Ohio, and commenced swimming for the opposite shore. Some bold spirits determined Mike should not so easily escape, and jumping into the only skiff at command, pulled swiftly after him. Mike watched their movements until they came within a hundred yards of him, then turning in the water, he supported himself by his feet alone, and raised his deadly rifle to his eye. Its muzzle, if it spoke hostilely, was as certain to send a messenger of death through one or more of his pursuers, as if it were lightning, and they knew it; dropping their oars and turning pale, they bid Mike not to fire. Mike waved his hands towards the little village of Louisville, and again pursued his way to the opposite shore.

The time consumed by the firing of Mike's rifle, the pursuit, and the abandonment of it, required less time than we have taken to give the details; and in that time, to the astonishment of the gaping crowd around Joe, they saw him rising with a bewildered air; a moment more and he recovered his senses and stood up—*at his feet lay his scalp-lock*! The ball had cut it clear from his head; the cord around the root of it, in which were placed feathers and other ornaments, held it together; the concussion had merely stunned its owner; farther, he had escaped all bodily harm! A cry of exultation rose at the last evidence of the skill of Mike Fink—the exhibition of a shot that established his claim, indisputable, to the eminence he ever afterwards held—the unrivalled marksman of all the flat-boatmen of the western-waters. Proud Joe had received many insults. He looked upon himself as a degraded, worthless being; and the ignominy heaped upon him he never, except by reply, resented; but this last insult was like seizing the lion by the mane, or a Roman senator by the beard—it roused the slumbering demon within, and made him again thirst to resent his wrongs with an intensity of emotion that can only be felt by an Indian. His eye glared upon the jeering crowd around like a fiend; his chest swelled and heaved until it seemed that he must suffocate. No one noticed this emotion. All were intent upon the exploit that had so singularly deprived Joe of his war-lock; and, smothering his wrath, he retreated to his associates with a consuming fire at his vitals. He was a different man from an hour before; and with that desperate resolution on which a man stakes his all, he swore by the Great Spirit of his forefathers that he would be revenged.

An hour after the disappearance of Joe, both he and Mike Fink were forgotten. The flat-boat, which the latter had deserted, was got under way, and dashing through the rapids in the river opposite Louisville wended its course. As is customary when nights sets in, the boat was securely fastened in some little bend or bay in the shore, where it remained until early morn.

Long before the sun had fairly risen, the boat was again pushed into the stream, and it passed through a valley presenting the greatest possible beauty and freshness of landscape the mind can conceive.

It was spring, and a thousand tints of green developed themselves in the half-formed foliage and bursting buds. The beautiful mallard skimmed across the water, ignorant of the danger of the white man's approach; the splendid spoon-bill decked the shallow places near the shore, while myriads of singing-birds filled the air with their unwritten songs. In the far reaches down the river, there occasionally might be seen a bear stepping along the ground as if dainty of its feet, and, snuffing the intruder on his wild home, he would retreat into the woods. To enliven all this, and give the picture the look of humanity, there might also be seen, struggling with the floating mists, a column of blue smoke that came from a fire built on a projecting point of land, around which the current swept rapidly and carried everything that floated on the river. The eye of the boatman saw the advantage of the situation which the place rendered to those on shore, to annoy and attack, and as wandering Indians, in those days, did not hesitate to rob, there was much speculation as to what reception the boat would receive from the builders of the fire.

The rifles were all loaded, to be prepared for the worst, and the loss of Mike Fink lamented, as a prospect of a fight presented itself, where he could use his terrible rifle. The boat in the meantime swept round the point; but instead of an enemy, there lay, in a profound sleep, Mike Fink, with his feet toasting at the fire. His pillow was a huge bear that had been shot on the day previous, while at his sides, and scattered in profusion around him were several deer and wild turkeys. Mike had not been idle. After picking out a place most eligible to notice the passing boat, he had spent his time in hunting, and he was surrounded by trophies of his prowess. The scene that he presented was worthy of the time and the man, and would have thrown Landseer into a delirium of joy, could he have witnessed it. The boat, owing to the swiftness of the current, passed Mike's resting place, although it was pulled strongly to the shore. As Mike's companions came opposite to him, they raised such a shout, half exultation at meeting him, and half to alarm him with the idea that Joe's friends were upon him. Mike, at the sound, sprang to his feet, rifle in hand, and as he looked around, he raised it to his eyes, and by the time he discovered the boat, he was ready to fire. "Down with your shooting-iron, you wild critter", shouted one of the boatmen. Mike dropped the piece, and gave a loud halloo, that echoed among the solitudes like a piece of artillery. The meeting between Mike and his fellows was characteristic. They joked, and jibed him with their rough wit, and he parried it off with a most creditable ingenuity. Mike soon learned the extent of his rifle-shot—he seemed perfectly indifferent to the fact that Proud Joe was not dead. The only sentiment he uttered was regret that he did not fire at the vagabond's head, and if he hadn't hit it, why he made the first bad shot in twenty years. The dead game was carried on board of the boat, the adventure was forgotten, and everything resumed the monotony of floating in a flat-boat down the Ohio.

A month or more elapsed, and Mike had progressed several hundred miles down the Mississippi; his journey had been remarkably free from incident; morning, noon, and night presented the same banks, the same muddy water, and he sighed to see some broken land, some high hills, and he railed and swore that he should have been such a fool as to desert his favourite Ohio for a river that produced nothing but alligators, and was never at best half finished.

Occasionally, the plentifulness of game put him in spirits, but it did not last long; he wanted more lasting excitement, and declared himself as perfectly miserable and helpless as a wild-cat without teeth or claws.

In the vicinity of Natchez rises a few abrupt hills, which tower above the surrounding lowlands of the Mississippi like monuments; they are not high, but from their loneliness and rarity they create sensations of pleasure and awe.

Under the shadow of one of these bluffs, Mike and his associates made the customary preparations to pass the night. Mike's enthusiasm knew no bounds at the sight of land again; he said it was as pleasant as "cold water to a fresh wound"; and, as his spirits rose, he went on making the region round about, according to his notions, an agreeable residence.

"The Choctaws live in these diggins", said Mike, "and a cursed time they must have of it. Now if I lived in these parts I'd declare war on 'em just to have something to keep me from growing dull; without some such business I'd be as musty as an old swamp moccasin. I could build a cabin on that thar hill yonder that could, from its location, with my rifle, repulse a whole tribe if they came after me. What a beautiful time I'd have of it ! I never was particular about what's called a fair fight; I just ask half a chance, and the odds against me, and if I then don't keep clear of snags and sawyers, let me spring a leak and go to the bottom. It's nature that the big fish should eat the little ones. I've seen trout swallow a perch, and a cat would come along and swallow the trout, and perhaps, on the Mississippi, the alligators use up the cat, and so on to the end of the row. Well, I will walk tall into varmint and Indian; it's a way I've got, and it comes as natural as grinning to a hyena. I'm a regular tornado, tough as a hickory, and long-winded as a nor'-wester. I can strike a blow like a falling tree, and every lick makes a gap in the crowd that lets in an acre of sunshine. Whew, boys!" shouted Mike, twirling his rifle like a walking-stick around his head, at the ideas suggested in his mind. "Whew, boys ! if the Choctaw divils in them thar woods thare would give us a brush, just as I feel now, I'd call them gentlemen. I must fight something, or I'll catch the dry rot—burnt brandy won't save me." Such were some of the expressions which Mike gave utterance to, and in which his companions heartily joined; but they never presumed to be quite equal to Mike, for his bodily prowess, as well as his rifle, were acknowledged to be unsurpassed. These displays of animal spirits generally ended in boxing and wrestling matches, in which falls were received, and blows were struck without being noticed, that would have destroyed common men. Occasionally angry words and blows were exchanged, but, like the summer storm, the cloud that emitted the lightning purified the air; and when the commotion ceased, the combatants immediately made friends and became more attached to each other than before the cause that interrupted the good feelings occurred. Such were the conversation and amusements of the evening when the boat was moored under the bluffs we have alluded to. As night wore on, one by one of the hardy boatmen fell asleep, some in its confined interior, and others protected by a light covering in the open air. The moon arose in beautiful majesty; her silver light, behind the highlands, gave them a power and theatrical effect as it ascended; and as its silver rays grew perpendicular, they finally kissed gently the summit of the hills, and poured down their full light upon the boat, with almost noonday brilliancy. The silence with which the beautiful changes of darkness and light were produced made it mysterious. It seemed as if some creative power was at work, bringing form and life out of darkness. In the midst of the witchery of this quiet scene, there sounded forth the terrible rifle, and the more terrible war-whoop of the Indian. One of the flat-boatmen, asleep on deck, gave a stifled groan, turned upon his face, and with a quivering motion, ceased to live. Not so with his companions—they in an instant, as men accustomed to danger and sudden attacks, sprang ready-armed to their feet; but before they could discover their foes, seven sleek and horribly painted savages leaped from the hill into the boat. The firing of the rifle was useless, and each man singled out a foe and met him with the drawn knife.

The struggle was quick) and fearful; and deadly blows were given amid screams and imprecations that rent the air. Yet the voice of Mike Fink could be heard in encouraging shouts above the clamour. "Give it to them, boys!" he cried, "cut their hearts out! choke the dogs! Here's hell a-fire and the river rising!" then clenching with the most powerful of the assailants, he rolled with him upon the deck of the boat. Powerful as Mike was, the Indian seemed nearly a match for him. The two twisted and writhed like serpents,—now one seeming to have the advantage, and then the other.

In all this confusion there might occasionally be seen glancing in the moonlight the blade of a knife; but at whom the thrusts were made, or who wielded it, could not be discovered.

The general fight lasted less time than we have taken to describe it. The white men gained the advantage; two of the Indians lay dead upon the boat, and the living, escaping from their antagonists, leaped ashore, and before the rifle could be brought to bear they were out of its reach. While Mike was yet struggling with his antagonist, one of his companions cut the boat loose from the shore, and, with powerful exertion, managed to get its bows so far into the current, that it swung round and floated; but before this was accomplished and before any one interfered with Mike, he was on his feet, covered with blood, and blowing like a porpoise: by the time he could get his breath, he commenced talking. "Ain't been so busy in a long time," said he, turning over his victim with his foot; "that fellow fought beautiful; if he's a specimen of the Choctaws that live in these parts, they are screamers; the infernal serpents! the d———d possums!" Talking in this way, he with the others, took a general survey of the killed and wounded. Mike himself was a good deal cut up with the Indian's knife; but he called his wounds blackberry scratches. One of Mike's associates was severely hurt; the rest escaped comparatively harmless. The sacrifice was made at the first fire; for beside the dead Indians, there lay one of the boat's crew, cold and dead, his body perforated with four different balls. That he was the chief object of attack seemed evident, yet no one of his associates knew of his having a single fight with the Indians. The soul of Mike was affected, and taking the hand of his deceased friend between his own, he raised his bloody knife towards the bright moon, and swore that he would desolate "the nation" that claimed the Indians who made war upon them that night, and turned to his stiffened victim, that, dead as it was, retained the expression of implacable hatred and defiance; he gave it a smile of grim satisfaction, and then joined in the general conversation which the occurrences of the night would naturally suggest. The master of the "broad horn" was a business man, and had often been down the Mississippi. This was the first attack he had received, or knew to have been made from the shores inhabited by the Choctaws, except by the white man, and he, among other things, suggested keeping the dead Indians until daylight, that they might have an opportunity to examine their dress and features, and see with certainty who were to blame for the occurrences of the night. The dead boatman was removed with care to a respectful distance; and the living, except the person at the sweep of the boat, were soon buried in profound slumber.

Not until after the rude breakfast was partaken of, and the funeral rites of the dead boatman were solemnly performed, did Mike and his companions disturb the corpses of the red men.

When both these things had been leisurely and gently got through with, there was a different spirit among the men.

Mike was astir, and went about his business with alacrity. He stripped the bloody blanket from the Indian he had killed, as if it enveloped something disgusting, and required no respect. He examined carefully the moccasins on the Indian's feet, pronouncing them at one time Chickasas, at another time, the Shawnese. He stared at the livid face, but could not recognise the style of paint that covered it.

That the Indians were not strictly national in their adornments, was certain, for they were examined by practiced eyes, that could have told the nation of the dead, if such had been the case, as readily as a sailor could distinguish a ship by its flag. Mike was evidently puzzled; and as he was about giving up his task as hopeless, the dead body he was examining, from some cause, turned on its side. Mike's eyes distended, as some of his companions observed, "like a choked cat", and became riveted. He drew himself up in a half serious, and half comic expression, and pointing at the back of the dead Indian's head, there was exhibited a dead warrior in his paint, destitute of his scalp-lock, the small stump which was only left, being stiffened with *red paint.* Those who could read Indians' symbols learned a volume of deadly resolve in what they saw. The body of Proud Joe was stiff and cold before them.

The last and best shot of Mike Fink cost a brave man his life. The corpse so lately interred was evidently taken in the moonlight by Proud Joe and his party as that of Mike's, and they had risked their lives, one and all, that he might with certainty be sacrificed. Nearly a thousand miles of swamp had been threaded, large and swift running rivers had been crossed, hostile tribes passed through by Joe and his friends, that they might revenge the fearful insult of destroying *without the life* the sacred scalp-lock.

DEATH OF MIKE FINK[33]

"The Last of the Boatmen" has not become altogether a *mythic* personage. There be around us those who still remember him as one of flesh and blood, as well as proportions simply human, albeit he lacked not somewhat of the *heroic* in stature, as well as in being a "perfect terror" to people!

As regards Mike, it has not yet become that favourite question of doubt—"Did such a being really live?" Nor have we heard the sceptic inquiry—"Did such a being really die?" But his death in half a dozen different ways and places has been asserted, and this, we take it, is the first gathering of the *mythic* haze—that shadowy and indistinct enlargement of outline, which, deepening through long ages, invests distinguished mortality with the sublimer attributes of the hero and the demi-god. Had Mike lived in "early Greece", his flat-boat feats would, doubtless, in poetry, have rivalled those of Jason, in his ship; while in Scandinavian legends, he would have been a river-god, to a certainty! The Sea-Kings would have sacrificed to him every time they "crossed the bar", on their return; and as for Odin, himself, he would be duly advised, as far as any interference went, to "lay low and keep dark, or, *pre*-haps", etc.

The story of Mike Fink, including *a* death, has been beautifully told by the late Morgan Neville, of Cincinnati, a gentleman of the highest literary taste as well as of the most amiable and polished manners. "The Last of the Boatmen", as his sketch is entitled, is unexceptionable in style, and, we believe, in *fact*, with one exception, and that is, the statement as to the manner and place of Fink's death. He did *not die* on the Arkansas, but at Fort Henry, near the mouth of the Yellow Stone. Our informant is Mr. Chas. Keemle of this paper,[34] who held a command in the neighbourhood, at the time, and to whom every circumstance connected with the affair is most familiar. We give the story as it is told by himself.

In the year 1822, steamboats having left the "keels" and "broadhorns" entirely "out of sight", and Mike having, in consequence, fallen from his high estate—that of being "a little bit the almightiest man on the river, *any* how"—after a term of idleness, frolic and desperate rowdyism, along the different towns, he, at St. Louis, entered the service of the Mountain Fur Company, raised by our late fellow citizen Gen. W. H. Ashley, as a trapper and hunter; and in that capacity was he employed by Major Henry, in command of the Fort at the mouth of Yellow Stone river, when the occurrence took place of which we write.

Mike, with many generous qualities, was always a reckless daredevil; but, at this time, advancing in years and decayed in influence, above all become a victim of whisky, he was morose and desperate in the extreme. There was a government regulation which forbade the free use of alcohol at the trading posts on the Missouri river, and this was a continual source of quarrel between the men and the commandant, Major Henry—on the part of Fink, particularly. One of his freaks was to march with his rifle into the fort, and demand a supply of spirits. Argument was fruitless, force not to be thought of, and when, on being positively denied, Mike drew up his rifle and sent a ball through the cask, deliberately walked up and filled his can, while his particular "boys" followed his example, all that could be done was to look upon the matter as one of his "queer ways", and that was the end of it.

This state of things continued for some time; Mike's temper and actions growing more unbearable every day, until, finally, a "split" took place, not only between himself and the commandant, but many others in the fort, and the unruly boatman swore he would not live among them. Followed only by a youth named Carpenter, whom he had brought up, and for whom he felt a rude but strong attachment, he prepared a sort of cave in the river's bank, furnished it with a supply of whisky, and, with his companion, *turned in* to pass the winter, which was then closing upon them. In this place he buried himself, sometimes unseen for weeks, his *protégé* providing what else was *necessary* beyond the whisky. At length attempts were used, on the part of those in the fort, to withdraw Carpenter from Fink; foul insinuations were made as to the nature of their connection; the youth was twitted with being a mere slave, etc., all which (Fink heard of it in spite of his retirement) served to breed distrust between the two, and though they did not separate, much of their cordiality ceased.

The winter wore away in this sullen state of torpor; spring came with its reviving influences, and to celebrate the season, a supply of alcohol was procured, and a number of his acquaintances from the fort coming to "rouse out" Mike, a desperate "frolic", of course, ensued.

There were river yarns, and boatmen songs, and "nigger breakdowns", interspersed with wrestling-matches, jumping, laugh, and yell, the can circulating freely, until Mike became somewhat mollified.

"I tell you what it is, boys", he cried, "the fort's a skunk-hole, and I rather live with the *bars* than stay in it. Some on ye's bin trying to part me and my boy, that I love like my own cub—but no matter. Maybe he's *pis*oned against me; but, Carpenter (striking the youth heavily on the shoulder), I took you by the hand when it had forgotten the touch of a father's or a mother's—you know me to be a man, and you ain't a going to turn out a dog!"

Whether it was that the youth fancied something insulting in the manner of the appeal, or not, we can't say; but it was not responded to very warmly, and a reproach followed from Mike. However, they drank together, and the frolic went on, until Mike, filling his can walked off some forty yards, placed it upon his head, and called to Carpenter to take his rifle.

This wild feat of shooting cans off each other's head was a favourite one with Mike—himself and "boy" generally winding up a hard frolic with this savage, but deeply-meaning proof of continued confidence as for risk, their eagle eyes and iron nerves defied the might of whisky. After their recent alienation, a doubly generous impulse, without doubt, had induced Fink to propose and subject himself to the test.

Carpenter had been drinking wildly, and with a boisterous laugh snatched up his rifle. All present had seen the parties "shoot", and this desperate aim, instead of alarming, was merely made a matter of wild jest.

"Your grog is spilt, for ever, Mike!"

"Kill the old varmint, young 'un!"

"What'll his skin bring in St. Louis?" etc., etc.

Amid a loud laugh, Carpenter raised his piece—even the jesters remarked that he was unsteady—crack!—the can fell—a loud shout—but, instead of a smile of pleasure, a dark frown settled upon the face of Fink! He made no motion except to clutch his rifle as though he would have crushed it, and there he stood, gazing at the youth strangely! Various shades of passion crossed his features—surprise, rage, suspicion—but at length they composed themselves into a sad expression; the ball had grazed the top of his head, cutting the scalp, and the thought of treachery had set his heart on fire.

There was a loud call upon Mike to know what he was waiting for, in which Carpenter joined, pointing to the can upon his head and bidding him fire, if he knew how!

"Carpenter, my son", said the boatman, "I taught you to shoot differently from that *last* shot! You've *missed* once, but you won't again!"

He fired, and his ball, crashing through the forehead of the youth, laid him a corpse amid his, as suddenly hushed, companions!

Time wore on—many at the fort spoke darkly of the deed. Mike Fink had never been known to miss his aim—he had grown afraid of Carpenter—he had murdered him! While this feeling was gathering against him, the unhappy boatman lay in his cave, shunning both sympathy and sustenance. He spoke to none—when he did come forth, 'twas as a spectre, and only to haunt the grave of his "boy", or, if he did break silence, 'twas to burst into a paroxysm of rage against the enemies who had "turned his boy's heart from him!"

At the fort was a man by the name of Talbott, the gunsmith of the station: he was very loud and bitter in his denunciations of the "murderer", as he called Fink, which, finally, reaching the ears of the latter, filled him with the most violent passion, and he swore that he would take the life of his defamer. This threat was almost forgotten, when one day, Talbott, who was at work in his shop, saw Fink enter the fort, his first visit since the death of Carpenter. Fink approached; he was careworn, sick, and wasted; there was no anger in his bearing, but he carried his rifle, (had he ever gone without it?) and the gunsmith was not a coolly brave man; moreover, his life had been threatened.

"Fink", cried he, snatching up a pair of pistols from his bench, "don't approach me—if you do, you're a dead man!"

"Talbott", said the boatman, in a sad voice, "you needn't be afraid;

you've done me wrong—I'm come to talk to you about—Carpenter—my boy !"

He continued to advance, and the gunsmith again called to him:

"Fink ! I know you; if you come three steps nearer, I'll fire, by——!"

Mike carried his rifle across his arm, and made no hostile demonstration, except in gradually getting nearer—*if* hostile his aim was.

"Talbott, you've accused me of murdering—my boy—Carpenter—that I raised from a child—that I loved like a son—that I can't live without! I'm not mad with you *now*, but you must let me show you that I *couldn't* do it—that I'd rather died than done it—that you've wronged me——"

By this time he was within a few steps of the door, and Talbott's agitation became extreme. Both pistols were pointed at Fink's breast, in expectation of a spring from the latter.

"By the Almighty above us, Fink, I'll fire—I don't want to speak to you now—don't put your foot on that step—don't."

Fink did put his foot on the step, and the same moment fell heavily within it, receiving the contents of both barrels in his breast! His last and only words were,

"I didn't mean to kill my boy!"

Poor Mike! we are satisfied with our senior's conviction that you did *not* mean to kill him. Suspicion of treachery, doubtless, entered his mind, but cowardice and murder never dwelt there.

A few weeks after this event, Talbott himself perished in an attempt to cross the Missouri river in a skiff.

PSEUDO BAD MEN

CROCKETT'S BRAG[35]

I'm that same David Crockett, fresh from the backwoods, half-horse, half-alligator, a little touched with the snapping-turtle; can wade the Mississippi, leap the Ohio, ride upon a streak of lightning, and slip without a scratch down a honey locust; can whip my weight in wild cats—and if any gentleman pleases, for a ten dollar bill, he may throw in a panther—hug a bear too close for comfort, and eat any man opposed to Jackson.

FINK'S BRAG[36]

I'm a Salt River roarer! I'm a ring-tailed squealer! I'm a reg'lar screamer from the ol' Massassip' ! WHOOP! I'm the very infant that refused his milk before its eyes were open, and called out for a bottle of old Rye! I love the women an' I'm chockful o' fight! I'm half wild horse and half cock-eyed alligator and the rest o' me is crooked snags an' red-hot snappin' turkle. I can hit like fourth-proof lightnin' an' every lick I make in the woods lets in an acre o' sunshine. I can outrun, out-jump, out-shoot, out-brag, out-drink, an' out-fight, rough-an'-tumble, no holds barred, any man on both sides the river from Pittsburgh to New Orleans an' back ag'in to St. Louiee. Come on, you flatters, you bargers, you milk-white mechanics, an' see how tough I am to chew! I ain't had a fight for two days an' I'm spilein' for exercise. Cock-a-doodle-do!

THE BOASTING DRUNK IN DODGE[37]

When a group of cowboys reached Dodge City from Texas, they had not slept in a bed for months; nor had they shaved or enjoyed a hot bath or a haircut. Their clothing was dirty, often ragged. They had not seen a woman perhaps for half a year. The saloons of Dodge never shut their doors (on the opening day the proprietor threw away the keys). The red lights in back of the saloons beckoned. First the cowboys got rid of their extra hair, bought new outfits of clothing, and then they tanked up. They were ready to go. Some were quiet in their dissipation. Others talked—perhaps to keep up their courage—as does the "Boasting Drunk". Dodge was the toughest town known in 1883.

Raised on six-shooters till I get big enough to eat ground shotguns,
When I'm cool I warm the Gulf of Mexico and bathe therein,
When I'm hot there's an equinoxical breeze that fans me fevered
    brow,
The moans of widows and orphans is music to me melancholy soul.

Me the boy that chewed the wad the goat eat that butted the goat off
    the bridge
Born in the Rocky Mountains, suckled by a grizzly bear,
Ninety-nine rows of jaw teeth and not a single hair.

Thirty-two inches 'tween the eyes and they feed me with a shovel,
Mount the wild ass and leap from crag to crag,
And roar like laughter in a tomb,
Jump from precipice to precipice and back to pice again.

Snatched him bald-headed and spit on the place where the hair come
     off;
Take a leg off him and beat him over the head with the bloody end of
     it,
Slap his head up to a peak and then knock the peak off,
Take his eye out and eat it for a grape.

Gimme one hundred yards start and I'll run plumb to Honolulu
     without even wettin' my feet,
Shoulder five hundred bushel of shot and wade through solid rocks up
     to my shoulder blades.
Any damn man don't believe it . . .

I'll lick him on a sheep hide and never tromp on the tail,
Knock a belch out of him that'll whiz like a nail,
Knock a belch out of him longer'n a rail,
Sharp enough to stick a pig with.

OTHER COWBOY BOASTING CHANTS[38]

I'm wild and woolly
And full of fleas;
Ain't never been curried
Below the knees.
I'm a wild she wolf
From Bitter Creek,
And it's my time
To h-o-w-l, whoop-i-e-e-ee.

Wasp nests and yeller jackets,
The higher you pitch, the sweeter my navy tastes.
Born on the Guadalupe,
Ten miles below Duck Pond,
Raised in the Rocky Mountains.
Hang one spur where the collar works

And the other where the crupper works.

Four rows of jaw teeth
And holes punched for more;
Steel ribs and iron backbone,
And tail put on with screws,
Double dew-clawed,
Knock-kneed and bandy-shanked,
Nine rows of teeth,
And holes punched for more.

COWBOY TO PITCHING BRONCO[39]

To be declaimed, not sung

Born on the Col-o-ra-do,

Sired by an al-li-ga-tor.

I'm a bold, bad man from Crip-ple Creek, Col-o-ra-do.

When I git back there'll be a tor-na-do!

Git high-er, git high-er,

The high-er you git's too low for me.

Want to git my po-ny back and throw my nig-gers through the crack.

I'm tell-in' you, flam-doo-zle-dum!

Born on the Colorado,
Sired by an alligator,
I'm a bold, bad man
from Cripple Creek, Colorado.
When I get back
    there'll be a tornado!

A practice, once common in Texas, called for boasting talk from the probably scared cowboy as the wild horse, ridden for the first time, began his frantic pitching to dislodge his rider. Each line of the chant measures the period while the horse is in the air. The chant goes on indefinitely, other verses being added or the first being repeated, until the final exclamation when the horse suddenly stops to breathe.

The above rote and time values can but poorly, approximately, and arbitrarily reproduce the cowboy's chant; its freedom of motion, unusual disposition of accent, and rising and falling of the voice are never twice the same.

—J. A. L. and A. L.

Git higher, git higher,
The higher you git's
    too low for me.
Want to git my pony back
and throw my riggers through the crack.
I'm tellin' you, flamdoozledum!

COWBOY YELLS[40]

"Half horse, half alligator, with a little touch of a snapping turtle, clumb a streak of lightning, and slid down a locust tree a hundred feet high, with a wild cat under each arm and never got a scratch. Whoopee-yip-ho!"

"I come to this country riding a lion, whipping him over the head with a .45 and picking my teeth with a .38 and wearing a .45 on each hip, using a cactus for a pilfer, whee-ee-e! I'm a two-gun man and a very bad man and won't do to monkey with. Whee-ee-o, I'm a bad man! Whoopee!"

"Raised in the backwoods, suckled by a polar bear, nine rows of jaw teeth, a double coat of hair, steel ribs, wire intestines, and a barbed wire tail, and I don't give a clang where I drag it. Whoopee-whee-a-ha!"

KILLERS

STACKALEE[41]

Gypsy told Stack's mother,
Told her like a friend,
Your double-jinted baby
Won't come to no good end.

HE WAS BORN WITH A VEIL OVER HIS FACE

And the gypsy woman shore said a hatful, cause it all come out that very way. And how comes Stackalee's mother to call in the fawchin teller was cause he come kickin into this wide world double-jinted, and with a full set of teeth. But what scared her most was he had a veil over his face, and everybody knows that babies born with veils on their faces kin see ghosts and raise 41 kinds of hell.

SOLD HIS SOUL TO THE DEVIL

And so when Stackalee growed up he got to be an awful rascal and rounder wit lots of triflin women and he staid drunk all the time. One dark night as he come staggerin down the road the devil popped up real sudden, like a grinnin jumpin jack. He carried Stackalee into the grave yahd and bought his soul. And that's how come Stack could go round coin things no other livin man could do, such as:

Makin himself so little he could git into a bottle on a shelf and you could look at him settin there—yes suh! And fillin a small bottle full of water and settin it in a big glass jar where it would sink to the bottom till he began to talk to it and make it rare up and crap back just howsoever he wanted it to. And by walkin barefoot on hot slag out of a pig iron furnace and never gettin burned and eatin all the hot fire you could hand him without burning his stummick and changin hissels into a mountain or varmint. Some old timers lowed they knowed him personal and that his favourite night time shape was a prowlin wolf. That's how it come they used to sing that old song about him:

Stackalee didn't wear no shoe;
Couldn't tell his track from horse or mule.

THE MAGIC HAT

You see, it happened like this: Stack was crazy about Stetson hats; specially them great big five gallon hats with dimples in the crown. And he had a whole row of em hangin on pegs and you could look at em along the wall of his rickety shanty on Market Street in St. Louis, where he lived with his woman, Stack o' Dollars, that I'm goin to tell you about later.

He had a dimpled and lemon coloured yeller hat, and a black Sunday one with two white eyes to wear to funerals with his new brogans, and lots of other ones, all kinds and colours.

But his favourite was an oxblood magic hat that folks claim he made from the raw hide of a man-eatin panther that the devil had skinned alive. And like I told you, how come Stack to have it was because he had sold his soul to old Scratch. You see, Satan heard about Stack's weakness, so he met him that dark night and took him into the grave yahd where he coaxed him into tradin his soul, promisin him he could do all kinds of magic and devilish things long as he wore that oxblood Stetson and didn't let it get away from him. And that's the way the devil fixed it so when Stack did lose it he would lose his head, and kill a good citizen, and run right smack into his doom.

HIS GIRL FRIEND

Now Stackalee had a girl friend and her name was Stack o' Dollars. She blew into St. Louis off Cincinnati's old Bucktown on the Levee where she used to run gamblin games at a saloon there called the Silver Moon, long, long, ago; and she always bet her whole stack of silver dollars.

> She walked into the Silver Moon
> Stacked her dollars, mountain high;
> Says they call me Stack o' Dollars
> Cause my limit is the sky.

She had two diamond teeth with gold fillin and when she opened her mouth with a sunburst smile, didn't they glitter! Proud of them sparklers, too, cause they shined like flashlights. Wouldn't pawn em, even to get old Stackalee out on bond. And since they was fastened to her haid they was safe cause she was a fat mama with the meat shakin on her bones and she didn't need no man for a bouncer. She feared nothin and nobody. Her motto was: "Come clean, or come dirty and get cleaned." She could put a knot on a bully's haid so big that he wouldn't know whether the knot was on him or he was on the knot.

She had a full bosom, wore an eight-gallon Stetson, smoked cheroots, and was tougher than Big Mag of Chicago's old Cheyenne District. She ruled the levees with her big fist, and even old double-jinted Stackalee, big enough to go bear huntin with a willow switch, had to light out when they had them Saturday night fist fights, cause she would roll up her sleeves and begin smackin him around till their shanty shook like when Joshua fit the battle of Jericho and the walls come tumblin down. But she was good-hearted, though, when she was sober; and old long tall Stack who was a gambler with plenty of good-lookin browns claimed he like her cause she whupped him so good.

STACKALEE GOES WEST

Now like I told you, Stack was popular with the women folks cause he could whup the blues on a guitar, and beat out boogie woogie music piano bass and the like of that, but what they liked about him most was he was so stout he could squeeze the breath out of em almost. And his favorite one was a voodoo queen down in New Orleans French market.

Any way, the women got to braggin on him bein so stout that they reckoned he could even give old Jesse James a good tussle. So Stack, with his gun handle filled with notches, knowed there was a reward out for him for men he had washed away. He lowed he was lucky 'count of his magic Stetson to keep in hidin, but he figgered he had better light out while the goin was good. So he thought he would just look up old Jesse James and give him a trial.

> Stackalee went out West,
> Met Jesse James, and did his best.

Yes, sir, that fool even got mixed up with Jesse James. But Jesse was too much for him—turned old Stack every way but loose. And Lord knows what might not have happened to Stack if the devil hadn't come down the road in a cloud that got in Jesse's eyes. Leastwise, it might have saved the city of San Francisco and it might have kept old Stack from gettin into all them other amazin things I'm going to tell you about later. And leastwise the devil wouldn't have changed hisself to look like Billy Lyons and get poor innercent Billy killed.

STACKALEE CHANGES HIMSELF INTO A HORSE

Anyway, after the devil had saved him from Jesse James, Stack, knowin the law was hot after him, lit out again, headin west. And it was on the way over the mountains that he run into two cullud deputies on the lookout for him in order to collect the $5,000 reward offered for his arrest. So Stack set down to swap a few words with 'em between two big mountains[42] before they had caught on who he was. Then he told em he didn't aim to hurt em, he just wanted to know what their names was. When they told him, that sucker hauled out his forty-five and shot their initials in their hats, changed hisself into a horse, and galloped away with a lot of little baby red devils ridin on his back. And did them deputies run the other direction! They knowed it was Satan's work and they thought maybe Stack was the devil hisself.

> Tell you the truth!
> Think I'm lyin?
> Had to run sideways
> To keep from flyin.

So skeered they tore out through a graveyahd, knockin tombstones over like ten pins in a bowlin alley. And so Stack he held his sides laughin, and set down between them two big mountains and thought and thought, and finally made up his mind to go on to Frisco, where he was later called "the black Samson".

STACKALEE LAYS SAN FRANCISCO LOW

Now here comes the most amazin part of the story. Stack had been in Frisco about a month, getting leapin drunk, and just about runnin hisself crazy. So one morning in April, 1906, after he had had a rocky night and had a headache built for a hippopotamus he was out lookin for a sudden jerk and an eye opener to cool the burnin thirst in his throat. Into the first barroom he staggered. He didn't have penny one on him but he had a fist full of tricks and his magic oxblood Stetson and he was sure he could pull off some kind of conjuration to get his morning's juice.

But the bartender told him: "Listen here, cullud man! I ain't wettin even the bottom of a glass with gin till you shows me the colour of your money."

Stack got all big at the nose and woofed: "All right, boss, you either fixes me up with that gin, or I pulls down this bar!"

The bartender he just stood there grinnin and lookin sassy. So Stack he laid a-holt of the bar with both hands and sweat as big as marbles rolled down his face while he huffed and puffed and blew.

Stack knowed that he didn't know his own strength, so when he give one last powerful jerk and down come the ceiling and whole building he said: "Mah goodness, I sure didn't aim to get so rough! Damned if I ain't gone and made a mess for sure!"

It happened so fast it almost skeered Stack hisself.

IT WAS THE WATAH PIPES

Outside was more wrecks than you could shake a stick at; buildings tumblin down all over town.

"Lordy! Sure didn't know mah own strength!" Stack said to a crowd of people in the street. They tried to tell him about an earthquake, but Stack didn't pay them no mind.

"It was the watah pipes", he said. "They was all fastened together all over town. When I give that last powerful jerk, I must have pulled out a faucet in the saloon and snatched down the whole town."

Then he lit out of there for St. Louis, where he run right smack into his doom.

HOW OLD SCRATCH TRICKED STACKALEE

You see, Stack was gettin into so much devilment that he even worried the devil, and old Satan was gettin tired waitin for Stack's soul, so he figgered out a way to trick him.

Old Scratch knowed that if Stack was killed fightin another bad man like Jesse James maybe God wouldn't let his soul go to hell. So this is the way the devil fixed it. He schemed it out to make hisself look like Billy Lyons, an innercent family man. So when Stack killed an honest family man, the Lord would be mad at him and let Satan have him.

One cold, frosty Friday night when Stack was havin one of his lucky streaks in a big coon can game down at Jack o' Diamond's place in St. Louis, he was so busy pickin up his money that he hung his oxblood Stetson on the back of his cheer. That's when Old Scratch, keepin his eye peeled, changed hisself to look like Billy Lyons. Then he snatched the magic hat and tore out toward the White Elephant

Barrel House where he knowed Billy was. When the devil got to the door he disappeared. Stack came runnin up and seen Billy standin by the door, lookin as innercent as you please, smokin, and watchin the can can dancers.

And there is where Stack shot him through and through. Billy pleaded for his life, on account of his wife and babies. But Stack, mad as blue blazes because he had lost the magic hat that kept the law from ketchin him, blazed away and blasted poor Billy down.

So the wagon come loaded with pistols and a big gatlin gun and hauled Stack off to jail. But the police didn't kill him like the devil, setting outside the window in the shape of a black cat, hoped they would.

Instead, they slapped Stack into jail where the judge sent him to Jefferson Pen for 75 years. He's already served 34 of em and got 41 more to serve there yet. The devil is waitin for him to die so he can snatch his soul just like the song tells you:

It was in the year of eighteen hundred and sixty-one
In St. Louis on Market Street where Stackalee was born.
Everybody's talkin 'bout Stackalee.*

It was on one cold and frosty night
When Stackalee and Billy Lyons had one awful fight,
All about an old Stetson hat.

Stackalee got his gun. Boy, he got it fast!
He shot poor Billy through and through; the bullet broke a lookin'
glass.
Oh, oh, Lord, Lord, Lord.

Stackalee shot Billy once; his body fell to the floor.
He cried out, "Oh, please, Stack, please don't shoot me no more."

The White Elephant Barrel House was wrecked that night;
Gutters full of beer and whisky; it was an awful sight.

Jewelry and rings of the purest solid gold
Scattered over the dance and gamblin hall.

The can can dancers they rushed for the door
When Billy cried, "Oh, please, Stack, don't shoot me no more."

"Have mercy", Billy groaned. "Oh, please spare my life;
I've got two little babies and an innocent wife."

Stack says, "God bless your children, damn your wife!
You stole my magic Stetson; I'm gonna steal your life."

"But", says Billy, "I always treated you like a man.
'Tain't nothin to that old Stetson but the greasy band."

He shot poor Billy once, he shot him twice,
And the third time Billy pleaded, "Please go tell my wife."

Yes, Stackalee, the gambler, everybody knowed his name;
Made his livin hollerin high, low, jack and the game.

Meantime the sergeant strapped on his big forty-five,
Says, "Now we'll bring in this bad man, dead or alive."

*Refrain:

> Everybody's talkin 'bout Stackalee. (Use this one most.)
> That bad man Stackalee.
> Oh tough man Stackalee.
> Oh oh, Lord, Lord, Lord.
> All about an old Stetson hat.

For variation the following were often used:

> Oh, treacherous Stackalee.
> Oh, oh, what a shame.
> Oh, foolish Stackalee.
> Oh, scared Stackalee.
> Oh, scheming Stackalee.

Oh worried Stackalee.
Oh oh. what a lie.—O. L. S.

And brass-buttoned policemen all dressed in blue
Came down the sidewalk marchin two by two.

Sent for the wagon and it hurried and come
Loaded with pistols and a big gatling gun.

At midnight on that stormy night there came an awful wail—
Billy Lyons and a graveyard ghost outside the city jail.
"Jailer, jailer," says Stack, "I can't sleep.
For around my bedside poor Billy Lyons still creeps.

"He comes in shape of a lion with a blue steel in his hand,
For he knows I'll stand and fight if he comes in shape of man."

Stackalee went to sleep that night by the city clock bell,
Dreaming the devil had come all the way from hell.

Red devil was sayin, "You better hunt your hole;
I've hurried here from hell just to get your soul."

Stackalee told him, "Yes, maybe you're right,
But I'll give even you one hell of a fight."

When they got into the scuffle, I heard the devil shout,
"Come and get this bad man before he puts my fire out."

The next time I seed the devil he was scramblin up the wall,
Yellin, "Come an get this bad man fore he mops up with us all."[43]

Then here come Stack's woman runnin, says, "Daddy, I love you true;
See what beer, whisky, and smokin hop has brought you to.

"But before I'll let you lay in there, I'll put my life in pawn."
She hurried and got Stackalee out on a five thousand dollar bond.

Stackalee said, "Ain't but one thing that grieves my mind.
When they take me away, babe, I leave you behind."

But the woman he really loved was a voodoo queen
From Creole French market, way down in New Orleans.

He laid down at home that night, took a good night's rest,
Arrived in court at nine o'clock to hear the coroner's inquest.

Crowds jammed the sidewalk, far as you could see,
Tryin to get a good look at tough Stackalee.

Over the cold, dead body Stackalee he did bend,
Then he turned and faced those twelve jury men.

The judge says, "Stackalee, I would spare your life.
But I know you're a bad man; I can see it in your red eyes."

The jury heard the witnesses, and they didn't say no more;
They crowded into the jury room, and the messenger closed the door.
The jury came to agreement, the clerk he wrote it down,
And everybody was whisperin, "He's penitentiary bound."

When the jury walked out, Stackalee didn't budge.
They wrapped the verdict and passed it to the judge.

Judge looked over his glasses, says, "Mr. Bad Man Stackalee,
The jury finds you guilty of murder in the first degree."

Now the trial's come to an end, how the folks gave cheers;
Bad Stackalee was sent down to Jefferson pen for seventy-five years.

Now late at night you can hear him in his cell,
Arguin with the devil to keep from goin to hell.

And the other convicts whisper, "Whatcha know about that?
Gonna burn in hell forever over an old Stetson hat!"
Everybody's talkin 'bout Stackalee.

FREE LANCES

ROY BEAN, "LAW WEST OF THE PECOS"

Necktie Justice[44]

"Hear ye! Hear ye! This honourable court's now in session; and if any galoot wants a snort afore we start, let him step up to the bar and name his pizen. Oscar, serve the gentlemen." Thus did Judge Bean open court to try one Carlos Robles, an opening typical of his original procedure.

"Carlos Robles", he said solemnly after witnesses and hangers-on had downed their liquor, "it is the findin' of this court that you are charged with a grave offense against the peace and dignity of the law West of the Pecos and the State of Texas, to wit: cattle-rustlin'. Guilty or not guilty?"

Not being able to speak or comprehend English, Robles merely grunted.

"Court accepts yore plea of guilt. The jury will now deliberate; and if it brings a verdict short of hangin' it'll be declared in contempt. Gentlemen, is yore verdict ready?"

The twelve nondescript citizens cleared their throats in unison. "It is, your honour," several spoke.

"Thank you, gentlemen. Stand up, Carlos Robles, and receive yore sentence. You got anything to say why judgment shouldn't be passed on you in this court?"

Of course Carlos had not, in view of the fact that he had only the vaguest idea of what was transpiring.

"Carlos Robles," Judge Roy continued, his voice almost quaking with the solemnity of the occasion, "you been tried by twelve true and good men, not men of yore peers, but as high above you as heaven is of hell; and they've said you're guilty of rustlin' cattle.

"Time will pass and seasons will come and go; Spring with its wavin' green grass and heaps of sweet-smellin' flowers on every hill and in every dale. Then will come sultry Summer, with her shimmerin' heat-waves on the baked horizon; and Fall, with her yeller harvest-moon and the hills growin' brown and golden under a sinkin' sun; and finally Winter, with its bitin', whinin' wind, and all the land will be mantled with snow. But you won't be here to see any of 'em, Carlos Robles; not by a dam' sight, because it's the order of this court that you be took to the nearest tree and hanged by the neck till you're dead, dead, dead, you olive-coloured son-of-a-billy-goat!"[45]

The Law West of the Pecos could be cruel in administering his brand of justice; but he was cruel only when he deemed the accused and the crime fully warranting such cruelty. He more frequently tempered justice with his own peculiar brand of mercy, especially if there was any means by which he could profit by that mercy.

One afternoon several ranchmen brought in a twenty-year old boy accused of horse-stealing. They demanded that he be tried and dealt with according to the enormity of the crime.

Judge Bean duly opened court. He appointed six men as jurors, the actual number meaning nothing to him and depending entirely upon men available. He would not appoint just any citizens to jury duty. They must be good customers of the liquid bar at the other end of the shack during intermissions, or their services as jurors no longer were desirable or acceptable. Every transaction must be made to return the utmost in profit, and non-drinking jurors were strictly dead timber.

"Hear ye! This honourable court is again in session. Anyone wishin' a snort, have it now. This here prisoner is charged with the grave offense of stealin' a horse and Oscar, where are the witnesses?" the Law West of the Pecos opened. He appreciated his own sense of humour in varying his court openings to relieve the monotony; but seldom varied to the extent of omitting the invitation to participate in a snort at the other bar.

"We caught him in the act of stealin' the animal", the ranchman testified. "He admitted his intentions."

"That right, young feller ? You was stealin' the cayuse?"

The young prisoner dropped his head, unruly red hair tumbling down over his high forehead. "Yes, your honour", he mumbled.

"Gentlemen of the jury", His Honor instructed, "the accused pleads guilty to horse theft. You know as well as I do the penalty. I'm ready for yore verdict." And it was promptly forthcoming.

Gravely the judge passed sentence. "If there's any last word, or anything, I'll give you a few minutes", he told the pale Easterner, thus extending an infrequent favour.

"I would like to write a note—to my mother back in Pennsylvania", the doomed prisoner mumbled with obvious emotion. "Thank you."

"Oscar, fetch the prisoner a piece of wrappin' paper and a pencil. I think we got a pencil back there behind that row of bottles." Bean gently handed the convicted thief these writing facilities, got up and tendered him the beer barrel and rickety table from which sentence had just been passed. Then he took a position directly behind the boy so that he could watch over his shoulder at what he wrote.

The victim wrote at length in apology for the grief and trouble he had caused his mother and earnestly sought her forgiveness. "In small part perhaps I can repay you for the money I have cost you in keeping me out of trouble. Enclosed is $400, which I've saved. I want you——
—"

Judge Bean started, cleared his throat, cut in at this point. "By gobs!" he exclaimed, "gentlemen, I got a feelin' there's been a miscarriage of justice, in this case. I hereby declare it reopened. Face the bar, young man."

The prisoner removed himself from the beer keg and stood erect in front of the judicial bench, befuddled at this sudden turn.

"After all, that wasn't much of a cayuse the lad tried to steal; and he didn't actually steal him. So I rule it's a finable case. I hereby fine the accused three hundred dollars and get to hell outer this country afore I change my mind!"

The boy gladly enough paid three hundred of his four hundred dollars and assured the court that the next setting sun would find his brow well beyond El Rio Pecos.

Practically every cattleman and law-abiding citizen of the Bean bailiwick had an indefinite appointment as deputy constable to the Law West of the Pecos. Thus any citizen who apprehended any person in the act of committing a crime or suspected any of crime had authority to bring him on forthwith for trial. Bean consistently encouraged such co-operation, for the more business they brought before the court, the greater the financial returns for the whole establishment. Naturally it was understood that such arresting constables did not in any manner participate in the fee accruing from such cases created by them. This doubtless was the only justice court in the State of Texas wherein only one official received all fees collected by the office.

Under authority as deputy constable, Reb Wise, Pecos rancher, brought in a cattle rustler on a hot August afternoon when business at the refreshment counter was exceptionally brisk. It was all both Roy and Oscar could do to handle the trade. Consequently Bean looked up with sour expression when Deputy Constable Wise approached the bar and informed the judge that a prisoner was awaiting attention at the bar of justice.

"What's he charged with, Reb ?" Roy asked, opening another foaming bottle of Triple-X beer.

"Cattle-rustlin', yuhr honour," Reb replied.

"Whose cattle ?"

"Mine".

"You positive he's guilty, Reb ?"

"Positive? Say, Judge, I caught him with a runnin' iron on one of my finest calves!" the rancher replied with emphasis.

For the first time Roy glanced up at the scowling prisoner. He noticed blood dripping from his left ear. "Who plugged his ear ?" he inquired.

"I did, yuhr honour, when he wouldn't stop."

"You ought'n shot at his head, Reb. You could 'a' killed him; and that would 'a' been bad, because he wouldn't have been saved for the punishment he deserves. You real shore he's guilty?"

"Didn't I say, Judge, I caught him runnin' a brand on my stuff?" "All right then", the judge said. "What'll it be for you, feller?" to a newcomer at the bar, " . . . All right then. The court finds the accused guilty as charged; and as there ain't no worse punishment I know of right handy, I hereby sentence him to be hung. Reb, I'm busy's hell here. You and some of yore compadres take him out and tie his neck to some handy limb—some place where his cronies'll be positive to see him; and that's my rulin'. Court's adjourned and what'll it be for you down there, Slim ?"

BUFFALO BILL'S "WILD WEST"[46]

BUFFALO BILL'S "WILD WEST"
PRAIRIE EXHIBITION, AND ROCKY MOUNTAIN SHOW,
A DRAMATIC-EQUESTRIAN EXPOSITION
OF
LIFE ON THE PLAINS,
WITH ACCOMPANYING MONOLOGUE AND
INCIDENTAL MUSIC
THE WHOLE INVENTED AND ARRANGED BY
W. F. CODY
W. F. CODY AND N. SALSBURY, PROPRIETORS AND
MANAGERS WHO HEREBY CLAIM AS THEIR
SPECIAL PROPERTY THE VARIOUS
EFFECTS INTRODUCED IN
THE PUBLIC PER-
FORMANCES
OF
BUFFALO BILL'S "WILD WEST"

———

MONOLOGUE

LADIES AND GENTLEMEN:

I desire to call your attention to an important fact. From time to time it will be my pleasure to announce to you the different features of the programme as they occur. In order that I may do so intelligently, I respectfully request your silence and attention while I am speaking. Our agents will pass among you- with the biographical history of the life of Hon. William F. Cody ("Buffalo Bill") and other celebrities who will appear before you this afternoon. The Management desires to vouch for the truth and accuracy of all the statements contained in this book, and respectfully submitted to your attention, as helping you to understand and appreciate our entertainment. Before the entertainment begins, however, I wish to impress upon your minds that what you are about to witness is not a performance in the common sense of that term, but an exhibition of skill, on the part of men who have acquired that quality while gaining a livelihood. Many unthinking people suppose that the different features of our exhibition are the result of what is technically called "rehearsals". Such, however, is not the fact, and anyone who witnesses our performance the second time will observe that men and animals alike are the creatures of circumstances depending for their success upon their own skill, daring and sagacity. In the East, the few who excel are known to all. In the far West, the names we offer to you this afternoon are the synonyms of skill, courage and individual excellence. At the conclusion of the next overture our performance will commence with a grand processional parade of the "Wild West".

> Overture, grand processional parade of cowboys, Mexicans, and Indians, with incidental music.

I will introduce the different groups and individual celebrities as they pass before you in review.

> Enter a group of Pawnee Indians. Music. Enter Chief. Music. Enter a group of Mexican vaqueros. Music. Enter a group of Wichita Indians. Music. Enter Chief. Music. Enter a group of American Cowboys. Music. Enter King of Cowboys. Music. Enter Cowboy Sheriff of the Platte. Music. Enter a group of Sioux Indians. Music. Enter Chief. Music.

I next have the honour of introducing to your attention a man whose record as a servant of the government, whose skill and daring as a frontiersman, whose place in history as the chief of scouts of the United States Army, under such generals as Sherman, Sheridan,

Hancock, Terry, Miles, Hazen, Royal, Merrit, Crook, Carr and others, and whose name as one of the avengers of the lamented Custer, and whose adherence throughout an eventful life to his chosen principle of "true to friend and foe", have made him well and popularly known throughout the world. You all know to whom I allude—the Honourable William F. Cody, "Buffalo Bill".

> Enter Cody. Bugle Call. Cody speaks.

Ladies and Gentlemen: Allow me to introduce the equestrian portion of the Wild West Exhibition.

> Turns to review.

Wild West, are you ready! Go !

> Exeunt omnes.

First on our programme, a————mile race, between a cowboy, a Mexican, and an Indian, starting at————. You will please notice that these horses carry the heaviest trapping, and that neither of the riders weigh less than 145 pounds.

————

Next on our programme, the Pony Express. The Pony Express was established long before the Union Pacific railroad was built across the continent, or even before the telegraph poles were set, and when Abraham Lincoln was elected President of the United States, it was important that the election returns from California should be brought across the mountains as quickly as possible. Mr. William Russell, the great government freighter, who at the time was in Washington, first proposed the Pony Express. He was told that it would take too long— 17 or 18 days. The result was a wager of $200,000 that the time could be made in less than ten days, and it was, the actual time being nine days, seventeen hours, leaving seven hours to spare, and winning the wager of two hundred thousand dollars. Mr. Billy Johnson will illustrate the mode of riding the Pony Express, mounting, dismounting and changing the mail to fresh horses.

> Music. Enter express rider, changing horses
> in front of the grandstand, and exit.

————

Next on our programme, a one hundred yard race between an Indian on foot, and an Indian on an Indian pony, starting at a given point, running fifty yards, and returning to the starting point—virtually a race of a hundred yards.

> Race as described above. Music.

Next on our programme, an historical representation between Buffalo Bill and Yellow Hand, fought during the Sitting Bull war, on the 17th of July, 1876, at War Bonnet Creek, Dakota, shortly after the massacre of Custer. This fight was witnessed by General Carr's command and the Sioux army, and resulted in the death of Yellow Hand, and the first scalp taken in revenge of Custer's fate.

> Duel as described above. Cody, supported by cowboys, etc., Yellow Hands by Indians. Music.

Mr. Seth Clover is introduced and proceeds to give an exhibition of his skill shooting with a Winchester repeating rifle at composition balls thrown from the hand. He is followed by Master Johnny Baker, of North Platte, Neb., known as the Cowboy Kid, 16 years of age, and the holder of the boy's champion badge for rifle and revolver shooting. Then comes:

Miss Annie Oakley, the celebrated wing and rifle shot. Miss Oakley gives an exhibition of her skill, shooting with a shot gun at Ligowsky patent clay pigeons, holding the gun in various positions.

> Shoots pigeons sprung from trap.

Shooting, double, from two traps sprung at the same time.

> Shoots as above.

Picking the gun from the ground after the trap is sprung.

> Shoots as above.

Shooting double in the same manner.

> Shoots as above.

Shooting three composition balls, thrown in the air in rapid succession, the first with the rifle held upside down upon the head, the second and the third with the shot gun.

> Shoots as above. Exit.

Next on our programme, the cowboy's fun, or the riding of bucking ponies and mules, by Mr.———, Mr.———, and Mr.———. There is an impression in the minds of many people that these horses are taught or trained to buck, or that they are compelled to do so by having foreign substances placed under their saddles. This, however, is not the fact. Bucking, the same as balking or running away, is a natural trait of the animal, confirmed by habit.

Riders announced, and mount in succession.
Watch Mr. Taylor pick up his hat.

Taylor rides past at full speed, leans out of his saddle and picks hat from the ground.

Watch Mr. Taylor pick up his handkerchief.

Taylor rides past at full speed, leans out of his saddle, and picks up handkerchief.

Hon. William F. Cody, champion all round shot of the world.

Enter Mr. Cody.

Mr. Cody will give an exhibition of his skill, shooting with shot gun, rifle and revolver at clay pigeons and composition balls, shooting first with a shot gun at clay pigeons, pulling the traps himself. (Shoots.)

Mr. Cody now gives an exhibition of shooting, holding the gun in all manner of positions, hitting clay pigeons and composition balls thrown into the air in rapid succession, ending by hitting two balls thrown into the air at the same time as he rides past at full speed.

Next on our programme, the Deadwood stage coach, formerly the property of Gilmore, Salsbury, & Co., and plying between Deadwood and Cheyenne. This coach has an immortal place in American history, having been baptized many times by fire and blood. The gentleman holding the reins, is Mr. John Higby, an old stage driver, and formerly the companion of Hank Monk, of whom you have all probably read.

Seated beside him is Mr. John Hancock, known in the West, as the Wizard Hunter the Platte Valley. Broncho Bill will act as out rider, a position he has occupied in earnest many times with credit. Upon the roof of the coach is seated Mr. Con Croner, the Cowboy Sheriff of the Platte, to whose intrepid administration of that office for several consecutive terms, covering a period of six years, Lincoln County, Neb., and its vicinity are indebted for the peace and quiet that now reigns. Mr. Croner's efforts having driven out the cattle thief and hoodlum element who formerly infested that section of the country, noticeably, the notorious Middleton gang. The coach will start upon its journey, be attacked from an ambush by a band of fierce and warlike Indians, who in their turn will be repulsed by a party of scouts and cowboys, under the command of Buffalo Bill. Will two or three ladies and gentlemen volunteer to ride as passengers.

After passengers are seated in coach.

It is customary to deliver parting instructions to the driver before he starts on his perilous journey, something in the following fashion: Mr. Higby, I have intrusted you with valuable lives and property. Should you meet with Indians, or other dangers, *en route*, put on the whip, and if possible, save the lives of your passengers. If you are all ready, go!

> Coach is driven down track, meets Indians, turns, followed by Indians. Battle back to stand. Cody and cowboys come to rescue. Battle past stand. Cody, coach and cowboys return to stand. Exit [*sic*] omnes.

———

Next on our programme, a one-quarter mile race between Sioux boys and on barebacked Indian ponies from the Honourable William F. Cody's ranche [*sic*] at North Platte, Neb., starting at———

> Race as above. Music.

———

I would next call your attention to an exciting race between Mexican thoroughbreds. These animals are bred with great care, and at considerable expense, their original cost being sixteen [hundred?] dollars per doz. All up! No jockeying! Go!

> Race as above. Music. "We Won't Come Home till Morning."

———

A portion of the Pawnee and Wichita tribes will illustrate their native sports and pastimes, giving first the war dance.

> War dance by Indians.

Next the grass dance.

> Grass dance by Indians.

Next, the scalp dance, in which the women of the tribe are allowed to participate.

> Scalp dance by Indians and squaws.

———

Keep your eyes on the burros!

> Burros return. Music. "Home Again!" or "We Never Speak as, Etc."

I have the pleasure of introducing "Mustang Jack", or as the Indians call him "Pet-se-ka-we-cha-cha", the great high jumper. Jack is the champion jumper among the cowboys of the West, and stands ready to jump with anybody in any manner or style for any amount of money. He will give you an exhibition of his skill, jumping over various animals, beginning with the small burro.

Jack jumps over burro.

Jumping twenty-four feet in two jumps, and clearing the burro in the second jump.

Jack jumps as above.

Jumping the Indian pony, Cha-sha-sha-na-po-geo, a feat which gave him his name of "Mustang Jack".

Jumps as above.

Next, jumping the tall white horse, "Doe. Powell", sixteen and a half hands high. The best recorded standing high jump is one of five feet and three inches made by Mr. Johnson, of England. In order to clear this horse, Jack is obliged to make a jump of nearly six feet, thus beating the record daily.

Jumps as above.

Next on our programme the roping, tying and riding of wild Texan steers by cowboys and Mexicans.

Performance as above.

Next on our programme the riding of a wild elf, by Master Voter Hall, a Feejee Indian from Africa.

Saddled elk ridden as above.

Next on our programme the attack upon a settler's cabin by a band of marauding Indians, and their repulse, by a party of scouts and cowboys, under the command of Buffalo Bill. After our entertainment you are invited to visit the Wild West camp. We thank you for your polite attention, and bid you all good afternoon.

Battle as above. Review before the grand stand.

Adieux and dismissal by Mr. Cody.

Finis

MIRACLE MEN

PAUL BUNYAN

Pipeline Days And Paul Bunyan[47]

It was evening. The sun hung like a sandy ball above the rim of dull mesquite that surrounded the pipeline camp. For three weeks the line had been extending through a lifeless country of mesquite and dust. For three weeks the men had been broiling under the August sun with not even a wind to make the heat less deadening. Now they were sprawled on the grass in easy after-supper positions. Forming a half circle about the cook-shack, they rested uncomfortably and "razzed" the lone fat man who had not yet finished eating. "Fat" was always last—last to start work, last to stop eating, and certainly last to stop talking. "Fat" ate on, unconcerned with their tired humour. Gradually the men drifted into small groups and lay droning a preparation for the evening's talk.

"Git a scoop. That's what you need, Fat."

"Move the chuck wagon and he'll starve to death. He's too damn lazy to follow it."

"Hey, Fat, did you ever get all you wanted to eat ?"

"They ought to grow square beans so he could get more of them on his knife."

"Talk about eating. Tell you what I saw once," said one who aspired to Fat's position as the camp's chief liar. "I saw a man eat a whole ham once—well, not exactly a whole ham, we had eaten a meal off it—not exactly we, my brother-in-law Jim and his family. The man came to the house one morning and wanted something to eat. Sis was busy and didn't have no time to be fooling with him; so she just set the table and put this ham on it and then went on about her housework or whatever she was doing. Well, when she come back the man was gone and so was the ham—all except the bone and it had been gnawed so dry that even the dog wouldn't touch it. That's the God's truth. Jim swears it's the truth."

The men howled derisively, and Fat, who had been listening half attentively, arose from his stool and sauntered into the centre of the group.

"Did you say something about eating?" he said. "Well, I had a funny thing happen to me the other day in Wichita Falls. I goes into one of them restaurants down by the railroad tracks to eat. When I come in I saw a couple of tough hombres setting at the counter and they looks me over kind of amused like. But I just goes on back and sets down a couple of seats from them. After a while the waiter comes out from behind and goes over to where they are setting and asks them what they want.

"They was sure tough-looking birds, and one of them speaks up and says, 'Gimme a T-bone steak a inch and a quarter thick. Just scorch it.' And he looks over at me kinda mean like.

"But I didn't pay him no mind but just set there. So the other one pulls his hat 'way down over his eye, and says, 'Gimme a hind quarter. Raw.' And then they both looks over at me.

"Well, when the waiter come over to where I am setting, I says to him, 'Gimme a sharp butcher knife and then just cripple a steer and run him through here. I'll cut off what I want!'"

"Speaking of steers," the Contender put in, "did you ever hear about the cattle line that Paul Bunyan laid from his ranch to Chicago?

"Well, Paul he got tired of paying such high freight to get his stock to market; so he just laid a pipeline all the way to the stockyards in. Chicago and pumped them through it. Everything went all right except that the pipe was so big that the calves and half-grown yearlin's would get lost in the threads and starve to death before they could get to the outside. And one time the line sprung a leak and Paul lost thirty-five carloads of cattle before he could get it corked [caulked]. But he sure did do a good job of corking when he did get to it."

"How the devil did he cork a hole that big?" asked Fat after a minute or two of silence.

"Why with B. S., you big windbag, same as that that you have been spouting off."

Fat sat for a moment trying to think of a way to get "back at" the Contender. Then he started off on a new trail.

"You know so much about Paul Bunyan", he said. "Did you ever hear about that big steer that he had? He called her Babe and she just measured forty-two pick-handles lengths and the width of a size seven derby hat between the eyes. And strong! Why that steer could pull anything!

"1 remember one time when we was drilling a well down Breckenridge way. Wasn't much of a hole, just sixteen inches. Well, we drilled and drilled and didn't ever strike nothing—except dust, and a God's plenty at that; so finally Paul he said we might as well give it up as a dry hole and let it go at that.

"But Paul was mad! He swore around for two or three days and smashed the derrick into kindling wood and was about to quit drilling when he saw a advertisement in the paper by some bird out on the plains that wanted to buy some post-holes. Ten thousand post-holes it was he wanted. Ten thousand holes three feet long.

"Well, Paul he hitched a chain around this duster hole and hooked up Babe and pulled fifteen thousand feet of it out of the ground. He got mad again because the hold broke off and left over half of it in the ground. But directly he said that they wasn't no use of a post-hole being sixteen inches across; so he just quartered the hole and then sawed it up into the right lengths.

"You know out on the plains they have a awful hard time digging post-holes, or any other kind of holes for that matter. The soil out there is only about a foot deep till you strike solid rock and they can't dig through this rock a-tall.

"Why, them guys used to come down into East Texas and buy all the old wells and dug-outs that they could get a-hold of and cut them up to use for post-holes. I used to know a feller down there that could dig and stack on cars more old wells than any man I ever saw before. He could stack twenty-nine of them on cars in a day and take two hours off for dinner.

"They finally moved so many wells down there that they ruined the water; so they was a ordinance passed against it. But that didn't stop it. They bootlegged them out to the plains. I knew one guy that got rich bootlegging them. He had a patented jack that would lift a well or a dug-out out of the ground.

"It don't do much good to build fences out on the plains, though. That there wind out there is awful. Soon as a man gets a good fence built, along comes the wind and blows it away, posts, post-holes, and all. Why, that wind even blows wells away and a guy told me that he seen it turn prairie dog holes wrong side out it blew so hard. But I never did believe it. Them guys are awful liars. One of them told me he had a horse throw him so high one time that he had to catch a-holt of a cloud to keep from falling and killing himself. It's cold out there too—"

"I'll say it is", a pipeliner broke in. "Like that guy that was up in

Canada somewheres when it was fifty degrees below. He come up to another guy and said, 'God, man, wouldn't you hate to be in Amarillo today?'"

"Ja ever hear about them wells out in Colorado where the oil freezes when it comes out of the ground?" asked the Contender. "They can't pipe it away; so they just let it spout out on the ground and then shovel it into wagons with scoops and haul it off."

"That's like some of them wells that Paul Bunyan drilled in over at Smackover", said someone. "They was gushers and blew in so strong that they had to put roofs over the derricks to keep the oil from spouting a hole in the sky."

"I worked for Paul out in Arizona on the biggest well that I ever worked on," resumed the Contender. "It was a seventy-five inch hole, it was, and we had to make a derrick so tall that it had to be hinged in two places and folded up before the sun and stars could pass. Took a man fourteen days to climb to the top of it. It did. And Paul had to hire thirty derrick men so we could have a man on top all of the time. They was always fourteen men going up and fourteen men coming down, a man on top and a man off tower,[48] all the time. And they was dog houses built a day's climbing apart for the men to sleep in while they was going up and down.

"Why, when that well blew in, it took three days for the oil to reach the top of the derrick, and it rained oil for a week after we had got it capped.

"It was some well. We drilled it with one of Paul's patented rotary rigs. Never could have drilled so deep—it was sixty thousand feet— if Paul hadn't used flexible drill pipe. We just wound the drill stem up on the draw-works. Take a devil of a long time to come out of the hole if we had had to stack it.

"Well, when we was down sixty thousand and three feet, the well blew in. And when we had come out of the hole we seen that we had forgot to case it. Well, Paul he called out both towers and made up the casing on the ground—about ten miles of seventy-five-inch casing— and then he just picked it up and dropped it down into place."

"I worked for Paul on one of them deep wells once", said Fat. "It was out in Arkansas. Jimmy Blue was running the rig and we was drilling with standard tools. We got down thirty thousand feet and struck a rock formation that a bit wouldn't touch. And we was using a pretty good sized bit too, drilling a fifty-inch hole.

"Well, we worked on this formation for three weeks without doing any good and then we called up Paul. Paul he came out there and took charge of the rig himself and worked for three more weeks, day and night, without doing anything except ruin a lot of bits. And finally he got so mad that he jumped down on the derrick floor and pulled up the bit with his hands. Then he threw it down into the hole as hard as he could throw it. Well, we busted the rock that time. The bit just kept on going and when the line run out it pulled derrick, rig, and all into the hole after it.

"We got a gusher that time. But when Paul seen that the rig had pulled Jimmy into the hole with it he was just about to plug off the hole and abandon it. But in a few days we got a telegram from Jimmy in China saying that he had a 100,000 barrel gusher and was spudding in on another location."

"Did any of you guys work for Paul on that big line he laid?" asked the Contender. "Well, I worked for him on that 101-inch aluminum line that he laid from Pennsylvania to California. We laid it to pipe buttermilk out to his camp out there. Paul liked buttermilk so well himself that he had a twenty-four-inch petcock running wide open all the time to catch enough for him to drink."

"Yeh", said Fat, "I know all about that. I helped Paul drill the buttermilk well that furnished that line. We drilled down thirty-two thousand feet and then struck a formation of cornbread. We drilled for five hundred feet through the cornbread and then for twelve hundred feet through solid turnip green—except that every few feet would be a layer of fried sow-belly. That's where the old song started: 'Cornbread, Buttermilk, and Good Old Turnip Greens'."

"Fat, did you ever see Paul's wife?" asked. a young boll-weevil who had started to work only a few days before. "She had a wooden leg and she was so homely that we used to scrape enough ugly off her face every day to mud off a well. The hardest six months' work I ever put in was painting that wooden leg of hers."

"When Paul worked on the highlines he had a wooden leg himself," added an ax-linesman. "It was ninety feet long and the men used to wear one out every three days climbing up to bum him for cigarettes."

"Paul discovered perpetual motion—of the jaw—when he got Fat to work for him", said the Contender.

"Huh", said Fat, "only perpetual motion Paul ever discovered was one time down in India. We was drilling a ninety-inch hole with standard tools. And when we got down twenty-seven thousand feet we struck the root of a rubber tree and the bit never did stop bouncing. Had to abandon the hole."

"I worked—" the Contender began.

"Yeh, and on another one of them wells we was drilling a eighty-inch offset. Had them big derricks all around us. And our camp was setting so far back in them derricks that we had to pipe the daylight in. We drilled down nearly fifty thousand feet and struck a flowing vein of alum water and the hole, rig, and everything drew up until we had to abandon it."

"Paul sure had drilling down to a fine point," said the Contender. "Why I worked for him on one hole where we was using rubber tools. We would just start the tools bouncing and then go to sleep until it was time to change the bit. And the men was so fast that the driller would just bounce the bit out of the hole and they would change it before it could fall back."

"Paul's camps wasn't nothing like this dump," said Fat. "I worked for him on a ninety-inch line once and we had so many men in the camp that it took fifteen adding machines running day and night to keep track of their time. Paul invented the first ditching machine while we was laying this line through Arkansas. He bought a drove of them razorback hogs and trained them to root in a straight line."

"You telling about that cattle line of Paul's a while back reminds me of the trees that used to grow down on the Brazos," said the "Old Man". "One time I was working through that country with a herd of cattle and come up to the river where I couldn't ford it. While I was setting on my horse looking at the water I heard a big crash up the river and when I went up to see what it was, it was a tree had fallen across the river. It was one of them big holler trees. So I just drove my herd across the river through the holler of it. But when I got to the other side and counted the herd I seen that they was nearly three hundred steers missing and I went back to look for them. They had wandered off into the limbs and got lost."

"That reminds me of the sand storms that they used to have down in East Texas," said the Contender. "One time they was a nigger riding along one of them sandy roads on a jackass and he stopped to go down to the creek and get a drink and tied his mule to a sapling by the side of the road. While he was gone it come one of them sand storms and when he come back he seen his ass hanging by the tie-rope about seventy feet up in a tree. The sand had blown away from under him and just left him hanging there."

"Say", said Fat, "did any of you guys ever see Paul Bunyan in a poker game. The cards he used were so big that it took a man five hours to walk around one of them. Paul used to play a lot of poker that time we was digging Lake Michigan to mix concrete in when he was building the Rocky Mountains. A little while after that we dug Lake Superior for a slush pit for one of them big wells we was drilling. Any of you birds want to play some poker ?"

This, from Fat, was the signal for retiring. The sun was long past set and mosquitoes were buzzing in the darkened mesquite. Silently the men stalked off toward their tents—all except two or three who followed Fat to his tent for a session at poker.

CASEY JONES

I. Casey Jones, Engineer

I[49]

On the last day of April [1928] occurs the 28th anniversary of the death of Casey Jones—probably the most famous of a long line of locomotive engineer heroes who have died at their post of duty, one hand on the whistle and the other on the airbrake lever. Casey Jones' fame rests on a series of nondescript verses, which can hardly be called poetry. They were written by Wallace Saunders, a Negro engine wiper who had been a close friend of the famous engineer, and who sang them to a jigging melody all his own.

Mrs. Casey Jones still lives in Jackson, Tenn. She has two sons and a daughter. Charles Jones, her younger son, lives in Jackson; Lloyd, the older son, is with a Memphis auto agency; and her daughter, Mrs. George McKenzie, lives at Tuscaloosa, Ala.

Although 41 years have flitted by since Miss Janie Brady said "I do" and became the bride of John Luther (Casey) Jones, Mrs. Jones still keeps green the memory of that glad occasion. Today, still on the sunny side of 60, the plump blonde woman with her cheery smile tells graphically the story of how her husband was killed, and how Wallace Saunders composed the original air and words that later swept the country for years as the epic ballad of the railroader.

"My husband's real name was John Luther Jones," she told her latest interviewer. "He was a lovable lad—6 feet 41/2 inches in height, dark-haired and grey-eyed. Always he was in good humour and his Irish heart was as big as his body. All the railroaders were fond of Casey, and his wiper, Wallace Saunders, just worshipped the ground he walked on."

The interviewer asked Mrs. Jones how her husband got the nickname Casey.

"Oh, I supposed everyone knew that!" she replied. "He got it from the town of Cayce, Kentucky, near which he was born. The name of the town is locally pronounced in two syllables, exactly like 'Casey'."

Mrs. Jones remembers Wallace Saunders very well, although she has not seen him for years.

"Wallace's admiration for Casey was little short of idolatry", she said. "He used to brag mightily about Mr. Jones even when Casey was only a freight engineer."

Casey Jones was known far and wide among railroad men for his peculiar skill with a locomotive whistle.

"You see", said Mrs. Jones, "he established a sort of trade mark for himself by his inimitable method of blowing a whistle. It was a kind of long-drawn-out note that he created, beginning softly, then rising, then dying away almost to a whisper. People living along the Illinois Central right of way between Jackson and Water Valley would turn over in their beds late at night and say: 'There goes Casey Jones', as he roared by."

After he had put in several years as freight and passenger engineer between Jackson and Water Valley, Casey was transferred early in 1900 to the Memphis-Canton (Miss.) run as throttle-puller of the Illinois Central's crack "Cannonball" train.

Casey and his fireman, Sim Webb, rolled into Memphis from Canton about 10 o'clock Sunday night, April 29. They went to the checking-in office and were preparing to go to their homes when Casey heard some body call out: "Joe Lewis has just been taken with cramps and can't take his train out tonight."

"I'll double back and pull Lewis' old No. 638", Casey volunteered.

At 11 o'clock that rainy Sunday night Casey and Sim Webb clambered aboard the big engine and eased her out of the station and through the South Memphis yards.

"All the switchmen knew by the engine's moans
That the man at the throttle was Casey Jones."

Four o'clock of the 30th of April. The little town of Vaughn, Miss. A long, winding curve just above the town, and a long sidetrack beginning about where the curve ended.

"There's a freight train on the siding," Casey yelled across to Sim Webb.

Knowing the siding there was a long one, and having passed many other freights on it, Casey figured he would do the same this night.

But there were two separate sections of a very long train on the side-track this night. And the rear one was a little too long to get all its length off the main line onto the siding. The freight train crews figured on "sawing by"; that is as soon as the passenger train passed the front part of the first train, it would move forward and the rear freight would move up, thus clearing the main track.

But Casey's speed—about fifty miles an hour—was more than the freight crews bargained for.

But when old 638 was within a hundred feet of the end of the siding the horrified eyes of Casey Jones and Sim Webb beheld through the gloom the looming shape of several boxcars in motion, swinging across from the main line to the side-track. In a flash both knew there was no earthly way of preventing a smashup.

"Jump, Sim, and save yourself!" was Casey's last order to his fireman. As for himself, Casey threw his engine in reverse and applied the air-brakes—all any engineer could do, and rode roaring 638 into a holocaust of crashing wood that splintered like match boxes. Sim Webb jumped, fell into some bushes and was not injured.

When they took Casey's body from the wreckage (old 638 had plowed through the cars and caboose and turned over on her side a short distance beyond) they found one hand on the whistle cord, the other on the air-brake lever.

"I remember", Sim Webb told Casey's widow, "that as I jumped Casey held down the whistle in a long, piercing scream. I think he must have had in mind to warn the freight conductor in the caboose so he could jump."

Probably no individual, excepting a member of Casey's family, was more affected by the sad news than Wallace Saunders.

A few days later he was going about singing a song to a melody all his own. The air had a lilt that caught the fancy of every one who heard it. But Wallace, honest old soul, had no idea of doing more than singing it as a sort of tribute to his white friend's memory.

But one day a song writer passed through Jackson and heard the song and details of Casey's tragic death. He went off and changed the words, but retained the lilting refrain and the name of Casey Jones. That was about 1902.

II[50]

There are many railroad men still living who knew and worked with Jones. The affection he aroused among all his acquaintances seems to have been an outstanding characteristic. He was 6 feet 4 1/2 inches tall, dark-haired and grey-eyed. An excellent photograph of him, which has just come to light from the Memphis Press-Scimitar, is reproduced as a frontispiece in this issue.

His old friend R. E. Edrington, a fellow engineer on the Illinois Central writes: "The reputation which Casey enjoyed was richly earned by numerous feats of resourcefulness, skill and downright daring. He could perform feats with his famous 638 that no other engineer could equal with locomotives of the same class, or even with the same engine. Firing for him was a back-breaking and hair-raising job, but his mulatto fireman, Sim Webb, was equal to every demand, and held Casey in almost idolatrous regard, following him from one run to another through his entire career."

A. J. ("Fatty") Thomas, who often ran as conductor on trains pulled by Casey and the 638, writes: "I had often heard the song about Casey Jones, but on account of the phrases in it about the Southern Pacific and the Santa Fe, rounder, Frisco, and 'another papa on the Salt Lake Line', I never figured that the song was intended for my Illinois Central Casey. For he was not a rounder but a car roller, and in my estimation the prince of them all. We had a number of fast men, and since then I have had hundreds of good engineers pull me on different western roads. But I never met the equal of Casey Jones in rustling to get over the road.

"The 'whistle's moan' in the song is right. Casey could just about play a tune on the whistle. He could make the cold chills run up your back with it, and grin all the time. Everybody along the line knew Casey Jones' whistle.

"I never saw him with his mouth closed—he always had a smile or a broad grin. The faster he could get his engine to roll, the happier he was. He would lean out of the cab window to watch his drivers, and when he got her going so fast that the side rods looked solid, he would look at you and grin all over, happy as a boy with his first pair of red boots. Yet he had a reputation as a safe engineer. With all his fast running I never knew of him piling them up, of any but a few derailments and never a rear-ender. He was either lucky, or else his judgment was as nearly perfect as human judgment can be."

Ed Pacey, another conductor who knew Casey Jones, writes: "In the early days of railroading there was a real glamour to the rails. Into this setting, Casey, engineer of the Cannonball Express, fitted perfectly. He was a giant and came of a great railroad family. His nickname was derived from his native village, Cayce, Tenn., pronounced 'Casey'.

"Jones was famous for two things: he was a teetotaler in days when abstinence was rare, and he was the most daring of all engineers in the days when schedules were simply 'get her there and make the time, or come to the office and get your time'."

Mr. Pacey lodges a protest against the popular song's line to the effect that Casey Jones' widow informed her orphan children that "you've got another papa on the Salt Lake line". Mr. Pacey chafes at the implied disrespect toward Mrs. Jones in that stanza. "There never was any other papa on the Salt Lake or any other line", he says. "Instead, the widow devoted her life to the hard struggle to maintain herself and educate her three children."

The common story of the wreck in which Jones was killed is that Casey had to meet two freight trains which were too long to clear the siding. For some reason, never clearly explained, Casey failed to stop and he piled them up when he struck the caboose and cars protruding out on the main line.

According to R. E. Edrington, however, the situation was even more complicated. "It was characteristic," he says, "of the desperate chances which were part of the period of railroading, when the engines were rapidly growing in size and the sidings, safety equipment and other appliances not keeping pace with them.

"There were not two but three trains. Two of these were north bound and had pulled into the siding. The third was racing, on short time, ahead of the Cannonball. As this train scurried down to the siding it dropped off a flagman but, after it had pulled down, this flagman rode in with the idea that the mother train would protest against the Cannonball.

"But the other train crew thought that he was still out and did not flag. So Casey came down, as fast as he could turn a wheel, with the result of one of the worst wrecks in the history of the road. . . . "

II. THE "CASEY JONES" SONG[47]

Four years ago the Erie Railroad Magazine gathered up the real story of Casey's life and death, as told by his widow, who still lives in Jackson, Tenn. The article was reprinted in railroad magazines and newspapers all over the world and has brought a continuous stream of letters ever since. Scores of correspondents have sent in various versions of the Casey Jones song, not only in English but in French, German and even in the language of the native labourers on the South African railways.

Every branch of railroading has at least one version of the song. The hobo jungles and the I.W.W. song books contribute others. Still others come from the campfires and boarding cars of construction gangs, and several weird and often unprintable variations were composed by dough-boys in France during the world war.

Come all you round-ers for I want you to hear The sto — ry told of a brave en — gi — neer ; Ca — sey Jones was the round-er's name, On a heav-y six—eight wheel-er he rode to fame.

Come all you rounders for I want you to hear
The story of a brave engineer;
Casey Jones was the rounder's name
On a heavy six-eight wheeler he rode to fame.

Caller called Jones about half-past four,
Jones kissed his wife at the station door,
Climbed into the cab with the orders in his hand,
Says, "This is my trip to the promised land."

Through South Memphis yards on the fly,
He heard the fireman say, "You've got a white-eye",
All the switchmen knew by the engine's moans,
That the man at the throttle was Casey Jones.

It had been raining for more than a week,
The railroad track was like the bed of a creek.
They rated him down to a thirty mile gait,
Threw the south-bound mail about eight hours late.

Fireman says, "Casey, you're runnin' too fast,
You run the block signal the last station you passed."
Jones says, "Yes, I think we can make it though,
For she steams much better than ever I know."

Jones says, "Fireman, don't you fret,
Keep knockin' at the firedoor, don't give up yet;
I'm gain' to run her till she leaves the rail
Or make it on time with the south-bound mail."

Around the curve and a-down the dump
Two locomotives were a-bound to bump.
Fireman hollered, "Jones, it's just ahead,
We might jump and make it but we'll all be dead."

'Twas around this curve he saw a passenger train;
Something happened in Casey's brain;
Fireman jumped off, but Casey stayed on,
He's a good engineer but he's dead and gone—

Poor Casey was always all right,
He stuck to his post both day and night;
They loved to hear the whistle of old Number Three
As he came into Memphis on the old K.C.

Headaches and heartaches and all kinds of pain
Are not apart from a railroad train;
Tales that are earnest, noble and gran'
Belong to the life of a railroad man.

THE SAGA OF JOE MAGARAC: STEELMAN[52]

While working in the steel mills along the Monongahela valley of
Pennsylvania, I often heard one of the many Slavs who worked in the
mills call one of his fellow-workers "*magarac*". Knowing that literally
translated the word *magarac* meant jackass, but knowing also, from
the tone of voice and the manner in which it was used, that it was
seldom used derisively, I questioned my Hunkie leverman as to its
meaning as understood by the Hunkie workers. He gave me a vivid
explanation. He said:

"Magarac! Dat is mans who is joost lak jackass donkey. Dat is
mans what joost lak eatit and workit, dats all."

Pointing a finger toward another of his race, a huge Hunkie by the
name of Mike, who was walking from the open hearth, he yelled:

"Hay! Magarac!"

At once, Mike's thumbs went to his ears, and with palms outspread
his hands waved back and forth while he brayed lustily in the best
imitation of a donkey that he could give.

"See", my leverman said, "dere is *magarac*. Dat is Joe Magarac for
sure."

Then they both laughed and spoke in their mother tongue, which I
did not understand.

It was evident enough there was some definite reason for the use of
the word, and obviously that reason was, to their way of thinking, very
humorous.

By working for a considerable number of years with a Hunkie on
my either side, by sitting many evenings in their homes, and, since
turning my thoughts to writing, by spending a good deal of my time
with them, I have been fortunate enough to hear considerably more
about Mr. Joe Magarac.

I find that Joe Magarac is a man living only in the imagination of
the Hunkie steel-mill worker. He is to the Hunkie what Paul Bunyan is
to the woodsman and Old Stormalong is to the men of the sea. With
his active imagination and his childlike delight in tales of greatness,

the Hunkie has created stories with Joe Magarac as the hero that may in the future become folklore of our country. Conceived in the minds of Hunkie steel-mill workers, he belongs to the mills as do the furnaces and the rolling-mills. Although the stories of Joe Magarac are sagas, they have no tangible connection so far as I have been able to find, with the folklore of any of the countries which sent the Hunkie to these United States. It seems that the Hunkie, with the same adaptability that has made him into the best worker within our shores, has created a character and has woven about him a legend which admirably fits the environment in which he, the Hunkie, has been placed. Basically, the stories of Joe Magarac are as much a part of the American scene as steel itself.

I did not hear the story which I have set down here as accurately as I have been able, at one time. Some of it I heard in the mill; some of it while sitting on the hill above the mill on pleasant Sunday afternoons; the most of it while sitting in Agnes's kitchen with Hunkie friends at my side and well-filled tin cups of prune-jack before us.

The saga of Joe Magarac is more typical of the Hunkie than any tale or incident or description I might write. It shows his sense of humour, his ambitions, his love of his work, and, in general, shows what I know the Hunkie to be: a good-natured, peace- and home-loving worker.

One time long time ago mebbe one, two hundred years, dere was living by Hunkietown, Steve Mestrovich. Steve he workit by open-hearth and he have daughter Mary. Oh, my, Mary was pretty girls: she have big, blue eyes, hairs yellow lak hot steel, hands so little lak lady, and big strong teethe. She was prettier as Hunkie girls from any place and all fellows what workit for mill comit around and say for Steve:

"Mebbe pretty soon now be plenty good tiny Mary gone catch hoosband."

Den Steve he always laughit and he say:

"Gone on home little mans. Mary no gone marry some one lak you who not catch much steam dis time. Mary gone marry only strongest mans what ever lived, ya betcha."

Mary say nothing. She joost sit around and hope dat pretty soon mans who be all right comit, for she was seventeen year old already and she no lak dat business of wait around. Steve get sick too from wait around and nobody comit. Steve say:

"What the hells kind business is cat. I catch best young girls as anybody: she pretty lak hell, she wanit mans, she wanit be good for mans and joost stay home and raise kids and no say nothing, cats all. And, by Gods, I catch two hundred dollar I give myself for wedding present and I no find mans for her. By Gods, I tink gone have party dis time and ask everybody comit and den we see who is best mans for Mary, ya damn right.

"So, Old Womans, next Sunday we gone have party. You makit plenty prune-jack and I gone to Pittsburgh and gone have two barrel beer sent out on truck."

Well, Steve's old lady she makit plenty prune-jack and all week she workit makit cake and Mary she help and she was glad lak anyting because Sunday gone be party and she tink mebbe she gone catch mans lak 'nother Hunkie girls who have mans who workit in mills. Steve tell everybody what gone be on Sunday and all dem young fellers start lift 'em up dolly bars in eighteen-inch mill, its big hunk steel what is heavy lak anyting, so dat dey strong for Sunday. Some people say dey betcha dat Pete Pussick be strongest man for Pete lift 'em up dolly bars same lak it was toothpicks; other peoples tink maybe Eli Stanoski be better mans and he gone catch fine girls lak Mary for *frau*. But everybody wish it gone be him who is best mans and everybody dey lookit at Mary and dey feel strong lak anyting.

So pretty soon next Sunday be dere and Hunkie mans comit from Monesson, comit from Homestead, comit from Duquesne, comit from every place along Monongahela River and dey gone show everybody how strong dey be dis time. Steve have everything fix 'em up: in big field down by river bank he put two barrel beer what comit from brewery, he put table what he makit where Old Lady gone put prune-jack and cakes, and he have three dolly bar what he get from mill.

One dose dolly bar its joost lime one what weigh three hundred fifty pound, 'nother dolly bars weigh five hundred pounds, and big ones she weigh more as 'nother two put together. On side of field Steve has fixed 'em up benches where womans can sit and nurse baby and see what gone happen and right by dere is platform lak have on Fourth July with red paper and flags and everyting. Mary she sit on platform where all young fellow can see good and see what dey gone get after dey lift 'em up dolly bars. Mary was dressed up lak dere was big funeral: she have on dress what mudder had made from wedding dress and it was pretty I tell you. It was all red and green, silk too, and on front was big bunch lace what *Groszmutter* in old country makit.

On finger was ring with nice red stone what Steve buy from company store and on head was nice scarf. Oh, sure, when Mary go on platform everybody say she was prettier as Queen.

Steve was happy mans dat day, I tell you. He was dressed up with sleeves down and tie on his neck and he walkit 'round lak he was Boss everyting and he yell lak dis:

"Hi, yah, Pete. You tink you feelit all right to-day? By Gods, better you no be sick and have lots steam. It take plenty strong mans to lift 'em up dolly bars."

And den he say:

"Hi, yah, Eli. What matter you? Mebbe better you take 'nother drink prune-jack. You lookit little bit white in face lak you was 'fraid Pete nor Sam gone be stronger as you. By Gods, was I young mans same as you I lift 'em up whole damn three bars one time to catch fine girls lak Mary."

Den he laughit and pull mustache and walkit up and down same like nigger mans on pay day.

After everybody visit 'round little bit and everybody havit one, two, three drink all around, Steve got on platform and makit speech. He say:

"For coople year now everybody what is young mans and feelit pretty good dey comit for me and dey say: 'Pretty soon Mary gone lookit for mans. Me! I catch good job for blast furnace. Me, I be best mans what workit for mills, best mans what ever poke 'em out tap hole. Sure! I be strong lak anyting. Whats matter Mary not be *frau* for me?'"

Den Steve he stopit speech and he stickit out tongue lak he was not feelit so good for stomach and he say:

"By Gods, I hear so many mans talk lak dat dat it makit me sick. So I fix 'em up plan and now we gone see who be good mans for marry Mary, daughter of Steve Mestrovich, me, by Gods, what is best mans who was cinderman for open hearth any place. First, everybody gone lift 'em up small dolly bars. If anybody no lift 'em up dat little one den he joost go and play smith little kids dats all. Next, everybody gone to lift 'em up second dolly bars. Anybody no lift 'em up dat second dolly bars den dey go and sit with womans and stay out road of strong mans while strong mans gone show him something. Den, everybody gone lift 'em up last dolly bars. By Gods, dis dolly bar she be from bloomer mill and she is so heavy dis time dat I no can lift him myself. Somebody gone lift 'em up dat hunk steel dens by Jezus, dats mans what gone marry Mary, ya damn right, ya betcha."

So all young fellows pull off shirt and get ready to lift dolly bars. First mans was Pete. Pete he walkit over by dolly bars and he lookit 'round for make sure everybody see and den he reach down and lift 'em up easy lak anyting. Everybody holler:

"Dats big mans, you Pete! Dats good fellow!"

Pete he no say nothing. He joost walkit away and he laughit lak he feel sure he gone be plenty strong dis time. Den Eli gone over by dolly bars and he lift 'em up easier as Pete and everybody yell some more. Two fellows what comit from Homestead try and lift 'em up and day no can move dolly bars from ground. Den everybody laughit and say:

"Ho! Ho! Ho! What kinds mans you have dat place, Homestead? At home I got boy joost two year old and I tink mebbe I better send him over by your mill to help you out little bit. Better you go and play with kids little mans so dat you no monkey 'round with big mans and get hurt dis time."

Well, after dat, dey lift 'em up second dolly bars and what you tink? Only three mans catch enough steam to do dat. Dat was Pete, dat was Eli, and dat was 'nother mans from Johnstown. Dis fellow from Johnstown was plenty big mans all right and he catch plenty steam to lift 'em up dolly bars. He do dat easy as anyting. Den all his friends dey yell hoorah for him and dey face at Pete and Eli same lak dey was sure dat dis fellow was gone be strongest mans and take Mary Mestrovich back to Johnstown with him. People from dis place no lak dat business. Dey lak much better Pete nor Eli gone be strongest and den Mary Mestrovich stay dis place which have better mills as Johnstown anytime. Dat mills at Johnstown is joost little place what when do best she can no makit more as one, two hundred tons steel a day. So peoples get mad at dese peoples from Johnstown and dey gone makit bet dat Pete nor Eli gone be stronger as dis fellow. Pete say dat is good business and nobody gone worry nothing, he gone lift 'em up big dolly bars joost same lak he lift 'em up little ones. Den Pete he gone over take big, big drink prune-jack and he spit on hands. Den he reach down and grab dat big dolly bars. His arm crack lak paper bag, his eyes stick out from head lak apple, sweat run down face same lak he was workit in front furnace in July. By Jezus, dat dolly bars no movit one inch from ground. Den Eli try it and he was no good dis time. People from dis place groan lak somebody kick in stomach when dey see dat. Dey tink for sure now dey gone lose Mary Mestrovich, dey gone lose money, and den dey must listen when peoples from Johnstown say:

"Ho! Ho! Ho! Over by dis place mans is joost same lak old womans who talkit all time and no doit nothing. Comit over by Johnstown where mans so strong dat doy tear down mill and fix 'em up again every day joost for fun."

Den dis fellow from Johnstown takit two big, big drinks prune-jack, he twist mustache so she look lak King, and he wave hand for everybody. Den he fixit his feets so he no be shaky and bend down and grabit dat dolly bars. He give big pull, and den another big pull and he grunt all time lak pig at dinner time. He pullit so damn hard on dat dolly bars dat his hand come loose and he fallit down on ground.

Peoples from dis place feelit much better: she is not so easy as dis fellow tink. Johnstown fellow mad lak *frau* when hoosband get drunk and spend all money on pay days. He joomp up from ground and he cuss lak hell and he grabit dolly bars again. No good dis time neither.

"Ho! Ho! Ho!"

A laugh lak dat comit from somebody in crowd. Everybody lookit 'round to see who laughit lak dat; mans from Johnstown straighten back and he say:

"Who laughit for me? By Jezus Christ a Mighty, if dat fellow who laughit tink he be so strong mans whets matter he no comit here and pick tem up dolly bars? Den after he do dat I gone broke his neck."

Den out from crowd walkit biggest mans whatever I see: he have back bigger as door, hands bigger as Pete nor Eli together, neck lak big bulls, and arm bigger as somebodys round waist. I betcha my life he was more as seven feets tall. Oh, he was prettiest mans whatever anybody ever see. Everybody lookit everybody and everybody say:

"Who is dat fellow anyhow?"

And everybody shake heads no dey never see before.

Dat fellow he walkit over to dolly bars and he was laughit so hard he have to holdit his belly so dat he can stand on feet. Dat fellow from Johnstown he takit pull at trousers, he spit on hands and he gone take slug at dat fellow. But dat mans he grabit fellow from Johnstown with one hands and with 'nother he pick 'em up dolly bars. Den he hold 'em out and shake until mans from Johnstown yell he was so 'fraid.

By Gods, everybody was white lak sheet. Dey never see before mans what was so strong lak dat. But dat fellow put dat fellow from Johnstown down so easy as little baby by mudder and he say:

"Nobody be 'fraid nothing. I no wanit hurt nobody, no wanit makit trooble. Joost havit little bit fun, dats all."

Steve Mestrovich walkit over and he say:

"What kind mans you are? Which place you comit from?"

And dat fellow answer:

"My name is Joe Magarac, what you tink of dat, eh?"

Everybody laughit for dat for *magarac* in Hunkie mean jackass donkey. Dey know dis fellow is fine fellow all right when he say his name is Joe Jackass. Den dis fellow say:

"Sure! Magarac, Joe. Dats me. All I do is etit and workit same lak jackass donkey. Me, I be only steelmans in whole world, ya damn right. Lookit for me; I show you something."

He pull 'em off shirt and everybody lookit. By Gods, he no tell lie. He was steelmans all right: all over he was steel same lak is from open hearth, steel hands, steel body, steel everything. Everybody say:

"What the hells you tink of dat?"

Joe Magarac say:

"Dats all right, dats good business for me. Me, I was born inside ore mountains many year ago. To-day I comit down from mountain in ore train and was over in ore pile by blast furnace."

Den he laughit and twist dolly bars in two with hands.

Steve Mestrovich smile lak somebody givit him cold beer on hot day and he takit Mary by hand and leadit her over to Joe Magarac: dis time he gone catch best hoosband for Mary dat was in whole country. Joe Magarac takit long look at Mary and he say:

"Oh, boy, I never see such pretty girls as dat. You makit fine *frau* for anybodies. But dat is no business for me. What you tink, I catch time for sit around house with womans? No, by Gods, not me. I joost catch time for workit dats all. Be better all right if Mary have hoosband and I tink I see her get little bit dizzy in head when she lookit for Pete. Dats good, for after me dis Pete is best mans in country."

Joe Magarac close one eyes for Steve and Steve close one eyes for Joe Magarac and Mary was happy lak anyting for she lak dat Pete all right better as anybody. Fellow from Johnstown get black in face and he stomp 'round mad lak anyting, but he 'fraid say anyting for fellow who was made out of steel and who comit from ore mountain. So he go away.

Everyting was fixed 'em up all right den: Priest comit with alter boy and Pete and Mary kneel down and pretty soon dey was hoosband

and *frau*. First one to dancit with bride was Joe Magarac. Den everybody get drunk, have big time and was happy as anyting.

So next day, Joe Magarac gone down to Mrs. Horkey, who catch
boarding-house by mill gate and he say:

"Howdy do, Mrs. Horkey. My but you lookit nice dis morning and
from kitchen comit smell of best breakfast whatever I smell anyplace.
Dis place lookit all right for me. I gone work in mill dis place and I
wanit good place for eat. I no wanit room, joost five big meals a day,
dats all, for I workit night turn and day turn all at same time."

So Joe Magarac livit by Horkey's boarding-house and he catch job
in mill. He workit on Noomber Seven furnace by open hearth and he
workit all night and all day without finish and he no get tired nothing.
He standit before Noomber Seven and he throw 'em in limestone, ore,
scrap and everyting and den he go sit in furnace door with fires from
furnace licking 'round chin. When steel melt 'em up, Joe Magarac put
in hands and stir steel 'round while she was cookit and when furnace
was ready for tap 'em out he crawl into furnace and scoop up big
handfuls steel and dump 'em into ingot mould. After dat he run down
to lower end and grab dat steel in hands and squeeze 'em out from
fingers and he makit rails. Eight rails one time, four by each hand, he
makit by Gods. Pretty soon he makit more steel as all other furnace
together. Nobody ever see before such business lak dat, so boss of
open hearth have big sign made and he put sign on mill fence where
everybody see and dis sign say:

The Home of Joe Magarac

Joe Magarac was workit every day and every night at mill and same
lak before he was makit rails with hands. Pretty soon dat pile of rails
in yard get bigger and bigger for Joe Magarac is workit so hard and
after coople months yard was full, everyplace was rails. When Joe
Magarac see dat he joost laughit and workit harder as ever. So one day
roller-boss he comit up from down by finishing mills and he say to Joe
Magarac who was workit by his furnace in open hearth. Roller-boss he
say:

"Well, Joe Magarac, I guess we gone shut mill down early dis
week. Dis time we catch plenty rails everyplace and we no catch many
orders. So by Gods, we gone shut mill down Thursday night and we
no start 'em up again until Monday morning. Mebbe you gone put
slow heat in furnace: you tell stockman give you fifty-ton stock. You

put 'em in stock and give furnace slow fire so dat she keepit warm and be ready for start 'em up on Monday."

Joe Magarac he act lak he gone say something and den he no say nothing and roller-boss tink everyting gone be all right dis time and he gone away.

When next Monday comit mans gone back to work for open hearth. Den dey see dat Joe Magarac is not workit on furnace dat morning. Everyplace dey lookit and dey no see Joe anyplace. 'Nother mans was workit on Noomber Seven and pretty soon when Noomber Seven was ready for tap 'em out melter-boss gone down to platform to see what kind steel dat slow heat makit. He was standit by ingot mould and pretty soon he hear voice what say:

"How she lookit dis time?"

Melter-boss lookit 'round and he no see nobody and den dat voice say again:

"It's me, Joe Magarac. I'm inside ladle."

Melter-boss turn around and he lookit inside ladle and he see Joe. Joe was sitting inside ladle with hot steel boiling up around neck. Melter-boss was scared lak anyting and he say:

"What the hells you do in dere, Joe Magarac? Better you gone crawl out dat ladle right 'way or I tink maybe for sure dat she gone melt you up."

Joe Magarac close one eyes for melter-boss and he say:

"Dats fine. Dats good business, dats joost what I wanit. By Gods, I be sick dis time of mill what shut down on Thursday and no start 'em up again until Monday. What the fuels I gone do all time mill is shut down anyway? I hear big boss say dat he was gone makit two, three good heats steel so dat he gone have best steel what we can makit for buildit new mill dis place. Dey gone tear down dis old mills and makit new ones what is gone be best mills in whole Monongahela valley, what gone be best mills in whole world. Den by Gods, I get plan: I gone joomp in furnace when steel is melted down and dey gone melt 'em up me, who was made from steel, to makit steel to makit dat mills. Now Mr. Boss you gone listen for me and I gone tell you someting. You gone take dis ladle steel what has me inside and you gone pour 'em out in ingot mould and den you gone roll 'em out and makit beam, channel, and maybe one, two piece angle and you gone take dat steel and makit new mills. You do lak I say for you and you gone see you gone have best mills for anyplace. Good-bye."

Den Joe Magarac sit back down in ladle and hold his chin down in boiling steel until he was all melted up. Pretty soon dey pour him out in ingot mould.

Well, after dey roll 'em out dat heat and dey cut 'em up dey see dat dis time dey have best steel what was ever made. Oh, my, dat steel was smooth and straight and it no have seam or pipe nothing. Den melter-boss he gone 'round for everybody and he say:

"Now we gone have best mills for sure. You see dat steel? By Gods, nobody ever see steel lak dat before and cats joost because Joe Magarac he makit dat steel. Sure, he's inside and now we gone takit dat beam and dat channel and we gone build finest mills what ever was."

Dey do lak melter-boss say and dat is why all young boys want to go for mill, and dat is why when somebody call Hunkie *magarac* he only laughit and feel proud as anyting, and dat is why we catch the best mill for anyplace, ya damn right!

Lastly, the hero of modern folklore in its most contemporary form— the comic strip—Popeye. This latest addition to the gallery of mythological miracle men has all the traditional characteristics of the giant, except that his strength is in his forearm and his spinach, and his stature remains that of a runt.

SONGS OF POPEYE[53]

I yam Popeye,
The Sailor Man.
  I yam what I yam
  'Cause tha's what I yam.
I yam Popeye,
The Sailor Man.

I yam Popeye,
The Sailor Man.
  Never more will I roam,
  Fer I feels right to home.
I yam Popeye,
The Sailor Man.

I yam Popeye,
The Sailor Man.
   I yam jus' a little feller,
   But I hasn't any yeller.
I yam Popeye,
The Sailor Man.

I yam Popeye,
The Sailor Man.
   I have said I hates strife,
   But I'll fight fer me life.
I yam Popeye,
The Sailor Man.

I yam Popeye,
The Sailor Man.
   When spinach I eat
   I kin not be beat.
I yam Popeye,
The Sailor Man.

I yam Popeye,
The Sailor Man.
   I fights fer the right
   With all of me might.
I yam Popeye,
The Sailor Man.

I yam Popeye,
The Sailor Man.
   I yam strong as the breezes
   Wich blows down big treeses.
I yam Popeye,
The Sailor Man.

I yam Popeye,
The Sailor Man.
   I yam strong at the finitch
   'Cause I eats me spinitch.
I yam Popeye,
The Sailor Man.

PATRON SAINTS

JOHNNY APPLESEED: A PIONEER HERO[54]

The "far West" is rapidly becoming only a traditional designation: railroads have destroyed the romance of frontier life, or have surrounded it with so many appliances of civilization that the pioneer character is rapidly becoming mythical. The men and women who obtain their groceries and dry-goods from New York by rail in a few hours have nothing in common with those who, fifty years ago, "packed" salt a hundred miles to make their mush palatable, and could only exchange corn and wheat for molasses and calico by making long and perilous voyages in flat-boats down the Ohio and Mississippi rivers to New Orleans. Two generations of frontier lives have accumulated stores of narratives which, like the small but beautiful tributaries of great rivers, are forgotten in the broad sweep of the larger current of history. The march of Titans sometimes tramples out the memory of smaller but more useful lives, and sensational glare often eclipses more modest but purer lights. This has been the case in the popular demand for the dime novel dilutions of Fenimore Cooper's romances of border life, which have preserved the records of Indian rapine and atrocity as the only memorials of pioneer history. But the early days of Western settlement witnessed sublimer heroisms than those of human torture, and nobler victories than those of the tomahawk and scalping-knife.

Among the heroes of endurance that was voluntary, and of action that was creative and not sanguinary, there was one man whose name, seldom mentioned now save by some of the few surviving pioneers, deserves to be perpetuated.

The first reliable trace of our modest hero finds him in the Territory of Ohio, in 1801, with a horse-load of apple seeds, which he planted in various places on and about the borders of Licking Creek, the first orchard thus originated by him being on the farm of Isaac Stadden, in what is now known as Licking County, in the State of Ohio. During the five succeeding years, although he was undoubtedly following the same strange occupation, we have no authentic account of his movements until we reach a pleasant spring day in 1806, when a pioneer settler in Jefferson County, Ohio, noticed a peculiar craft, with a re-markable occupant and a curious cargo, slowly dropping down with the current of the Ohio River. It was "Johnny Appleseed", by which name Jonathan Chapman was afterward known in every log-cabin from the Ohio River to the Northern lakes, and westward to the prai-ries of what is now the State of Indiana. With two canoes lashed together he was transporting a load of apple seeds to the Western frontier, for the purpose of creating orchards on the farthest verge of white settlements. With his canoes he passed down the Ohio to Marietta, where he entered the Muskingum, ascending the stream of that river until he reached the mouth of the Walhonding, or White Woman Creek, and still onward, up the Mohican, into the Black Fork, to the head of navigation, in the region now known as Ashland and Richland coun-ties, on the line of the Pittsburgh and Fort Wayne Railroad, in Ohio. A long and toilsome voyage it was, as a glance at the map will show, and must have occupied a great deal of time, as the lonely traveller stopped at every inviting spot to plant the seeds and make his infant nurseries. These are the first well authenticated facts in the history of Jonathan Chapman, whose birth, there is good reason for believing, occurred in Boston, Massachusetts, in 1775. According to this, which was his own statement in one of his less reticent moods, he was, at the time of his appearance on Licking Creek, twenty-six years of age, and whether impelled in his eccentricities by some absolute misery of the heart which could only find relief in incessant motion, or governed by a benevolent monomania, his whole after-life was devoted to the work of planting apple seeds in remote places. The seeds he gathered from the cider-presses of Western Pennsylvania; but his canoe voyage in 1806 appears to have been the only occasion upon which he adopted that method of transporting them, as all his subsequent journeys were made on foot. Having planted his stock of seeds, he would return to Pennsylvania for a fresh supply, and, as sacks made of any less sub-stantial fabric would not endure the hard usage of the long trip through forests dense with underbrush and briers, he provided himself with leathern bags. Securely packed, the seeds were conveyed, sometimes on the back of a horse, and not unfrequently on his own shoulders, either over a part of the old Indian trail that led from Fort Duquesne to Detroit, by way of Fort Sandusky, or over what is styled in the appen-dix to "Hutchins's History of Boguet's Expedition in 1764" the "sec-ond route through the wilderness of Ohio", which would require him

to traverse a distance of one hundred and sixty-six miles in a west-
north-west direction from Fort Duquesne in order to reach the Black
Fork of the Mohican.

This region, although it is now densely populated, still possesses a
romantic beauty that railroads and bustling towns cannot obliterate—a
country of forest-clad hills and green valleys, through which numerous bright streams flow on their way to the Ohio; but when Johnny
Appleseed reached some lonely log-cabin he would find himself in a
veritable wilderness. The old settlers say that the margins of the streams,
near which the first settlements were generally made, were thickly
covered with low, matted growth of small timber, while nearer to the
water was a rank mass of long grass, interlaced with morning-glory
and wild pea vines, among which funereal willows and clustering
alders stood like sentinels on the outpost of civilization. The hills, that
rise almost to the dignity of mountains, were crowned with forest
trees, and in the coverts were innumerable bears, wolves, deer, and
droves of wild hogs, that were as ferocious as any beast of prey. In the
grass the massasauga and other venomous reptiles lurked in such numbers that a settler named Chandler has left the fact on record that
during the first season of his residence, while mowing a little prairie
which formed part of his land, he killed over two hundred black rattlesnakes in an area that would involve an average destruction of one of
these reptiles for each rod of land. The frontiersman, who felt himself
sufficiently protected by his rifle against wild beasts and hostile Indians, found it necessary to guard against the attacks of the insidious
enemies in the grass by wrapping bandages of dried grass around his
buckskin leggings and moccasins; but Johnny would shoulder his bag
of apple seeds, and with bare feet penetrate to some remote spot that
combined picturesqueness and fertility of soil, and there he would
plant his seeds, place a slight inclosure around the place, and leave
them to grow until the trees were large enough to be transplanted by
the settlers, who, in the mean time, would have made their clearings in
the vicinity. The sites chosen by him are, many of them, well known,
and are such as an artist or a poet would select—open places on the
loamy lands that border the creeks—rich, secluded spots, hemmed in
by giant trees, picturesque now, but fifty years ago, with their wild
surroundings and the primal silence, they must have been tenfold more
so.

In personal appearance Chapman was a small, wiry man, full of restless activity; he had long dark hair, a scanty beard that was never shaved, and keen black eyes that sparkled with a peculiar brightness. His dress was of the oddest description. Generally, even in the coldest weather, he went barefooted, but sometimes, for his long journeys, he would make himself a rude pair of sandals; at other times he would wear any cast-off foot-covering he chanced to find—a boot on one foot and an old brogan or a moccasin on the other. It appears to have been a matter of conscience with him never to purchase shoes, although he was rarely without money enough to do so. On one occasion, in an unusually cold November, while he was travelling barefooted through mud and snow, a settler who happened to possess a pair of shoes that were too small for his own use forced their acceptance upon Johnny, declaring that it was sinful for a human being to travel with naked feet in such weather. A few days afterward the donor was in the village that has since become the thriving city of Mansfield, and met his beneficiary contentedly plodding along with his feet bare and half frozen. With some degree of anger he inquired for the cause of such foolish conduct, and received for reply that Johnny had overtaken a poor, barefooted family moving Westward, and as they appeared to be in much greater need of clothing than he was, he had given them the shoes. His dress was generally composed of cast-off clothing, that he had taken in payment for apple-trees; and as the pioneers were far less extravagant than their descendants in such matters, the homespun and buckskin garments that they discarded would not be very elegant or serviceable. In his later years, however, he seems to have thought that even this kind of second-hand raiment was too luxurious, as his principal garment was made of a coffee sack, in which he cut holes for his head and arms to pass through, and pronounced it "a very serviceable cloak, and as good clothing as any man need wear". In the matter of head-gear his taste was equally unique; his first experiment was with a tin vessel that served to cook his mush, but this was open to the objection that it did not protect his eyes from the beams of the sun; so he constructed a hat of pasteboard with an immense peak in front, and having thus secured an article that combined usefulness with economy, it became his permanent fashion.

Thus strangely clad, he was perpetually wandering through forests and morasses, and suddenly appearing in white settlements and Indian villages; but there must have been some rare force of gentle goodness dwelling in his looks and breathing in his words, for it is the testimony of all who knew him that, notwithstanding his ridiculous attire, he was always treated with the greatest respect by the rudest frontiersman, and, what is a better test, the boys of the settlements forbore to jeer at him. With grown-up people and boys he was usually reticent, but manifested great affection for little girls, always having pieces of ribbon and gay calico to give to his little favourites. Many a grandmother in Ohio and Indiana can remember the presents she received when a child from poor homeless Johnny Appleseed. When he consented to eat with any family he would never sit down to the table until he was assured that there was an ample supply for the children; and his sympathy for their youthful troubles and his kindness toward them made him friends among all the juveniles of the borders.

The Indians also treated Johnny with the greatest kindness. By these wild and sanguinary savages he was regarded as a "great medicine man", on account of his strange appearance, eccentric actions, and, especially, the fortitude with which he could endure pain, in proof of which he would often thrust pins and needles into his flesh. His nervous sensibilities really seem to have been less acute than those of ordinary people, for his method of treating the cuts and sores that were the consequences of his barefooted wanderings through briers and thorns was to sear the wound with a red-hot iron, and then cure the burn. During the war of 1812, when the frontier settlers were tortured and slaughtered by the savage allies of Great Britain, Johnny Appleseed continued his wanderings, and was never harmed by the roving bands of hostile Indians. On many occasions the impunity with which he ranged the country enabled him to give the settlers warning of approaching danger in time to allow them to take refuge in their block-houses before the savages could attack them. Our informant refers to one of these instances, when the news of Hull's surrender came like a thunderbolt upon the frontier. Large bands of Indians and British were destroying everything before them and murdering defenceless women and children, and even the block-houses were not always a sufficient protection. At this time Johnny travelled day and night, warning the people of the approaching danger. He visited every cabin and delivered this message: "The Spirit of the Lord is upon me, and he hath anointed me to blow the trumpet in the wilderness, and sound an alarm in the forest; for, behold, the tribes of the heathen are round about your doors, and a devouring flame followeth after them." The aged man who narrated this incident said that he could feel even now the thrill that was caused by this prophetic announcement of the wild-looking herald of danger, who aroused the family on a bright moon-light with his piercing voice. Refusing all offers of food and denying himself a moment's rest, he traversed the border day and night until he had warned every settler of the approaching peril.

His diet was as meagre as his clothing. He believed it to be a sin to kill any creature for food, and thought that all that was necessary for human sustenance was produced by the soil. He was also a strenuous opponent of the waste of food, and on one occasion, on approaching a log-cabin, he observed some fragments of bread floating upon the surface of a bucket of slops that was intended for the pigs. He immediately fished them out, and when the housewife expressed her astonishment, he told her that it was an abuse of the gifts of a merciful God to allow the smallest quantity of anything that was designed to supply the wants of mankind to be diverted from its purpose.

In this instance, as in his whole life, the peculiar religious ideas of Johnny Appleseed were exemplified. He was a most earnest disciple of the faith taught by Emanuel Swedenborg, and himself claimed to have frequent conversations with angels and spirits; two of the latter, of the feminine gender, he asserted, had revealed to him that they were to be his wives in a future state if he abstained from a matrimonial alliance on earth. He entertained a profound reverence for the revelations of the Swedish seer, and always carried a few old volumes with him. These he was very anxious should be read by everyone, and he was probably not only the first colporteur in the wilderness of Ohio, but as he had no tract society to furnish him supplies, he certainly devised an original method of multiplying one book into a number. He divided his books into several pieces, leaving a portion at a log-cabin, and on a subsequent visit furnishing another fragment, and continuing this process as diligently as though the work had been published in serial numbers. By this plan he was enabled to furnish reading for several people at the same time, and out of one book; but it must have been a difficult undertaking for some nearly illiterate backwoodsman to endeavour to comprehend Swedenborg by a backward course of reading, when his first instalment happened to be the last fraction of the volume. Johnny's faith in Swedenborg's works was so reverential as almost to be superstitious. He was once asked if, in travelling barefooted through forests abounding with venomous reptiles, he was not afraid of being bitten. With his peculiar smile, he drew his book from his bosom, and said, "This book is an infallible protection against all danger here and hereafter".

It was his custom, when he had been welcomed to some hospitable log-house after a weary day of journeying, to lie down on the puncheon floor, and, after inquiring if his auditors would hear "some news right fresh from heaven", produce his few tattered books, among which would be a New Testament, and read and expound until his uncultivated hearers would catch the spirit and glow of his enthusiasm, while they scarcely comprehended his language. A lady who knew him in his later years writes in the following terms of one of these domiciliary readings of poor, self-sacrificing Johnny Appleseed: "We can hear him read now, just as he did that summer day, when we were busy quilting up stairs, and he lay near the door, his voice rising denunciatory and thrilling—strong and loud as the roar of wind and waves, then soft and soothing as the balmy airs that quivered the morning-glory leaves about his grey beard. His was a strange eloquence at times, and he was undoubtedly a man of genius." What a scene is presented to our imagination! The interior of a primitive cabin, the wide, open fireplace, where a few sticks are burning beneath the iron pot in which the evening meal is cooking; around the fire-place the attentive group, composed of the sturdy pioneer and his wife and children, listening with a reverential awe to the "news right fresh from heaven"; and reclining on the floor, clad in rags, but with his grey hairs glorified by the beams of the setting sun that flood through the open door and the unchinked logs of the humble building, this poor wanderer, with the gift of genius and eloquence, who believes with the faith of apostles and martyrs that God has appointed him a mission in the wilderness to preach the Gospel of love, and plant apple seeds that shall produce orchards for the benefit of men and women and little children whom he has never seen. If there is a sublimer faith or a more genuine eloquence in richly decorated cathedrals and under brocade vestments, it would be worth a long journey to find it.

Next to his advocacy of his peculiar religious ideas, his enthusiasm for the cultivation of apple-trees in what he termed "the only proper way"—that is, from the seed—was the absorbing object of his life. Upon this, as upon religion, he was eloquent in his appeals. He would describe the growing and ripening fruit as such a rare and beautiful gift of the Almighty with words that became pictures, until his hearers could almost see its manifold forms of beauty present before them. To his eloquence on this subject, as well as to his actual labours in planting nurseries, the country over which he travelled for so many years is largely indebted for its numerous orchards. But he denounced as absolute wickedness all devices of pruning and grafting, and would speak of the act of cutting a tree as if it were a cruelty inflicted upon a sentient being.

Not only is he entitled to the fame of being the earliest colporteur on the frontiers, but in the work of protecting animals from abuse and suffering he preceded, while, in his smaller sphere, he equalled the zeal of the good Mr. Bergh. Whenever Johnny saw an animal abused, or heard of it, he would purchase it and give it to some more humane settler, on condition that it should be kindly treated and properly cared for. It frequently happened that the long journey into the wilderness would cause the new settlers to be encumbered with lame and broken-down horses, that were turned loose to die. In the autumn Johnny would make a diligent search for all such animals, and, gathering them up, he would bargain for their food and shelter until the next spring, when he would lead them away to some good pasture for the summer. If they recovered so as to be capable of working, he would never sell them, but would lend or give them away, stipulating for their good usage. His conception of the absolute sin of inflicting pain or death upon any creature was not limited to the higher forms of animal life, but everything that had being was to him, in the fact of its life, endowed with so much of the Divine Essence that to wound or destroy it was to inflict an injury upon some atom of Divinity. No Brahmin could be more concerned for the preservation of insect life, and the only occasion on which he destroyed a venomous reptile was a source of long regret, to which he could never refer without manifesting sadness. He had selected a suitable place for planting apple seeds on a small prairie, and in order to prepare the ground he was mowing the long grass, when he was bitten by a rattlesnake. In describing the event he sighed heavily, and said, "Poor fellow, he only just touched me, when I, in the heat of my ungodly passion, put the heel of my scythe in him, and went away. Some time afterward I went back, and there lay the poor fellow dead." Numerous anecdotes bearing upon his respect for every form of life are preserved, and form the staple of pioneer recollections. On one occasion, a cool autumnal night, when Johnny, who always camped out in preference to sleeping in a house, had built a fire near which he intended to pass the night, he noticed that the blaze attracted large numbers of mosquitoes, many of whom flew too near his fire and were burned. He immediately brought water and quenched the fire, accounting for his conduct afterward by saying, "God forbid that I should build a fire for my comfort which should be the means of destroying any of His creatures!" At another time he removed the fire he had built near a hollow log, and slept on the snow, because he found that the log contained a bear and her cubs, whom, he said, he did not. wish to disturb. And this unwillingness to inflict pain or death was equally strong when he was a sufferer by it, as the following will show. Johnny had been assisting some settlers to make a road through the woods, and in the course of their work they accidentally destroyed a hornets' nest. One of the angry insects soon found a lodgment under Johnny's coffee-sack cloak, but although it stung him repeatedly he removed it with the greatest gentleness. The men who were present laughingly asked him why he did not kill it. To which he gravely replied that "It would not be right to kill the poor thing, for it did not intend to hurt me."

Theoretically he was as methodical in matters of business as any merchant. In addition to their picturesqueness, the locations of his nurseries were all fixed with a view to a probable demand for the trees by the time they had attained sufficient growth for transplanting. He would give them away to those who could not pay for them. Generally, however, he sold them for old clothing or a supply of corn meal; but he preferred to receive a note payable at some indefinite period. When this was accomplished he seemed to think that the transaction was completed in a businesslike way; but if the giver of the note did not attend to its payment, the holder of it never troubled himself about its collection. His expenses for food and clothing were so very limited that, notwithstanding his freedom from the *auri sacra fames*, he was frequently in possession of more money than he cared to keep, and it was quickly disposed of for wintering infirm horses, or given to some poor family whom the ague had prostrated or the accidents of border life impoverished. In a single instance only he is known to have invested his surplus means in the purchase of land, having received a deed from Alexander Finley, of Mohican Township, Ashland County, Ohio, for a part of the southwest quarter of section twenty-six; but with his customary indifference to matters of value, Johnny failed to record the deed, and lost it. Only a few years ago the property was in litigation.

We must not leave the reader under the impression that this man's life, so full of hardship and perils, was a gloomy or unhappy one. There is an element of human pride in all martyrdom, which, if it does not soften the pains, stimulates the power of endurance. Johnny's life was made serenely happy by the conviction that he was living like the primitive Christians. Nor was he devoid of a keen humour, to which he occasionally gave vent, as the following will show. Toward the latter part of Johnny's career in Ohio an itinerant missionary found his way to the village of Mansfield, and preached to an open-air congregation. The discourse was tediously lengthy, and unnecessarily severe upon the sin of extravagance, which was beginning to manifest itself among the pioneers by an occasional indulgence in the carnal vanities of calico and "store tea". There was a good deal of the Pharisaic leaven in the preacher, who very frequently emphasized his discourse by the inquiry, "Where now is there a man who, like the primitive Christians, is travelling to heaven barefooted and clad in coarse raiment?" When this interrogation had been repeated beyond all reasonable endurance, Johnny rose from the log on which he was reclining, and advancing to the speaker, he placed one of his bare feet upon the stump which served for a pulpit, and pointing to his coffee-sack garment, he quietly said, "Here's your primitive Christian!" The well-clothed missionary hesitated and stammered and dismissed the congregation. His pet antithesis was destroyed by Johnny's personal appearance, which was far more primitive than the preacher cared to copy.

Some of the pioneers were disposed to think that Johnny's humour was the cause of an extensive practical joke; but it is generally conceded now that a widespread annoyance was really the result of his belief that the offensively odoured weed known in the West as the dog-fennel, but more generally styled the May-weed, possessed valuable antimalarial virtues. He procured some seeds of the plant in Pennsylvania, and sowed them in the vicinity of every house in the region of his travels. The consequence was that successive flourishing crops of the weed spread over the whole country, and caused almost as much trouble as the disease it was intended to ward off; and to this day the dog-fennel, introduced by Johnny Appleseed, is one of the worst grievances of the Ohio farmers.

In 1838—thirty-seven years after his appearance on Licking Creek—Johnny noticed that civilization, wealth, and population were pressing into the wilderness of Ohio. Hitherto he had easily kept just in advance of the wave of settlement; but now towns and churches were making their appearance, and even, at long intervals, the stage-driver's horn broke the silence of the grand old forests, and he felt that his work was done in the region in which he had laboured so long. He visited every house, and took a solemn farewell of all the families. The little girls who had been delighted with his gifts of fragments of calico and ribbons had become sober matrons, and the boys who had wondered at his ability to bear the pain caused by running needles into his flesh were heads of families. With parting words of admonition he left them, and turned his steps steadily toward the setting sun.

During the succeeding nine years he pursued his eccentric avocation on the western border of Ohio and in Indiana. In the summer of 1847, when his labours had literally borne fruit over a hundred thousand square miles of territory, at the close of a warm day, after travelling twenty miles, he entered the house of a settler in Allen County, Indiana, and was, as usual, warmly welcomed. He declined to eat with the family, but accepted some bread and milk, which he partook of sitting on the door-step and gazing on the setting sun. Later in the evening he delivered his "news right fresh from heaven" by reading the Beatitudes. Declining other accommodation, he slept, as usual, on the floor, and in the early morning he was found with his features all aglow with a supernal light, and his body so near death that his tongue refused its office. The physician, who was hastily summoned, pronounced him dying, but added that he had never seen a man in so placid a state at the approach of death. At seventy-two years of age, forty-six of which had been devoted to his self-imposed mission, he ripened into death as naturally and beautifully as the seeds of his own planting had grown into fibre and bud and blossom and the matured fruit.

Thus died one of the memorable men of pioneer times, who never inflicted pain or knew an enemy—a man of strange habits, in whom there dwelt a comprehensive love that reached with one hand downward to the lowest forms of life, and with the other upward to the very throne of God. A labouring, self-denying benefactor of his race, homeless, solitary, and ragged, he trod the thorny earth with bare and bleeding feet, intent only upon making the wilderness fruitful. Now "no man knoweth of his sepulchre"; but his deeds will live in the fragrance of the apple blossoms he loved so well, and the story of his life, however crudely narrated, will be a perpetual proof that true heroism, pure benevolence, noble virtues, and deeds that deserve immortality may be found under meanest apparel, and far from gilded halls and towering spires.

PART TWO

BOOSTERS AND KNOCKERS

*Everything is upon a great scale upon this con-
tinent. The rivers are immense, the climate violent in heat and cold, the prospects magnificent, the thunder and lightning tremendous. The
disorders incident to the country make every
constitution tremble. Our own blunders here,
our misconduct, our losses, our disgraces, our
ruin, are on a great scale.*
                    —LORD CARLISLE TO GEORGE SEEWYN (1778)

Introduction to Part Two

TALL TALK

The language of the ring-tailed roarer—and without his language he
was like Samson without his hair—was tall talk. Tall talk may be
defined as the art of making a noise in language. As such, it is characterized by grandiloquence, and exaggeration. At its best it is a kind of
poetry. At its worst it is bombast and buncombe. For the most part,
however, it is comic in effect or intention, insofar as exaggeration is a
source of humour or as tall talk has been associated with the local-
colour sketches, yarns, and tall tales of the old Southwest. "Froth and
specks" of the "fermentation processes" of language (as that tall-talk-
ing poet, Whitman, described slang), tall talk is the slang of the frontier movement, when windy bragging and laughing at bragging were
at their height.

Tall talk is not only "frontier" in spirit; it is also national and regional. Since "broad exaggeration" has been identified with American humour and through it with the character of the people and the physical features of the country, tall talk has come to be considered a part of our national heritage, along with tall tales and tall heroes. During the growth of nationalism and the "new nation" after the War of 1812, "rankness and protestantism in speech" accompanied the release of political and industrial energies in this country. Robert Kempt, the British compiler of *The American Joe Miller*, wrote in 1865 of his American cousins: "Their ordinary speech is hyperbole, or tall talk. They never go out shooting unless with the long bow."

Regional characteristics are clearly stamped upon tall talk. In the United States what has been called the "dividing line of loquacity" runs East and West as well as North and South. It corresponds roughly to the Mason and Dixon line and the Mississippi or Missouri River. The tradition of good talk and talkativeness has been at home South by West. Here country frolics and public gatherings—parties, picnics, barbecues, camp and political meetings, muster and court days—have invited talk—folk talk, man talk, back talk—and encouraged yarn-swapping and stump-speech eloquence. Such backwoods eloquence is "expansive eloquence", in contrast to the "reluctant" Yankee cracker-box philosopher brand.

It must not be thought, however, that tall talk was illiterate. In its "bundle of crooked and stupendous" words and phrases it possessed many of the features of a "literary dialect".

"Gentle reader", admonishes the anonymous author of *Sketches and Eccentricities of Col. David Crockett, of West Tennessee*, in a prefatory statement belied by "A Vote for Crockett", "I can promise you, in no part of this volume, the wild rhodomontades of 'Bushfield'; nor can I regale you with the still more delicate repast of a constant repetition of the terms *'bodyaciously'*, *'tetotaciously'*, *'obfisticated'*, etc. Though I have had much intercourse with the West, I have never met with a man who used such terms unless they were alluded to, as merely occupying a space in some printed work. They have, however, thus been made to enter, as a component part, into the character of every backwoodsman. . . . "

Like most literary dialects, tall talk was spread on thick by its practitioners. The picturesque, grotesque tropes and expletives attributed to backwoodsmen and boatmen in fiction, for all their allusions to everyday objects and activities of the time and place, constitute a species of literary folklore. Basic to this "strong language" is, of course, what John Russell Bartlett (in his *Dictionary of Americanisms*, 1848) refers to as the fondness of Americans, especially in the South and West, for "intensive and extravagant epithets"—awful, powerful, monstrous, dreadful, mighty, almighty, all-fired. Tall talk was "strong language" constantly striving to outdo itself. Thus Bartlett defines *teetotaciously* as "A strange Western term, meaning a little more than teetotally, if such a thing be possible". By means of strained blends and coinages, coupled with far-fetched comparisons and extravagant conceits—as shaggy and rambunctious as the backwoodsmen who were supposed to utter them—tall talk went the whole hog.

Tall talk also had its mythology, in which animal allusions figure prominently. These point to a hunting and trapping existence and to love of sports of "turf and field", such as produced the hunting and sporting yarns that filled William T. Porter's virile journal of oral and anecdotal humour, *The Spirit of the Times* (1883–1861). Like the woods, the Crockett almanacs were full of bear, catamount, beaver, panther, moose, wolf, raccoon, possum, turkey, etc. Of the word *screamer* ("a bouncing fellow or girl"), Bartlett notes: "This, like the word roarer, is one of the many terms transferred from animals to men by the hunters of the West." It is not too fantastic to see in this transfer of names as in nicknames, a totemic transfer of traits, reflected in the application to humans of such terms as hoss (old hoss), colt (a pretty severe colt), coon (a right smart coon, a gone coon), varmint, critter.

In a wild country, it was good business for "wild men" to go about scaring people with strange noises and by "making terrible faces playfully". But as the hunter was displaced by the second and third orders of "back settlers", the squatter and the homesteader, the roarers and screamers were not only out-hollered but out-licked by a new type of boaster and tall talker. This was the boomer and booster, drunk not with his own powers but with the bigness of the country and the illusion of inexhaustible resources and opportunities.

Here history repeated itself. As the backwoodsman's antics and war-cries were partly in imitation of the Indian,[55] so the advocates of Western expansion and settlement borrowed from the backwoodsman the elbow-room motif. This had been given expression for all time by Daniel Boone when in 1799, at the age of 65, he was asked why he was leaving Kentucky for frontier Missouri: "Too many people! Too crowded! Too crowded! I want more elbow room!" The frontier also had a saying: "When you see the smoke of your neighbour's chimney, it's time to move."

"The backwoodsman", says the Crockett Almanac for 1838, "is a singular being, always moving westward like a buffalo before the tide of civilization. He does not want a neighbour nearer than ten miles; and when he cannot cut down a tree that will fall within ten rods of his log house, he thinks it is time to sell out his betterment and be off."

But to the expansionists and the promoters of free land and the West, elbow-room meant room for improvements, for free enterprise, and so for more neighbours—in terms of nothing less than a continent and manifest destiny.

With the movement for territorial expansion and free land, the country entered upon one of the greatest advertising campaigns in history—the booming of the West. This was a campaign in which statesmen and orators joined with land and railroad companies, farmers' organizations, departments of agriculture, bureaus of immigration, boards of trade, and chambers of commerce. The theme of countless speeches, immigrant handbooks, emigrants' and railroad guides, state and regional guidebooks and gazetteers, state year books, rural almanacs, real estate directories, and government reports was "The sky's the limit", "Watch us grow", "We don't have to prove it—we admit it."

In style this propaganda rivalled the "expansive eloquence" of the ring-tailed roarer and the stump-speaker. Its flamboyant ballyhoo proved that, more than the protective colouration of the homespun hero playing the tough guy and the smart aleck, tall talk is the highfalutin style of all provincial Americans whose motto is "Braggin' saves advertisin'."

In the vanguard of Western expansion was another screamer, the American eagle. This "favourite fowl of orators" was derived from the American emblem in the Great Seal and in coinage—not, according to Franklin, the most appropriate emblem of America. But the bird suffers not so much from the "bad moral character"—"generally poor, and often very lousy" and a "rank coward"—ascribed to it by Franklin, as from sheer triteness.

From the apex of the Allegheny to the summit of Mount Hood, the bird of America has so often been made to take flight, that his shadow may be said to have worn a trail across the basin of the Mississippi. . . . [56]

The scream of the expansionist eagle is heard in the swelling per-oration of Samuel C. Pomeroy's impassioned plea for the Homestead Bill, whose passage climaxed the ten-years' debate in Congress on the free land question.

State nicknames, which have become part of the folklore of Ameri-can places, crystallized local aspirations or pretensions to uniqueness and excellence: the Boomer's Paradise (Oklahoma), the Garden of the West (Illinois, Kansas), the Land of Heart's Desire, or the Land of Sunshine (New Mexico), the Land of Plenty (New Mexico, South Dakota), the Wonder State (Arkansas).[57]

As an instance of the willingness with which state governments took the lead in "telling the world of our wonderful possibilities", one may point to the concurrent resolution of the Arkansas Senate approv-ing the nickname, "The Wonder State"—virtually an argument in favour of changing the name of Arkansas. The objection to the earlier nick-name of "The Bear State" is typical of the desire of the self-conscious West to live down its frontier past, commemorated in such uncompli-mentary terms as the Puke State (Missouri) and the Grasshopper State (Kansas).

The prince of state greeters and boosters was Robert Love Taylor (1850–1912), the "Fiddling Governor" of Tennessee and the apostle of "Love, Laughter, and Sunshine", who devoted his sky-painting talents as orator, editor, and writer chiefly to booming the South. His "village apocalypse quality" and "inventive, epic earnestness" have been praised by another village improver, Vachel Lindsay, in his poem, "Preface to Bob Taylor's Birthday". For all his Pollyanna optimism and mush-and-syrup sentiment, Taylor had something of the folk touch in his art of improvisation and a backwoodsy homeliness in his native figures and allusions. Above all, he had a big heart, which went out to all things big, such as Uncle Sam, Dixie, and Tennessee, or any state that exerted or felt the influence of the sunny South. Here is tall talk in the plug hat, swallow-tailed coat, and striped trousers of a "glad-handed" Uncle Sam.

The advertising pages of *Bob Taylor's Magazine*, a monthly ad-dressed to "all Parts of the Prosperous South", were filled with the "come-on" invitations of Southwest railroad and land companies and "commercial clubs"; for whose promotion Taylor set the pace in his editorials and essays and. in October, 1906, gave the cue with the following query:

Have you a Board of Trade, or a Chamber of Commerce, or a Boosters' Club? . . . A Southern Town now without a live Board of Trade might as well disincorporate and go back into the woods.

One of the most elaborate of these advertisements rivalled Taylor's lush pen in depicting the farm lands of the Nueces River Valley as a paradise on earth worthy of Theodore Roosevelt's characterization of Texas as the "garden spot of the land".

Besides manifest destiny, free land, and state pride, the West had another string to its bow—the long bow which it drew in order to live down its wild and woolly reputation and to attract settlers. This was the myth of a land flowing with milk and honey—part of the American dream of a promised land of plenty, opportunity, and "beginning", which had first attracted settlers from the Old World to the New and was now transferred to the fabulous, far-off West. To make its ardours outweigh its endurances, orators, promoters, and guidebook writers painted this unknown country in the rosy hues of fairyland.

The land of "nature's bounty" was "God's country", defined as "a special part of the United States or the country as a whole, viewed nostalgically as almost a paradise."[58] "God's country" was sometimes the country one was going to—perhaps always going to and never reaching, like the pot of gold at the end of the rainbow; and it was sometimes the place that one was going back to. Or perhaps it was only in the heart—not a place but a state of mind. To Boone in retrospect it was real enough—the Kentucky he had left behind him. " 'I have travelled", he said in his old age, 'over many new countries in the great Mississippi Valley; I have critically examined their soils; their mineral wealth; their healthful climates; their manufacturing situations; and the commercial advantages given them by nature. I have discovered where these endowments were given most bountifully in many localities, singly and in groups, *but I have never found but one Kentucky—a spot of earth where nature seems to have concentrated all her bounties'*."[59] For many a pioneer settler, however, who, while in quest of God's country, often had to ask: "Is this God's Country or not?" and "Had God forsaken us?" there was only this consolation left at the end of the search:

We learned that God's Country isn't in the country. It is in the mind. As we looked back we knew that all the time we was hunting for God's country we had it. We worked hard. We was loyal. Honest. We was happy. For 48 years we lived together in God's Country.

The potency of this phrase was part of the "pioneer myth". This assumed that land, which should be as free as the air and the sunshine, was a symbol of the inalienable rights of man; that all land was good land and all settlers were good farmers; that in its "green pastures" one should not want; that the land had certain imperishable values of its own from which one could derive, not only sustenance and profit, but also strength and courage; and that the pioneer, "inured to self-reliance" through hardship and discouragement, was a soldier of civilization and of God.

In a land of violent extremes and abrupt contrasts of weather and climate, the quest for health and happiness put a premium on optimum environment. Land advertisements boasted of such advantages as dry, bracing air; three hundred (or more) days of sunshine a year; and—negatively—no killing frosts, hail, blizzards, hot winds, heat waves, tornadoes, cyclones, whirlwinds, hurricanes, earthquakes, and similar afflictions. "Why Shovel Snow and Shiver?" was one rhetorical question. "No chills, no negroes, no saloons, no mosquitoes", went a sweeping statement from Arkansas.

The guidebooks were equally reassuring.

> It is complained that the "wind blows". As it blows elsewhere, so it blows in Colorado—occasionally. Sometimes these winds are momentarily disagreeable, but they serve nature as one of her sanitary measures and their effect is refreshing and beneficial.[60]
>
> Withal there is an effect of climate, and something of freedom caught from the outdoorness of life. Sunshine and green salads all the year will promote cheerfulness. Where there are no bitter winds, no sleet or hail, no blizzards to kill flocks and herds, no "cold snaps" to freeze poultry on the perch or water-pipes in the kitchen. it is not at all surprising that people laugh and are affected by the great world of sun and summer in which they dwell.[61]

Emigrant and Western songs fell in line with the chauvinism, utopianism, and arcadianism of the guidebooks, reflected in many a state song and poem of the "sweet singer" or boosting variety and many a popular song of nostalgia for this, that, or the other "wonder state".[62]

The boast of a climate "so healthy that people rarely die, except from accident or old age", as in the Nueces River Valley land advertisement, was a common one.[63] One of the best of the stories on this theme is related by Barnum, as he heard it from a sleight-of-hand artist named Henry Hawley.

Related to the stories of life-prolonging air are the stories of air that restores life.

In East Texas it is the wind that revives corpses.

> Truth of it is, Dad was dead, but when that coffin bust open and that strong healthy plains wind hit him it just filled his lungs full of good revivin air, and Dad nor no one else could stay dead.

In Florida it is the sunshine, as on the occasion when the corpse of a gangster had been imported from Chicago so that a funeral could be staged by the local dealer in cemetery lots.

> The coffin was taken to the graveside and the lid was opened to give the bystanders a glimpse of the beautiful way the corpse had been laid out, a master-piece of the undertaker's art. As the Florida sunshine hit the body, there was an immediate stir. The gangster arose with a yell, feeling for his gun. The bystanders had to kill him again before they could go on with the funeral.[64]

Variations on the theme are found in the stories of a dying person being revived by the air expelled from a bicycle or automobile tire, which had been pumped up in California or Arizona, or of an incur-able victim of tuberculosis being healed by a single ray of Florida sunshine.[65]

Rival claims of salubrious climate are accompanied by mutual re-crimination in which state rivalry is keen. Thus Florida papers cast aspersions on California as a "terrible place, going rapidly to the bad from frost, storms, earthquakes, and other calamities. California and other resort places reciprocate".[66] To the older feud between Florida and California has more recently been added the competition between California and the Rio Grande Valley.

> But we have the healthiest climate in California. It is so healthy we had to shoot a man in order to start a graveyard.
> That's no comparison with our Valley climate for health. One of our citizens went out to California, took sick and died there. They shipped his remains back to the Valley, the friends of the deceased were gathered around the corpse. When they opened the casket he raised up, greeted his friends and walked off.[67]

Tacked on to Hawley's yarn is the tale of the "monstrous large gun", which "required one pound of powder and four pounds of shot to load it properly" and with which Hawley shot off four-and-a-half bushels of wild pigeons' feet and legs (without killing a single bird) when the flock rose off the ground just a half second ahead of his shot.

The great number of pigeons and the large field of buckwheat which it was feared they would destroy reflect the abundance of crops and game associated with the marvels of climate and soil. Here brags about rich land and big crops shade off into yarns of varying degrees of exaggeration. The boosters' club gives way to the liars' club—with an occasional knock for the famine that often followed the feast or the bust that followed the boom.

In 1851 the Commissioner of Patents reported an "address delivered by A. Williams, Esq., at a meeting in San Francisco, for presenting the premium of a silver goblet, offered by Mr. C. A. Shelton for the best varieties of vegetables and grains". Among other prize products are an onion weighing 21 pounds, a turnip "which equalled exactly in size the top of a flour barrel", another weighing 100 pounds, a cabbage measuring 13 feet, 6 inches around, a beet weighing 63 pounds, and carrots three feet in length, weighing 40 pounds, not to mention a single potato, "larger than the size of an ordinary hat," of which twelve persons partook at a dinner in Stockton, "leaving at least the half untouched". Then the speaker added ironically:

> And we have some still larger and taller specimens of other things nearer home, here in our own city, to which many who hear me will bear witness from experience, and which come to maturity *"monthly in advance"*—rents, the tallest kind of rents, put up higher than the pines, and sometimes harder to get around than red-wood![68]

Praise of the wonders and glories of the new country was offset by a healthy scepticism which viewed with alarm instead of pointing with pride. Hardship and failure gave rise to inverse exaggeration and defensive boasting—of the kind that proceeds from having too little rather than too much.

A common symbol of disillusionment was the returning emigrant or prospector admonishing the westward traveller to turn back. In the frontispiece of "Major Wilkey's" *Narrative*,[69] the fashionable young man in the smart chaise behind the spirited horse, proclaims: "I am going to Illinois!" whereas from the lips of the broken-down owner of a "broken down waggon!—a broken winded horse!—a brokenhearted wife!—a broken legged dog! and, what is still more to be lamented, the irreparable broken constitutions of my three Fever and Ague sons, Jonathan, Jerry, and Joe!"—the reply emanates: "I have been!" A modern parallel is furnished by *The Grapes of Wrath*, in which the Joads, on their way to "where it's rich an' green", and they can get work and a "piece a growin' land with water", are laughed at by a ragged man who inquires:

> "You folks all goin' to California, I bet." "I tol' you that", said Pa. "You didn' guess nothin'." The ragged man said slowly, "Me—I'm comin' back. I been there. . . . I'm goin' back to starve. I ruther starve all over at oncet."[70]

Disappointed victims of gold fever, who had been advised "not to be too sanguine of success", turned back with mottoes properly amended to express their disgust. "Busted, by thunder!" set the pattern in slogans for all settlers who did not have the "grit, grace, and gumption" necessary to tough it out in a tough country.

Disillusionment in turn was seasoned with stoical humour of the type known as "laughing it off", or smiling in the face of adversity. Grasshopper plagues were commemorated in the wagon inscription, "Hoppers et all but the wagonsheet", in the saying that the grasshoppers had eaten everything except the mortgage, and in the story of the grasshopper who ate the farmer's team of mules and then pitched the horseshoes for the wagon. In Nebraska one could stand by the side of a field and hear the grasshoppers threatening. "On the potato vines they would eat downward, and when they came to a potato bug would calmly kick it and go on their devastating way."[71]

On the Great Plains, it has been said, "If you ain't burned up by drought and winds hot as hell or frozen out by blizzards and hail storms, you're eat up by grasshoppers, speculators, and politicians,"[72]— and, it might have been added, centipedes, snakes, bedbugs, fleas, and other pests that infested the primitive shelters of pioneer settlers. This is the plaint of Western "hard times" songs like "The Lane County Bachelor", which prove that only a thin line separates stoicism from revolt.

LOCAL CRACKS AND SLAMS

> *Crack* . . . Slang. *A gibing retort; a quip.*
> *Slam* . . . Colloq. *A violent criticism.*
> —WEBSTER'S COLLEGIATE DICTIONARY,
> FIFTH EDITION (1936)

> *From time immemorial . . . pointing sarcasm or*
> *humour at localities has been recognized as an*
> *element in human nature and its literature.*
> —SAMUEL S. COX

NAMES AND NICKNAMES

In all times and places popular tradition embraces terms, phrases, sayings, allusions, rhymes, songs, and jokes that poke fun at a particular locality or group.[73] In America geographical and cultural diversity intensifies rather than modifies the spirit of clannishness, provincialism, and rivalry which motivates local gibes. Minority and sectional conflicts and the mobility of the population are contributing factors. The restlessness of travel and internal migration makes local differences stand out in sharp relief and heightens the power of observation and the sense of the incongruous. Corresponding to "local colour" in fiction, the humour of local characters and customs is an integral part of our folklore.

From another point of view, local taunts and insults are inspired by reaction against the excessive optimism and confidence of boasting and boosting. This boosting in reverse has already been noted in mock brags and orations, inverse brags, and "laughing it off". Mockery and scepticism also break out in open scoffs and jeers, pricking the inflated self-opinion of places. Exaggeration is the weapon as well as the object of attack.

The thrusts and shots of deflating sarcasm are also related to the national habit of "knocking" or fault-finding. The fact that knocking is as much at home in America as boosting may be attributed to the see-saw of American life, with its ups and downs of feasts and famines, booms and busts—"always up in the clouds or down in the dumps". More than the opposite of boosting, however, knocking is the spirit of social criticism and protest at work on the inequalities and contradictions of "individual competitive aggressiveness". When accompanied by wit and humour, knocking is relieved of rancour and in the guise of panning or razzing becomes not only good fun but an effective form of debunking.

In the matter of name-calling nicknames go even further and call a spade a shovel. Slang names of the states and their inhabitants popular during the last century were mostly uncomplimentary. One of the harshest of these is Puke, for a Missourian. "Early Californians christened as 'Pukes' the immigrants from Missouri, declaring that they had been vomited forth from that prolific State."[74] Collections of these sportive and slighting sobriquets illustrate not only local pride and prejudice but also the fondness for "intensive and extravagant epithets" noted by Bartlett and the "perennial rankness and protestantism" in speech which Whitman identified with slang.

A simple form of local witticism is nomenclature. Out of a realistic sense of humour and the apt phrase, frontier communities assumed disreputable, hard-sounding names, with a rough-and-ready appropriateness and facetious raciness. Bret Harte has capitalized and popularized such places as Roaring Camp, Poker Flat, Red Gulch, One Horse Gulch, Rough and Ready.

In these hardy, improvised names, born out of the moment's humour—good or bad—the American expressed the same irreverence and impudence as in the "barbaric yawp" of tall talk and boasting. "The appetite of the people of These States", wrote Whitman in *An American Primer*, "is for unhemmed latitude, coarseness, directness, live epithets, expletives, words of opprobrium, resistance . . . Words of Names of Places are strong, copious, unruly, in the repertoire for American pens and tongues."

Such names, far from being confined to the West, had been anticipated in the East, where they have entered into mountain speech and thence into mountain fiction. John Fox, Jr.'s readers are familiar with the grotesque or whimsical sound and the native salt and savour of Hell fer Sartain, Cutshin, Frying Pan, Kingdom Come, Troublesome, Lonesome.

Poor Country

A common butt of ridicule is "poor country", whose lack of fertility and productiveness has given rise to almost as many jests as rich land has to brags.[75] In the East, especially the South-east, "poor country" is apt to be exhausted or impoverished land, eroded and inefficiently farmed.

The typical "poor country" of the West is dry country. In the geography books of the last century the Great American Desert extended as far east as the Mississippi Valley, but as more and more of the land was put under cultivation or grazing, the desert was pushed farther and farther west. Recently, as a result of overgrazing and plowing under of the grassland, the desert—this time man-made—has moved east again, in what, since the dust storms of May, 1933, has become known as the Dust Bowl.

At their best, however, the Great Plains are semi-arid or sub-humid. The formula has thus been stated by Walter Prescott Webb: "east of the Mississippi civilization stood on three legs—land, water, and timber; west of the Mississippi not one but two of these legs were withdrawn—water and timber—and civilization was left on one leg—land."[76]

In this land where "You can see farther and see less than anywhere else on earth" and "Between Amarillo and the North Pole there is nothing to stop the wind but a barbed wire fence", many a jest and saying speak of too much wind and too little water.

Although applicable to and diffused over the entire Plains area, "dry country" jests become attached to individual states. Thus the genial "hymn of hate" describing the "hell" of the arid South-west is known variously as "Hell in Texas", "The Birth of New Mexico", and "Arizona".[77] Similarly, "Dakota Land", "Kansas Land", and "Nebraska Land" (cited above) are essentially the same song about another "land of little rain". In other cases a song, in spite of many parallels, is more or less definitely associated with a single state.

"—Who Would Sooner be Funny than Accurate"

According to the author of *The Truth about Arkansas* (1895), "Probably about no other State are there so many misconceptions and so many inaccurate ideas as about Arkansas. . . . For this we may credit the class of writers who would sooner be funny than accurate. The chronicler of the wanderings of that noted personage, 'The Arkansas Traveller', for example, may be said to have cost the State millions of dollars. . . . In spite of all that the State has suffered at the hands of traducers and thoughtless writers, it is undergoing a wonderful development."[78]

As a form of criticism or propaganda, local satire may be a power for good as well as for evil. Beyond its uses for mere entertainment, in the hands of journalists and politicians the humorous treatment of localities has had a serious purpose. Proceeding on the theory that "every knock's a boost", Dick Wick Hall (1877–1926), of Salome (rhymes with "home"), Arizona (population, 100), put the town and himself on the map by playing the rôle of Salome's "best friend and severest critic". Homesteading, ranching, and mining had given him an intimate knowledge of the region. As postmaster, garage owner, and editor and publisher of a one-man, single-sheet mimeographed newspaper, the Salome *Sun* (issued monthly beginning in January, 1921), he combined civic responsibility and business with literature. His puns, whoppers, and wisecracks, often in rhymed prose, are in the "Bingville Bugle" tradition of the comic country newspaper. His frog who had never learned to swim is straight out of American folklore. And his small town stuff—overtly good fun and covertly agitation for improved roads—sums up a whole phase of American life and humour, best described by the sign on his "Laughing Gas" filling station: "Smile—You Don't Have to Stay Here but We Do."[79]

The classic of American humorous folklore is *The Arkansas Traveller* (1840). Local in origin and allusion, it belongs to the older and larger tradition of the saucy, riddling dialogue, or cross questions and crooked answers, between a traveller and a crotchety innkeeper.[80] The wit and humour of the dialogue are largely elementary—a mixture of puns, paradoxes, insults, involving misunderstanding, the matching of wits, the naïveté of the rustic, the discomfiture of the stranger, and the solecisms of dialect. In style it is characterized by the humour of understatement, more typically identified with Yankee laconic wit or "reluctant eloquence", as opposed to the "expansive eloquence" of the backwoods.[81] Here the grudging response of the Squatter is associated with the stubborn cantankerousness of the native, due in part to suspicion and dislike of strangers (which in the Crockett almanacs inspired pugilistic encounters, including those of the purely verbal order) and in part to the low standard of living of the "unfit of the frontier", with its shiftless wantlessness and attendant ills of malaria, hookworm, and pellagra. Certainly the piece, for all its broadness, is far from a caricature; and the spoofing of the well-groomed Traveller on his milk-white horse (as pictured in the famous painting of the same name by Edward Payson Washbourne, 1858) derives an added social interest and significance from its realism as well as an extra satirical fillip from the outwitting of the socially superior by the socially inferior.

The Arkansas Traveller has other backwoods connotations. In the love of music that unites the Traveller and the Squatter when the former supplies the "Turn of the Tune" (also pictured by Washbourne in the companion painting of that name) is reflected the popularity of the fiddle as a socializing agent, following the frontier. Again, the character of the Squatter may be a reflection of the dislike and contempt which the yeomanry has felt for the "poor white", as signified in such derogatory nicknames as poor white trash, no 'count, po' buckra, peckerwood, mean whites, low downers, sand-hillers, pineywoods tackles, hill-billies, dirt-eaters, clay-eaters.[82] Something, too, of the conservative's distrust of the pioneer and "coonskin" democracy enters into the treatment of backwoods hospitality, which is here taken off as somewhat less spontaneous and generous than usually represented in backwoods sketches and travel accounts.

The dialogue is not only a piece of folk humour; it is also a popular entertainment. Essentially a folk drama, it is known to have been acted out by wagoners in at least one tavern bar-room, at Salem, Ohio,[83] and has inspired a play, *Kit, the Arkansas Traveller*, besides being used in plays like Paul Green's *Saturday Night*, for folklore colour. As a recitation, with or without music, it has circulated in songbooks and jokebooks, to many of which it has given its name.[84] The tune itself (first printed in 1847)[85] rivals *Turkey in the Straw* (*Zip Coon*) as the liveliest and most popular of American fiddle tunes.

Apart from its local colour interest, *The Arkansas Traveller* remains one of the most American of folklore themes, in both its symbolism— that of the backwoods, defined as a "state of society where rusticity reigns supreme"—and its form—that of a question-and-answer "frame" dialogue which has attracted to itself a number of typically rural jokes.

No less vigorous, if more scurrilous, is that other Arkansas classic, *Change the Name of Arkansas? Hell, No!*, a mythical speech which takes off the fulminating rhetoric of backwoods legislators. Though the unprintable version smacks more of the smoking car than of the halls of state, it represents the less seemly side of tall talk, which in another version has been cleaned up with the aid of passages lifted from the raftsman talk in Mark Twain's *Life on the Mississippi*.

In the rôle of inquiring traveller American humorists have developed a type of humorous travelogue, which has been made popular by jokebooks and has served as a vehicle for monologists and lectures. Its origin may be traced, on the one hand, to serious and imaginary travel literature and, on the other, to the humorous travel or local colour sketch of the almanac variety. It has developed mainly in two directions: the comic account of "'scapes and scrapes" and the satiric commentary on local manners. Various "literary comedians"—William Tappan Thompson ("Major Jones"), Bill Nye, Artemus Ward, and Mark Twain—have worked this vein of local humour in one form or another.

On the popular or quasi-folk level it is almost pure vaudeville—rapid-fire, sure-fire stuff, interspersing wisecracks with gags and puns. Thomas W. Jackson's *On the Slow Train through Arkansaw* (1903)[86] has had many imitators, including a dozen or so jokebooks on the same pattern by Jackson himself. On a more sophisticated level it has produced the "hick-baiting" and "Babbitt-baiting" "Americana" of the *American Mercury* type. The inquiring traveller, with his gibes at local fads, freaks, and follies, is one of the many incarnations of the "cracker-box philosopher", providing material for a comic social history of the U.S.A.

Part Two

TALL TALK

STRONG LANGUAGE

I. Fanciful, Facetious, and Factitious Intensifying Words

(From the Specimens in Part One)

absquatulate, v. (cf. *abscond* and *squat*), to depart, run away

anngelliferous, a. angelic

bodaciously bodyaciously, adv. (cf. *bold* and *audacious*; or, possibly "an absurd exaggeration of bodily") wholly, completely (Southern dialect; "bodaciously tired", "bodaciously ruint")

boliterated, p. p. see exfluncted

exfluncted, exfluncticated, exflunctificated, explunctified, explunctificated, p. p. (cf. *flunkt, flunked*, overcome, outdone) exhausted, crushed, demolished, beaten thoroughly

obflisticated, obflusticated, obfusticated, p. p. obfuscated, bewildered, confused, put out of the way

ramsquaddled, rumsquaddled, p. p. see *exfluncted*

ring-tailed roarer or *squealer*, n. a stentorian braggart (Thornton)

ripstaver, n. a first-rate person or thing (Thornton); a dashing fellow (Bartlett)

screamer, n. a bouncing fellow or girl (Bartlett)

slantindicular, adv. in a slanting direction

tarnal, tarnacious, a. eternal, a Yankee form of swearing (Thornton)

tetotal, teetotal, a. total

tetotaciously, teetotaciously, adv. totally

wolfish, wolfy, a. savage

II. Figurative Expressions

I[87]

Shut pan, and sing dumb, or I'll throw you into the drink.

Hold your tongue, you beauty, or you shall smell brimstone through a nail hole.

I wish I may run on a sawyer if I didn't.

I'll be choked with a saw-log if I do.

See if I don't row you up Salt River before you are many days older.

I wouldn't risk a huckleberry to a persimmon that we don't every soul get treed and sink to the bottom like gone suckers.

Drive him like a flash of lightning through a gooseberry-bush.

A mighty grist of rain.

I'll be shot.

Prayed like a horse.

He had turned the edge of a razor in attempting to cut through a fog.

I'll wool lightning out of you if you interrupt me.

He'll find I'm from the forks of Roaring River, and a bit of a screamer.

I told him I knew him as well as a squirrel knows a hickory-nut from an acorn.

I told him stories that were enough to set the Mississippi afire.

You do take the rag off the bush.

Poking his nose everywhere like a dog smelling out a trail.

You don't know a B from a Buffalo's foot.

II[88]

Hang me up for bar-meat, ef I don't push off without them.

Bile me fur a sea-horse, ef I wouldn't rather crawl into a nest o' wild-cats, heels foremost, than be cotched alone with you in the night-time.

Quicker nor a alligator can chew a puppy.

Choked to death like a catfish on a sandbank.

Dumb as a dead nigger in a mud-hole.

Harder nor climbin' a peeled saplin', heels uppard.

Travel like a nigger in a thunder-storm.

ANIMAL COMPARISONS

I'm a hoss what never war rode.[89]

I can walk like an ox, run like a fox, swim like an eel . . . make love like a mad bull.[90]

I'm shaggy as a bear, wolfish about the head, active as a cougar, and can grin like a hyena, until the bark will curl off a gum log.

There's a sprinkling of all sorts in me, from the lion down to the skunk; and before the war is over, you will pronounce me an entire zoological institute, or I miss a figure in my calculation.[91]

A man that comes to settle in these parts must be wide awake, and rip and tear away like a horse in a canebrake.

A man must begin with the eggshell on him, as the partridge learns to run, and get up before daylight many a year in and year out, before he can get to be worth much—I mean in the way of living in these parts.[92]

Ar'n't I the leaping trout of the waters?[93]

One said, "I am a man; I am a horse; I am a team. I can whip any man *in all Kentucky*, by G-d."

The other replied, "I am an alligator; half man, half horse; can whip any *on the Mississippi*, by G-d."

The first one again, "I am a man; have the best horse, best dog, best gun, and handsomest wife in all Kentucky, by G-d."

The other, "I am a Mississippi snapping turtle: have bear's claws, alligator's teeth, and the devil's tail; can whip *any man*, by G-d."[94]

—AND NOTHING BUT THE CONTINENT[95]

"MR. SPEAKER: When I take my eyes and throw them over the vast expanse of this expansive country: when I see how the yeast of freedom has caused it to rise in the scale of civilization and extension on every side; when I see it growing, swelling, roaring, like a spring-freshet—when I see all *this*, I cannot resist the idea, Sir, that the day will come when this great nation, like a young schoolboy, will burst its straps, and become entirely too big for its boots!

"Sir, we want *elbow-room*—the continent—the *whole* continent—and nothing but the continent! And we will *have* it! Then shall Uncle Sam, placing his hat upon the Canadas, rest his right arm on the Oregon and California coast, his left on the eastern sea-board, and whittle away the British power, while reposing his leg, like a freeman, upon Cape Horn! Sir, the day *will*—the day *must* come!"

THE PROUDEST BIRD UPON THE MOUNTAIN[96]

. . . Our country is yet but in the infancy of its being, not yet three centuries old. And our settlements are but specks dotted round upon the edge of the map of the continent. The great heart of America, with treasures as precious as the lifestrings, is as yet unexplored, and almost unknown.

This bill, enacted into a law, shall give civilization and life throughout the silent gorges and gentle sleeping valleys, far away into the deep recesses of the continent. Where it leads the way, there shall go in triumph the American standard, the old flag of the Union. And when once thus planted, it shall never again be trailed in the dust. The proudest bird upon the mountain is upon the American ensign, and not one feather shall fall from her plumage here. She is American in design, and an emblem of wildness and freedom. I say, again, she has not perched herself upon American standards to die here. Our great Western valleys were never scooped out for her burial place. Nor were the everlasting untrodden mountains piled for her monument. Niagara shall not pour her endless waters for her requiem; nor shall our ten thousand rivers weep to the ocean in eternal tears. No, sir; no. Unnumbered voices shall come up from the river, plain and mountain, echoing the songs of our triumphant deliverance, while lights from a thousand hilltops will betoken the rising of the sun of freedom, that shall grow brighter and brighter until a perfect day.

NUECES RIVER VALLEY PARADISE[97]

. . . Located on that middle plain between East Texas, where it rains too much, and the arid section or West Texas, where it does not rain enough; . . .

Where the constant sea breeze makes cool summers and warm winters without snow or hard freezes;

Where there are no blizzards, nor tornadoes, nor earthquakes, nor cyclones;

Where the flowers bloom ten months in the year;

Where the greatest variety of products can be grown;

Where the farmers and gardeners, whose seasons never end, eat home-grown June vegetables in January, and bask in midwinter's balmy air and glorious sunshine;

Where the land yield is enormous, and the prices always remunerative;

Where something can be planted and harvested every month in the year;

Where the climate is so mild that the Northern farmer here saves practically all his fuel bills and three-fourths the cost of clothing his family in the North;

Where the country is advancing and property values rapidly increasing;

Where all stock, without any feed, fatten, winter and summer, on the native grasses and brush which equal any feed pen;

Where the same land yields the substantials of the temperate and the luxuries of the tropic zones;

Where the farmer does not have to work hard six months in the year to raise feed to keep his stock from dying during winter, as they do in the North and North-west;

Where the winter does not consume what the summer produces, and there are markets for all produced;

Where two full crops of the same kind, three vegetable crops, or four mixed crops, can be raised from the same land in one year;

Where vegetation is so rapid that in two years the home is surrounded by trees and shrubs which would require five years to develop in a colder climate;

Where there are no aristocrats and people do not have to work hard to have plenty and go in the best society;

Where ten acres, judiciously planted in fruits, will soon make one independent, all varieties being wonderfully successful and profitable;

Where the natives work less and have more to show for what they do than in any country on earth;

Where houses, barns and fences can be built for less than half the cost in the North;

Where the average temperature is about 60 degrees, varying from 50 in winter, to 90 in summer, which is rendered cool by constant sea breezes;

Where the average rainfall for the past five years is over 39 inches, and well distributed, as shown by the government's report, which is more than some of the older States have;

Where sun-strokes and heat-prostrations are unknown;

Where the residents have charming homes surrounded by trees and flowers of a semi-tropical climate;

Where sufferers with Asthma, Bronchitis, Catarrh, Hay-Fever and Throat troubles find relief;

Where one can work out of doors in shirt sleeves, without inconvenience, 29 out of every 30 days of the year around;

Where, surrounded by fruits and vegetables, which ripen every month in the year, the living is better and less expensive than in the North;

Where the water is pure, soft and plentiful;

Where the laws protect both the investor and the settler;

Where the people are so law abiding that usually only two days of District Court every six months are required to dispose of all the Civil and Criminal business;

Where the taxes are so low that the amount is never missed;

Where Public and Private schools and Churches of all denominations are plentiful;

Where peace, plenty and good will prevail to such an extent that the people sleep with their doors and windows open the year around, without danger of molestation;

Where it is so healthy that people rarely die, except from accident or old age; . . .

GOING TO GOD'S COUNTRY[98]

We were going to God's Country. Eighteen hunderd and go. With a husle and busle to get things ready. With five litel childern and the oldest only 10 years old. And geting food and clothing for a long journey. We could do that job very well for we did not realise what we were geting into. We had some cousens that had gone 2 years before to the Indian Territory way down on what was called the Fleet Wood Farms in the Chicksaw Nation. Its part of Oklahoma now. And that was where we were going. (P. 11.)

It was prety hard to part with some of our things. We didn't have much but we had worked hard for everything we had. You had to work hard in that rocky country in Missouri. I was glad to be leaving it. We were going to God's Country. (Pp. 12–13.)

Toughf Missouri

Old Missouri was after all a prety toughf place. I hated to leave it though for it was all I knew. But we were going to God's Country. We were going to a new land and get rich. Then we could have a real home of our own. But we didn't know what was ahead of us. (P. 41.)

We All Drive In

We were all tired from the long wearysome trip. And it seemed that
every river we crossed was up. Our first was Sock, the next bad river
was the Arkansaw and the next was the Cimarron. And then the North
Canadian and the South Canadian and hundreds of others it seemed.
We went through part of Missouri, Kansas, Osage Nation, Pawnee
Nation, Old Oklahoma proper, Chicksaw Nation and then we landed
on the Fleet Wood Farms. It was the Red River just across from
Texas. So there we were at our cousens. And was we ever so hapy.
We all drove in his lot with the seven coverd wagons. And so tired
from thirty three days drive. But at last we were in God's Country.
(Pp. 56–57.)

We Sleep with Centipeads

The dug out was so full of centipeads that we had to sleep with a
bucher knife under our pillows so we could have something to protect
our selfs.

Sleeping with the bucher knives under our pillows at night to kill
the centipeads in our half dug out was exciting. The dug out was made
of logs with mud in between so when we would put the lights out at
night the centipeads would go runing in the cracks. Then we would
whak them to pieces. Some nights we would kill as many as twenty.
Next morning first thing was to move the beds and sweep the dead
ones out. But that was pioneering in God's Country. (Pp. 59–60.)

We Count Blessings

We thought that it was indeed God's Country. We had worked hard
for eleven years in Missouri and left there with eight hunderd dolars
and our teams and wagons. And after we paid for picking and gining
and all expenses we had eight hundred and twenty dolars left. And
besides we had our corn and our garden truck.

And our garden was the best garden that we ever had. It seemed
like every seed came up. And how the garden did grow. We had
onions, tomatose, cabages, peas, beans, potatose, pepers, letuce, pars-
nips, musk melons, water melons and every thing in that line. People
came from all around to see that garden. So when fall came we went
to Henrietta for groceries. But this time it was for barels. I made one
barel of catchup and a barel of soar crout

But many things hapend while we were living on the small lease. Many hardships along with the pioneering. But we tried to overlook all for everything was so difernt and new to us with heaps of excitement. And besides we were in God's Country. (Pp. 70–71.)

SOWING WHEAT

We picked coton most all fall but when October came it was geting time for wheat sowing. Then there was a wheat drill to buy and that was eighty five more dolars of the coton money gone. So that was that. It seemed like we never looked ahead untell we had to have some implements to work with. Then it was another long trip to the rail road. But that was done with good grace. We were in God's Country.

But at least we had a drill to sow the wheat. Back in Missouri we would sow by hand. You would put about a peck of wheat in a sack and swing it across your shoulder. Then you would take out a hand full and sling it around. You could just sow about ten feet at once. You would have to walk around the field till you got it all done. Then harrow the ground to cover the wheat. The harrow was made by tying some brush together with a chain and fastening the brush to a double tree. Then two singel trees were fastened to the double tree and horses fastened to them. That was the way it was done for a good many years. But in God's Country we had a drill to sow the wheat. (Pp. 83–84.)

A PRARIE FIRE

In 1892 the prarie grass was most as high as our coverd wagons. One day by some means a fire got started. We never knew how but any way it was exciting. You could see the blaze leap. It looked like it was fifty feet in the air. We had burned a very small patch around our house. Perhaps one half an acer. We had just built us a shed for our teams and a chicken house for a cow corell. Our horses were all tied in the shed and the fire was coming so fast that we could not tell whether we would have time to get them out or what to do. It looked like our horses and our milk cows and our family too would go up in the flames. We did manage to get the teams and harness out of the shed and close to the house. But the fire was getting very close. Just about half mile away I should judge.

We were so frightent. The litel childern crying and screaming and the horses snorting and I was praying and working too. We had a well that we had dug in front of the house. We had to draw the water by hand with a bucket and I was drawing water so as we might try to save our house and childern. The fire was geting prety close and we could see jack rabits, prarie dogs, prarie chickens, cyotes, all kinds of birds and antilopes, runing in front of the fire. While we were watching the animels and birds I had every available thing full of water that I had drawn from the well. We could hear the fire roaring and see the flames leaping. We were all covered with the burning grass. We put the six litel childern all in the house and fastened the door and the one window.

While we were standing in front of the hut watching the fire I just hapend to turn my head to get some of the burned grass out of my eyes and I thought that I could see some moving objects coming from the north. I wiped my eyes again and looked. Then I said to my husband, "Look, there is something coming from the north." He wiped his eyes and looked. It looked like a herd of stampeded cattle. And if it was that, we were goners for they were coming toward us. We watched for a moment but it was smokey and so much burned grass flying in the air, for the fire was coming from the south west and was blowing very hard, we couldn't see. All that we could do was to stand there and wait.

There we were, we thought, between two fires. We could plainly see the fire coming from the south west and my husband said if it was a stampeded herd of catle that we were in for something. I ask him if we hadnt better go in the house with the children and he said that I might but that he would watch. But I never did go in, for just about that time I wiped my eyes again and I could see that it wasnt catle. But we couldn't make out just what it was. It looked like men the best we could see through all that smoke. We just stood and looked and I told my husband perhaps it was Indians on the war path. He said it might be but he did not think so. But I do believe he thought it was Indians for he turned white. So white that I could see he was scerd. And so was I. The fire coming one way and the Indians or stampeded catle the other.

We just stood there most petrified for a few seconds and then I could see that it was men. But what kind of men. Cow boys or Indians? But all at once one man whiped ahead of the rest and then I felt like it was cow boys. And shure enoughf he just came chargen up. I felt some relief but I was shakin so I could hardly stand on my feet and so was my husband. The six litel childern in the house got over being scerd and were just playing. When we opened the door they looked so surprised to see so many cow boys. They never said a word but just looked so amazed.

Cow Boys Save The Day

Then the boys said that Roof Benton had sent them for he could see the fire and thought we might be in danger and some of his catle might too. All the water I had drawd out of the well was used for when the cow boys got there they got off their horses, droped their briedl reins, went to the shed, gathered up all the old feed sacks and two of them picked up the water and walked out to the edge of the high grass. Then they all wet the feed sacks and began to set the grass a fire but they did not tell us what they were going to do. We soon found out. They were back firing.

Back Firing Works

They burned all along past the shed and then let it burn quite a ways. But they would whip it out with the wet sacks. So when the fire got to the burned grass it would stop. They had a very hard time of it because the wind was so strong and they were burning against the wind.

They worked most all that night and when they began it was about three o'clock in the afternoon. About six o'clock my husband said that we would give them something to eat. I tried to get them something nice to eat but it was a hard job for most every thing we had in the house was black with burned grass. But anyway I made some buisquit and some coffe. They ate and drank the coffe but they told my husband that they would stay untell we was out of danger. Later we made some more coffe and some more buisquit and by that time I had goten some of the burnt grass washed off of the things so we could cook some food.

When my husband took the food to them the second time they told him for us to go to bed and rest for we had gone through some exsperence. And they was right too for we had. I washed the litel folks the best that I could and put them to bed. Of course they thought it funny to have the burnt black grass all over them and their rag dolls.

Finly we did try to sleep but I did not sleep very much and was up early next morning. I wanted to see how things looked. It all looked black. The cow boys were gone and the fire was all out. But every thing did look so queer. We looked around, fed the litel folks and went to work to clean our house. Every thing was so black we had to wash all our beding and every thing that we had. And wash the house outside and inside. We worked all day. Then the childerns heads and my own head was to wash. It was a long time before I could get the black off of things.

Is This God's Country or Not?

In just a few days we noticed the buzards sailing over where the fire had burned. So we hitched a team to the wagon and piled the childern in and drove over the prarie. Was we surprised to see the dead rabits, snakes and all kinds of birds. And when the wind blew from the south west we could smell some thing that smelled like burned hair.

Well it wasnt very long untell it came a big rain and that helps to wash the black off things and prety soon the grass came up so green and every thing did look so beautifull and before long it was covered with cattle.

After several days of hard work I got every one cleaned up and the house cleaned too. While I was doing that, H. H. went to the rail road and brought some fence posts and the hired man back with him. The hired man had gone to visit some one. He said that he was sorry that he had missed all the fun. I told him that it wasnt much fun but that he could have the fun of seting the fence posts back where the fire had burned them out. They went to work but it took several days. We finly got every thing in shape again. But I never looked over the prarie that way but what I could imagin that I could see smoke. It took me a long time to forget it. In fact I never did and it makes my flesh creep today when I think about that terable fire and smoke. I said to myself, "Is this God's Country or not?" I didn't talk about it to my husband but just kept saying, "go on for every thing will be O. K." But some times I all most gave up. Then something kept saying. "It must be God's Country. Go on." (Pp. 90–96.)

Rock Botem

As time went on every thing went to rock botem. Wheat, corn, coton, hogs, catle and every thing.

One of the men that was in the drunken spree was wanting to go back to Texas. He had raised quite a lot of corn and fed a bunch of hogs and they were very nice. But he could not sell them on the market for there wasnt any market. So he came to our place and wanted us to buy them. We told him that we could not handle them for the weather was too warm to butcher. He just stayed and stayed and talked and cussed the country and finly he said that if we would buy them that we could have them for a dolar a head. We didn't know what to do but we finly said that we would take them if he would bring them over. He said that he had his wagon in the shop for he was geting ready to leave the damned country. "Well", I told him, "This is God's Country". "But", he said, "It's a hell of a country." He was one of those good Methodists, but he did get drunk and got in jail. Foster was his name. Any way we felt sory for him, so we told him that we would take the hogs and we would come that evening when it got cool to get them.

We got a top on the wagon and went to get the hogs. They were nice young hogs and very fat. He put his dog in the pen to help catch them. One of the hogs got too hot and keeled over so H. H. just cut his throat. One of the hogs dead out of the whole batch wasn't so bad. We got the rest loaded and put the dead one on top of the planks that we had to keep the hogs from jumping out. We gave Foster eight dolars and went home.

We heated some water and cleaned the dead one and put the others in the pen. We worked most all night before we got our work done, and the next day I worked all day frying the meat down in big stone jars. It was lovly meat too. The Texas man was ready to go back to Texas. We never did see him again but hope he got back to his good old Texas.

Things just was on the bed rock but we staid and fought it out and came out all right in the end. But it was a toughf go. We raised thirty five bales of coton that year and sold three bales early and had the rest jined and hauled home. We piled it in the yard untell the next spring and then we sold it for three and a half cents a pound. It did not even pay for the picking. But we were in God's Country. Or so they said. (Pp. 101–102.)

A Sand Storm

The very day that the school was out we had the worst sand storm. It came up about two o'clock in the afternoon. It was so bad that we could not see fifty yards. We went in the house and closed all the doors and windows. But that did not make any diference. The house was just made of boxing lumber. And the sand came through the cracks. Every thing was coverd. We just had to sit and take it. We could not cook nor do any thing but try to keep from choking to death. There was two hired men at that time and my brother and nine of our own family so there we all sat and the sand poring in. No super. We could not cook nor even get out to milk our cows. It lasted eighteen hours. We had to just sit.

Besids the sand blowing it was an electric storm. Every thing was so full of electricity that we would not tuch any thing. If you tuched any thing the fire would fly like you had struck a match. The sun was shining but the air was full of electricity. Abe Gunn, a hired man, came in from the field, threw his lines on the fence and the electricity flew down the fence. The children would get drinks of water so they could slide the tin cup over the stove to see the sparks fly. And the electricity killed streaks of wheat and oats. Some places in the fields for fifty feet looked like the fire had run over it and that was dead. It never did grow any more and there was streaks all over the whole country. We estimated about one fifth of our crop was killed. We sure wondered if that was God's Country.

Well the next morning, first thing was to dig out the sand from the house. We moved every thing outside, swept out the best we could and then we tried to cook some breakfast. But every thing was so grity we could hardly eat. Most all our groceries were ruined. So was every ones else for the sand storm was all over the country where the land was plowed. The house was cleaned the best we could, the cows milked, and breakfast over. Every one went to work.

Was we ever blue and home sick. But our cousen, Joe Parker, came over to cheer us up. He said that it was the worst storm that he ever saw. I laughft and said that I thought so, for it was God's Country. He did not like it. He said that he was sory for me for I had worked so hard and had been such a good sport about every thing but he thought every thing would be allright.

Then in a few days we had a good rain. Things began to look pretty good. We felt beter. But we did not have a very good crop. Wheat was short and corn not very good, coton pretty fair. But the price of coton was down. It looked like we were going back from where we started from in 91. One thing, we had our big lease for four more crops so we tried to console our selfs and look ahead for beter times. (Pp. 112–114.)

Had God Forsaken Us?

It was July 1895. I comenced to wonder if God had forsaken this country. Crops was bad. And most all our money gone. And all those teams to feed. The corn all burned. Five hunderd acers of wheat and not one grain cut. It was all too short. Just a very few oats cut. The coton was about a foot high, then the jack rabits cleaned it up. We had about fifty acers of cotton but it did not last long when the jack rabits took to it. And it looked like the grass was going to dry up too. No gardens. No feed for our hogs. No feed for the childern. But our credit was good so we still bought goods.

The Post Office was still going. Not much pay for we just got what we canceled. That wasnt very much for every body was too poor to buy stamps. Then we had a big rain that pepped things up. We would make some hay and have some feed and the grass would green up so our cows. could give some milk.

We plowed some ground and went to town and bought a bushul of black eyed peas and planted them. We planted a new garden of most every thing. Our neighbors laughft at us. But when fall came they did not laughf. So did H. H. laughf when I told him that I was going to plant a garden. I said, "Why not for we are in God's Country." So he didn't say any more.

He helped me plant the garden and we had a nice garden and lots of black eyed peas. I sold some of them peas.

Every body in the neighborhood, what did not leave the country, went to plowing. Turning under their wheat land and the wheat that did not make any thing. A lot of people left. Some left in the night and took all their belongings and some things that did not belong to them. They had bought plows and other implements and my husband had gone on their notes. So that left us to pay for their things. And nothing to pay with.

We went to Ryan and told the merchants what had hapened. So they said, "Well H. H. you go and put in your crop. We will carry you over and let you have money to buy your seed." They bought a car load of seed wheat and a car load of oats for seed and the merchants let every body have seed. But most of them had to give a morgage on their teams and impliments. They said that they would trust us. I felt like we were favord. And we was too. (Pp. 123–124.)

PERHAPS THE CHEYENNE ARAPAHO WAS GOD'S COUNTRY

We were still working on, but all the time wishing that we could really have a home. We were not afraid of work but it seemed that just when you thought you had something it would burn up or it would rain so much that everything would be ruined. The childern were growing up and we knew that we must get a home.

So we went up to the town of Geary. We looked around and saw some nice places for sail. We made a deal for one claim and that would be one hunderd and sixty acers. And another claim was to be relinquished. The man relinquished and H. H. filed on the eighty acers.

We paid the man three hunderd dolars for his claim. I had the money in gold. We had sold part of our catle for twenty dolars a head and I had made a litel sack and fasened it to my under skirt band. When I gave him the three hunderd dolars in gold the mans eyes got as big as a hen egg. He was so sceard that he jumped on his horse and started to El Reno. We told him that it was thirty miles and the bank would be closed. But he said that if he couldn't get to the bank he would hide out untell morning. If people knew that he had that much money he would be robed before morning.

We put up the money for the other farm in the bank at El Reno. We had to write to Washington and prove up on it, so that took quite a while. We got what is called a paton from the government. That hunderd and sixty acers cost us about seven hunderd dolars and the other eighty, three hunderd.

It was a beautiful land in the valey on the south side of the North Canadian River. We had about made up our minds that the Chicksaw Nation wasnt God's Country. But we had hopes of finding it in this new territory. So we started back home. Or what we caled home. It was our seven year home and five of that was lived out.

We thought we would stay one more year and then sell our box houses. We had kept building one most every year as the family would grow till we had five litel box houses, the store and Post Office combined, the litel black smith shop and the chicken houses. Those we could move if we wished to. All we had to leave was the four wire fence.

We had sold all of our milch cows to get money to buy the two farms. So I told my husband that something would have to be done. I couldn't go out and round up one like I did in the ninetys. He laughft and said, "Wasnt them good old days." I told him that he might think so but I didn't. Then he joked me and said that when I was a young girl that I had debated the question that "Persuit is beter than possession". "Yes", I told him and that I still believed that persuit was the beter. That I was still in persuit of the home we had talked about. That I did not believe that I could have fought the snakes, centipeeds, cyotes, and all the rest of the varments and live like we did if I all ready had a home. And I was still thinking that persuit was beter than posession. He laughft and said, "You are a queer old woman but one that will stay with it." But anyway we knew that we had to do something about some milch cows. (Pp. 146–148.)

Looking Ahead

This new God's Country was much farther north and we would camp out while we were building. One thing was that we had a lumber yard in Geary, the place where we were going, and it wouldn't be so far to hall lumber. Our new place was just four miles from Geary. We had been going so much farther four miles would seem just like play.

We sold our building to Charley Willis, the man that had worked for us for four years. He bought all of our improvements and was going to run the farm.

When it came time for us to move I felt like I wanted to stay for we had had lots of excitement and lots of fun, lots of hardships too and lots of hard work. But it was all over now. We did like pioneering very much for you would get something out of it.

We had not found God's Country but we were sure we would find it in our new home in the Cheyenne Country. So again we were on our way. We were going to God's Country. (Pp. 155–156.)

The Wind and Plaster

We were going to build a two story house but every one said that was too high. So we just built one story and a half. We wanted to plaster. "No", the people said, "The wind will shake the plaster all off." So we just sealed and papered. But that was all a mistake. The people did not know what they were talking about for we have built two story houses and plastered too. But later. So I think it does not pay to take every ones advice. Just do like you want to. But anyway we built. And it was the show house of the whole country. You could see it for miles. At last we were in God's Country. (Pp. 159–160.)

We Sell Again

We stayed about four years and then one day a man came to our place looking for a home. Ours being the best improved and the best looking farm, he wanted to know what we would take for the place. "Well" I said, "I wont sell for I am tired of moving." Then H. H. said that he would sell if he could get his price and that was sixty five hundred. The man said that he would take it if we would wait for part of the money. We said what we guessed we could. So we sold.(Pp. 163–164.)

Another House, Another Baby

Then it was to look out for some place to live. We had to give posession in May so we moved in a small house again and looked for another place. On August the twenty fourth, 1901, while we were still living in the litel house, we had another baby. We called her Daisy Lincoln.

H. H. was still looking for a beter place to live. There was much talk of the Caddo Country coming in for setlement. That was a good place to setle if you got the right farms. Some places were bad. So H. H. went to El Reno to regester. When you regestered you would get the numbers in a sealed envelope. Then you would have to go and locate your land. He regestered but he never drew. (Pp. 164–165.)

A Big Place

We finly bought a lovly place just south of our old place. . . . It was a new place and a beautiful place. But again it was too small so we had to build on a big kitchen twenty feet long and eighteen feet wide. And a big back porch. It was a lovly place with all kinds of fruits and berys. Apricots, all kind of buded fruit, and all kind of ornimentel trees. So we could work very haply with such a lovly home. And we thought that we would be there for life. We were sure that we had landed in God's Country. Or almost sure. (Pp. 165–166.)

Another Baby

In 1904 there was another baby girl, Lily, on hand. This was our twelfth child. She was born in November so work was slacked up for some time. (P. 170.)

We Buy Some Texas Land

We heard of good land that was selling around Vernon, Texas, so we desided that we would go to Texas and see. We thought that we were in God's Country now and might take a chance on something. We went to Geary and took the train to Texas. Of course we were met by a lot of real estate men. They drove us all over the country. . . . But anyway we bought seven hundered and forty acers. We just paid five hunderd dolars down. . . . We had paid ten dolars per acer. And that was quite a lot of money. We let a man have the place to sow wheat but it did not make very much. So then did some of the Geary people laugh and say that we were crazy. We didn't say very much for we began to think that maby we had made a mistake.

Pay day came around and we had to pay five hunderd dolars and the interest so that was over one thousand dolars gone. And no crop. We didn't say much to our neighbors about it. Some of them felt sory and some of them were tickled. It didn't weary me for I knew that we had been in so many tight places before and had all ways come out all right and I felt that we would this time. And we did.

That fall we got a telegram from the same man that we bought from saying that we could get fifteen dolars per acer. So we talked it over and sent him a telegram saying, "Twenty dolars an acer and no less." The next day here came a telegram saying, "Sold. Deeds will folow." Was we ever hapy.

But since then that land was worth lots of money for there was big produsing oil wells all over the seven hunderd acers. So you see one never knows what to do. But we made good for we cleard four thousand dolars. We thought that was prety good and we bought another farm close to us with what we made. We thought that was the easiest money we had ever made. And only one thousand dolars invested for eight months. And then we wondered if maybe Texas wasnt God's Country. (Pp. 170–172)

We Sell Again

It was not long untell a man from Kentucky came to our place and wanted to know how much we wanted for our home place. I said that I wanted to quit moving but he kept hanging around so H. H. told him that he would take ten thousand dolars. He said, "Sold." I had to have a big cry for we had bought a lot of new furnature and we also had the other farm. But I didn't say any thing. I wonderd where we were going to go this time.

The next thing was to sell the other place just across the road. That did not take long. We just put up a sign, "For Sail", and in a few days a man from Kansas came by looking for a farm. We sold our farm that we had bought with the money we had made from the Texas deal. We paid four thousand and sold it for forty five hunderd. (Pp. 172–173.)

HUNTING AGAIN

So now we were all set for another search for God's Country. For another wild goose chase. And this time it was Oregon. My father was there and I had a sister there too and they had been writing what a wonderful country it was. They wrote that "Oregon is really God's Country". We had been in search of God's Country ever since we left Missouri so we decided we would taken another chance. We decided that it was—on to Oregon. (P. 173.)

A TREK ACROSS COUNTRY

That was nineteen and eight. And there were seven childern and H. H. and myself. Two of the boys were in college, one was about twelve, three litel girls and the baby boy, Harley. He was born in nineteen and seven, the money panic year and the year Oklahoma became a State.

It was a husel around to get off but this time we were going on the train and not in the coverd wagons. I thought it would be much beter. And of course it was. We were only five days on the train. But believe me it was some job even then with all those litel folks. It was a big trek across the country. Easy though. For it was made by train.

We landed in Salem Oregon about the midle of June. It was so difernt but it was a lovly country. Somehow I did not like it. But we thought that we would try it.

We had to have some place to live and we could not find anything to rent that was fit to live in so we began to look for something to buy. (Pp. 174–175.)

ANOTHER HOME

The real estate men hauled us all over the country. In spring wagons. Some with tops and some without. And the dust was about three inches deep on all the roads but anyway we did get to see lots of country. And it was very beautiful! with all the groves of tall fir trees and the Royal Ann cherys. Salem was noted for its cherys.

We soon found a big two story house that belonged to a widow and two girls. They wanted to sell and buy a smaller house. We bought it. And it was more furnature to buy and it took quite a lot of money. (Pp. 175–176.)

WE LOOK BACK TOWARD OKLAHOMA

It was getting fall now and we began to think of going back to our old stomping ground. We did not like it in Oregon. It was a very good place but just wasnt what we thought it would be.

I was geting discouraged hunting for God's Country. I knew there must be such a place. But where? We decided that maybe Oklahoma wasn't so bad. Any way we decided to go back. (P. 179.)

WE FIND GOD'S COUNTRY

We found just about every kind of person in every part of the country we lived. We worked, made friends, helped out where we could and usually found that others were willing to help us when we had our troubles. We were comencing to wonder if there was a certain place that was God's Country. Or if God's Country was everywhere? Or if God wasnt in the country—then in what?

H. H. and I did a lot of thinking and a litel talking. We had been living out on the farm in Woodward County for three years when H. H. had a stroke of paralysis. We moved back to Enid so we could be near good doctors. He lived for two years. Then my beloved died. We had spent 48 years together hunting for God's Country. Before he died we learned something. Something teribly important.

We learned that God's Country isnt in the country. It is in the mind. As we looked back we knew that all the time we was hunting for God's Country we had it. We worked hard. We was loyal. Honest. We was happy. For 48 years we lived together in God's Country. (Pp. 185–186.)

BEAUTIFUL AND HEALTHFUL IOWA

I[99]

Iowa is noted for the glory and beauty of its autumns. That gorgeous season denominated "Indian Summer" cannot be described, and in Iowa it is peculiarly charming. Day after day, for weeks, the sun is veiled in a hazy splendour, while the forests are tinged with the most gorgeous hues, imparting to all nature something of the enchantments of fairyland. Almost imperceptibly, these golden days merge into winter, which holds its stern reign without the disagreeable changes experienced in other climes, until spring ushers in another season of life and beauty. And so the seasons pass, year after year, in our beautiful and healthful Iowa.

II[100]

Our climate is one of the most delightful in nature. Our spring usually commences in March, and by the middle of April the prairies are green with mild, beautiful weather. In May, all the face of nature is covered with flowers and the foliage of the prairies bends before the breeze like the waves of an enchanted lake, whilst the whole atmosphere is scented with the breath of flowers. At all seasons of the year, a gentle breeze is fanning the prairies, and a day is never so sultry but that a cooling breath comes to moderate the melting temperature.

THE KINKAIDERS[101]

Air: "Maryland, My Maryland."

1   You ask what place I like the best,
     The sand hills, O the old sand hills;
     The place Kinkaiders make their home,
     And prairie chickens freely roam.

Chorus:
     In all Nebraska's wide domain
     'Tis the place we long to see again;
     The sand hills are the very best,
     She is the queen of all the rest.

2   The corn we raise is our delight,
     The melons, too, are out of sight.[102]
     Potatoes grown are extra fine
     And can't be beat in any clime.

3   The peaceful cows in pastures dream
     And furnish us with golden cream,
     So I shall keep my Kinkaid home
     And never far away shall roam.

Chorus:
     Then let us all with hearts sincere
     Thank him for what has brought us here,
     And for the homestead law he made,
     This noble Moses P. Kinkaid.[103]

A HOME ON THE RANGE[104]

Oh, give me a home where the buffalo roam,
Where the deer and the antelope play;
Where seldom is heard a discouraging word
And the skies are not cloudy all day.

Chorus:
Home, home on the range,
Where the deer and the antelope play;
Where seldom is heard a discouraging word
And the skies are not cloudy all day.

Where the air is so pure, the zephyrs so free,
The breezes so balmy and light,
That I would not exchange my home on the range
For all the cities so bright.

The red man was pressed from this part of the West,
He's likely no more to return
To the banks of Red River where seldom if ever
Their flickering campfires burn.

How often at night when the heavens are bright
With the light of the glittering stars,
Have I stood here amazed and asked as I gazed
If their glory exceeds that of ours.

Oh, I love these wild flowers in this dear land of ours;
The curlew I love to hear scream;
And I love the white rocks and the antelope flocks
That graze on the mountain-tops green.

Oh, give me a land where the bright diamond sand
Flows leisurely down the stream;
Where the graceful white swan goes gliding along
Like a maid in a heavenly dream.

Then I would not exchange my home on the range,
Where the deer and the antelope play;
Where seldom is heard a discouraging word
And the skies are not cloudy all day.

HAWLEY'S YARN[105]

. . . Emboldened by his success, Hawley proceeded to relate that there was, in that same section, an area of twenty miles where the air was so pure that people never died, unless by accident.

"Never died!" exclaimed several of his hearers in astonishment.

"No, gentlemen, it was quite possible. The rare purity of the atmosphere prevented it. When persons got too old to be useful, they would sometimes be blown away, and, once outside of the charmed circle, they were lost."

"Is that really possible ?" asked one of his hearers, in some doubt.

"A fact, upon my honour", rejoined old Hawley. "Indeed, some years ago several philanthropic gentlemen erected a museum at that place, where persons who became too old for usefulness were put into sacks, labelled, registered at the office, and hung up. If at any subsequent period their friends wished to converse with them, for a fee of fifty cents the old friend would be taken down, placed in a kettle of tepid water, and would soon be enabled to hold a conversation of half an hour, when he would be taken out, wiped off, and hung up again."

"That *seems* incredible!" remarked one of the listeners.

"Of course it does," replied Hawley. "It is nevertheless true. Why, gentlemen," he continued, "on one occasion I went to the museum, and asked if they had a subject there named Samuel Hawley. I had an uncle by that name who went to the Rocky Mountains thirty years before, and we had not heard from him in a long time. The clerk, having examined the register, replied that Samuel Hawley was in Sack No. 367, and had been there nineteen years. I paid the fee and called for an interview. The contents of that particular sack were placed in the warm water, and in a short time I proceeded to inform my old uncle who I was. He seemed pleased to see me, although I was a child when he left our part of the country. He inquired about my father and other friends. His voice was very weak, and after a conversation of twenty minutes, he said his breath was failing him, and if I had nothing more to say he would like to be hung up again. I remarked that I believed he formerly owned a large gun, and asked him where it was. He informed me that it was lying on the cross-beam in my father's garret, and that I was welcome to it. I thanked him, and bidding him good-bye, the keeper of the museum took him in hand, and soon placed him in his proper locality. If any of you should ever go that way, gentlemen, I hope you will call on my uncle and present him my compliments. Remember his number is 367."

THE FIRST CALIFORNIA BOOSTER STORY[106]

The wear and tear of this covered-wagon life on the plains discourages many, although (who can doubt it?) we are journeying to a land unexcelled in all the world—even if there isn't a single nugget of gold within its boundary lines! This is illustrated by the yarn of a man who had lived in California, until he had reached the interesting age of 250 years. In most countries a man that old would be pretty feeble and decrepit, but not in California—Oh no! In fact such were the exhilarating, life-giving, and youth-preserving qualities of that climate that our hero at 250 was in the perfect enjoyment of his health and every faculty of mind and body. But he had become tired of life. The perpetual responsibility of managing a large fortune made him long for a new state of existence, unencumbered with this world's cares, passions, and strifes. Yet, notwithstanding his desire—for which he daily and hourly prayed to his maker—health and vigour typical of residents of California clung persistently to him. He could not shake them off. At times he contemplated suicide; but the holy padres (to whom he confessed his thoughts) admonished him that that was damnation; being a devout Christian, he would not disobey their injunction. A lay friend, however, no doubt the heir to his estate, with whom he daily consulted on this subject, at last advised him to a course which, he thought, would produce the desired result. It was to make his will and then travel into a foreign country. This suggestion was pleasing to our California patriarch in search of death, and he immediately adopted it. He visited a foreign land; and very soon, in accordance with his plan and his wishes, he fell sick and died. In his last will and testament, however, he required his heir and executor, upon pain of disinheritance, to transport his remains to his own beloved country and there entomb them. This requisition was faithfully complied with. His body was interred with much be-candled pomp and ceremony in his own California, and prayers were duly rehearsed in all the churches for the rest of his soul. He was happy it was supposed, in Heaven, where, for a long series of years, he had prayed to be; and his heir was happy that he was there. But who can safely mock Providence? Being brought back and interred in Californian soil, with the health-breathing, youth-preserving, Californian zephyrs rustling over his grave, the energies of life were immediately restored to his inanimate corpse! Herculean strength was imparted to his frame and, bursting the prison-walls of death, he appeared before his chapfallen heir reinvested with all the vigour and beauty of early manhood! He submitted to his fate with Christian resignation and determined bravely to live his appointed time.[107]

TIMID BUT WISE[108]

In times of adversity the faint-hearted forsake the country. Even after a few weeks of drouth many timid ones desert their farms, some remain away only a year, and others give them up entirely or sell them for a small amount to some sharp speculator. . . .

Consternation seizes the settlers in these districts when the real condition dawns upon them, and they begin at once to fix up a "prairie schooner" preparatory to going East to make a protracted visit among their relations. . . .

. . . One covered wagon had written on it: "In God we trusted in Kansas we busted." It was in all probability the same fellow who, returning next year, wrote: "We fled Kansas' sun and dust, and in Missouri's mud stuck fast." One man who had left Kansas several times, while returning the last time silenced any who might question or ridicule by posting these words: "Wise men change their minds; fools, never."

"OKLAHOMA RAIN"[109]

It was reported that dust had been found in the vault at the bank, that a banana crate used as a wastepaper basket by the local editor was full and running over with dust. One man claimed that gravel had come through his windowpane and wakened him during the night. Another, finding his car stalled by the grit in the engine, opened the door and shot ground squirrels overhead which were tunnelling upward for air! A local paper reported finding gold nuggets in the street which had been blown from the mines in New Mexico. The country farm agent advised his clients that it would be unnecessary to rotate crops in the future, since the wind was rotating soils. One of the natives proposed a test for wind velocity: "Fasten one end of a logchain to the top of a fence-post. If the wind does not blow the chain straight out from the post, the breeze is moderate. You have a calm day."

Allergy in its various forms became so common that, it was said, even the snakes had learned to sneeze; in the night you could tell when a duster was coming by the sneezing of the rattlesnakes on the prairie. Everyone jestingly referred to a dust storm as an "Oklahoma rain". A man caught some huge bullfrogs, so he said, and put them in his watertank to multiply; but, he said, the poor things all drowned immediately. It hadn't rained for so long that they had never had a chance to learn to swim.

A housewife claimed that she scoured her pans by holding them up to a keyhole. The sand coming through in a stream polished them better than she could by the usual method. One old lady, on hearing a man compare the climate to that of hell, put her chin up and declared that if the good Lord sent *her* to hell, he'd have to give her a constitution to stand it.

They laughed about the Black Snow which covered their fields. One farmer said he was going to leave Texas and move to Kansas to pay taxes—"There's where my farm is now."

Another said he could not keep up with his farm, which had taken a trip north. "But next week she'll be back," he said. "I can plow then."

One leather-faced dry farmer said, "I hope it'll rain before the kids grow up. They ain't never seen none." . . .

Those who left the Plains generally did so unwillingly, and, in the midst of their disaster, with a joke on their lips: "Well, the wind blew the dirt away. But we haven't lost everything. We still got the mortgage !"

DAKOTA LAND[110]

Air: After "Beulah Land".

We've reached the land of desert sweet,
Where nothing grows for man to eat.
The wind it blows with feverish heat
Across the plains so hard to beat.

Chorus:
> O Dakota land, sweet Dakota land,
> As on thy fiery soil I stand,
> I look across the plains
> And wonder why it never rains,
> Till Gabriel blows his trumpet sound
> And says the rain's just gone around.

We've reached the land of hills and stones
Where all is strewn with buffalo bones.
O buffalo bones, bleached buffalo bones,
I seem to hear your signs and moans.

We have no wheat, we have no oats,
We have no corn to feed our shoats;
Our chickens are so very poor
They beg for crumbs outside the door.

Our horses are of bronco race;
Starvation stares them in the face.
We do not live, we only stay;
We are too poor to get away.

THE LANE COUNTY BACHELOR[111]

My name is Frank Bolar, 'nole bachelor I am,
I'm keepin' ole bach on an elegant plan.
You'll find me out West in the County of Lane
Starving to death on a government claim;
My house it is built of the national soil,
The walls are erected according to Hoyle,
The roof has no pitch but is level and plain
And I always get wet when it happens to rain.

Chorus:
> But hurrah for Lane County, the land of the free,
> The home of the grasshopper, bedbug, and flea,
> I'll sing loud her praises and boast of her fame
> While starving to death on my government claim.

My clothes they are ragged, my language is rough,
My head is case-hardened, both solid and tough;
The dough it is scattered all over the room
And the floor would get scared at the sight of a broom;
My dishes are dirty and some in the bed
Covered with sorghum and government bread;
But I have a good time, and live at my ease
On common sop-sorghum, old bacon and grease.

Chorus:

But hurrah for Lane County, the land of the West,
Where the farmers and labourers are always at rest,
Where you've nothing to do but sweetly remain,
And starve like a man on your government claim.

How happy am I when I crawl into bed,
And a rattlesnake rattles his tail at my head,
And the gay little centipede, void of all fear
Crawls over my pillow and into my ear,
And the nice little bedbug so cheerful and bright,
Keeps me a-scratching full half of the night,
And the gay little flea with toes sharp as a tack
Plays "Why don't you catch me?" all over my back.

Chorus:

But hurrah for Lane County, where blizzards arise,
Where the winds never cease and the flea never dies,
Where the sun is so hot if in it you remain
'Twill burn you quite black on your government claim.

How happy am I on my government claim,
Where I've nothing to lose and nothing to gain,
Nothing to eat and nothing to wear,
Nothing from nothing is honest and square.
But here I am stuck, and here I must stay,
My money's all gone and I can't get away;
There's nothing will make a man hard and profane
Like starving to death on a government claim.

Chorus:

Then come to Lane County, there's room for you all,
Where the winds never cease and the rains never fall,
Come join in the chorus and boast of her fame,
While starving to death on your government claim.

Now don't get discouraged, ye poor hungry men,
We're all here as free as a pig in a pen;
Just stick to your homestead and battle your fleas,

And pray to your Maker to send you a breeze.
Now a word to claim-holders who are bound for to stay:
You may chew your hard-tack till you're toothless and gray,
But as for me, I'll no longer remain
And starve like a dog on my government claim.

Chorus:

Farewell to Lane County, farewell to the West,
I'll travel back East to the girl I love best;
I'll stop in Missouri and get me a wife,
And live on corn dodgers the rest of my life.

THE STATE OF ARKANSAS[112]

My name is Sanford Barney, and I came from Little Rock Town,
I've travelled this-a wide world over, I've travelled this-a wide world
    round.
I've had many ups and downs through life, better days I've saw,
But I never knew what misery was till I came to Arkansas.

'Twas in the year of '82 in the merry month of June,
I landed at Hot Springs one sultry afternoon.
There came a walking skeleton, then gave to me his paw,
Invited me to his hotel, 'twas the best in Arkansas.

I followed my conductor unto his dwelling place.
It was starvation and poverty pictured on his face.
His bread it was corn dodgers, and beer I could not chaw.
He charged me fifty cents a meal in the state of Arkansas.

I started back next morning to catch the early train.
He said, "Young man, you better work for me. I have some land to
    drain.
I'll give you fifty cents a day, your washing and all chaw.
You'll feel quite like a different man when you leave old Arkansas."

I worked for the gentleman three weeks, Jess Harold was his name.
Six feet seven inches in his stocking length, and slim as any crane.
His hair hung down like ringlets beside his slackened jaw.
He was a photygraft of all the gents that 'uz raised in Arkansas.

His bread it was corn dodgers as hard as any rock.
It made my teeth begin to loosen, my knees begin to knock.
I got so thin on sage and sassafras tea I could hide behind a straw.
I'm sure I was quite like a different man when I left old Arkansas.

I started back to Texas a quarter after five;
Nothing was left but skin and bones, half dead and half alive.
I got me a bottle of whisky, my misery for to thaw;
Got drunk as old Abraham Linkern when I left old Arkansas.

Farewell, farewell, Jess Harold, and likewise darling wife,
I know she never will forget me in the last days of her life.
She put her little hand in mine and tried to bite my jaw,
And said, "Mr. Barnes, remember me when you leave old Arkansas."

Farewell, farewell, swamp angels, to canebrake in the chills.
Fare thee well to sage and sassafras tea and corn-dodger pills.
If ever I see that land again, I'll give to you my paw,
It will be through a telescope from here to Arkansas.

LOCAL CRACKS AND SLAMS

MINING LOCALITIES PECULIAR TO CALIFORNIA[113]

Jim Crow Canon
Happy Valley
Ground Hog's Glory
Red Dog
Hell's Delight
Jackass Gulch
Devil's Basin
Bogus Thunder
Ladies' Canon
Dead Wood
Last Chance
Miller's Defeat
Gouge Eye
Greenhorn Canon
Loafer Hill
Lousy Ravine
Humpback Slide
Hungry Camp
Lazy Man's Canon
Swellhead Diggings
Coon Hollow
Murderer's Bar
Whiskey Bar
Pepper-Box Flat
Poor Man's Creek
Poverty Hill
Nigger Hill
Humbug Canon
Greasers' Camp
Seventy-Six
Bloomer Hill
Christian Flat
Piety Hill
Grizzly Flat

Puke Ravine
Shanghai Hill
Mad Canon
Plug-Head Gulch
Shirt-tail Canon
Guano Hill
Slap Jack Bar
Skunk Gulch
Rattlesnake Bar
Quack Hill
Snow Point
Wild Cat Bar
Paradise
Nary Red
Dead Mule Canon
Rough and Ready
Hog's Diggings
Rat Trap Slide
Ragtown
Brandy Gulch
Pike Hill
Sugar-Loaf Hill
Liberty Hill
Port Wine
Poker Flat
Love-Letter Camp
Mud Springs
Logtown
Cayote Hill
Skinflint
Git-up-and-git
Poodletown
American Hollow
Gopher Flat

Blue-Belly Ravine
Gas Hill
Dead Man's Bar
Wild Goose Flat
Sluice Fork
Ladies' Valley
Brandy Flat
Shinbone Peak
Graveyard Canon
Gridiron Bar
Seven-up Ravine
Gospel Gulch
Hen-Roost Camp
Loafer's Retreat
Chicken-Thief Flat
Yankee Doodle
Gold Hill
Stud-Horse Canon
Horsetown
Pancake Ravine
Bob Ridley Flat
Petticoat Slide
Centipede Hollow
One Eye
Chucklehead
  Diggings
Nutcake Camp
Push-Coach Hill
Mount Zion
Seven-by-nine
Valley
Puppytown
Barefoot Diggings
Paint-Pot Hill

"BIZARRE AND ORIGINAL PLACE NAMES"[114] OF APPALACHIA

The qualities of the raw backwoodsman are printed from untouched negatives in the names he has left upon the map. His literalness shows in Black Rock, Standing Stone, Sharp Top, Twenty Mile, Naked Place, The Pocket, Tumbling Creek, and in the endless designations taken from trees, plants, minerals, or animals noted on the spot. Incidents of his lonely life are signalized in Dusk Camp Run, Mad Sheep Mountain, Dog Slaughter Creek, Drowning Creek, Burnt Cabin Branch, Broken Leg, Raw Dough, Burnt Pone, Sandy Mush, and a hundred others. His contentious spirit blazes forth in Fighting Creek, Shooting Creek, Gouge-eye, Vengeance, Four Killer, and Disputanta.

* * * * *

A sardonic humour, sometimes smudged with "that touch of grossness in our English race", characterizes many of the backwoods place-names. In the mountains of Old Virginia we have Dry Tripe settlement and Jerk 'em Tight. In West Virginia are Take in Creek, Get In Run, Seldom Seen Hollow, Odd, Buster Knob, Shabby Room, and Stretch Yer Neck. North Carolina has its Shoo Bird Mountain, Big Bugaboo Creek, Weary Hut, Frog Level, Shake a Rag, and the Chunky Gal. In eastern Tennessee are No Time settlement and No Business Knob, with creeks known as Big Soak, Suee, Go Forth, and How Come You. Georgia has produced Scataway, Too Nigh, Long Nose, Dug Down, Silly Cook, Turkey Trot, Broke Jug Creek, and Tear Breeches Ridge.

* * * * *

...Rip Shin Thicket, Dog-hobble Ridge, the Rough Arm, Bearwallow, Woolly Ridge, Roaring Fork, Huggins's Hell, the Devil's Racepath, his Den, his Courthouse, and other playgrounds of Old Nick—they, too, were well and fitly named.

HOOSIER

I[115]

HOOSIER. A nickname given at the West to a native of Indiana. A correspondent of the Provincial Journal, writing from Indiana, gives the following account of the origin of this term: "Throughout all the early Western settlements were men who rejoiced in their physical strength, and on numerous occasions, at log-rollings and house-railings, demonstrated this to their entire satisfaction. They were styled by their fellow citizens, 'hushers', from their primary capacity to still their opponents. It was a common term for a bully throughout the West. The boatmen of Indiana were formerly as rude and as primitive a set as could well belong to a civilized country, and they were often in the habit of displaying their pugilistic accomplishments upon the Levee at New Orleans. Upon a certain occasion there, one of these rustic professors of the 'noble art' very adroitly and successfully practiced the 'fancy' upon several individuals at one time. Being himself not a native of this Western world, in the exuberance of his exultation he sprang up, exclaiming, in foreign accent, 'I'm a *hoosier*, I'm a *hoosier.*' Some of the New Orleans papers reported the case, and afterwards transferred the corruption of the epithet 'husher' (*hoosier*) to all the boatmen from Indiana, and from thence to all her citizens.

There was a long-haired *hoosier* from Indiana, a couple of smart-looking *suckers* from Illinois, a keen-eyed, leather-belted *badger* from Wisconsin; and who could refuse to drink with such a company?—*Hoffman, Winter in the West*, p. 210.

The *hoosier* has all the attributes peculiar to the backwoodsmen of the West. . . . One of them visited the city [New Orleans] last week. As he jumped from his flat-boat on to the Levee, he was heard to remark that he "didn't see the reason of folks livin' in a heap this way, where they grew no corn and had no *bars* to kill."—*Pickings from the Picayune.*

II[116]

"The citizens of this State, known as Hoosiers, who gave the State its name, are proverbially inquisitive. They are said to have got their nick-name, because they could not pass a house without pulling the latchstring and crying out, Who's here?" (W. Ferguson, *America by River and Rail*, p. 338.) Another version derives the name from the word huskier, denoting a man of superior strength and skill, who could hush or overcome every adversary, and hence an equivalent for the modern "bully".

SUCKER[117]

SUCKER. A nickname applied throughout the West to a native of Illinois.

The origin of this term is as follows:

The Western prairies are, in many places, full of the holes made by the "crawfish" (a fresh water shell-fish similar in form to the lobster) which descends to the water beneath. In early times, when travellers wended their way over these immense plains, they very prudently provided themselves with a long hollow weed, and when thirsty, thrust it into these natural artesians, and thus easily supplied their longings. The crawfish-well generally contains pure water, and the manner in which the traveller drew forth the refreshing element gave him the name of "Sucker".—*Let. from Illinois, in Providence Journal.*

A correspondent of the *New York Tribune*, writing from Illinois, says:

> We say to all friends of association, come West; to the land of *suckers* and liberal opinions.

A POOR COUNTRY

I[118]

Please goodness! but that's a poor country down yander; it makes the tears come into the kildear's eyes when they fly over the old fields. Dod drot me, if you can even get a drink of cider!! They a'n't got no apples but little runts of things, about as big as your thumb, and so sour, that when a pig sticks his tooth into 'em, he lays back his jaw, and hollers, you might hear him a mile; but its "eat, pig, or die"—for it's all he's got. And then again, they're great for huntin of foxes; and if you were to see their hounds! lean, lank, labber-sided pups, that are so poor they have to prop up agin a post-and-rail fence, 'fore they can raise a bark at my tin-cart. It's the poorest place was ever made.

II[119]

The dogs, in a certain county in Maryland, are so poor, that they have to lean against the fence to bark. The kildees are so poor, that they have to let down the draw-bars to enable them to go into a field; and the pigs are so poor, that to prevent them from upsetting as they run down hill, they are compelled to suspend a lump of lead to their tails to balance them.

III[120]

An eastern editor, in alluding to a rival town, says, that it takes several of their pigs to pull up a blade of grass; that they are so poor, the foremost seizes the spear in his mouth, the balance having taken each other by the tail, when they give a pull, a strong pull, and a pull altogether, and if it breaks, the whole tumble to the ground for want of sufficient strength to support themselves. It must take three or four such pigs to make a shadow.

WHAT THEY SAY ON THE PLAINS[121]

I

"Does the wind blow this way here all the time?" asked the ranch visitor in the West.

"No Mister", answered the cowboy; "it'll maybe blow this way for a week or ten days, and then it'll take a change and blow like hell for a while."

* * * * *

"This", said the newcomer to the Plains, "would be a fine country if we just had water."

"Yes", answered the man whose wagon tongue pointed east, "so would hell."

"In this country", said the cowboy, "we climb for water and dig for wood."[122]

"No woman should live in this country who cannot climb a windmill or shoot a gun."

"On the plains", said another, "the wind draws the water and the cows cut the wood."

II[123]

Where you can go farther and see less,
Where there are more creeks and less water,
Where there are more cows and less milk,
Where there is more climate and less rain,
Where there is more horizon and fewer trees,
Than any other place in the Union.

SALOME—"WHERE SHE DANCED"[124]

I

Many tourists and easterners ask about the past, present and future history of Salome—so here is it. Salome is the principal stopping point on the Santa Fe Railroad and the International Auto and Air Route, between Phoenix and Los Angeles—which means that when you are not in the auto you ought to be in the air—and Salome put the air in Arizona.

The train stops here twice each day—when it goes from Phoenix and when it comes back from Los Angeles. Some folks have wondered why it comes back from Los Angeles but the engineer's wife has the asthma and lives in Phoenix—so he comes back. The train stops here because Salome has the only good water for a long ways—and the engine has to have water. The train goes through here becuz it can't get through the Granite Wash Mountains without going right through Salome—otherwise some of the natives might not know what a train looks like.

Some sweet day someone with a trained and talcum powdered tongue and an unlimited vocabulary of alluring and entrancing adjectives will attempt to describe the wonders and beauties of Salome. Meantime, it is a good place to live, if you like it—and a good place to die, if you don't.

Salome is not as large as Los Angeles, but larger than Phoenix used to be—and a much better town than either of them to live in—if you like them small and quiet—not dead, but sleeping.

Twenty years ago there was no one here but me—and now there's folks a listing as far as you can see. On some nights when the Tourists are thick and the section men all in town and a good game going at Blarney Castle. as many as 75 or 90 people have been counted here—which is a big increase from nothing in twenty years.

It is a characteristic of the country, however, as one cow man who now has over a thousand head of cattle is said to have come here riding a blind mule and driving one red steer. It really would be fine cattle country if we had more grass and water.

Almost everything grows well here. Squint Eye Johnson built a barn last year and on account of the high price of lumber cut four big cottonwood posts and set them in the ground for the corners, nailing boards on to complete the barn. It rained soon after and the corner posts started to grow—and it kept Squint Eye busy all summer nailing on more boards at the bottom to keep the cows from getting out—and now he has a two story barn and uses the top story for a hen house. Squint Eye says one more wet year and he will have to buy an aeroplane to feed his chickens.

Melons don't do very well here becuz the vines grow so fast they wear the melons out dragging them around the ground—and in dry years we sometimes have to plant onions in between the rows of potatoes and then scratch the onions to make the potatoes eyes water enough to irrigate the rest of the garden—and the kids sure do hate to scratch the onions on moonlight nights.

Salome has the purest water and the clearest air in the whole world—including Texas. Don't mix Salome with Yuma, where the bad soldier lived, and when he died—well, he sent for his blankets and overcoat. Yes, it was through the streets of Yuma that the coyote chased the jack rabbit—and they were both walking—and it wasn't more than three figures in the shade at midnight either. Just warm.

II

Stop when you get to Salome—where she danced and fill your tires with that soft Salome air—it rides easier and is used to dodging bumps—use our laughing gas—a free smile with every quart—we laugh becuz we like to live here—we have to and you don't—you just keep on riding by and buy asking which road and dodging bumps and chucks coming and going—we wonder where—and why becuz we've been here a long time—a 1-o-n-g time trying to save something for a rainy day—Rockefeller and Henery Ford used to get all the money before we started.

But we haven't saved anything—and it hasn't rained—there's frogs here seven years old that haven't learned to swim yet—so why should we worry about rainy days? We thank you—and if you have to come this way again why—stop and say hello! Maybe Salome will dance again or the frog learn to swim by that time. Adios!

THE ARKANSAS TRAVELLER[125]

A lost and bewildered Arkansas Traveller approaches the cabin of a Squatter, about forty years ago, in search of lodgings, and the following dialogue ensues:

DIALOGUE

Traveller.—Halloo, stranger.
Squatter.—Hello yourself.
T.—Can I get to stay all night with you?
S.—No, sir, you can't get to—
T.—Have you any spirits here?
S.—Lots uv 'em; Sal seen one last night by that ar ole hollar gum, and it nearly skeered her to death.
T.—You mistake my meaning; have you any liquor?
S.—Had some yesterday, but Ole Bose he got in and lapped all uv it out'n the pot.
T.—You don't understand; I don't mean pot liquor. I'm wet and cold and want some whisky. Have you got any?
S.—Oh, yes—I drunk the last this mornin.
T.—I'm hungary; havn't had a thing since morning; can't you give me something to eat?
S.—Hain't a durned thing in the house. Not a mouffull uv meat, nor a dust uv meal here.
T.—Well, can't you give my horse something?
S.—Got nothin' to feed him on.
T.—How far is it to the next house?
S.—Stranger! I don't know, I've never been thar.
T.—Well, do you know who lives here?
S.—Yes sir!
T.—As I'm so bold, then, what might your name be?
S.—It might be Dick, and it might be Tom; but it lacks right smart uv it.
T.—Sir! will you tell me where this road goes to?
S.—It's never gone any whar since I've lived here; it's always thar when I git up in the mornin'.

T.—Well, how far is it to where it forks?

S.—It don't fork at all; but it splits up like the devil.

T.—As I'm not likely to get to any other house to night, can't you let me sleep in yours; and I'll tie my horse to a tree, and do without anything to eat or drink?

S.—My house leaks. Thar's only one dry spot in it, and me and Sal sleeps on it. And that thar tree is the ole woman's persimmon; you can't tie to it, 'caze she don't want 'em shuk off. She 'lows to make beer out'n um.

T.—Why don't you finish covering your house and stop the leaks?

S.—It's been rainin' all day.

T.—Well, why don't you do it in dry weather?

S.—It don't leak then.

T.—As there seems to be nothing alive about your place but children, how do you do here anyhow?

S.—Putty well, I thank you, how do you do yourself?

T.—I mean what do you do for a living here?

S.—Keep tavern and sell whisky.

T.—Well, I told you I wanted some whisky.

S.—Stranger, I bought a bar'l more'n a week ago. You see, me and Sal went share. After we got it here, we only had a bit betweenst us, and Sal she didn't want to use hern fust, nor me mine. You see I had a spiggin in one eend, and she in tother. So she takes a drink out'n my eend, and pays me the bit for it; then I'd take un out'n hern, and give her the bit. Well, we's getting long fust-rate, till Dick, durned skulking skunk, he born a hole on the bottom to suck at, and the next time I went to buy a drink, they wont none thar.

T.—I'm sorry your whisky's all gone; but, my friend, why don't you play the balance of that tune?

S.—It's got no balance to it.

T.—I mean you don't play the whole of it.

S.—Stranger, can you play the fiddul?

T.—Yes, a little, sometimes.

S.—You don't look like a fiddlur, but ef you think you can play any more onto that thar tune, you kin just try it.

(The traveller takes the fiddle and plays the whole of it.)

THE TURN OF THE TUNE.

S.—Stranger, tuck a half a duzen cheers and sot down. Sal, stir yourself round like a six-horse team in a mud hold. Go round in the hollar whar I killed that buck this mornin', cut off some of the best pieces, and fotch it and cook it for me and this gentleman, d'rectly. Raise up the board under the head of the bed, and get the old black jug I hid from Dick, and gin us some whisky; I know thar's some left yit. Til, drive ole Bose out'n the bread-tray, then climb up in the loft, and git the rag that's got the sugar tied in it. Dick, carry the gentleman's hoss round under the shead, give him some fodder and corn; much as he kin eat.

Til.—Dad, they ain't knives enuff for to sot the table.

S.—Whar's big butch, little butch, old case, cob-handle, granny's knife, and the one I handled yesterday! That's nuff to sot any gentleman's table, outer you've lost um. Durn me, stranger, ef you can't stay as long as you please, and I'll give you plenty to eat and to drink. Will you have coffey for supper?

T.—Yes, sir.

S.—I'll be hanged if you do, tho', we don't have nothin' that way here, but Grub Hyson,[126] and I reckon it's mighty good with sweetnin'. Play away, stranger, you kin sleep on the dry spot to-night.

T.—(After about two hours' fiddling.) My friend, can't you tell me about the road I'm to travel to-morrow?

S.—To-morrow! Stranger, you won't git out'n these diggins for six weeks. But when it gits so you kin start, you see that big sloo over thar? Well, you have to git crost that, then you take the road up the bank, and in about a mile you'll come to a two-acre-and-a-half cornpatch. The corn's mitely in the weeds, but you needn't mind that: jist ride on. About a mile and a half or two miles from that, you'll cum to the damdest swamp you ever struck in all your travels; it's boggy enouff to mire a saddle-blanket. Thar's a fust rate road about six feet under that.

T.—How am I to get at it?

S.—You can't git at it nary time, till the weather stiffens down sum. Well, about a mile beyant, you come to a place what thar's no roads. You kin take the right hand ef you want to; you'll foller it a mile or so, and you'll find its run out; you'll then have to come back and try the left; when you git about two miles on that, you may know you're wrong, fur they ain't any road thar. You'll then think you're mity lucky ef you kin find the way back to my house, whar you kin cum and play on thata'r tune as long as you please.

"CHANGE THE NAME OF ARKANSAS? HELL, NO!"[127]

I[128]

Mr. Speaker, you blue-bellied rascal! I have for the last thirty minutes been trying to get your attention, and each time I have caught your eye, you have wormed, twisted and squirmed like a dog with a flea in his hide, damn you!

Gentlemen, you may tear down the honoured pictures from the halls of the United States Senate, desecrate the grave of George Washington, haul down the Stars and Stripes, curse the Goddess of Liberty, and knock down the tomb of U. S. Grant, but your crime would in no wise compare in enormity with what you propose to do when you would change the name of Arkansas ! Change the name of Arkansas— hell-fire, no!

Compare the lily of the valley to the gorgeous sunrise; the discordant croak of the bull-frog to the melodious tones of a nightingale; the classic strains of Mozart to the bray of a Mexican mule; the puny arm of a Peruvian prince to the muscles of a Roman gladiator—but never change the name of Arkansas. Hell, no!

II[129]

The member arose, shook his head, looked fierce, rolled up his sleeves, pounded the table, and saying, "Hear me, gentlemen", waded in:

Mr. Speaker: The man who would CHANGE THE NAME OF ARKANSAS is the original iron-jawed, brass-mounted, copper-bellied corpsemaker from the wilds of the Ozarks! Sired by a hurricane, dammed by an earthquake, half-brother to the cholera, nearly related to the smallpox on his mother's side, he is the man they call Sudden Death and General Desolation! Look at him! He takes nineteen alligators and a barrel of whiskey for breakfast, when he is in robust health; and a bushel of rattlesnakes and a dead body when he is ailing. He splits the everlasting rocks with his glance, and quenches the thunder when he speaks!

Change the name of Arkansas! Hell, no! stand back and give him room according to his strength. Blood's his natural drink! and the wails of the dying is music to his ears ! Cast your eyes on the gentleman, and lay low and hold your breath, for he's 'bout to turn himself loose! He's the bloodiest son of a wild-cat that lives, who would change the name of Arkansas! Hold him down to earth, for he is a child of sin! Don't attempt to look at him with your naked eye, gentlemen; use smoked glass. The man who would change the name of Arkansaw, by gosh, would use the meridians of longitude and the parallels of latitude for a seine, and drag the Atlantic ocean for whales! He would scratch himself awake with the lightning, and purr himself asleep with the thunder! When he's cold, he would "bile" the Gulf of Mexico and bathe in it! When he's hot, he would fan himself with an equinoctial storm! When he's thirsty, he would reach up and suck a cloud dry like a sponge! When he's hungry, famine follows in his wake! You may put your hand on the sun's face, and make it night on the earth; bite a piece out of the moon, and hurry the seasons; shake yourself and rumble the mountains; but, sir, you will never change the name of Arkansaw!

The man who would change the name of Arkansaw, would massacre isolated communities as a pastime. He would destroy nationalities as a serious business! He would use the boundless vastness of the Great American Desert for his private grave-yard! He would attempt to extract sunshine from cucumbers! Hide the stars in a nail-keg, put the sky to soak in a gourd, hang the Arkansas River on a clothesline; unbuckle the belly-band of Time, and turn the sun and moon out to pasture; but you will never change the name of Arkansaw! The world will again pause and wonder at the audacity of the lop-eared, lantern-jawed, half-breed, half-born, whiskey-soaked hyena who has proposed to change the name of Arkansaw! He's just starting to climb the political banister, and wants to knock the hay-seed out of his hair, pull the splinters out of his feet, and push on and up to the governorship. *But change the name of Arkansaw, hell, no!*

PART THREE

JESTERS

Amerikans luv caustic things; they would pre-
fer turpentine to colone water, if they had to
drink either. So with the relish of humour; they
must hav it on the half-shell with cayenne. An
Englishman wants his fun smothered deep in
mint sauce, and he is willing tew wait till next
day before he tastes it. If yu tickle or convince
an Amerikan yu have got tew do it quick. An
Amerikan luvs to laff, but he don't luv to make
a bizziness ov it; he works, eats, and hawhaws
on a canter. I guess the English hav more wit,
and the Amerikans more humour. We havn't
had time yet to bile down our humour and get
the wit out ov it.

—JOSH BILLINGS

Introduction to Part Three

PRANKS AND TRICKS

> *Of course all boys are not full of tricks, but the best of them are. That is, those who are readiest to play innocent jokes, and who are continually looking for chances to make Rome howl, are the most apt to turn out to be first-class business men.*
>
> —GEORGE W. PECK

GIBES, SELLS AND PRACTICAL JOKES

The lore of "sells" (which, as Peck indicates, are only a step removed from sales) centres in the Yankee peddler. As the "American Autolycus", the Yankee has been the peddler not only of wares but also of wit and wisdom—"Yankee notions" in the intellectual sense— to the nation. In fact, as cracker-box philosopher, he has become a national type, from Seba Smith to Will Rogers, much as Cousin Jonathan has become Brother Jonathan or Uncle Sam.

During the last century the feud between the backwoodsman and the Yankee peddler, who sold the other things he didn't want, assumed the proportions of a comic contest of wits. As a butt of ridicule and the victim of counterplots, the Yankee was penalized for his superior sagacity. "You might as well try to hold a greased eel as a live Yankee." For Yankee trickiness or slickness the name Sam Slick has become proverbial. The original clockmaker of that name (who has had many namesakes) was the creation of a Nova Scotia judge, T. C. Haliburton, and was in reality half Yankee or down-easter and half ring-tailed roarer, by a curious blend of rival traits.[130] Perhaps a truer embodiment of the Yankee spirit of sharpness of wit and trade was P. T.

Barnum, of whom one of his friends said: "If he was shipwrecked and thrown on a desert island, he would try to sell maps of the island to the inhabitants."[131]

Back of the similar libels of sheepherders are the feuds between cowmen and sheepmen and, within the ranks of the latter, between herders and shearers, old hands and new, and bosses and men.

In popular tradition the spirit of mischief and roguery has been embodied in trickster heroes of varying degrees of innocence and malice—Robin Goodfellow, Tyl Eugenspiegel, Reynard the Fox, and Brer Rabbit. It has also inspired the countless pranks and tricks that are part of the folkways and folk humour of everyday life, from the wild-goose chases and ridiculous deceptions of April Fool's Day[132] to what Governor Bob Taylor calls the "eternal war between the barefooted boy and the whole civilized world".

The apotheosis of the "bad boy" in American humour is Peck's Bad Boy.[133] George W. Peck saw no contradiction between the vagaries of the Bad Boy—"wide awake, full of vinegar"—and success in life, and in fact admitted the possibility of a correlation between toughness and smartness. The charm of the Bad Boy, as distinguished from such plaguy brats as the Katzenjammer Kids, lies not so much in pure deviltry as in ingenuity and gumption, the horse sense in his horseplay taking the form of sly, shrewd digs at grown-up frauds and shenanigans.

A modern, sophisticated, feminine counterpart of Peck's Bad Boy is Little Audrey (as she is generally known), whose rôle is that of a spectator at life's little tragedies rather than a perpetrator of mischief. The catastrophes, however, are in the nature of ironic tricks or pranks of fate; and Little Audrey has a trick of her own, that of just laughing and laughing, followed by an I-knew-it-all-the-time observation involving a pun or a surprise.

In backwoods, frontier, and small-town America practical jokes (ranging from the low comedy of badger fights and snipe hunts to pure orneriness) are similarly both a pastime and a means of getting along by hook or by crook. Together with fighting, drunkenness, blackguarding, boasting, and savage sports, horseplay and fool stunts afford relief from monotony, loneliness and strain; an outlet for surplus energy and animal spirits; and an opportunity for exhibitionism. Western humorists have used the practical joke as a form of democratic attack on presence and affectation. To realists and satirists village japes and monkeyshines are an expression of the sadistic or moronic in American life.[134]

The practicalness of a "practical joke" is said to consist in the fact that something is done rather than said. Such a joke differs from a mere gibe in that the butt of the joke is also its victim. Functionally, a practical joke is intended to take advantage of ignorance, in the person of the newcomer or the green hand, and as such is related, on the one hand, to the dislike of strangers, and, on the other, to the exploitation of the weak. From the point of view of the victim, practical jokes exemplify the gullibility of human nature.

Even verbal jests may partake of the nature of a practical joke when a whopper or a riddle ends with a "sell", which pulls the leg of the victim or leaves him holding the sack.

> "There I was out in that prairie, not a tree or a bush in a thousand miles, and a bald-faced bull took after me. I run about fifty feet and climbed up a tall tree."
> "Why, you————liar, you said there was no trees or bushes in a thousand miles."
> "There had to be one—just had to be one."[135]

Or the narrator gets himself cornered-by hostile Indians or wild animals in order to elicit a query as to what happened to him and to permit the solemn announcement: "Why—then them damn redskins killed me", or "They got me."

Riddles often conceal a surprise which is akin to a sell. Lincoln liked to ask: "'If three pigeons sit on a fence and you shoot and kill one of them, how many will be left?'...The answer was, 'Two, of course.' To which Lincoln responded, 'No, there won't, for the other two will fly away.'"[136]

Here, too, belong children's riddling tricks and catches, such as "Just like me", "I'm a gold lock", "Adam and Eve and Pinchme",[137] and arithmetical jokes like Barnum's.

In almost every occupation, part of the education or initiation of the new hand consists in sending him on foolish errands, usually in search of a mythical or impossible object, such as left-handed monkey wrench, a bottle stretcher, a four-foot yard stick, or a sky-hook, or in otherwise exposing his ignorance ridiculously and perhaps painfully.

> The youngest fellow on the works always had to take the "rawhiding", but I soon learned to hold my own. I was hired to work on "macaroni" farms, sent to buy "striped paint", but was not as bad as the fellow who looked all day in a mud puddle for a frog, because they needed it on the railroad.[138]

Greenhorns and tenderfeet are pranked by falsifying narratives and dialogues (often acted out in a little by-play) as well as by practical jokes. These recitals usually involve animals surrounded by mystery and terror, such as inhabit Paul Bunyan's woods. Yarns of "fearsome critters" have the double purpose of taking in the newcomer and entertaining the old-timers, and so belong to the kingdom of lies as well as of pranks. Sometimes the hazing narratives take the form of circular stories, or "long-winded tales that ingeniously held the listener's interest, but eventually disclosed that they had no point, making this disclosure sometimes by reverting to the starting-place and reiterating word for word".[139] In national parks and on Western ranches the hazing of "dudes" and tenderfeet has produced many classics among sells.

Besides "breaking in" new hands, practical jokes also serve the purpose of getting even with enemies or getting rid of intruders. Where the element of revenge is present, as in "Casting Anchor", the idea is to give "trick for trick". Where the presence of the victim is unwelcome, the aim is to frighten him away. In any case, as in love or war, all is what Davy Crockett calls "fairation" when one is dealing with a rival.

The ruses of trade and swindling are more practical than practical jokes in that they are a means to an end—the end being gain—rather than an end in themselves. At the same time, many swindling dodges, such as selling a greenhorn gold bricks, the Brooklyn Bridge, Grant's Tomb, or the Woolworth Building, are hoaxes. The hoax differs from the ordinary prank in that it is played for greater stakes and before a larger audience. As a "deliberately concocted untruth, made to masquerade as truth",[140] the hoax differs also from true superstition or myth as deliberate falsification differs from erroneous observation or false inference. Yet in their fictitious build-up, hoaxes involve mythical elements and are "folklore in the making". In between the more elaborate hoaxes, like Barnum's Mermaid, which belong to history and journalism rather than to folklore, and the myth-making stunts involving freaks and monsters, such as sea serpents, petrified men, and "fearsome critters" of the hodag type, are the hoaxing, cheating tricks akin to practical jokes—the pretty cute little stunts by which one outsmarts a customer in a trade, whether it be selling or swapping.

HUMOROUS ANECDOTES AND JESTS

> *It was common in the bar-rooms, the gather-*
> *ings in the "country store", and finally at pub-*
> *lic meetings in the mouths of "stump orators".*
> *Arguments were clinched, and political prin-*
> *ciples illustrated by a "funny story". It in-*
> *vaded even the camp meeting and the pulpit.*
> *It at last received the currency of the public*
> *press. But wherever met it was so individual*
> *and characteristic, that it was at once known*
> *and appreciated abroad as "an American*
> *story."*
> —BRET HARTE

The anecdote may be defined as a story with a point or a point with a story, depending upon where the emphasis falls. Unlike the fable or parable, the anecdote is not allegorical and is generally based on an actual occurrence. Because the point of an anecdote is wise or witty rather than moral, it is close to the aphorism; and in its use to enliven or illustrate conversation and oratory, it resembles the allusion and the figure of speech. All these values are embodied in Lincoln's remark— an anecdote in epitome—on the lawyer's paper: "It's like the lazy preacher that used to write long sermons, and the explanation was, he got to writin' and was too lazy to stop."

Typically, the anecdote is associated with character and custom, being commonly used to illustrate a trait of an individual or a commu- nity. Thus we are familiar with anecdotes (etymologically, "unpub- lished" stories) of famous persons and of places. In the broad sense, however, the anecdote is any traditional narrative of a single incident and of a realistic and usually humorous character, which is intended to be believed. Although all anecdotes are not humorous, all jests involv- ing a narrative situation, with some development and elaboration, may be classed as anecdotes.

The evolution of an anecdote from a mere joke is illustrated by two versions of "Ain't Lost". In its simplest form the gag is a comeback, as given by Carl Sandburg in *The People, Yes*: "Which way to the post office, boy?" "I don't know." "You don't know much, do you?" "No, but I ain't lost."

In general, three types of anecdotes may be distinguished: the anec- dote based on a witty remark, or *jeu d'esprit*, such as "Ain't Lost", involving repartee, quibbles, and quiddities; the anecdote of character; and the social or cultural anecdote, which involves a comment on a way of living. In the United States, all three types are given local colouring and significance in what may be called the local anecdote.

It is perhaps in the local anecdote of character that one may best see the American anecdote on its way to becoming a short story, in line with Bret Harte's theory that the American anecdote was the "parent of the American 'short story'."

On the one hand, story-telling is a pastime or a form of social intercourse, associated with leisure, gregariousness, and travel. On the other hand, it may have a practical application, enforcing a point and enlivening a discourse with a parable or example. Because wit and humour add an extra seasoning to the sauce of narrative, the humorous anecdote has always been effective for the purposes of homiletic or forensic illustration, as demonstrated by the popularity of collections of stories and jokes for speakers. Thus the medieval Latin collections of *exempla*, or illustrative stories for use in sermons, which drew upon the storehouses of classical legend, fable, and merry tales, served as a link between the folk literatures of ancient and modern times and as a forerunner of the jest-book.

In America the practical value of the humorous anecdote lies not so much in teaching a lesson as in making a point. Hence the wide use of the practical story in business and politics. The master of the story with a point was Lincoln, unique among story-tellers and presidents in his ability "to tell his stories, and by them to illustrate matters of great pith".

Lincoln touches the art of the humorous American anecdote at almost every point. In young manhood he discovered the secret that the Yankee peddler had learned before him and that travelling salesmen, storekeepers, lawyers, and politicians have always known—how to mix business and sociability by making a good story break down resistance, build up good will, clinch or bolster an argument, or simply pass the time of day. Whether his business was floating a flatboat or raft down the river, logging, clerking in a store, practicing law, representing his district in the state legislature or Congress, or directing the destiny of his country in a great Civil War, he knew that the apt saying or anecdote, expressive of a principle or truth, constituted one of his greatest assets.[141]

From the prize story-teller of his community and its spokesman at all the neighbourhood gatherings, he rose to be story-teller to the nation and the voice of the people. He is our only folk hero who is also a folk artist. Akin to Aesop and Poor Richard, he differs from our other great folk story-teller, Mark Twain, in that he was not a professional humorist, and from other "funny men" in Congress—Hardin, Corwin, Knott, and Cox—in that with him the anecdote rather than repartee or satire was the weapon. Drawing his homely incidents, allusions, figures, aphorisms, and idioms from backwoods experience, he differs from all the ordinary raconteurs who have used funny stories to garnish oratory or tickle an audience. At the same time, steeped in the lore of humour, he learned many of his tricks from the cracker-box philosophers and jesters before him, including Joe Miller. He raised the wisecrack to the level of scripture.

The practical anecdote also has its religious uses, as parables, to illustrate sermons, to point the meaning of true religion, or perhaps to satirize a rival sect.

Rural Jests

Both Lincoln and Crockett, in common with many of our popular humorists and comedians, had hayseed in their hair. Near the end of the last century the vogue of rural humour coincided with the vogue of rural and provincial drama, fiction, and poetry of the *Old Homestead, David Harum*, and James Whitcomb Riley stamp. The appeal of rural character and illiteracy in American literature is based on various motives and related to various movements in American life. The frontier, the democratic tradition of the common man, local colour, and naturism, with their cults of the soil, the "homely pathetic", and the "native", have conspired to make the dry wit and the slow drawl of the countryman the most effective and characteristic expression of American independence, ingenuity, and irreverence. In rural humour, with its blend of Yankee shrewdness, backwoods eccentricity, and Western breeziness, the central trait is the contrast between apparent simplicity and underlying wit and wisdom or between pretended knowledge and actual ignorance, coupled in either case with gumption and nerve. The spectacle of rustic follies and blunders affords entertainment not only to the city-dweller, who is something of a hick-baiter, but also to the countryman ruminating on the odds and ends of his daily life. The best of rural jests are local anecdotes of character and custom. On the "make-it-yourself-or-do-without" level of culture, moreover, story-telling is one of the chief leisure-time activities and an integral part of fun-making.

On the credit side, the countryman is as commonsensical as he is unlearned; on the debit side, he is apt to be as nonsensical as he is simple. The humour of rustic ignorance and gullibility, with the stupid person being taken in by the clever one, is part of the larger humour of mistakes and misunderstandings. From ancient times men have laughed at "that droll stupidity which is the characteristic of noodles or simple-tons" and which, as in the following drolleries, takes the form of Irish bulls, Gaulardisms, pedantry, making easy things hard, absentminded-ness, imagining troubles, and literal following of directions.[142]

NEGRO JESTS

The laughter of the Negro, like that of other minorities' is a solace and a source of courage; but it is on the attack rather than merely on the defensive, emphasizing the Brer Rabbit resourcefulness of a highly adaptive and infinitely patient folk. Negro jests strike a note of defi-ance rather than of protest, as in the case with Negro blues and folk rhymes. As High John de Conquer (the folk name for the marsh St. John's wort, whose root wards off evil, in the form of disease, hants, witches, nightmares, and the like), the "John" of slavery anecdotes is a symbol of the Negro's briar-patch-bred ability to land on his feet in the briers and "skip out des ez lively ez a cricket in de embers". Old John gets out of tight places and turns the joke on Old Massa, by dint of what Zora Neale Hurston calls "hitting a straight lick with a crooked stick". "Now, High John de Conquer, Old Massa couldn't get the best of *him*. That Old John was a case!" High John de Conquer's laughter is a secret laughter, with a subtle power like that of the root of the same name—the power to help Negroes "overcome things they feel that they could not beat otherwise."[143]

GAGS AND WISECRACKS

From the perennial humour of wit and nitwit emerge stock themes, such as the absent-minded man, Scotch jokes, the ugliest man, the meanest man, as well as certain vogues, such as slow train and Ford jokes and, among sayings, "knock knocks" and "You tell 'em" En-glish. The ephemeral humour of gags and wisecracks—the temporal counterpart of local anecdotes and sayings—provides a laboratory for the study of the patterns, variations, and diffusion of popular material. The idiom is largely urban and sophisticated, since the principal means of transmission is by press, stage, film, and radio, but the mould is the folk mould of popular fantasy patterned by repetition.

Almost every form of wit and rhetorical device is employed in the wisecrack or "jocular smart remark": puns, malapropisms, boners, and other varieties of word play and humorous mistakes (She was so dumb she thought a subordinate clause was one of Santa's offspring; He is a big needle and thread man from So-and-So; She is not my best girl— just necks best; Lettuce is a proposition); Wellerisms (As the pencil sharpener said, "Now to get down to the point"); Irish bulls and paradoxes (I couldn't commit suicide if my life depended on it; She would be cute if it wasn't for her face); extravagant impossibilities (Yours till elephants roost on rose bushes); nonsense (More fun than I've had since the day the cow catcher had a calf); exaggeration (She was so thin that she could fall through a flute and never strike a note); the fabulous or the tall tale (It was so cold the cows gave ice cream); *reductio ad absurdum* (If steam-ships sold for a nickel, I couldn't buy the echo of a whistle); *non sequitur* (Let's you and him fight until I get tired).

The use of the formula is basic to the wisecrack: so dumb, so tight, you tell 'em, they call, she was only, you don't have to, you may be. Certain formulae are identified with disparaging or insulting wisecracks, or "slams" (They call her a toe dancer because she dances on other people's toes; You don't have to hang from a tree to be a nut; You may be bread in old Kentucky but you're just a crumb around here).

The habit of wisecracking is related to the American trait of "laughing it off" and to the love of mottoes and slogans. Many trade slogans are nothing but wisecracks: We wash everything but the baby; You can whip our cream but you can't beat our milk; You furnish the girl, we furnish the rest; Look at your hat, everyone else does; Why kill your wife? Let us do the dirty work; You wreck 'em, we fix 'em.

The value of this floating linguistic material for both the poet and the social historian is evinced by the successful use of talk, jokes, and lingo made by Carl Sandburg in both *Abraham Lincoln, the Prairie Years* and *The People, Yes*.

Part Three

PRANKS AND TRICKS

Some English readers, especially members of the Stock Exchange, who at one time seemed to make her particularly their own, may be surprised to find Little Audrey amongst the mythological heroines of folklore. The exact date and place of her origin, as with so many characters in folklore, is uncertain. With her peculiar brand of naïve, desperate cynicism, she perhaps dates from the depression period.

THE ADVENTURES OF LITTLE AUDREY[144]

Little Audrey is a folk-lore character about whom thousands of nonsensical short tales have been told. Sometimes Little Audrey parades as Little Emma or Little Gertrude, but she usually is recognizable by a catch phrase—she "just laughed and laughed". The amusing incident is typically a catastrophe. Little Audrey sees the humour in any situation.

A nice thing about Little Audrey is her integrity. She is no hypocrite; she does what she wants to do, says what she wants to say, and makes no bones about it. Little Audrey will never have inhibitions. Further, she is a very modern girl. She is having new adventures constantly, as indicated by the puns on floating power automobiles and the carioca dance steps. To her, irony predominates over sentiment. She has few illusions.

Little Audrey is nation-wide in distribution. In Texas she is well-known, particularly in universities and high schools. Approximately one out of ten students is a Little Audrey fan with a number of her adventures tucked away in his mind. The following are some of the stories known and collected by the author:

Little Audrey and her papa were out riding one day in their new stream-lined car. Papa was proud of the car, and he was giving it the gas; he wanted to see how much it would make. All of a sudden the road turned, but papa did not; he went straight on and into the lake.

Little Audrey saw what was going to happen, and she just laughed and laughed. She knew all of the time that their car had floating power.

Once upon a time all the children in Little Audrey's neighbourhood were taking lessons. It was the proper thing to do; if you did not take lessons, you simply were not in the social swim. So Little Audrey cried and cried, 'cause she was not taking lessons.

After a while her mama said, "Little Audrey, if you will just stop that bawling, I'll let you take lessons." That made Little Audrey awful happy; so she sat down to think about what kind of lessons she would take. Well, after a long time she decided to take parachute lessons. So Little Audrey practiced and practiced, and after a while it was time to give her recital; you know if you take lessons you just have to give recitals.

Well, people came from far and near to see Little Audrey parachute jump. She went way up high in the airplane and got ready to jump. She looked down and saw all those people watching her, and then she jumped out. On her way down she just laughed and laughed, 'cause she knew she was going to fool those people; she didn't have on her parachute.

Once upon a time Little Audrey got lost on a desert island. Along came a big bunch of black cannibals and kidnapped her. They tied her up to a tree and started their pot to boiling. Little Audrey knew they were going to make stew out of her; so she looked around at those lean, hungry cannibals and counted them. There were nineteen. Little Audrey just laughed and laughed, 'cause she knew she was not big enough to make enough stew to go around.

One day Little Audrey and her mother went for a walk in the forest where some lumbermen were felling trees. Just as they came along, the men cut down a big oak, and it fell right on mother! Little Audrey just laughed and laughed, 'cause she knew all the time that Mother couldn't carioca.

That night Little Audrey and her mama and papa and her little brunette sister were sitting at the dinner table. Papa said, "Little Audrey, pass the cream, please." So Little Audrey passed the cream to her papa, and he poured some into his coffee. Then he put the pitcher down, and Little Audrey noticed that right on the tip end of the spout there was a little drop of cream all ready to fall. Little Audrey just laughed and laughed, 'cause she knew all the time that the little cream pitcher couldn't go *sniff, sniff.*

One day Little Audrey was standing on the corner just a-crying and a-crying, when along comes a cop, who said, "Little Audrey, why are you crying?" And Little Audrey said, "Oh, I've lost my papa!" The cop said, "Why, Little Audrey, I wouldn't cry about that. There's your papa right across the street leaning against that bank building." Little Audrey was overjoyed; without even looking at the traffic she started across the street. Along came a big two-ton truck that ran over Little Audrey and killed her dead. The cop just laughed and laughed. He knew all the time that that was not Little Audrey's papa leaning against the bank building.

One time Little Audrey and her little brother were inspecting a ship. They went over it from top to bottom, and then little brother decided he wanted to go way up high to the crow's nest. Little Audrey told him he better not go, but he was awful hard-headed; so up he went. When he got up there he waved to Little Audrey, lost his balance, and came tumbling down. Little Audrey looked at the remains and just laughed and laughed, 'cause she knew all the time that her brother just could not stand hard ships.

One time Little Audrey took her grandpa out walking. Little Audrey got awful hot; so she said, "Grandpa, let's go down to the old swimming hole and take a swim." But grandpa didn't much want to, 'cause he was blind. But Little Audrey begged and begged, and finally grandpa agreed to go. So they went down to the old swimming hole and put on their bathing suits. There was a big tree, growing out over the water, that the kids used as a diving board. Little Audrey told her grandpa to climb up the tree and dive off. But he didn't want to; so Little Audrey had to make him. When he jumped off, Little Audrey just laughed and laughed. She knew all the time that the swimming hole had dried up.

Little Audrey's brother was a jailbird. One time when he was up for three years he broke out of jail. The sheriff looked and looked for him, but he couldn't find him anywhere. After about a month the sheriff decided to put the bloodhounds on the trail. And that made Little Audrey just laugh and laugh, 'cause she knew all the time that her brother was anaemic.

One day Little Audrey and her mother were driving along when all of a sudden the car door flew open and Little Audrey's mother fell out. Little Audrey just laughed and laughed, 'cause she knew all the time that her mother had on her light fall suit.

The nurse was going to take Little Audrey out for a walk; but the nurse was absent-minded, and she forgot until she was outside to take Little Audrey with her. So she called up to the cook and said, "Cook, throw Little Audrey out the window, and I'll catch her on the second bounce." The cook threw Little Audrey out the window and then she just laughed and laughed. She knew all the time that Little Audrey was not a rubber ball.

One day Little Audrey's mama went to town, and while she was gone Little Audrey decided to bake a cake, 'cause she wanted to show her mama how smart she was. She got down the recipe book and mixed the cake according to directions. She sifted the flour, creamed the butter and sugar, beat the eggs, and stirred the ingredients together. Then she was ready to cook the cake; so she looked at the recipe book and it said: "Now set in the oven for thirty minutes." So Little Audrey crawled into the oven and closed the door.

By and by Little Audrey's mama came home. She looked everywhere for Little Audrey, but she couldn't find her. All of a sudden she smelled something burning. She opened the oven door, and there was Little Audrey, burned to a crisp. Her mother just laughed and laughed. She didn't know that Little Audrey could read.

The next day Little Audrey and her grandma were standing on their front porch watching the men pave their street. There was a cement mixer, a steam roller, and all kinds of things to watch. All of a sudden grandma saw a quarter out there right in the middle of the street. She dashed right out to get it, but just as she picked it up along came that old steam roller and rolled her out flatter than a sheet of theme paper. Little Audrey just laughed and laughed, 'cause she knew all the time it was only a dime.

One day Little Audrey was playing with matches. Mama said, "Ummm, you better not do that." But Little Audrey was awful hard-headed; she kept right on playing with matches, and after a while she set the house on fire, and it burned right down to the ground. Mama and Little Audrey were looking at the ashes, and mama said, "Uh huh, I told you so! Now, young lady, just wait until your papa comes home. You certainly will catch it!" Little Audrey just laughed and laughed. She knew all the time that papa had come home an hour early and had gone to bed to take a nap.

The next night Little Audrey and her date were sitting on the sofa when all of a sudden the lights went out. "Oh", said Little Audrey's boy friend, "it sure is dark in here. I can't even see my hand in front of me." Little Audrey just laughed and laughed, 'cause she knew all the time that his hand wasn't in front of him.

CONCERNING BALD-HEADED WHIZZERS[145]

Typical adjunct to life in the hell-roarin' days of the Argonauts when camps reeked gold and the humours of men were raw as new-plowed prairie land, was that effervescent phenomenon known as the Whizzer.

The Whizzer was the high ace in the deck of life as it was dealt over gravel bar and auriferous stream bank. Individuals and towns reaped fame by it. A successful Whizzer not only crowned its originator and perpetrator with glory, but shed an enviable light upon the entire community that witnessed—or suffered—its execution. Whizzers of superlative merit have been embalmed in the memories of very old men who still sun themselves in the ghost towns of gold and who can be led, with much chuckling, to recount them. In a few rare volumes of reminiscences long out of print you'll find samples of this long extinct genus pinned like gorgeous butterflies to the pages.

A noteworthy swindle, a practical joke, a brilliant hoax: these were the magic components of which the Whizzer was made. They were of two classes, the plain and the bald-headed. A bald-headed Whizzer was one so adroitly built upon a human foible or frailty, so carefully exploited by its author as to bring a whole community into the arena of mocking laughter. The distinction between the two varieties was comparative; the gage, you might say, of genius.

One of the earliest Whizzers of the gold diggin's to gain immortality was that one perpetrated by a genius whose name comes down as Pike Sellers—undoubtedly one of the Wild Missouri hellions generically lumped as "Pikes", in the vocabulary of the mines. This Pike had an imagination and a devilishly sly humour which would qualify him to-day for one of our highly specialized lines of salesmanship.

It was in the spring of '50 when word of the incredible richness of Downie's Flat, away up near the headwaters of Yuba's north fork, swept downstream and set a crowd of wild-eyed boomers hurrying thither. Original discoverers of Downie's Flat were digging a pound of gold a day to the man out of crevices under the rim rock with the point of a butcher knife. Major Downie himself had sifted downstream to Bullard's Bar with $3000 in nuggets, result of three days' work! So rumour exploded.

When the first of the rush commenced to lower themselves hand over hand down the precipitous wall of the gorge to Downie's camp on the forks of white water they were not very cordially received by the ten or a dozen original discoverers who'd spent a hard winter there. It was, in fact, quite true that Downie and his associates had been hitting raw gold out of the bank with butcher knives and iron spoons over several months; and they did not welcome a division of riches.

Then it was that Pike Sellers had his inspiration.

He was working away at the soft dirt of the stream bank one day when he saw one of the boomers, pack on back, crawling precariously down trail. Pike, unseen himself; scrambled up out of the stream bed and commenced furiously prying with his long knife at the bark slabs on a jack-pine. Just as the stranger came up one of the rough shags of bark became loosened. Pike pushed two fingers behind it and withdrew a fat gold nugget.

Eyes of the stranger popped. Pike tackled another bark slab without so much as a glance over shoulder at the fascinated onlooker. By a simple trick of legerdemain that hunk yielded a second alluring gold pebble.

"My Gawd!"—from the tenderfoot. "I hearn ye was diggin' the yeller stuff outa cracks in the rocks, but I didn't know she grew on trees."

"Gits lodged thar when th' tree's pushing up through th' soil", indifferently from Pike. "Most of th' nuggets is up higher, but too dam'd much trouble to shin up th' trees. Me, I'm jist satisfied to peck round nigh th' ground."

Under the believing eyes of the newcomer Pike found a couple more nuggets. Then the former whipped out his bowie-knife and started to work on a near-by jack-pine.

"Hold on thar!" commandingly from the Sellers person. "Yo're on my claim. Rule in this camp ev'ry fella's entitled to ten gold bearin' pines; that thar one belongs to me."

The boomer wanted to know in an excited whine where he could stake himself to a tree. Reluctantly Pike Sellers abandoned his work to stride through the forest to where a jack-pine of smaller growth reared.

"Like I said, she's richest nigh th' top. Ye can climb this one 'thout a ladder iffen yo're so minded." Pike showed a commendable interest in seeing the newcomer make his first strike of jack-pine gold. The latter dropped his pack and, bowie in teeth, commenced to shin up the rough trunk.

"Higher up's better", bawled Pike when his protégé had come to the first limbs. "Nothin' but flake gold low down mostly."

Up went the avid tenderfoot, before his eyes the vision of a man prying nuggets from beneath tree bark. Pike let him risk his neck until the luckless light-wit was fifty or sixty feet from the ground.

"That's likely 'nough place to begin on. Only be mighty keerful not to drop any nuggets. I kain't be held responsible fer losses like that."

The searcher after tree gold began to attack the bark with his bowie knife. Pike Sellers sifted back to the stream bed to bring an audience for the farce comedy he had staged. Thereafter "jack-pine gold" became a synonym through all the Northern Mines.

Pike Sellers reaped enduring fame as the father of a Whizzer.

HUMOROUS ANECDOTES AND JESTS

AIN'T LOST[146]

A fine city man had a brand-new buggy and a prize-winning pair of trotters that he wished to try out. He drove along the country roads, speeding a little here and walking a little there, studying the good points and admiring the beauty of his new rig. He was so delighted with the prospect that he failed to notice the road. Later on he realized that he was lost, but he hoped by driving on to find his way, or at least to meet someone who could tell him how to get back to the city.

But it was a long lonesome road. For a long time he followed the windings, hoping every hilltop would bring him within sight of some dwelling. When it was almost dark he saw in front of him a cotton patch and a good-sized country boy chopping away in the rows. He reined his tired team near the fence and called out, "Hello, boy."

"Hello yourself", the boy replied, still wielding his hoe.

"Where does this road go to?"

"Hadn't never seed it go nowhars. Hit allus stays right whar hit is", said the boy, still digging away.

"How far is it to the next town?"

"Don't know; never measured it", replied the boy.

Thoroughly disgusted, the man said with some heat, "You don't know anything. You are certainly the biggest fool I ever saw."

The boy looked a long time in the man's eyes; then he said with contempt, "I knows I don't know nothing. I knows I'se a fool. But I ain't lost."

WEATHER PROPHETS[147]

It has been said that George B. Erath, the famous German pioneer and Indian fighter, was the author of the expression: "Nobody prophesies about Texas weather except newcomers and damn fools."

For many years this has been a favourite gag in Texas social life. It was one of the sells in the old saloon days, and the unfortunate tenderfoot who fell for it always had to set up the drinks to the crowd.

One dull, slow evening when things were at an absolute standstill in the saloon, a fresh young guy with a derby hat and store-bought clothes breezed into the place, walked up to the bar, and ordered a drink. The usual crowd of loafers looked on disapprovingly but said nothing. Leisurely finishing his drink and wiping his mouth with a bright silk handkerchief, the newcomer said, "Well, I believe it's going to rain."

The golden opportunity had arrived; the whole crowd was alert and watchful. Then the old nester, the leader in all the local wars of wits, said very fatherly, "My friend, did you know that there were only two kinds of people who prophesy about Texas weather?"

"Two kinds of people who prophesy on Texas weather?" mused the stranger. "That's very queer. Who are they?"

Then the old nester, with all the contempt and sarcasm in his power, sneered, "Newcomers and damn fools."

The crowd rose with a mighty shout and gathered around the newcomer shouting, "Haw, haw, haw." "He got you that time." "You are it." "He got you good." "Set um up. Set um up." "You owe the drinks to the house." "Come on, set em up."

The young fellow stood smiling at all their hurrah. He was not the least troubled about their demands for the drinks. When the hubbub had died down and they were all properly up against the bar, he said very calmly and slowly, "You say there are only two kinds of people who prophesy about Texas weather—newcomers and damn fools. You are right. Those are the only two kinds in Texas."

ALL FACE[148]

On a cold dreary day an Indian and a white man were making a journey together. The Indian had on no clothing except a blanket while the white man was bundled up in all the clothes he possessed.

The white man continued to complain about the cold and to wonder why the Indian was not freezing. He said to the Indian, "I don't understand it. With all my clothes I am about to freeze, and you, with only a thin blanket, do not seem to be cold at all."

"Is your face cold?" asked the Indian.

"No, my face is not cold, but I'm just about to freeze everywhere else."

"Me all face," said the Indian.

PREDESTINATION FOR THE INDIAN[149]

In the early days of the Republic of Texas when the Indians were especially bad, an old Primitive Baptist preacher was preparing for a long trip across the Indian country. He was especially careful in cleaning and loading the long rifle that was to accompany him. A friend, seeing his preparation and knowing his belief in predestination, said to him, "Uncle Billie, why are you so careful about your gun? If you meet the Indians and you are predestined to die at that time, why you will die anyway; so why worry about the gun? 'What is to be will be anyway', you know."

"Yes, I know all about that," said Uncle Billie, "but it might be the Indian's time."

CONTRADICTORY DREAM REVELATIONS[150]

It is said of this same minister that a notorious character of the community thought he would be able to take advantage of him because of his belief in mystic visions. So one morning he drove his wagon up to Uncle Billie's crib and said to him, "The Lord told me in a dream last night to come to your crib and get a load of corn."

Uncle Billie reached up over the door and took down his long rifle and said, "Yes, but the Lord must have changed His mind, for He told me this morning not to let you have it."

G. P. C.[151]

The church was in an uproar. The congregation was badly divided on the question of whether or not they should grant a certain young brother, whose reputation for piety was none too good, a licence to preach.

A few of the older conservative members were a little doubtful about the sudden call to the ministry, and wanted to put him off until they could be a little surer about the reality of the call. Many of the younger brethren were very enthusiastic about the wonderful conversion and vocation of the applicant. They thought a real miracle had happened, and they were anxious to see him licensed and put to work in the Lord's vineyard. They recounted with great seriousness how, according to the young man's own testimony, the Lord had appeared to him in a vision and had shown him the three letters "G. P. C." flaming in the sky, and how a still small voice had said, "Follow these." There could be no doubt about the interpretation. G. P. C. meant "Go Preach Christ." And the young man should be sent on his way.

But the old deacon was on his feet, replying, "Brethren, I do not deny the vision. I am sure that the Lord has spoken to this young man. But knowing this young man as I do, and appreciating to some degree the great wisdom of the Lord, I am sure that you all misinterpret what this vision meant. 'G. P. C.' in this case can only mean, 'Go Pick Cotton'."

ESSENCE OF RURAL HUMOUR[152]

The scene is Kennicott's store at Blue Eye, a situation but slightly commercial. The group includes Dave Beatty, Forgy Dell, Marcus Feitz, Henstep Creaseley, Tola Summerlin, Homer Bullteeter, Homer's hired boy Bill Skeats, and the storekeeper. These occupy poultry crates and such. They whittle matches into infinitesimal slivers. They draw strange diagrams on the dusty porch floor and whistle tunes that take after nothing in particular. They indulge in slight sounds, slow gyrations, slight parleying, patterings of feet, uproarous yawnings, and stretchings in the form of capital Xs and Ys.

Their relish for the wisecrack inevitably forthcoming is enhanced a dozenfold by such interludes of speculative waiting. The first spiel is by Bill Skeats, since hired boys are among the most cherished perpetrators of store-porch mirth.

Bill Skeats, then, sitting in sunny oblivion on the lowest estate of the store-porch steps, opens in dialect at his boss:

"Homer, how's hit do for me to ride your hoss home?"

The employer quivers slightly.

"It wouldn't do so good, I've got to ride him myse'f." Then with a soft ripple of merriment: "Mought be you could walk alongside me though."

"No, I reckon I'd better jest be pattin' down the road now by myself. If I was to walk aside you, I'd have to open and shet ever' gate and fence-gap between here and thar."

Backbrush humour hangs upon pegs that are unashamedly obvious: the old gentleman who can't get any satisfaction out of reading the dictionary because it changes the subject too often; the itinerant parson who agrees that a spring wagon and a span of mules are fool proof, but not necessarily damn-fool proof; the upbrush politician who craves a postmastership within easy walking distance of a distillery; the clodhopper who overwhelms the school-teacher's suggestion that the burning of Mart Miller's barn must have been the work of an incendiary with, "Incendiary, hell! Somebody sot it."

The humour carries an amiable plenitude, too, of anecdotes of stupidity.

The sheriff of a brush county in Southwestern Missouri was forming a posse to recapture a depraved culprit who had broken jail while the defender of justice was away investigating. A store-porch commentator reported that the fugitive had spent half the afternoon strolling about the village; that he had last been seen taking out westward down the old wire road. Then the observing countryman added that he had seen the sheriff pass by the escaped prisoner not an hour before. The upholder of sovereign justice admitted it.

"Oh, yes, yes! I seed him all right—passed him on the town branch bridge a while after dinner time—passed him and spoke howdy to him. But I didn't know the low hound reprobate was out of jail."

The store-porcher relishes so simple an episode as that of the rural lad and his first banana. The youth from Alpena was taking his first train ride, and when the newsman came through acclaiming "chawklets—bernanners!" the mountain lad invested readily in the latter. On the next round the caller stopped to ask after the qualities of his wares.

"Well, Mister, I can't say so bodaciously much for it. In the first place it was mainly all cob; and when I'd thronged that away, what little they was left was bitter and sort of 'ornery to eat."

Sometimes the gentleman of the store-porch is tickled almost beyond endurance by ignorance of rural ways, by unfamiliarity with the dictates of soil and season which he himself knows so well. The newcomer who figures to get rich off a few slanting acres of stump ground; who would bear down on his plow handles, tie up fodder with string, buckle the throat-latch of a bridle before he set the bit, undertake to keep the birds from his cherries or the squirrels from his corn—such a yahoo provides material for slow perceptive smiles based upon first-hand understanding of the ways and wiles of wooded hill and brushy dale.

The store-porch humorist is not, of course, above a pun. An old codger from Red Star was telling of his family.

"Yes, suh, they come three boys, then a girl, then another boy. So I named 'em Matthew, Mark, Luke, Ann, John."

And he knows the value of hyperbole. One time I asked an old countryman why he preferred cushaws (large hooked squashes) to pumpkins. He spat.

"Well, suh, if I was to grow punkins on them slopin' fields, they'd likely break loose from the vines and roll down and kill somebody. But cushaws—they hook theirselves to corn stalks and ketch on."

Nor is the store humorist immune to the potency of slap-stick. There is no good reason why he should be. Mimicry can also put him into the high rhapsodies of mirth. And the countryside idiot is a dependable source of laughter.

Backwoods fondness for burlesque mingles mirthfully with the liking for the humour of ignorance. For that very reason countrymen enjoy country jokes and relish the opportunity for embellishment and parody.

"You know, over at Post Oak Hill where we come from, that there's the reel brush. Pap Eason he's about the only feller down that there creek bend as knows how to read and write. So about seven or eight of us chipped in and taken the Springfield newspaper, figgerin' as how Pap could read it to us.

"Well, we done hit, and one day we was settin' around listenin' and

Pap was readin' about where the paper said as how ever'body ought to plant a lot of corn and plow hit a lot because some mighty bad droughts was comin'. Mart Miller set and puzzled awhile and then he says:

" 'Pap, what's a drought?'

"Pap chawed his terbaccer a minute and stroked his chin-whiskers and then says:

" 'Well, I couldn't be jest shore, but if I ain't mighty mistaken, a drought is one of them new-fangled varmints that's a cross betwixt a coon and a wildcat. Anyhow they shore is hell on corn.' "

Another tale of the same timbre tells of a rural countryside in the throes of a summertime political campaign. Squire Techstone was running for circuit clerk against a slicked-up county seat lawyer. The two were orating at an August picnic. The legal member was offering belligerent argument.

"That man is as ignorant of the law as he is of the responsibilities of office. I would even defy my opponent to define so simple a legal term as *habeas corpus.*"

Squire Techstone lifted off his battered felt hat and cogitated.

"Well, unless I'm mighty fur wrong that term means a red Jersey heifer fresh with a first calf."

There are rural epics of the sort that came about when Newt Finnen's wife prevailed upon Newt to take all their children to the protracted meeting.

"Newt said he couldn't rightfully bear to set and listen to preachin's, but one time his wife got come over with holiness and she hawg-an'-pantered him till he had to take her an' the young 'uns to meetin'. Newt set out on the back porch till the preachin' was all over, then he commenced gettin' on easy about was the young 'uns still there. He figgered he'd better round 'em up. So he strolled inside and brushed back the black bristles from his forehead and says,

" 'emmy, Dan'l, Sady, Jude, Prosey, Tom, Virgil, Dessie, Newtie, Violeeny, you-all-here?'

"They says, 'Yes, Pa, we're here.'

"So then Newt lined 'em up and struck out for home."

There are times when the edge of satire may become a bit cutting. A countryside revival meeting had reached the stage of spiritual orgies. The parson preached, the congregation rolled and grovelled and kicked up straw. Then came the hour for testifying.

Brother Amos, the countryside cripple, squatted upon a convenient corner bench. He was a paralytic, an invalid hopelessly cramped and drawn, with gangling and unruly limbs. During the course of the testifying the parson called upon the crippled one to rise and tell what the Lord had done for him.

Brother Amos roused jerkily, raised his chin a bare inch from his chest in painful deliberation and struggled to manipulate his lagging limbs. There was a silence of expectation and awaited revelation. Then the lame one shrilled:

"You was askin' what the Lord done for me. Well, I'll tell you. He jest blamed near ruint me."

The run of store-porch humour is withal a gentle humour, a garnishment for extensive leisure, cornmeal mush, sun and rain, dew and moonlight, and backwoods stillness. It rarely carries bitterness. It may be brusque but it is seldom vengeful. It is rarely ulterior. A man does not use it to sell his hen's eggs, or to acquire a soft job, or to swarm with the village social bees. The peasant laughs because he sees no reason why he shouldn't.

As an example of the kindliness of the humour, there is a recitation dealing with a lad from Gulch Hollow, who on first coming to Eureka, was lured by the tempting yellowness of the store-window lemons. The youth had never seen lemons before and he figured to sample them. So he bought a dime's worth and proceeded to try out the purchase. A first attempt to bite through the tough rind revealed an appalling mistake. But in the sight of a half-dozen onlookers the lad from Gulch Hollow did not once hesitate. He ate the first lemon whole; then the second and third. Nobody laughed. There was not even the suggestion of a smile. The rural youth addressed a sober audience.

"Yessir, fer a considerable spell I've been honin' to get my fill of these here tropical fruits because I shorely do pleasure in the flavour of 'em and now I aim to revel in it."

Then with puckering lips he retreated toward the village pump, his departure unmarred by laughter, his sensitive spirit unchafed.

And one time the folks were having a moonlight supper up at the Brush Ford schoolhouse. Uncle Zeb Hatfield, who hadn't been out to any manner of funmaking in a month of moons, was a bit unsteady about his etiquette, and in consequence chanced to pour buttermilk into his coffee instead of cream. An observing farm wife moved to fetch him another cup. But Uncle Zeb would be the subject of no such bother. He blew at the murky fluid and assured the company that taking buttermilk in coffee was to him an invariable habit. Steady faces accepted that declaration. There was not even an adolescent snigger.

Backwoods humour has its subtle side, too. The commoner from Low Gap is capable of a cerebral chuckle now and then, fully as capable of it as his brethren of the town.

He enjoys his Aunt Lulu Pettigrew's complaint of pains in her abominable muscles, or that most of her family have died of nobility, or that with one of them New Fords her son Wid can climb any manner of mountain in neutral. He relishes such picturesque generalities as those of Judge-Patton of Kentucky, who once offered these instructions to his jury:

"Gentlemen, whenever you see a big overgrown buck a-settin' at the mouth of some holler or the fork of some road, with a big slouch hat on, a blue collar, a celluloid rose in his coat lapel and a banjo strung across his chist, fine that man, gentlemen. Fine him! Because if he ain't done somethin' already, he blame soon will."

He enjoys hearing the Tannehill child assure a younger brother that if he will only stop hollerin' he can watch the old gentleman fall off the hay wagon.

He enjoys the strategy of the thrifty old lady of didactic leanings who in remonstrating with some little boys for their stealing a pocketful of pears, assured them that if they would only be forward and honest about it and bring along something in which to carry the fruit home, she would be glad to give them the pears. Five minutes later she was faced by the pack of youngsters who brought an old-style clothes basket capable of holding at least four bushels.

There is an ephemeral freshness to backwoods humour due in part to its nearness to earth; in part to the ways of its perpetrators—their slowness of speech and droll manoeuvrings of expression; their posture and inflections which cannot be adequately reproduced even in the most accommodating of type.

The great majority of upcountry jests are neither scrupulously original nor sparklingly clever. Often enough a rustic gem will shine for generations. And this fact is easier to understand when one understands that in Elizabethan America one generation is very much like another.

TWO PLANTATION TALES[153]

I. According to How the Drop Falls

"Is I gwine tell you a tale right now?" said Uncle Remus, in response to a question by the little boy. "Well, I ain't right certain en sho' 'bout dat. It's 'cordin ter how de drap falls."

"Pshaw!" exclaimed the youngster, "I've heard you say that before. I don't know what you mean when you say it's according to how the drop falls."

"Ah-yi!" retorted Uncle Remus triumphantly, "den I'm a punkin ahead er yo' 'simmon, is I?"

"It's according to how the drop falls", rejoined the little boy, laughing.

"De way dat sayin' come 'bout", said Uncle Remus, "may be funny, but 't ain't no tale. It des happen so. One time dey wuz a 'oman call on a neighbor 'oman des' fo' dinner-time. I dunner whedder de neighbor 'oman like dis mighty well, but she 'uz monst'us perlite all de same.

"She 'low, 'Come right in, en take off yo' things an make yo'se'f at home. You'll hatter skuzen my hens', kaze I'm makin' up dough. Fling yo' bonnet on de bed dar, en take a seat en be seated.'

"Well, de tudder 'oman, she sot afar en talk, en watch de neighbor 'oman mix dough fer de bread, en dey run'd on des like wimmin folks does. It seem like de neighbor 'oman got a bad col', en her eyes run water twel some un it crope down ter de een er her nose en hang dar. De tudder 'oman, she watch it, whiles dey er talkin'. De neighbor 'oman she work up de dough, en work it up, en talk. Sometimes she'd hol' her head fum over de tray en talk, en den ag'in she'd hol' it right spang over de dough, en shake 'er head en talk.

"Bimeby she 'low, 'Won't you stay ter dinner? I'll have dis bread done in two shakes uv a sheep's tail.'

"De tudder 'oman say, 'I can't tell you, ma'am; it's 'cordin' ter how de drap falls.'

"De tudder 'oman say, 'Dey ain't a cloud in de sky, so 't ain't gwine ter rain. You des ez well stay.'

"De tudder 'oman 'low, 'I dont tole you de trufe; hit's 'cordin' ter how de drap falls.'

"So, atter dat, when folks wan' right certain en sho' 'bout what dey gwine do, dey'd up en say 't wuz 'cordin' ter how de drap fall."

"Well, how did it fall, Uncle Remus—in the bread-tray, or on the table, or on the floor?" the little boy inquired.

"Lawsy, honey!" responded the old man, "ef I 'uz er tell you, I'd hatter dream it, en dreamin' ain't gwine do you er me any mo' good den it done de nigger man what had de possum."

"I never heard of that", said the little boy.

"Oh, yes you is!" Uncle Remus asserted with some emphasis. "You been hearin' 'bout it off'n on sence you 'uz knee-high ter a duck, en you ain't much mo'n dat right now. No, suh! You des got de idee in you' min' dat when I set down fer ter tell you sump'n hit's bleedz ter be a tale, en when yuther folks tells it 't ain't nothin' but talk. I ain't got no secret 'bout dish yer nigger man what had de possum, but I tell you right now, 'tain't no tale. Too many folks done been fool wid it.

II. The Man Who had the Possum

"Well, den, one time dey wuz a nigger man, en dish yer nigger man had a big fat possum en a half er peck er sweet 'taters. He tuck de possum en de taters home, en he lay um down—de possum on one side de fireplace en de taters on tudder side. Den he get some wood and chips en make 'im a firer, en den he fotch out de skillet. He put de possum in dar, he did, en he put de taters in de ashes close by fer ter keep 'im comp'ny. Den he raked out some hot embers en sot de skillet on um, en he put on de skillet led, en piled some embers 'pon topper dat.

"He sot dar, he did, en wait fer de possum fer ter git done, en whiles he wuz a-waitin' he struck up a song. Maybe you done hear it 'fo' now, but dat ain't make no diffunce ter me, kaze when I git started dis away, I'm like de bull yearlin' gwine down de lane; dem what gits in de way gwine ter git run'd over—dey mos' sholy is!"

Uncle Remus leaned back in his chair, closed his eyes, and began to pat his foot. Then, after a little pause, he sang this fragment of a song:

"Virginny cut, chew terbacker,
Nigger dance ter merlatter;
Hoe de corn, dig er tater,
Plant terbacker, 't is no matter.

"Mix de meal, fry de batter,
Nigger dance ter merlatter;
Warm de cake in er platter,
Fry um in de cooney fat.

"Grab er tater out de ash,
Nigger dance ter merlatter;
Possum meat afar in der platter,
Shool he make de nigger fatter."

Uncle Remus's voice was full of melody, and he sang the song to a rollicking tune. The little boy was so much pleased that he asked the old man to sing it again.

"Bless yo' soul, honey. If I git in a fa'r way er singin', de niggers 'll all quit der work en crowd 'roun' here en jine in wid me, en we'll have a reg'lar ole-timey camp-meetin' gwine on here 'fo' you know it. I ain't got no time fer dat.

"Now, den, dish yer nigger man, what I been tellin' you 'bout, he got his taters in de ashes en his possum in de skillet, en he sot afar en sing de song, en watch um all cook. Atter so long a time dey got done, en he pull de taters out'n de embers, en push de skillet 'way fum de fier. He 'low ter hisse'f, he did, dat col' possum is better'n hot possum, dough bofe un um is good nuff fer anybody. So he say he'll des let it set afar en cool, en soak in de gravy. Den he say he b'lieve he'll do some noddin', kaze den he'll dream he eatin' de possum, en den he'll wake up en eat 'im sho nuff, en have de 'joyment er eatin' 'im two times.

"Well, suh, dat des de way he done. He sot back in his cheer, de nigger man did, en he nodded en nodded, en he work his mouf des like he eatin' possum, en he grunt in his sleep like he feelin' good. But whiles he settin' afar sleepin', a nudder nigger man smell de possum, en he crope up ter de door en peep in. He seed how de lan' lay en he slipped off his shoes en stole in. He lif' up de led er de skillet, en dar wuz de possum. He look on de side er de h'ath, en dar wuz de taters. Now, den, when dat de case, what gwine ter happen? Possum, en tater, en hongry nigger! Well, suh, de fust news you know, de possum wuz all bones, de taters wuz all peelin's, en de nigger wuz mo' dan a nigger. He fix de bones in one little pile, en he fix de peelin's in anudder little pile, en den he tuck some er de possum gravy en rub it on de tudder nigger's mouf en hen's, en den he went on 'bout his business.

"'T wan't so mighty long atter dat 'fo' de noddin' nigger wake up. He open his eyes he did, en stretch hisse'f, en look at de skillet en laugh.

"He 'low, You er dar, is you? Well, I'll tell you howdy now, en terreckly I'll tell you good-by!'

"He tuck de led off'n de skillet, en dey ain't no possum dar. He look 'roun' fer de taters, en dey ain't no taters dar. Dey ain't nothin' dar but a pile er bones en a pile er tater-peelin's. De nigger sot down in his cheer en went ter studyin'. He look at his han's, en he see possum grease on um. He lick out his tongue, en he tas'e possum gravy on his mouf. He shuck his head en study. He look at his hen's: 'Possum been dar!' He lick his mouf: 'Possum been dar, too!' He rub his stomach: 'But I be bless ef any possum been here!'"

THE TALKING MULE[154]

Ole feller one time had uh mule. His name wuz Bill. Every mornin' de man go toh ketch 'im he say, "Come round, Bill!"

So one mornin' he slept late, so he decided while he wuz drinkin' some coffee he'd send his son tuh ketch Ole Bill.

Told 'im say, "Go down dere, boy, and bring me dat mule up here."

Boy, he sich a fast Aleck, he grabbed de bridle and went on down tuh de lot tuh ketch Ole Bill.

He say, "Come round, Bill!"

De mule looked round at 'im. He told de mule, "Tain't no use you rollin' yo' eyes at *me*. Pa want yuh dis mawnin'. Come on round and stick yo' head in dis bridle."

Mule kept on lookin' at 'im and said, "Every mornin' it's 'Come round, Bill! Come round, Bill!' Don't hardly git no night rest befo' it's 'Come round, Bill!"

De boy throwed down dat bridle and flew back tuh de house and told his Pa, "Dat mule is talkin'."

"Ah g'wan, boy, tellin' you' lies! G'wan ketch dat mule."

"New suh, Pa, dat mule's done gone tuh talkin'. You hatta ketch dat mule yo' ownself. Ah ain't gwine."

Ole man looked at old lady and say, "See what uh lie dat boy is tellin'?"

So he gits out and goes on down after de mule hisself. When he got down dere he hollered, "Come round, Bill!"

Ole mule looked round and says, "Every mornin' it's come round, Bill!"

De old man had uh little fice dog useter foller 'im everywhere he go, so he lit out wid de lil fice right behind 'im. So he told de ole lady, "De boy ain't told much of uh lie. Dat mule *is* talkin'. Ah never heered uh mule talk befo'."

Lil fice say, "Me neither."

De ole man got skeered agin. Right through de wood he went wid de fice right behind 'im. He nearly run hisself tuh death. He stopped and commenced blowin' and says, "Ah'm so tired Ah don't know whut tuh do."

Lil dog run and set down in front of 'im and went to hasslin'[155] and says, "Me too."

Dat man is runnin' yet.

THE VENTRILOQUIST[156]

TAD: Is you hear de tale 'bout de white man an' de nigger an' de mule?

VOICE: I hear a heap er tales 'bout white folks an' niggers an' mules. Wuh you have in mind?

TAD: One time dere was a white man an' he runned a big farm, an' he notice one er he mule was gitten mighty poor, so he got to watchin'. He s'picion dat de nigger wuh was workin' de mule was stealin' he feed. Dis white man was one er dem people wha' kin pitch dey voice any way dey wants. He could throw he voice into a cow or dog or any kind er animal an' have 'em talkin'—make 'em carry on reg'lar compersation.

VOICE: I has heared dem kind er people.

TAD: Well, he git to de crack er de stable an' he seed de nigger wid a bag reach in de mule' trough an' take out some corn an' put it in de bag. When de nigger do dat, de white man pitched he voice right into de mule' mout' an' make de mule say:

"Nigger, don't take my little bit er feed."

When he say dat, de nigger walk off an' look at de mule for awhile an' de mule ain' say nothin' more. Den he walk back an' dip in de trough again an' start takin' de mule' corn, an' de white folks make de mule say again:

"Nigger, please don't take my feed."

An' again de nigger walk off an' look at de mule.

VOICE: Ain' no mule ever would er spoke but one time to me.

TAD: Dis here nigger ain' have good sense, an' he went back de third time an' dive into dat corn. An' dis time de mule turn he head an' look at him, an' de white folks th'owed he voice into de mule' mout' one more time an' make de mule say:

"Nigger, ain' I axe you please for God' sake quit takin' my feed. You mighty nigh done perish me to de'te."

When he say dat, de nigger drap he bag an' bu's' out er dat stable, an' de next mornin' he went to he boss an' say:

"Boss, I guh quit."

An' he boss say:

"John, I ain' want you to quit me. I satisfy wid you."

An' de nigger say:

"Well, Boss, I ain' zackly satisfy. You mought as well gee me my time, kaze I done quit."

SCIP: Dere ain' no nigger ever would er been zackly satisfy atter he heared a mule talkin'.

VOICE: It was quittin' time.

TAD: Dat ain' all. De white folks paid de nigger he wages an' de nigger walk off a piece down de road an' turn 'round an' walk back to de white folks an' say:

"Boss, I done quit. Dere ain' no nuse for nobody to say nothin' to me. I done quit an' I is guine, but 'fore I goes I got one thing to say to you."

An' de white folks look at him jes as kind an' say:

"Wha' it is, John?"

An' de nigger say:

"Boss, I done quit sho' 'nough, but 'fore I goes I wants to tell you one thing. Anything dat mule say to you is a damn lie."

An' den he leff.

SCIP: I knowed in de first place dat de white folks done loss a nigger.

OLE MASSA AND JOHN WHO WANTED TO GO TO HEAVEN[157]

You know befo' surrender Ole Massa had a nigger name John and John always prayed every night befo' he went to bed and his prayer was for God to come git him and take him to Heaven right away. He didn't even want to take time to die. He wanted de Lawd to come git him just like he was—boot, sock and all. He'd git down on his knees and say: "O Lawd, it's once more and again yo' humble servant is kneebent and body-bowed—my heart beneath my knees and my knees in some lonesome valley, crying for mercy while mercy kin be found.

O Lawd, Ah'm astin' you in de humblest way I know how to be *so* pleased as to come in yo' fiery chariot and take me to yo' Heben and its immortal glory. Come Lawd, you know Ah have such a hard time. Ole Massa works me *so* hard, and don't gimme no time to rest. So come, Lawd, wid peace in one hand and pardon in de other and take me away from this sin-sorrowing world. Ah'm tired and Ah want to go home."

So one night Ole Massa passed by John's shack and heard him beggin' de Lawd to come git him in his fiery chariot and take him away; so he made up his mind to find out if John meant dat thing. So he goes on up to de big house and got hisself a bed sheet and come on back. He thronged de sheet over his head and knocked on de door.

John quit prayin' and ast: "Who dat?"

Ole Massa say: "It's me, John, de Lawd, done come wid my fiery chariot to take you away from this sin-sick world."

Right under de bed John had business. He told his wife: "Tell Him Ah ain't here, Liza."

At first Liza didn't say nothin' at all, but de Lawd kept right on callin' John: "Come on, John, and go to Heben wid me where you won't have to plough no mo' furrows and hoe no mo' corn. Come on, John."

Liza says: "John ain't here, Lawd, you hafta come back another time."

Lawd says: "Well, then Liza, you'll do."

Liza whispers and says: "John, come out from underneath dat bed and g'wan wid de Lawd. You been beggin' him to come git you. Now g'wan wid him."

John back under de bed not sayin' a mumblin' word. De Lawd out on de doorstep kept on callin'.

Liza says: "John, Ah thought you was so anxious to get to Heben. Come out and go on wid God."

John says: "Don't you hear him say 'You'll do'? Why don't you go wid him?"

"Ah ain't a goin' nowhere. Youse de one been whoopin' and hollerin' for him to come git you and if you don't come out from under dat bed Ah'm gointer tell God youse here."

Ole Massa makin' out he's God, says: "Come on, Liza, you'll do."

Liza says: "Oh, Lawd, John is right here underneath de bed."

"Come on John, and go to Heben wid me and its immortal glory."

John crept out from under de bed and went to de door and cracked it and when he seen all dat white standin' on de doorsteps he jumped back. He says: "Oh, Lawd, Ah can't go to Heben wid you in you' fiery chariot in dese ole dirty britches; gimme time to put on my Sunday pants."

"All right, John, put on yo' Sunday pants."

John fooled around just as long as he could, changing them pants, but when he went back to de door, de big white glory was still standin' there. So he says agin: "O, Lawd, de Good Book says in Heben no filth is found and I got on dis dirty sweaty shirt. Ah can't go wid you in dis old nasty shirt. Gimme time to put on my Sunday shirt!"

"All right, John, go put on yo' Sunday shirt."

John took and fumbled around a long time changing his shirt, and den he went back to de door, but Ole Massa was still on de doorstep. John didn't had nothin' else to change so he opened de door a little piece and says:

"O, Lawd, Ah'm ready to go to Heben wid you in yo' fiery chariot, but de radiance of yo' countenance is *so* bright, Ah can't come out by you. Stand back jus' a li'l way please."

Ole Massa stepped back a li'l bit.

John looked out agin and says: "O, Lawd, you know dat po' humble me is less than de dust beneath yo' shoe soles. And de radiance of yo' countenance is so bright Ah can't come out by you. Please, please, Lawd, in yo' tender mercy, stand back a li'l bit further."

Ole Massa stepped back a li'l bit mo'.

John looked out agin and he says: "O, Lawd, Heben is so high and wese so low; youse so great and Ah'm so weak and yo' strength is too much for us poor sufferin' sinners. So once mo' and agin yo' humber servant is knee-bent and body-bowed askin' you one mo' favor befo' Ah step into yo' fiery chariot to go to Heben wid you and wash in yo' glory—be so pleased in yo' tender mercy as to stand back jus' a li'l bit further."

Ole Massa stepped back a step or two mo' and out dat door John come like a streak of lightning. All across de punkin patch, thru de cotton over de pasture—John wid Old Massa right behind him. By de time dey hit de cornfield John was way ahead of Ole Massa.

Back in de shack one of de children was cryin' and she ast Liza: "Mama, you reckon God's gointer ketch papa and carry him to Heben wid him?"

"Shet yo' mouf, talkin' foolishness!" Liza clashed at de chile. "You know de Lawd can't outrun yo pappy—specially when he's barefooted at dat."

"GOD AN' DE DEVIL IN DE CEMETERY"[158]

Two mens dat didn't know how tuh count good had been haulin' up cawn and they stopped at de cemetery wid de last load 'cause it wuz gittin' kinda dark. They thought they'd git thru instead uh goin' 'way tuh one of 'em's barn. When they wuz goin' in de gate two ear uh cawn dropped off de waggin, but they didn't stop tuh bother wid 'em, just then. They wuz in uh big hurry tuh git home. They wuz juste 'vidin' it up. "You take dis'un and Ah'll take dat'un, you take dat'un and Ah'll take dis'un."

An ole nigger heard 'em while he wuz passin' de cemetery an' run home tuh tell ole Massa 'bout it.

"Masse, de Lawd and de devil is down in de cemetery 'vidin' up souls. Ah heard 'em. One say, 'You take that'un an' Ah'll take dis'un.'"

Ole Massa wuz sick in de easy chear, he couldn't git about by hisself, but he said, "Jack, Ah don't know whut dis foolishness is, but Ah know you lyin'."

"Naw Ah ain't neither, Ah swear it's so."

"Can't be, Jack, youse crazy."

"Naw Ah ain't neither; if you don't believe me, come see for yo'self."

"Guess Ah better go see whut you talkin' 'bout; if you fool me, Ah'm gointer have a hundred lashes put on yo' back in de mawnin' suh."

They went on down tuh de cemetery wid Jack pushin' Massa in his rollin' chear, an it wuz sho dark down dere too. So they couldn't see de two ears uh cawn layin' in de gate.

Sho nuff Ole Massa heard 'em sayin', "Ah'll take dis'un", and de other say, "An' Ah'll take dis'un." Old Massa got skeered hisself but he wuzn't lettin' on, an' Jack whispered tuh 'im, "Unh hunh, didn't Ah tell you de Lawd an' de devil wuz down here 'vidin' up souls?'

They waited awhile there in de gate listenin' den they heard 'em say, "Now, we'll go git dem two at de gate."

Jack says, "Ah knows de Lawd gwine take you, and Ah ain't gwine let de devil get me—Ah'm gwine home." An' he did an' lef' Old Massa settin' dere at de cemetery gate in his rollin' chear, but when he got home, Ole Massa had done beat 'im home and wuz settin' by de fire smokin' uh seegar.

THE FORTUNE TELLER[159]

In slavery time dere was a coloured man what was named John. He went along wid Old Massa everywhere he went. He used to make out he could tell fortunes. One day him and his Ole Massa was goin' along and John said, "Ole Massa, Ah kin tell fortunes." Ole Massa made out he didn't pay him no attention. But when they got to de next man's plantation Old Massa told de landlord, "I have a nigger dat kin tell fortunes." So de other man said, "Dat nigger can't tell no fortunes. I bet my plantation and all my niggers against yours dat he can't tell no fortunes."

Ole Massa says: "I'll take yo' bet. I bet everything in de world I got on John 'cause he don't lie. If he say he can tell fortunes, he can tell 'em. Bet you my plantation and all my niggers against yours and throw in de wood lot extry."

So they called Notary Public and signed up de bet. Ole Massa straddled his horse and John got on his mule and they went on home.

John was in de misery all that night for he knowed he was gointer be de cause of Ole Massa losin' all he had.

Every mornin' John useter be up and have Ole Massa's saddle horse curried and saddled at de door when Ole Massa woke up. But *this* mornin' Ole Massa had to git John out of de bed.

John useter always ride side by side with Massa, but on de way over to de plantation where de bet was on, he rode way behind.

So de man on de plantation had went out and caught a coon and had a big old iron wash-pot turned down over it.

There was many persons there to hear John tell what was under de wash-pot.

Ole Massa brought John out and tole him, say: "John, if you tell what's under dat wash-pot Ah'll make you independent, rich. If you don't, Ah'm goin' to kill you because you'll make me lose my plantation and everything I got."

John walked 'round and 'round dat pot but he couldn't git de least inklin' of what was underneath it. Drops of sweat as big as yo' fist was rollin' off of John. At last he give up and said: "Well, you got de ole coon at last."

When John said that, Ole Massa jumped in de air and cracked his heels twice befo' he hit de ground. De man that was bettin' against Ole Massa fell to his knees wid de cold sweat pourin' off him. Ole Massa said: "John, you done won another plantation fo' me. That's a coon under that pot sho 'nuff."

So he give John a new suit of clothes and a saddle horse. And John quit tellin' fortunes after that.

MASSA AND THE BEAR[160]

One day Ole Massa sent for John and tole him, says: "John, somebody is stealin' my corn out de field. Every mornin' when I go out I see where they done carried off some mo' of my roastin' ears. I want you to set in de corn patch tonight and ketch whoever it is."

So John said all right and he went and hid in de field.

Pretty soon he heard somethin' breakin' corn. So John sneaked up behind him wid a short stick in his hand and hollered: "Now, break another ear of Ole Massa's corn and see what *Ah'll* do to you."

John thought it was a man all dis time, but it was a bear wid his arms full of roastin' ears. He thronged down de corn and grabbed John. And him and dat bear!

John, after while got loose and got de bear by the tail wid de bear tryin' to git to him all de time. So they run around in a circle all night long. John was so tired. But he couldn't let go of de bear's tail, do de bear would grab him in de back.

After a stretch they quit runnin' and walked. John swingin' on to de bear's tail and de bear's nose 'bout to touch him in de back.

Daybreak, Old Massa come out to see 'bout John and he seen John and de bear walkin' 'round in de ring. So he run up and says: "Lemme take holt of 'im, John, whilst you run git help!"

John says: "All right, Massa. Now you run in quick and grab 'im just so."

Ole Massa run and grabbed holt of de bear's tail and said: "Now, John you make haste to git somebody to help us."

John staggered off and set down on de grass and went to fanning hisself wid his hat.

Ole Massa was havin' plenty trouble wid dat bear and he looked over and seen John settin' on de grass and he hollered:

"John, you better g'wan git help or else I'm gwinter turn dis bear aloose!"

John says: "Turn 'im loose, then. Dat's whut Ah tried to do all night long but Ah couldn't."

THE BEAR FIGHT[161]

Deacon Jones an' he gal live in a section of de country way dere been a heap er bears. An' one night he been guine to an experience meetin', an' dere been two roads, an' he gal say:

"Papa, le's we don't go through de woods road, kaze I seen a bear dere today."

An' de deacon say:

"I ain' care notin' 'bout no bear. I a Christian an' loves God an' God loves me, an' I puts my trust in Him. I loves God. God is good. I'm guine through dem woods."

An' de gal say:

"Papa, le's we don't make no mistakes. Le's we go 'round."

An' de deacon say:

"I'm guine through dem woods. I trust God. I puts my faith in God. God is good an' will pertec' me."

An' de gal say:

"I ain' trustin' all dat. I'm guine 'round."

An' de deacon say:

"Well, I'm guine through de woods. God is my pertecter."

An' he went through de woods, an' de gal went 'round.

An' when de deacon git half way through de woods, a bear jumped on him an' he had a terrible time fightin' wid dat bear. De bear tored mighty nigh all he clothes off, an' bit him up an' mighty nigh ruint him. But when he git loose, he made he way to de experience meetin'. An' when he git dere, dem niggers been tellin' 'bout dey experience wid God an' Jesus an de devil an' wid angels an' a passel er lies.

An' den dey spied Deacon Jones in de back er de congregation, an' dey call on him for his experience an' he say he ain' got nothin' to say. An' all dem brother an' all dem sister keep on hollerin' for him. An' atter while de deacon git up an' say:

"My brothers an' sisters, all I kin say is: God is good. God is good. I loves God. I sho' loves Him, an' I puts my faith in Him. God is good an' He'll help you in a lot er little things, but, my brothers an' sisters, good as God is, He ain' worth a damn in a bear fight."

"LITTLE MORON"[162]

I

The little moron was nailing shingles on the house Somebody noticed that he was throwing about half the nails away, and asked him why. "Because", said the little moron, "the heads are on the wrong ends." "Well, you dope", said the other, "those are for the other side of the house."

The little moron got up in the middle of the night to answer the telephone. "Is this one one one one?" says the voice. "No, this is eleven eleven." "You're sure it isn't one one one one?" "No, this is eleven eleven." "Well, wrong number. Sorry to have got you up in the middle of the night." "That's all right, mister. I had to get up to answer the telephone anyway."

Two little morons went hunting. The first one shot at a duck, and when it fell at his feet he felt bad that the little duck had died when he shot it. The other said, "Oh, don't feel so bad. The fall would have killed it anyway."

Little moron was painting the house when another one came up and said, "Got a good hold on that brush?", "Yep." "Well, if you are sure you got a good hold on that brush I'll borrow your ladder for a second." "O.K. but don't keep it long. The handle of this paint brush is kind of slippery."

Little moron's wife sent him down town after a bucket of ice. He came back with a pail of water. "I got this for half price because it was melted."

Little moron took two slices of bread and went down and sat on the street corner waiting for the traffic jam. A big truck came along and gave him a jar.

Why did the little moron go to the lumber yard?—To look for his draft board.

Then there was the little moron who broke his leg when he threw his cigarette butt down the manhole and tried to step on it.

And the one who took his nose apart to see what made it run.

Little moron tried to light his cigarette. He struck the first match on the seat of his pants, but it wouldn't light. He tried another. It wouldn't light. The third one finally lit. He lit his cigarette, carefully blew the match out and put it in his vest pocket. "What for did you put that match in your vest pocket." "That's a good match. I'll use it again."

Two little morons were in jail. They were trying to find a way out. "I know. I'll shine the flash light up to that window, you crawl up the beam and open that window." The other little moron objected. "Nothing doing. I'd get halfway up the beam and you'd turn the light off."

II[163]

Why did the little moron lock his papa in the icebox? Because he wanted cold pop.

Do you know why the little moron took some hay to bed with him? Because he wanted to feed his nightmare.

Can you tell me why the little moron took his clock to bed with him? Because it was fast.

What did the little moron do when he was told he was dying? He moved into the living room.

* * * *

A little moron went to a show. The usher asked him, "Would you like to sit down front?" The little moron answered, "I'm sorry, sir, but I don't bend that way."

And did you hear about the little moron who stayed up all night to study for his blood test? And the little moron who took some sugar and cream with him to the movie because he heard there was going to be a serial? And the little moron who saved burnt-out light bulbs to use during blackouts? And the little moron who took some pepper out with him because he heard it was hot stuff? And the little moron who ate some dynamite so his hair would grow out with bangs? And the little moron who put a chair in the coffin for rigor mortis to set in? And the little moron who slept on the chandelier because he was a light sleeper? And the little moron who went to a football game because he thought a quarter-back was a refund? And the little moron who took off his knee cap to see if there was any beer in the joint? And the little moron who sat up all night on his wedding night gazing out of the window because his mother had told him it would be the most wonderful night he ever saw?

There were two little morons who were waiting for a street car. One asked the other if he thought the car had already gone. "Yes, it must have gone", the other exclaimed. "There's it's tracks!"

Did you hear about the little moron who cut his arms off? He wanted to wear a sleeveless sweater.

Did you hear about the little moron bride who sat down and cried bitterly when her husband went out to shoot craps? She didn't know how to cook them.

Did you hear about the little moron who went strolling along the beach and saw a nude woman come out of the water? He said, "Boy wouldn't she look good in a bathing suit!"

Have you heard about the little moron who was so bashful that he had to go into another room to change his mind?

There was the one about the two little morons who were walking along a railroad track and spied a human arm beside the rails. "That looks like Joe's arm", exclaimed the first little moron. "It is Joe's arm", said the other. They walked a little farther and saw a human leg lying beside the rails. "That looks like Joe's leg", exclaimed the first little moron. "It is Joe's leg", said the other. A short way farther they saw a head lying beside the rails. "That looks like Joe's head", exclaimed the first little moron. "It is Joe's head", said the other little moron, and he stooped, picked the head up by the ears, shook it, and cried, "Joe, Joe, are you hurt?"

Then there was the one about a group of little morons who were building a house. One of the little morons went to the boss and asked if they should start building the house from the top down or from the bottom up. "Why, start from the bottom and build up, of course!" replied the boss. The little moron turned and yelled to his fellow workers: "Tear 'er down, boys! Gotta start all over!"

The little moron told his friend, "I only weighed three pounds when I was born." "Did you live?" asked the friend. "Did I live! Say, you oughta see me now!"

ABSENCE OF MIND[164]

I

A man, thinking he was at home, one evening lately, lay down on the common, and put his boots outside the gate to be blacked in the morning. Another person, after getting home one rainy night, put his umbrella in the bed, and leaned up in the corner himself.

We have just heard of a truly distressing instance of absence of mind, of which, we understand, our venerable friend, and contemporary, Mr. Bot Smith, was the victim. The other evening he proceeded bed-ward, as usual, and, in a fit of absence of mind, put the candle into the bed, *and blew himself out!*

III

The last "modern instance" recorded in the Yankee papers, is that of a Vermont waggoner going to market, who lifted his horse into the waggon, and tacked himself to the traces. The veracious chronicler adds, the waggoner did not discover his error until he endeavoured to neigh!

T'other day a man in Baltimore, intending to wind up his watch, through a sudden attack of absence of mind, wound up himself. . . .

The *Nashville Observer* informs us of the following case of absence of mind, which took place in the person of an old lady, who, after stirring the fire with her knitting needle, proceeded to knit with the poker, and did not discover her error till she commenced scratching her head with it.

A woman in Ohio put her baby into the washing-tub, and its dirty frock and petticoat into the cradle, and set her little boy to rock it. She did not discover her mistake until the baby cried out when she pinned its left leg to the line, as she hung it out in the yard to dry.

We learn from the *Nashville Banner*, that a land-agent down there, by name Hiram S. Botts, having to ride out in great haste one day last week, actually clapped the saddle upon his own back instead of his mare's, and never found out the mistake till he was quite fatigued with vainly trying to get upon himself.

IV

A highly respectable inhabitant of the city of New York lately died under very remarkable circumstances. He was subject to fits of extreme absence of mind from childhood, and one night, upon retiring to bed, having carefully tucked his pantaloons under the bed-clothes, he threw himself over the back of a chair, and expired from the severe cold he experienced during the night. The editor of the *New York Morning Herald*, who relates this extraordinary fact, assures his readers, as a guarantee of its truth, that he received his information from the individual in question!

BIG TALK

I. Colour[165]

Then Gold spoke up and said, "Now, lemme tell one. Ah know one about a man as black as Gene."

"Whut you always crackin' me for?" Gene wanted to know. "Ah ain't a bit blacker than you."

"Oh, yes you is, Gene. Youse a whole heap blacker than Ah is."

"Aw, go head on, Gold. Youse blacker than me. You jus' look my colour cause youse fat. If you wasn't no fatter than me you'd be so black till lightnin' bugs would follow you at twelve o'clock in de day, thinkin' it's midnight."

"Dat's a lie, youse blacker than Ah ever dared to be. Youse lam' black. Youse so black till they have to throw a sheet over yo' head so de sun kin rise every mornin'. Ah know yo' ma cried when she seen you."

"Well, anyhow, Gold, youse blacker than me. If Ah was as fat as you Ah'd be a yaller man."

'Youse a liar. Youse as yeller as you ever gointer git. When a person is poor he look bright and de fatter you git de darker you look."

"Is dat yo' excuse for being so black, Gold?"

II. An Ugly Man[166]

"Hey, Jim, where the swamp boss? He ain't got here yet."

"He's ill—sick in the bed Ah hope, but Ah bet he'll git here yet."

"Aw, he ain't sick. Ah bet you a fat man he ain't", Joe said.

"How come?" somebody asked him and Joe answered:

"Man, he's too ugly. If a spell of sickness ever tried to slip up on him, he'd skeer it into a three weeks' spasm."

Blue Baby[167] stuck in his oar and said: "He ain't so ugly. Ye all jus' ain't seen no real ugly man. Ah seen a man so ugly till he could get behind a jimpson weed and hatch monkeys."

Everybody laughed and moved closer together. Then Officer Richardson said: "Ah seen a man so ugly till they had to spread a sheet over his head at night so sleep could slip up on him."

They laughed some more, then Clifford Ulmer said:

"Ah'm goin' to talk with my mouth wide open. Those men y'all been talkin' 'bout wasn't ugly at all. Those was pretty men. Ah knowed one so ugly till you could throw him in the Mississippi river and skim ugly for six months."

"Give Cliff de little dog", Jim Allen said. "He done tole the biggest lie."

"He ain't lyin'", Joe Martin tole them. "Ah knowed dat same man. He didn't die—he jus' uglied away."

III. A MEAN MAN[168]

Allen asked: "Ain't dat a mean man? No work in the swamp and still he won't let us knock off."

"He's mean all right, but Ah done seen meaner men than him", said Handy Pitts.

"Where?"

"Oh, up in Middle Georgy. They had a straw boss and he was so mean dat when the boiler burst and blowed some of the men up in the air, he docked 'em for de time they was off de job."

Tush Hawg up and said: "Over on de East Coast Ah used to have a road boss and he was so mean and times was so hard till he laid off de hands of his watch."

Wiley said: "He's almost as bad as Joe Brown. Ah used to work in his mine and he was so mean til he wouldn't give God an honest prayer without snatching back 'Amen'."

SLOW TRAIN

I[169]

Some trains in northern Idaho are as slow as the one out of Salmon City. Between Lewiston and Kamiah it's so slow that farmers who load hay at Kamiah discover that the cars are empty by the time they reach Lewiston, because cows along the way have eaten it. One time a salesman was so indignant that he swore to high heaven he could get out and walk and arrive more quickly. The conductor gazed at him for a moment and sighed. "So could I", he said, "but the company won't let me."

Among intolerably slow trains in Idaho is the branch to the Twin Falls area. Once an impatient passenger wanted to know of the conductor why the train had stopped. "There's a cow on the track", he said. "We have to chase her off." When, a little later, the train stopped again, the passenger roared: "Now what's wrong?" "Oh", said the conductor serenely. "We just caught up with the cow."

II[170]

Talk about your slow trains through Arkansaw and your snail specials over the Rockies, but I struck a train in Indiana that was sure enough slow. I got on it to go up the state about seventy-five miles. The thing ran so slow that I went to the conductor and said, "Look here, if you don't ginger the gait of this thing up a little, I'll get out and walk." He flared up and said, "Who's the boss of this train?" I said, "I suppose you are." He said, "Then dry up." I said, "Whose dead body have you on board?" He said, "Nobody's; why?" I said, "Because you're running so slow I thought maybe you were bossing a funeral procession." That made him still madder, and we hooked up. We jumped out on the right-o'-way, and the train running at full speed, and had a fight, and I knocked the breath out of him and ran down to a pond and got my hat full of water and poured it in his face and brought him to, and we both caught the hind end of the train as it came by—and it wasn't a long train either.

But the walloping I gave the conductor didn't make the thing go any faster. A fellow standing on the side of the track held up a knife and hollered, "Got a frog-sticker yer want to swap?" I lit out and looked his knife over, swapped with him and skinned him too bad to talk about, and caught the hind end of the train again as it came by. I went to the conductor next day and apologized for banging him up. He said, "Oh, that's all right. The only thing I regret is, I lost my cap back where we had the fight." I said, "I'll go back and get it." He said, "Don't put yourself to any trouble." I said, "It won't be any trouble." I went back and got his cap and caught up with the train at the next station.

I was on the slow outfit so long that I wore out one of the cushion seats, and had train sores. You may think I'm overdrawing it, but I'm not, when I tell you that a fellow took down with typhoid fever on the thing just after I got on, and when I got off at the end of my journey, he was sound and well, and he had a long siege of it, too.

ORIGIN OF NAMES[171]

A young Oil Citizen calls his sweetheart Revenge, because she is sweet.—*Oil City Derrick*.

And the young married man in South Hill calls his mother-in-law Delay, because she is dangerous.—*Burlington Hawkeye*.

And a South End man calls his wife Fact, because she is a stubborn thing.—*Boston Globe.*

And a fourth wife of a district attorney calls him Necessity, because he knows no law.—*New Orleans Times.*

And a Cincinnati man names his coachman Procrastination, because he stole his watch.—*Breakfast Table.*

And we called a beautiful schoolma'am that we used to go to Experience, because she was a dear teacher.—*Eli Perkins.*

And a Yonkers man names his wife Frailty, because Shakespeare says: "Frailty, thy name is woman."—*Yonkers Gazette.*

Eli Perkins calls his wife Honesty, because he says it is the best policy.—*N. Y. Herald.*

UMPIRE BAIT, AND JOLLYS FOR PITCHERS AND BATTERS[172]

THAT base isn't made for a shelter, get into the open.

My kindergarten was the Polo Ground bleachers.

The first spiral staircase was built after the design of my fast curve.

Every time I swing the bat they have to give the ball a hydraulic treatment to coax it back into shape.

He couldn't hit a bunch of bananas with a bass fiddle.

Every time that Umps starts talking his tongue gets twisted around his eye tooth and he can't see what he's saying.

Data boy smoke, hit him on the head, you can't hurt him there.

Long fly to the pitcher, that's his noise.

Like a gate the way he swings.

Let him hit, let him hit, I got it.

He hasn't any more on that ball than September Morn wears.

Shut the gate, Nanny is wandering.

He hasn't got a thing today, but a grin and a belt buckle.

On the hill with nothing but a glove and a prayer.

You're not so rotten, kid, in about forty years you'll be a ball player.

This fellow is made to order for you, get up there and sting one.

Let's pick him to pieces, piece by piece, and see what makes him tick.

Take him out, get the hook, the hook.

He never touched me, Umps, I'll leave it to you.

If rags were ribbon, you'd be silk.

Look out, you fellows on the bench, this bloat at bat is liable to spike you.

Come on, Smoke, old boy, give him the spitter.

That ball was so low it would have to reach up to touch bottom.

Put on your chains, Umps, you're skidding.

Cancel that rave, Umps.

A cozy corner in the nuttery for yours.

Back to the oven, you aren't done yet.

Is this a union of some kind? Does everybody strike?

Come on fellows, keep working. We gotta beat ten men, but one of them is blind.

SLANG AND NEAR SLANG OF SOME LENGTH[173]

BACK to the oven, you're not done yet—Repartee. Conveys the impression of a lack of intelligence. Implies that the person's intelligence is in a "half baked" condition.

Come down from the walls—Be natural. Get down to facts. "Get off your high horse."

Come wipe your feet on our welcome mat—An invitation to make a visit.

Daggers at eighty paces—A mock challenge to a duel.

Do you follow me or do I go alone?—Do you understand what I am saying?

If you took a glass of water, the fumes would go to your brains—Repartee.

If you took laughing gas, you would cry—Repartee.

It was old when St. Louis was a blue print—It is old, old as the hills.

Jump on the bread wagon and loaf with the rest of the bundles—An invitation to become more idle and do things easier.

Put grease in your pan, your fish is burning—An intimation that what you are saying is incorrect.

Put in a quarter, your gas is low—You are getting out of breath or ideas.

Put on your chains, you're skidding—You are getting away from the idea or off the track.

Ring off, your wires are crossed—You are talking nonsense.

Ring the bell, conductor, I'm on, I'm on—I get your meaning.

Sit down, you're rocking the boat—You're causing a disturbance.

Six men will walk slow with you—You will be on your way to your funeral.

Sneeze, your brains are dusty—Your brain is not in good working order.

Snow again, I don't get your drift—I don't get your meaning. I don't understand you.

You are so low you have to reach up to touch bottom—Means your lowness almost surpasses description or imagination.

You've got more stalls than a stable—You abound in subterfuges and excuses.

I SHOULD WORRY————[174]

Like a ball and get bounced.
Like a button and get the hook.
Like a chandelier and get lit up every night.
Like dice and get shaken.
Like an elephant and carry my trunk.
Like a fresh clam and get the lemon.
Like a fireman and lose my hose.
Like glue and stick around.
Like a hat and order a coloured band.
Like a lump of butter and get strong.
Like the ocean and get fresh like the lakes.
Like a patrol wagon and do in a pinch.
Like a peanut and get roasted.
Like a peninsula and stretch out to see.
Like a pin cushion and get all stuck up.
Like a piano stool and go for a spin.
Like a plumber and get all around the joints.
Like a railroad track and get some new ties.
Like a raisin and go on a bun.
Like a rolling pin and gather the dough.
Like a smokestack and get all puffed up.
Like a tree and get trimmed.
Like a washboard and get full of wrinkles.
Like a window washer and feel a pain.

"YOU TELL 'EM" ENGLISH[175]

You tell 'em, mail carrier,
You're a man of letters!

You tell 'em,
My tongue's in my shoe!

You tell 'em, powder puff,
My lips stick.

You tell 'em, parcel post,
I can't express it.

You tell 'em, pony,
I'm a little horse.

You tell 'em, corsets,
You've been around women longer than I have.

You tell 'em, salad,
I'm dressing.

You tell 'em, Sahara,
You've got the sand.

You tell 'em, pieface,
You've got the crust.

You say it, goldfish,
You've been around the globe.

You tell 'em, victrola,
You've got the record.

You tell 'em, coffee,
You've got the grounds.

You tell 'em, little stream,
You've been through the mill.

You tell 'em, toothache,
You've got the nerve.

SHE WAS ONLY A DAUGHTER[176]

She was only a professor's daughter, but she learned her lesson.
She was only a fireman's daughter, but she sure did go to blazes.
She was only the tailor's daughter, but she pressed well.
She was only a photographer's daughter, but she delivered the goods.
She was only an electrician's daughter, but she had good connections.
She was only a blacksmith's daughter, but she knew how to forge ahead.
She was only a milkman's daughter, but she was the cream of the crop.
She was only a convict's daughter, but she knew all the bars.
She was only the parson's daughter, but she had her following.
She was only an acrobat's daughter, but she never turned over.
She was only a convict's daughter, but she knew when to faint.
She was only a florist's daughter, but she potted all the pansies.
She was only a dairyman's daughter, but what a calf.
She was only a woodcutter's daughter, but she hadn't been axed.
She was only a barber's daughter, but what a mug she had.
She was only a surgeon's daughter, but oh what a cut-up.

KNOCK KNOCK, WHO'S THERE?[177]

CHESTER. Chester who? Chester song at twilight.
Cecil. Cecil who? Cecil have music wherever she goes.
Hoffman. Hoffman who? I'll hoffman I'll puff an' I'll blow yer house in.
Gretta. Gretta who? Gretta long little doggie—gretta long.
Gwen. Gwen who? Gwen an' outthewinda. Gwen an' outthewinda.
Shixa. Shixa who? Shixa one half dozen of another.
Argo. Argo who? Argo chase yerself.
Hiram. Hiram who? Hiram I coin' hey hey.
Morris. Morris who? Morris Saturday—next day's Sunday.
Marcella. Marcella who? Marcella's fulla water.
Major. Major who? Major answer the door didn't I?
Thermos. Thermos who? Thermos be some one wait-ting who feels the way I do.
Arthur. Arthur who? Arthur any more at home like you?
Agatha. Agatha who? Agatha feeling you're foolin'.

Mortimer. Mortimer who? Mortimer pitied than scorned.
Akron. Akron who? Akron give you anything but love baby.
Alby. Alby who? Alby glad when you're dead you rascal you.
Hassan. Hassan who? Hassan a body here seen Kelly?
Irving. Irving who? Irving a good time wisha were here.
Upton. Upton who? Just upton and downtown.
Dick. Dick who? Dick 'em up—I'm tongued-tied.
Bob. Bob who? Bob ba black sheep havya any wool?
Cigarette. Cigarette who? Cigarette life if you don't weaken.
Domino. Domino who? Domino thing if ya ain't got that swing.
Fletcher. Fletcher who? Fletcher self go—relax an' fletcher self go.
Wendy. Wendy who? Wendy moon comes over the mountain.
Sonia. Sonia who? Sonia shanty in ol' shanty town.
Igloo. Igloo who? Igloo through here—the music goes down an' round.
Caesar. Caesar who? Caesar jolly good fellow, caesar jolly good fellow.
Ennui. Ennui who? I'm a dreamer, ennui all?
Thistle. Thistle who? Thistle be a lesson to me.
Tex. Tex who? Tex us to pull a good one, don't it?
Pettygil. Pettygil who? Pettygil is like a melody.
Edsall. Edsall who? Edsall there is—there is no more.

SMALL TOWN STUFF[178]

A MAN appears on the streets with more than a day's growth of stubble on his face. "Say, John, yah gonna have to pay dog tax pretty soon!"

A desperate man has cranked his fliver for thirty minutes and the motor has not coughed once. "What'll yah take fer it; spot cash?"

An ugly man or a handsome man, or a fairly respectable-looking man is having his picture made. "Mr. Photographer, yah gonna bust yah machine taking a picture o' Frank Goza."

Some brave soul, for vanity's sake, begins the culture of a moustache. "Say, guy, yah eyebrow has slipped", or "Why didn't yah swallow all o' the horse, Jim?"

A man loses his house by fire. "Sam, did yah have time to git the furniture out befo' yah sot her afire?"

John Purdy and his wife stand at the depot waiting for the train. "Yah goin' on a pleasure trip, John?" "Nope, the wife's goin' along."

A shining straw hat appears upon the head of a native. "Say, feller, the cows are gonna take after yah!"

The circus comes to town. "Goin' to the circus? "Sure, mike!" "Goin' in?" "Naw, I reckon not."

A man trudges home with a chicken swinging from his hand. "All right, Sim! Much oblige; I'll be up fer supper."

PHRASES OF THE PEOPLE[179]

PUT YO' brains in a jaybird's head an' he'd fly backwards.

Jump down your throat an' gallup your insides out.

Yessuh, my little boy he's tol'able honest for his age.

Dat road got littler an' littler til it jest run up a tree.

Been ponderin' so hard I ain't had time to think.

Got de hookworm hustle.

Mouth's so wide ef 'twarn't for his ears de top of his head would be an island.

Steppin' high like a rooster in deep mud.

When dat preacher leaves my house I steps out in de backyard an' counts my chickens.

* * * * *

I give him thunder an' lightning stewed down to a fine pizen.

Dat white cussed me from de birth o' Saul an' Silas to de death o'de devil, an' called me ev'ything 'cept a child o' God.

Cunnel, dat nigger sprinkled dis here peedee root an' love powders over me, an' dat's what fust injuced me to commit love.

So lazy yo' vittles don't taste good.

Water's so low dat de garfishes is gittin' freckle-faced.

Got tuk down drunk.

A fool's tongue is long enough to cut his throat.

Money thinks I'm dead.

You ain't got enough sense to deliver a chew of tobacco in a spittoon.

The bosom of his trousers.

* * * * *

Make your face look like a dime's wuth o' dog meat.

Jaybird jabber. [Gabble of women.]

Ef you wants to see how much folks is goin' to miss you, jest stick
yo' finger in de pond den pull it out an' look at de hole.
Cavortin' like a fat pony in high oats.
Make a straight coattail. [Scared man running.]
Grinnin' like a baked 'possum.
Lean hound for a long race and a poor man for chillun.
So hongry my belly think's my throat's cut.
Cluttered with trouble.
Dat nigger ain't skeered o' work; he'll lie down beside de biggest kind
    o' job an' go to sleep.

* * * * *

Enjoyin' poor health.
Swamp's so dry dere's four million bullfrogs ain't never learned how
    to swim.
Dat ooman's nine years older'n God.
A mighty miration. [Make a to-do.]
De devil gits up when de sun goes down, an' comes to plow his field.
Life is short an' full o' blisters.
Wish I was at home sick in bed.
"How is you today?" "Po'ly, thank God!"
Heap o' stir an' no biskits.
Busy as a bumblebee in a bucket of tar.
Don't remember yo' name, but I knows yo' favour.
Why don't you put sugar in yo' shoes to coax yo' breeches down?
Rather tell a lie on credit den de truth for cash.
Yo' head's a-blossomin' fer de grave.
Overspoke myself.
Got d' runnin off at de mouth.
Honest farmer puts straight wood on de outside his load.
On dat day seven women shall take hold of one man.
Dey 'scused me wrongful. [False charge of crime.]
A dunghill gentleman.
Beat him into doll rags.
It's agin nature and can't be did.
Afterclaps can go to the devil.
In a turkey dream.
Handful o' the dockyments. [Playing cards].
Wake, snakes, day's a-breakin'.

Busted to flinderjigs.
See him deep in hell as a pigeon can fly in a week.
Rich as mud.
A dog will cry if you beat him with a bone.
Tread in my footsteps ef you can spraddle far enough.
Full of wrath and cabbage.
Manhood distended his hide.
Whip you from the point of a dagger to the anchor of a ship.

PART FOUR

LIARS

An authentic liar knows what he is lying about, knows that his listeners—unless they are tender-feet, green- horns—know also, and hence makes no presence of fooling either himself or them. At his best he is as grave as a historian of the Roman Empire; yet what he is after is neither credulity nor the establishment of truth. He does not take himself too seriously, but he does re-gard himself as an artist and yearns for recogni-tion of his art. He may lie with satiric intent; he may lie merely to make the time pass pleasantly; he may lie in order to take the wind out of some egotistic fellow of his own tribe or to take in some greener; again, without any purpose at all and directed only by his ebullient and compan-ion-loving nature, he may "stretch the blanket" merely because, like the redoubtable Tom Ochiltree, he had "rather lie on credit than tell truth for cash". His generous nature revolts at the monotony of everyday facts and overflows with desire to make his company joyful.

—J. FRANK DOBIE

Introduction to Part Four

YARNS AND TALL TALES

> *To string, incongruities and absurdities to-*
> *gether in a wandering and sometimes purpose-*
> *less way, and seem innocently unaware that*
> *they are absurdities, is the basis of the Ameri-*
> *can art, if my position is correct. Another fea-*
> *ture is the slurring of the point. A third is the*
> *dropping of a studied remark apparently with-*
> *out knowing, it, as if one were thinking aloud.*
> *The fourth and last is the pause.*
>
> —MARK TWAIN

A yarn is a long, rambling, extravagant tale, with that quality of deliberate casualness and improvisation which stamps the "humorous story", in Mark Twain's view, as the distinctive development of story-telling in America.

The humorous story may be spun out to great length, and may wander around as much as it pleases, and arrive nowhere in particular; but the comic and witty stories must be brief and end with a point.

In Mark Twain's distinction between the comic or witty story and the humorous story is implied the difference between the anecdote and the yarn—a difference in form, style, and structure, based on a difference in purpose. Since the purpose of the anecdote as a wise or witty story is to make or illustrate a point, its business is to get to the point as quickly as possible (but not too quickly) and to make it clear and unmistakable. To that end the anecdote is bright and snappy, as brisk in movement as it is sharp in point. Since the purpose of the yarn is to create an effect of the odd, grotesque, or whimsical and to accumulate a certain kind of detail in order to produce that effect, the yarn takes its time, building up a good case for itself and delaying the ending or let-down, which is frequently an anti-climax.

The difference is essentially one of timing. The anecdote is closer to the short story, and the yarn to the sketch or tale in tempo. Whereas the former moves directly toward its goal, with, as the short-story textbooks put it, the greatest economy of means that is consistent with the utmost emphasis, the latter is leisurely, even to the point of being long-winded, and profuse to the point of diffuseness. The prolixity of the yarn is an oral quality, reflecting the relaxed mood of men who sit around and swap stories. While the anecdote suggests the give-and-take of conversational repartee, the yarn tends towards the monologue and garrulousness, with all the repetitions and digressions of monopolizing talk. In print the yarn becomes a mock-oral tale, imitating the slow drawl and sprawling ease of spoken, spontaneous narrative.

The enormous popularity of the mock-oral yarn which was the vehicle of backwoods and frontier humorists in the thirties is due as much to the naturalness and informality of the medium as to the genuineness of its humour. The humble art of humble life, the yarn presupposes leisure and loquacity. It was something both the teller and the listener could sink their teeth into. Though it may have lost its appeal for a generation used to a snappier lore, it still has the freshness that marked the discovery made by its first literary practitioners—the discovery that "something old in talking might look new in writing".[180]

A special, and to some the most distinctive, type of yarn is the tall tale. "Exuberant combinations of fact with outrageous fiction", in Walter Blair's definition, tall tales originate when the delicate balance between truth and untruth is turned in favour of the latter.

This improving on actual happenings rather than outright lying is the distinguishing feature of the tall tale, which carries it beyond the mere incongruity or absurdity of the yarn and saves it from the wholecloth invention of the ordinary whopper. The tall tale has a twofold relation to fact. On the one hand, as in the tall tales which were the chief stock-in-trade of Southern and Western humorists of the 1830's and 1840's, the eccentric or outlandish traits of backwoods and frontier life are singled out for realistic portrayal, the object being to create a "cumulative effect of the grotesque, romantic, or humorous". On the other hand, as in the later development of the genre, the prevailing interest is in the freaks of nature and in establishing a circumstantial basis for subhuman or superhuman marvels. In either case, the incongruity proceeds partly from the contrast between fact and fancy and is enhanced by enclosing the story in a realistic framework and employing the traditional device of the frame-tale, or group of stories within a story. This tendency of tall tales to grow and move in cycles also leads to their attraction about a central figure or hero of the Paul Bunyan variety.

Old-timers' reminiscences seem to make the best tall tales, all things considered, because the tricks of memory and distance come to the aid of the imagination in improving on actual happenings, while the exaggerations themselves are mellowed by time and immunized against criticism by the venerability that belongs to the narrator's years. Personal reminiscences gain further credence from the fact that they are the first-hand accounts of eye-witnesses or participants, backed up by the expressed or implied guarantee of "I saw or heard (if not actually did) these things myself." Sometimes the narrator employs the device of quoting an informant, named or unnamed, "long since dead" or lost track of, or of drawing upon travels (his own or some one else's) to report the wonders of distant places beyond checking up on. Credibility is also established by liberal use of local colour and circumstantial detail.

In spite of the presence of verisimilitude, which smacks of a hoax, the tall tale deals frankly with marvels, with the remarkable or prodigious, as the epithet signifies. As J. Frank Dobie points out, the tall-tale teller does not expect to be believed, except by the uninitiated. His task is essentially that of the poet; namely, to heighten fact and deal in illusions by creating a mood and an atmosphere favourable to the "willing suspension of disbelief that constitutes poetic faith".

The use of freaks of nature for tall tale material is associated not only with the experience of old-timers and travellers in their capacity as historians of the primitive type of a Herodotus or as naturalists of the credulous order of a Pliny but also with the American habit of boosting (as in stories of healthful climate and fertile soil) or boasting (as in brags of hunting and fishing) and with the pioneer trait of "laughing it off", or making light of misfortunes. Next to rural brags and gags, the most fertile source of tall tales is industry and remarkable inventions—an expression of the mechanical genius of Americans which has flowered in folklore ranging from Yankee contraptions like the bonepicking machine to the large-scale contrivances of Paul

Bunyan. The hone-picking machine is of the same breed as the automatic feeder in Chaplin's *Modern Times*.

> "I've got a new machine", said a Yankee pedlar, "for picking bones out of fish. Now, I tell you, it's a leetle bit the darndest thing you ever did see. All you have to do is to set it on a table and turn a crank, and the fish flies right down your throat and the bones right under the grate. Well, there was a country greenhorn got hold of it the other day, and he turned the crank the wrong way; and, I tell you, the way the bones flew down his throat was awful. Why, it stuck that fellow so full of bones, that he could not get his shirt off for a whole week!"[181]

Most yarns of occupational groups—cowboys, miners, lumberjacks, farmers—may be considered occupational in the sense of involving experiences encountered in the course of making a living. A true occupational tale, however, is told by as well as about workers and gives the feel of the job—something of how the work is done and how the workers feel about it. Although frequently incorporating sayings, jokes, and anecdotes that go the rounds, occupational tall tales are traditional tales which fall midway between the more esoteric or technical lore of the group and popular jokes and stories. They are to be distinguished also from the stories of practical jokes in which new hands are sent in search of impossible objects and from the legendary cycles of the Paul Bunyan type, into which these occupational tall tales may grow.

Like the best tall tales, occupational tall tales have a strong realistic and sociological colouring, even to a note of social criticism and protest. Although boastful, in the ring-tailed roarer tradition, they temper their brags with humorous complaints of hard work and bad conditions and with satire at the expense of bosses and fellow-workers.

At the same time occupational tall tales tell us much of the inside story of craftsmanship and industry and what happens when machine labour displaces hand labour and when one kind of tool is outmoded by another. Technological changes and differences give rise to feuds and contests, involving deeds of prodigious strength or skill. Rivalries take such subtle forms as the feud between cable-tool drillers and rotary workers in the oil fields or such obvious forms as the feud between old and new hands. Resentment against the machine and nostalgia for the good old days also creep in as normal reactions of displaced hand workers.

The language of the tales is coloured by occupations, both in the use of technical terms and trade slang and in the sprinkling of tall talk of men who work with their hands. In spite of the fact that freaks of machinery have replaced freaks of nature as subjects of these tall tales, there is a distinct hangover of the frontier-hero tradition of strong men and tough customers—hell-raisers or star performers. "I'm a man as is work-brickle", says the Demon Bricksetter from Williamson County. "I'm a man as can't say quit. While I lay a-holt, I'm like a turtle and I don't let loose till it thunders. I'm from Williamson County, and maybe you've heerd of the men they raise down there where the screech owls roost with the chickens."

FROM THE LIARS' BENCH

> *These men weren't vicious liars. It was love of romance, lack of reading matter, and the wish to be entertainin' that makes 'em stretch facts and invent yarns.*
>   —CHARLES M. RUSSELL

As a product of the untrammelled imagination, lying tales, whoppers, big windies, or big lies are a further specialization of the yarn and tall tale in the direction of the fabulous and mythical. Outside the realm of both probability and possibility, the world of lies is the world of supermen who perform miracles midway between nonsense and magic and who inhabit a land of giant vegetables and delightfully preposterous canny or composite creatures. Although more nearly akin to fairyland, this other world bears a faint resemblance and direct relation to the earthly paradise of Western guidebooks and land advertisements, out of whose boasts of marvels of climate and soil many whoppers have sprung.

In a land of vast distances and vast natural resources, where topographical features and human enterprises alike are on a grand scale, the line between fact and fantasy is hard to draw. Especially is this true in the "enchanted" South-west, amidst flat, shining expanses of plain and desert, where the atmosphere, light, and distance play queer tricks with one's vision and imagination, making for mirage and legend.

The rabbits have somehow. gotten the body of the hare and the ears of the ass; the frogs, the body of the toad, the horns of the stag-beetle, and the tail of the lizard; the trees fall up-hill, and the lightning comes out of the ground.[182]

Equally intense and dramatic is the history of the South-west, with its kaleidoscope of land-openings, migrations, and industrial developments, centring in the kingdoms of cattle and oil, cotton and citrus fruit. Landscape and history thus combine to keep one in a state of restless excitement and stimulation, in which it is easy to confuse illusion with reality, and a highly sharpened dramatic sense causes travellers and old-timers to feed their own and others' love of marvels, relating not what they have seen but what they think they have seen and what their listeners want to hear.

A similar enchantment is bred by the mountains and valleys of the South and the West. Among the concealments and surprises of winding creek trails, mysterious woods, and misty hollows, the marvellous hunters and fishermen of Appalachia and Ozarkia keep alive the name or tradition and the fictions of Davy Crockett and Baron Münchausen. Amidst the less intimate and more frigid wonders of the Rockies and the coastal range, where "streams run uphill and Nature appears to lie some herself", scouts, trappers, hunters, and explorers like Jim Bridger, Jim Beckwourth, Joe Meek, and Black Harris acquired a reputation as spectacular windjammers.[183]

Since whoppers are based on extravagant claims, artistic lying, like artistic boasting, thrives on competition. And once the element of competition or contest is introduced, the artistic lie gives rise to the burlesque lie, as the artistic boast gives rise to the burlesque boast. The whopper then becomes a monstrous take-off, a lie to end all lies.

As a convenient device for lying contests, the tradition of the Liars' Bench has sprung up in rural America. Generally, this is a purely figurative expression for a mythical gathering of story-tellers in any setting, from courthouse steps or square, country store, barber shop, or bar-room to campfire or bunkhouse. In some cases, however, the bench is an actual one rather than a mere symbol.[184] Thus in Indiana:

> In Nashville, county seat of Brown County, the bench stands beneath the locust trees on the courthouse lawn. It is an old wooden seat with iron legs, and a single arm, and has occupied the same position winter and summer for a number of years. Its seating capacity is limited to six. Here the Brown County story-tellers swap yarns.
> There is an unwritten law that when this bench is full and other tale-tellers come to join those seated there, the one at the foot—the end without the arm—is pushed off to make room for the new recruits. Efforts are sometimes made to dislodge the man at the head, but the iron arm blocks this move and as a result one of the middle men is pushed out when the grand shove begins. It is to this comfort-

able loafing place that Nashville women come whenever they cannot find their husbands nearer home.

Gentryville has always had its loafing place since the days when the Gentry boys, Baldwin the blacksmith, Abe Lincoln, and Dennis Hanks used to congregate around Jones' store. But it was not until 1894 that a definite place was established where a man might go and be sure of an audience any time of day. A large heavy bridge plank was wedged between two locust trees near the entrance to one of the crossroad stores. The plank was thick and long, and with a brace in the centre gave enough room for a number of men and boys who kept the bench full throughout the day and far into the night. As fast as one would leave some other would take his place.[185]

In response to the same urge for competitive lying and an audience, Liars' Clubs have also arisen, ranging from such hoaxes as the Sazerac Lying Club to regular organizations like the Tall Story Club of Lowell Thomas, the Burlington, Wisconsin, Liars' Club ("Originators and Promoters of the National Liars' Contest"), and the Goofy Liars' Club of Decatur, Illinois ("Organizers and Promoters of International Liars' Contest"). The Sazerac Lying Club was the creation of Fred H. Hart, born of a dearth of "local" copy to fill the columns of the *Reese River Reveille*, an Austin, Nevada, daily, of which he became editor in 1873.[186] The Tall Story Club grew out of a flood of fan-mail mosquito stories following a *Literary Digest* radio news commentary in which Lowell Thomas had cited the fact that the Arctic tundras rather than the tropics breed the biggest and worst mosquitoes.[187] The Burlington Liars' Club, like the Sazerac Lying Club, grew out of a newspaper hoax:

Back in 1929 a Burlington newspaper reporter wrote a story to the effect that these "old timers" got together each New Year's day at the police station, and lied for the championship of the city. He told a brother reporter of his plan, and the story was "sprung" just before New Year's.

They considered the story a good local joke, and after it had appeared in their respective newspapers, forgot about it. However, city editors, with an eye for interesting features, "put it on the wire", and the following December the Associated Press and other news agencies began phoning Burlington to find out if the city's annual contest would be repeated. By this time one of the reporters had left Burlington, but the other one, feeling it would be a shame to miss an opportunity to hornswoggle the public, concocted a story and sent it on its way. Letters began to trickle in from the four corners of the country commenting on the "contest". They furnished the inspiration for a real contest instead of a phoney one, national in scope, and the Burlington Liars' Club was formed to carry it on.[188]

The themes of whoppers are the perennial ones of weather, climate, soil, pests, monsters, hunting, fishing, marksmanship, in any extreme or excess that constitutes an asset or a liability, or both. On the asset side, stories of fertile land are perhaps the most common. From nearly all states comes a chorus of brags of giant vegetables—turnip, pumpkin, beet, potato, cucumber, corn—harking back to old world stories of the great cabbage and the pot that matched it, with disaster following in the trail of phenomenally large or rapid growth. On the liability side, stories of grasshoppers and potato bugs vie with those of mosquitoes as most destructive of crops or most annoying to mankind. Side by side with traditional whoppers are the individual inventions of professional humorists and literary men. Through all this lavish, contagious, and expansive mendacity runs a strain of elaborate hoaxing and jesting that belongs to the humour of exaggeration and deception but more often borders on pure nonsense or fantasy.

Nonsense and fantasy reach their height in the freakish behaviour of animals and the lore of mythical monsters. Harking back to the "unnatural natural history" and bestiaries of ancient and medieval times, the most fearsome of these fabulous creatures are those that haunt the big woods, from Maine to Vancouver Island, where, as part of the lore of the lumberjack, they have been attracted into the Paul Bunyan cycle.

Part Four

YARNS AND TALL TALES

THE SISSY FROM THE HARDSCRABBLE COUNTY ROCK QUARRIES[189]

The men that work in the rock quarries of Hardscrabble County are so tough they crack great big rocks just by spitting on them. The farther you go west in the county the tougher the men get, and the rock quarries are right on the western boundary line. When they set off a blast, those bullies are right out there with ten-year-old white oaks in their hand batting those big boulders around, or else they're playing catch without any gloves.

When they get constipated in the rock quarry camp they never use anything but blasting powder, and they whip their children with barb wire until the kids get to ten years old and then they thresh their parents.

Strangers almost never travel into the rock quarry country, because no man, woman, beast or child that dared to try it ever returned to tell about it no more than any soul ever fetched back a report from hell.

When the quarrymen leave their camp, everybody but invalids, little children, and cripples take to the hills till danger's past. It's lucky that they usually come in a drove, and you can see their dust for miles away and hear their fearsome blackguarding and whooping for a good hour and a half before they strike the city limits.

Gentlemen, it's no lie nor fairy tale when I tell you that those Hardscrabble County quarrymen are enough to plague a saint. They use them in the farm villages to scare little children and make them behave, but the grown-ups are even scareder than the young ones.

One day a lone wolf got right into town before anybody knew he was on the way. He came riding two snapping, snarling panthers, straddling them with a foot on each, and he was lashing them into a lather with a whip made of three six-foot rattlesnakes knotted together.

This fellow was a sight to behold, and everybody knew in a minute that he was a quarryman. He stood a good eight feet without tiptoeing, and not enough fat on him to grease a one-egg skillet. That man was muscled like a draft mule, and he moved around like a bolt of lightning on its holiday.

First thing off he went to the shoe store and bought him a pair of brogans. Then he got a nickel's worth of stout roofing nails from the hardware store and asked for the loan of a hammer. He drove these roofing nails right through the soles and heels of the shoes and put the shoes back on his feet. He wore a size fifteen, broad last.

"That's the way I like it", he said. "It gives you a good grip and all you got to do when your foot itches is to wiggle it around a little.

"I want to get prettied up a little", the quarryman said, and went into the barber shop. The barber took the edge off his shears when he tried to cut his hair.

"Ain't you got no tinsmiths in this town?" asked the quarryman. "Get a pair of tinsnips, extra large. And fetch a blowtorch from the plumber's. I ain't had a decent shave for a month of Sundays."

He dropped in the Blue Moon Saloon then and asked for a good stiff drink, talking as polite as chips. The bartender planked down a bottle of his strongest brand of fortyrod. Some of it sloshed over and ate a spot of varnish off the bar the size of a five-dollar bill. The quarryman lost his temper then, and snorted and fumed fit to kill.

"None of that bellywash for me! I'd as soon have a pinky, sticky ice cream sody with a cherry on it."

"What sort of a charge do you crave, stranger?" asked the bartender, his false choppers almost shaking out of his mouth.

"Gimme a prussic acid cocktail with a little sulphuric for a chaser", ordered the quarryman, "and see that you don't go diluting it with no carbolic, neither. What are you, anyway? One of them temperance cranks? You must think I'm a plumb teetotaler!"

The bartender dashed out the back way and hotfooted it to the drug store and got the stuff for the drinks. The quarryman got in a little better humour then, and began passing the time away by spitting on the floor and burning holes right through to the ground underneath.

"Not bad!" he said. "A little weak. Only trouble with this tipple is that it's hell on underwear. Every time you break wind it burns a hole in them."

"I guess you aim to get back to the quarries before nightfall, don't you, stranger?" said the bartender, hoping to God it was so.

"No, no!" answered the quarryman, shaking his head kind of sad. "I don't reckon I'll ever go back."

He grabbed a can of tomatoes off the shelf behind the bar and gulped it down without chewing it open.

"Don't it lay heavy on your stomach, stranger?" asked the bartender, terribly put out that the quarryman wasn't leaving that night.

"Not long", answered the quarryman. "I soon digest the can from around the tomatoes. It's easy. A doorknob is harder, but I can do it easy as pie when I set my head to it."

"You aim to make your home in our little Magic City?" asked the bartender, still hoping he had heard wrong.

"Hell's fire and damnation no, man!" said the quarryman, so riled he bit a foot long chunk out of the mahogany bar and spat it right in the bartender's face. "I wouldn't live here for love nor money. I wouldn't be caught dead here."

"Well, then", said the bartender, getting a little bolder, "why did you leave the quarries?"

"Aw, I didn't want to", answered the quarryman. "I had to."

"You had to? Why? Get in a fight or some kind of trouble there?"

"A fight? Are you plumb stark, staring looney, man? Whoever heard of a man getting into trouble over fighting in the Hardscrabble County rock quarries?"

"Why did you have to leave then?"

"Well", said the quarryman, looking like a sheepkilling dog. "They chased me out because they said I was a sissy."

THE DEMON BRICKSETTER FROM WILLIAMSON COUNTY[190]

A man that sets brick in a pavement only needs to have a weak mind, a strong back, and a great big hand with long fingers that will stretch and won't strain easy. It ain't no job for a violin player, you can bet your sweet life. You've got to kneel down on your prayerbones, or stoop over up and down like a little clown on a peanut roaster if your poor old backbone can stand it, and set the bricks three rows at a time. For every other row you set down a half brick to break the joints. Right ahead of you there's a crew smoothin' out the sand bed with a drag, hollerin' "Yo, drag!" all day long and humptediddyin' to keep ahead of the setters. The bricks are piled alongside the street, and a crew of men keep trottin' up to the setters with a pair of tongs holdin' four or five bricks. They ain't overly careful the way they drop the bricks, and if a setter ain't watchful he's liable to have his finger dressed in mournin'.[191] And whilst you're watchin' your fingers, they're apt as not to dump a load on your feet.

Behind the bricksetters there's a tar kettle, with the tar bubblin' hot. They draw it out of a spigot into coal scuttles, and then spread it as thin as possible, like molasses on a slice of bread, over the bricks. Two or three fellows push it into the cracks with long, stiff brushes. Their shoe soles get to be a foot thick from the tar stickin' on 'em. They're like flies on Tanglefoot, and long about the time that evening sun goes down and it's mighty hard to pick 'em up and lay 'em down anyhow, they're hardly able to walk about, let alone do their work.

The bricksetters, though, have the hardest job. There's a sand hard as diamonds that sticks to the bricks closer'n a brother and eats through a rawhide mitt damned nigh as quick as hell could scorch a feather. If you kneel down to save your poor old back, the little grains of sand eat into your prayerbones same as a rat would gnaw a hunk of cheese.

The Wild Man from Williamson County blew into town ridin' a panther broke to saddle and usin' a rattlesnake sportin' seventeen rattles and a button for a whip. First thing he done he dropped in a bar and called for a nitric acid cocktail with a lysol chaser. When he spat, he melted the copper spittoon till it ran along the floor like a crick when the snows melt in the spring. He thronged two-bits on the bar, and it went plumb through slick as a bullet. His muscles looked like they had been blowed up with a bicycle pump and was about to bust out with a big "pouf". When that man walked, I tell you he shook the earth for miles about and the windows cracked and dishes fell off the shelves. He was that much of a man, and that's the God's truth.

When the Wild Man asked for a job on the paving gang, the boss was glad enough to give it to him. It was sizzlin' hot in July and you could fry a steak to a cinder anywheres on the sidewalk or on a cake of ice, as far as that goes. Three or four of the setters had keeled over and was pantin' in the shade with their tongues hangin' out a foot, like dogs that had been chasin' a spry rabbit for days and days and days.

"I'm a man as is work-brickle", said the Wild Man. "I'm a man as can't say quit. When I lay a-holt, I'm like a turtle, and I don't let loose till it thunders. I'm from Williamson County, and maybe you've heer'd of the men they raise down there where the screech owls roost with the chickens. I'm a rambunctious, ruttin' rookaroo with fourteen tits and holes bored for more."

"Brother", said the foreman, "if it's labour your heart craves for, you got it right here on the premises. Just lay your lily whites on some of them brick, slap 'em down on that there sand, and show me you know how to back up your mouth. The wind blows where I come from, too, but it takes that old willy and some backbone to git by here."

Well, sir, when that Wild Man started in, he jumped up ten feet in the air and cracked his heels together three times before he ever touched the ground, crowin' like a Dominecker rooster on a frosty mornin'. He wouldn't take the buckskin mitts, and the first brick he nailed a-holt of was mashed into a red powder. The sparks flew like Fourth of July. After that he was more careful. The way he dropped them bricks sounded like a terrible, awful hailstorm on a tar roof. The carriers done their best to slow him down, because these pavin' jobs they don't last none too long, nohow. They slammed bricks on his heels and they bounced 'em off his fingers, but he never paid 'em the least teensy bit of mind. Fourteen men was huffin' and puffin' on the sand drag, clippin' along fifteen miles an hour, and then he had to wait for 'em lots of times. While he was waitin' he packed two hundred bricks under each arm back and forth across the street just to keep limbered up. Or sometimes he lay on the flat of his back and juggled ten brick at once with his feet.

Pretty soon he was the only setter left; all the rest was packin' brick to him and fallin' all over one another's feet. They went so fast they'd meet theirselves comin' back. You couldn't get enough men on that street, I tell you, to keep that Wild Man satisfied. He was the doin'est man that ever hit this burg, and that ain't no lie nor whore's dream.

It was time to give up when he taken off his shoes and started in to layin' 'em with his toes.

What do they feed 'em in Williamson County, for God's sakes?

Well, nothin' but punkins and crick water, they tell me. It's sure a wonder to nature.

We had aimed to have us a job all winter, but soon that old wind got to whistlin': "What have you done with your summer's wages?" The job was finished in three days, and would have been in one if they could have kept brick and sand on hand.

I tell you, good peoples, if you want to work on any paving gang, be sure to ask and inquire if they's a man from Williamson County on the job or if one has been seen in them parts lately. If there is, or if he has, don't never bother to start.

What do they raise them on down there in Williamson County, for God's sakes? Is it wildcat's milk or wild boar's meat that puts that old willy and double-jointed backbone in 'em?

Well, I can't say as to that, stranger. I heer'd they touch nothin' but turnip greens and weak well water down there, but it sure is a curiosity to nature how they get that way. If any man can tell *me*, I'll fetch him one of the finest pretties you ever clapped eyes on.

THE BOOMER FIREMAN'S FAST SOONER HOUND[192]

A boomer fireman is never long for any one road. Last year he may have worked for the Frisco, and this year he's heaving black diamonds for the Katy or the Wabash. He travels light and travels far and doesn't let any grass grow under his feet when they get to itching for the greener pastures on the next road or the next division or maybe to hell and gone on the other side of the mountains. He doesn't need furniture and he doesn't need many clothes, and God knows he doesn't need a family or a dog.

When the Boomer pulled into the roadmaster's office looking for a job, there was that sooner hound of his loping after him. That hound would sooner run than eat and he'd sooner eat than fight or do something useful like catching a rabbit. Not that a rabbit would have any chance if the sooner really wanted to nail him, but that crazy hound dog didn't like to do anything but run and he was the fastest thing on four legs.

"I might use you", said the roadmaster. "Can you get a boarding place for the dog?"

"Oh, he goes along with me", said the Boomer. "I raised him from a pup just like a mother or father and he ain't never spent a night or a day or even an hour far away from me. He'd cry like his poor heart would break and raise such a ruckus nobody couldn't sleep, eat or hear themselves think for miles about."

"Well, I don't see how that would work out", said the roadmaster. "It's against the rules of the road to allow a passenger in the cab, man or beast, or in the caboose and I aim to put you on a freight run so you can't ship him by express. Besides, he'd get the idea you wasn't nowhere about and pester folks out of their wits with his yipping and yowling. You look like a man that could keep a boiler popping off on an uphill grade, but I just don't see how we could work it if the hound won't listen to reason while you're on your runs."

"Why, he ain't no trouble," said the Boomer. "He just runs alongside, and when I'm on a freight run he chases around a little in the fields to pass the time away."

> "That may be so, I do not know;
> It sounds so awful queer.
> I don't dispute your word at all,
> But don't spread that bull in here",

sang the roadmaster.

"He'll do it without half trying", said the Boomer. "It's a little bit tiresome on him having to travel at such a slow gait, but that sooner would do anything to stay close by me, he loves me that much."

"Go spread that on the grass to make it green", said the roadmaster.

"I'll lay my first paycheck against a fin[193] that he'll be fresh as a daisy and his tongue behind his teeth when we pull into the junction. He'll run around the station a hundred times or so to limber up."

"It's a bet", said the roadmaster.

On the first run the sooner moved in what was a slow walk for him. He kept looking up into the cab where the Boomer was shovelling in the coal.

"He looks worried", said the Boomer. "He thinks the hog law[194] is going to catch us, we're making such bad time."

The roadmaster was so sore at losing the bet that he transferred the Boomer to a local passenger run and doubled the stakes. The sooner speeded up to a slow trot, but he had to kill a lot of time, at that, not to get too far ahead of the engine.

Then the roadmaster got mad enough to bite off a drawbar. People got to watching the sooner trotting alongside the train and began thinking it must be a mighty slow road. Passengers might just as well walk; they'd get there just as fast. And if you shipped a yearling calf to market, it'd be a bologna bull before it reached the stockyards. Of course, the trains were keeping up their schedules the same as usual, but that's the way it looked to people who saw a no-good mangy sooner hound beating all the trains without his tongue hanging out an inch or letting out the least little pant.

It was giving the road a black eye, all right. The roadmaster would have fired the Boomer and told him to hit the grit with his sooner and never come back again, but he was stubborn from the word go and hated worse than anything to own up he was licked.

"I'll fix that sooner", said the roadmaster. "I'll slap the Boomer into the cab of the Cannon Ball, and if anything on four legs can keep up with the fastest thing on wheels I'd admire to see it. That sooner'll be left so far behind it'll take nine dollars to send him a post card."

The word got around that the sooner was going to try to keep up with the Cannon Ball. Farmers left off plowing, hitched up, and drove to the right of way to see the sight. It was like a circus day or the county fair. The schools all dismissed the pupils, and not a factory could keep enough men to make a wheel turn.

The roadmaster got right in the cab so that the Boomer couldn't soldier on the job to let the sooner keep up. A clear track for a hundred miles was ordered for the Cannon Ball, and all the switches were spiked down till after that streak of lightning had passed. It took three men to see the Cannon Ball on that run: one to say, "There she comes", one to say, "There she is", and another to say, "There she goes". You couldn't see a thing for steam, cinders and smoke, and the rails sang like a violin for a half hour after she'd passed into the next county.

Every valve was popping off and the wheels three feet in the air above the roadbed. The Boomer was so sure the sooner would keep up that he didn't stint the elbow grease; he wore the hinges off the fire door and fifteen pounds of him melted and ran right down into his shoes. He had his shovel whetted to a nub.

The roadmaster stuck his head out of the cab window, and— whosh!—off went his hat and almost his head. The suction like to have jerked his arms from their sockets as he nailed a-hold of the window seat.

It was all he could do to see, and gravel pinged against his goggles like hailstones, but he let out a whoop of joy.

"THE SOONER! THE SOONER!" he yelled. "He's gone! He's gone for true! Ain't *nowhere* in sight!"

"I can't understand that", hollered the Boomer. "He ain't *never* laid down on me yet. It just ain't like him to lay down on me. Leave me take a peek."

He dropped his shovel and poked out his head. Then he whooped even louder than the roadmaster had.

"He's true blue as they come!" the Boomer yelled. "Got the interests of the company at heart, too. He's still with us."

"Where do you get that stuff?" asked the roadmaster. "I don't see him nowhere. I can't see hide nor hair of him."

"We're going so fast half the journal boxes are on fire and melting the axles like hot butter", said the Boomer. "The sooner's running up and down the train hoisting a leg above the boxes. He's doing his level best to put out some of the fires. That dog is true blue as they come and he's the fastest thing on four legs, but he's only using three of them now."

SLAPPY HOOPER, WORLD'S BIGGEST, FASTEST, AND BESTEST SIGN PAINTER[195]

Slappy Hooper wasn't big because he was six foot nine and wide between the eyes, no more than he weighed three hundred pounds without his cap on or his bucket in one hand and his brush in the other. It was just that there wasn't no job any too big for Slappy, and he never wanted a helper to mess around with.

Even when he was painting a high- stack, he didn't want any rube staggering and stumbling around the lines to his bosun's chair. He knew too well that lots of times a helper can be more trouble than he's worth. He'll yawn and gape around or send up the wrong colour or the wrong brush, or he'll throw rocks at birds, or he'll make goo-goo eyes at dames passing by. Like as not, he'll foul the lines or pull the wrong one and send you butt over appetite to kingdom come.

At any rate, a helper keeps a man uneasy, and when a man's uneasy he ain't doing his best work. They ought to make it a penitentiary act for a helper "gapering, mopering, and attempting to gawk". Slappy said his life was too short to take a helper to raise up. He could let himself up and down as fast as a monkey could skin up a cocoanut tree or a cat lick its hind leg up and its tongue out. Anything Slappy wanted on the ground he could lasso with his special long and tough rawhide lariat and pull it up to where he was working.

Slappy done some big jobs in his day, and he done them right and fast. He says if there ever was a crime against nature it's this way they got here of late of blowing paint on with a spray gun like you was slaying cockroaches or bedbugs or pacifying a cow to keep the flies off until she can get milked. Slappy liked to splash it on with a good old eight-inch brush, and he never was known to leave a brush lap or a hair on the surface when the job was finished. Slapping it on up and down or slapping it on crossways or anti-goggling[196] you couldn't tell the difference. It was all of a solid sheet.

With all these new inventions like smoke-writing from airplanes and painting signs from a pounce[197] (even pictures they do that way), it's hard to appreciate an old-timer like Slappy.

He used to get jobs of lettering advertising on the sky, and it didn't fade away in a minute like smoke that pours out of a plane and gets torn to pieces by the wind before you can hardly spell out what it says. It was all pretty and fancy colours, too; any shade a man's heart could wish for, and it'd stay right there for days if the weather was fair. Of course, birds would fly through it, and when it'd rain the colours would all run together and when the clouds rolled by, there'd be what folks got to calling a rainbow. It really was nothing but Slappy. Hooper's sky-writing all jumbled together. It seems that no man, woman, child or beast, alive or dead, was ever able to invent waterproof sky paint. If it could have been done, Slappy would have done it.

His biggest job was for the Union Pacific Railroad, and stretched from one end of the line to the other. The only way you could read it all was to get on a through train and look out of the window and up at the sky all the time. Everybody got stiff necks, of course, so Slappy had the bright idea of getting Sloan's Liniment to pay him for a big sign right at the end of the Union Pacific sign.

Nobody ever did understand how Slappy managed to do the sky painting. He'd have been a chump to tell anybody. He always used to say when people asked him: "That's for me to know and you to find out," or, "If I told you that, you'd know as much as I do."

The only thing people was sure of was that he used sky hooks to hold up the scaffold. He used a long scaffold instead of the bosun's chair he used when he was painting smokestacks or church steeples. When he started in to fasten his skyhooks, he'd rent a thousand acre field and rope it off with barbed wire charged with electricity. He never let a living soul inside, but you could hear booming sounds like war times and some folks figured he was firing his skyhooks out of a cannon and that they fastened on a cloud or some place too high for mortal eyes to see or mortal minds to know about. Anyways, after a while—if you took a spy glass—you could see Slappy's long scaffold raising up, up, up in the air and Slappy about as big as a spider squatting on it.

But that played out, somehow. It wasn't that people didn't like his skypainting any more, but the airplanes got to buzzing around as thick as flies around a molasses barrel and they was always fouling or cueing Slappy's lines, and he was always afraid one would run smack into him and dump over his scaffold and spill his paint if nothing worse. Besides, he said, if advertisers was dumb enough to let a farting airplane take the place of an artist, the more he'd fool them, and it wasn't no skin off his behind. He could always wangle three squares a day and a pad at night by putting signs on windows for shopkeepers if he had to. If I can stay off public works,[198] I'll be satisfied, he thought to himself.

So Slappy said to hell with the *big* jobs. I'll just start painting smaller signs, but I'll make them so real and true to life that I can still be the fastest and bestest sign painter in the world, if I ain't the biggest any more. It's pure foolishness for a man to try to match himself against an airplane at making *big* signs.

He knew he could do it with one hand tied behind and both eyes punched out. Some sign painters couldn't dot the letter "i" without a pounce to go by. It was enough to make a dog laugh to see some poor scissorbills wrestling around with a pounce, covered all over with chalk wet by sweat until they looked like a plaster of Paris statue.

Then, like as not, they'd get a pounce too small for the wall or billboard they was working on. When it was all on there was a lot of blank space left over. The boss'd yell: "Well, well, Bright Eyes! Guess the only thing to do is fetch a letter stretcher!" If the pounce happened to be too big, it was every bit as bad. "A fine job, Michael Angelo", the boss'd holler, "except you'll have to mix the paint with alum so's it'll shrink enough that we can squeeze it in with a crowbar."

One of Slappy's first jobs after he took to billboard painting was a picture of a loaf of bread for a bakery. It would make you hungry just to look at it. That was the trouble. The birds began to flying on it to peck at it, and either they'd break their bills and starve to death because they didn't have anything left to peck with, or they'd just sit there perched on the top of the billboard trying to figure out what was the matter until they'd just keel over. Some of them'd break their necks when they dashed against the loaf, and others'd try to light on it and slip and break their necks on the ground. Either way, it was death on birds. The humane societies complained so much and so hard that Slappy had to paint the loaf out, and just leave the lettering.

He didn't like this a bit, though, because, as he often said, any monkey who can stand on his hind legs and hold anything in his fingers can make letters. The loaf of bread business sort of gave Slappy a black eye. People was afraid to hire him.

Finally the Jimdandy Hot Blast Stove and Range Company hired him to do a sign for their newest model, showing a fire going good inside, the jacket cherry red, and heat pouring off in ever which direction. In some ways it was the best job Slappy ever done. The dandelions and weeds popped right out of the ground on the little plot between the billboard and the sidewalk, and in middle January of the coldest winter ever recorded by the Weather Bureau.

It was when the bums started making the place a hangout that the citizens and storekeepers of the neighbourhood put in a kick. The hoboes drove a nail into the billboard so they could hang kettles and cans against the side of the heater and boiled their shave or boilup[199] water. They pestered everybody in the neighbourhood for meat and vegetables to make mulligan stews. They found it more comfortable on the ground than in any flophouse in the city, so they slept there, too. They ganged up on the sidewalk so that you couldn't push through, even to deliver the United States mails. Mothers was afraid to send their little children to school or to the grocery store.

The company decided to hire a special watchman to shoo hoboes away, but this was a terrible expense. Not only that, but the watchman would get drowsy from the warmth, and no sooner did he let out a snore than the bums would come creeping back like old home week. Finally, the Company got the idea of having Slappy make the stove a lot hotter to drive the bums clean away.

So he did. He changed the stove from a cherry red to a white hot, and made the heat waves a lot thicker.

This drove the bums across the street, but it also blistered the paint off all the automobiles parked at the kerb. Then one day the frame building across the way began to smoke and then to blaze. The insurance company told the Jimdandy Hot Blast Stove and Range Company to jerk that billboard down and be quick about it, or they'd go to law.

Slappy says now he feels like locking up his keister[200] and throwing away the key. They don't want big sign painting and they don't want true-to-life sign painting, and he has to do one or the other or both or nothing at all.

FROM THE LIARS' BENCH

BLACK HARRIS AND THE PUTREFIED FOREST[201]

They were a trapping party from the north fork of Platte, on their way to wintering-ground in the more southern valley of the Arkansas; some, indeed, meditating a more extended trip, even to the distant settlements of New Mexico, the paradise of mountaineers. The elder of the company was a tall, gaunt man, with a face browned by twenty years' exposure to the extreme climate of the mountains; his long black hair, as yet scarcely tinged with grey, hanging almost to his shoulders, but his cheeks and chin clean shaven, after the fashion of the mountainmen. His dress was the usual hunting-frock of buckskin, with long fringes down the seams, with pantaloons similarly ornamented, and moccasins of Indian make. Whilst his companions puffed their pipes in silence, he narrated a few of his former experiences of western life; and whilst the buffalo "hump-ribs" and "tenderloin" are singing away in the pot, preparing for the hunters' supper, we will note down the yarn as it spins from his lips, giving it in the language spoken in the "far west":—

"'Twas about 'calf-time', maybe a little later, and not a hundred year ago, by a long chalk, that the biggest kind of rendezvous was held 'to' Independence, a mighty handsome little location away up on Old Missoura. A pretty smart lot of boys was camp'd thar, about a quarter from the town, and the way the whisky flowed that time was 'some' now, *I* can tell you. . . .

"Surely Black Harris[202] was thar; and the darndest liar was Black Harris—for lies tumbled out of his mouth like boudins out of a bufler's stomach. He was the child as saw the putrefied forest in the Black Hills. Black Harris come in from Laramie; he'd been trapping three year an' more on Platte and the 'other side'; and, when he got into Liberty, he fixed-himself right off like a Saint Louiy dandy. Well, he sat to dinner one day in the tavern, and a lady says to him:—

" 'Well, Mister Harris, I hear you're a great travler.'

" 'Travler, marm', says Black Harris, 'this niggur's no travler; I ar' a trapper, marm, a mountain-man, wagh!'

" 'Well, Mister Harris, trappers are great travlers, and you goes over a sight of ground in your perishinations, I'll be bound to say.'

" 'A sight, marm, this coon's gone over, if that's the way your "stick floats".[203] I've trapped beaver on Platte and Arkansas, and away up on Missoura and Yaller Stone; I've trapped on Columbia, on Lewis Fork, and Green River; I've trapped, marm, on Grand River and the Heely (Gila). I've fout the "Blackfoot" (and d—d bad Injuns they ar); I've raised the hair[204] of more *than one* Apach, and made a Rapaho "come" afore now; I've trapped in heav'n, in airth, and h—; and scalp my old head, marm, but I've seen a putrefied forest.'

"'La, Mister Harris, a what?'

"'A putrefied forest, marm, as sure as my rifle's got hind-sights, and *she* shoots centre. I was out on the Black Hills, Bill Sublette knows the time—the year it rained fire—and everybody knows when that was. If thar wasn't cold coins about that time, this child wouldn't say so. The snow was about fifty foot deep, and the bufler lay dead on the ground like bees after a beein'; not whar we was tho', for *thar* was no bufler, and no meat, and me and my band had been livin' on our moccasins (leastwise the parflesh[205]) for six weeks; and poor doins that feedin' is, marm, as you'll never know. One day we crossed a "cañon" and over a "divide", and got into a peraira, what was green grass, and green trees, and green leaves on the trees, and birds singing in the green leaves, and this in Febrary, wagh! Our animals was like to die when they see the green grass, and we all sung out, "hurraw for summer doins."

"'Hyar goes for meat', sais I, and I jest ups old Ginger at one of them singing birds, and down came the crittur elegant; its darned head spinning away from the body, but never stops singing, and when I takes up the meat, I finds it stone, wagh! 'Hyar's damp powder and no fire to dry it', I says, quite skeared.

" 'Fire be dogged,' says old Rube. 'Hyar's a hos as 'll make fire come'; and with that he takes his ax and lets drive at a cotton wood. Schr-u-k—goes the ax agin the tree, and out comes a bit of the blade as big as my hand. We looks at the animals, and thar they stood shaking over the grass, which I'm dog-gone if it wasn't stone, too. Young Sublette comes up, and he'd been clerking down to the fort on Platte, so he know'd something. He looks and looks, and scrapes the trees with his butcher knife, and snaps the grass like pipe stems, and breaks the leaves a-snappin' like Californy shells.

" 'What's all this, boy?' I asks.

" 'Putrefactions', says he, looking smart, 'putrefactions, or I'm a niggur'.

" La, Mister Harris', says the lady, 'putrefactions! why, did the leaves, and the trees, and the grass smell badly?'

"'Smell badly, marm!' says Black Harris, 'would a skunk stink if he was froze to stone? No, marm, this child didn't know what putre-faction was, and young Sublette's version wouldn't "shine" no how, so I chips a piece out of a tree and puts it in my trap-sack, and carries it in safe to Laramie. Well, old Captain Stewart (a clever man was that, though he was an Englishman), he comes along next spring, and a Dutch doctor chap was along too. I shows him the piece I chipped out of the tree, and he called it a putrefaction too; and so, marm, if that wasn't a putrefied peraira, what was it? For this hos doesn't know, and *he* knows "fat cow" from "poor bull", anyhow.' . . ."

LARKIN SNOW, THE MILLER, AND HIS FAST-RUNNING DOG[206]

Fox-hunting was a favourite sport with many; indeed, all loved it, but only a few kept hounds and gave chase to mischievous Reynard. Foxes were quite plenty, and renowned for deeds of daring. The women hated hounds most cordially, yet they would endure them for the sake of their fowls. If their fowls were destroyed, they could neither make soup nor their rich pot-pies, both of which were much admired. Wylie Franklin was a great favourite with chicken-raisers, for if a hen-roost was invaded a *hint* to him was all that was needed, and the marauder was soon taken. The compositions of Mozart, Handel, and Haydn were no music to these fox-hunters compared with the voice of hounds in the chase. Sometimes there would be a great rally of fox-hunters at some point to have a united chase, to see who had the fastest and the toughest hound. This must be kept in view in reading the story of Larkin's fast-running dog.

"You see", said Larkin, "a passer uv fellers cum frum 'bout Rock-ford, Jonesville, and the Holler to have a fox-hunt, and kep' a-boastin' uv thar fast dogs. I told 'um my little dog Flyin'-jib could beat all thar dogs, and give 'um two in the game. I called him up and showed him to 'um, and you mout a hearn 'um laugh a mile, measured with a 'coonskin and the tail thronged in. I told 'um they'd laugh t'other side o' thar mouths afore it were done. They hooted me.

"We went out with 'bout fifty hounds, and, as good luck would hev it, we started a rale old Virginny red fox, 'bout three hours afore day,

on the west side uv Skull Camp Mountin'. He struck right off for the
Saddle Mountin', then whirled round over Scott's Knob, then to Cedar
Ridge, up it, and over Fisher's Peak, round back uv the Blue Ridge,
then crossed over and down it at Blaze Spur, then down to and over
Round Peak, then down Ring's Creek to Shipp's Musterground, and
on agin to'ads Skull Camp. Not fur from Shipp's Musterground they
passed me, and Flyin'-jib were 'bout half a mile ahead on 'um all,
goin' fast as the report of a rifle gun. Passin' through a meader whar
thar were a mowin' scythe with the blade standin' up, Flyin'-jib run
chug aginst it with sich force that it split him wide open frum the eend
uv his nose to the tip uv his tail. Thar he lay, and nuver whimpered,
tryin' to run right on. I streaked it to him, snatched up both sides uv
him, slapped 'um together, but were in sich a hurry that I put two feet
down and two up. But away he went arter the fox, scootin' jist in that
fix. You see, when he got tired runnin' on two feet on one side, he'd
whirl over, quick as lightnin', on t'other two, and it seemed rusher to
hev increased his verlocity. He cotch the fox on the east side uv Skull
Camp, a mile ahead uv the whole kit uv 'um.

"Now when the fellers cum up, and seen all thar dogs lyin' on the
ground pantin' fur life, and Flyin'-jib jist gittin' his hand in, they was
mighty low down in the mouth, I warrant you. All the conserlation
they had was seein' my dog in sich a curious fix. But I jist kervorted,
and told 'um that were the way fur a dog to run fast and long, fust one
side up, then t'other—it rested him."

RICH LAND, POOR LAND[207]

"Yeah", said Sack Daddy, "you sho is tellin' de truth 'bout dat big old
mosquito, 'cause my old man bought dat same piece of land and raised
a crop of pumpkins on it and femme tell y'all right now—mosquito
dust is de finest fertilizer in de world. Dat land was so rich and we
raised pumpkins so big dat we et five miles up in one of 'em and five
miles down and ten miles across one and we ain't never found out
how far it went. But my old man was buildin' a scaffold inside so we
could cut de pumpkin meat without so much trouble, when he dropped
his hammer. He told me, he says, 'Son, Ah done dropped my hammer.
Go git it for me.' Well, Ah went down in de pumpkin and begin to
hunt dat hammer. Ah was foolin' 'round in there all day when I met a
man and he ast me what Ah was lookin' for. Ah tole him my ole man

had done dropped his hammer and sent me to find it for him. De man tole me Ah might as well give it up for a lost cause, he had been lookin' for a double mule-team and a wagon that had got lost in there for three weeks and he hadn't found no trace of 'em yet. So Ah stepped on a pin, de pin bent and dat's de way de story went."

"Dat was rich land but my ole man had some rich land too", put in Will House. "My old man planted cucumbers and he went along droppin' de seeds and befo' he could git out de way he'd have ripe cucumbers in his pockets. What is the richest land you ever seen?"

"Well", replied Joe Wiley, "my old man had some land dat was so rich dat our mule died and we buried him down in our bottom-land and de next mornin' he had done sprouted li'l jackasses."

"Aw, dat land wasn't so rich", objected Ulmer. "My old man had some land and it was so rich dat he drove a stob[208] in de ground at de end of a corn-row for a landmark and next morning there was ten ears of corn on de corn stalk and four ears growin' on de stob."

"Dat lan' y'all talkin' 'bout might do, if you give it plenty commercial-nal[209] but my old man wouldn't farm no po' land like dat", said Joe Wiley. "Now, one year we was kinda late puttin' in our crops. Everybody else had corn a foot high when papa said, 'Well, chillun, Ah reckon we better plant some corn.' So I was droppin' and my brother was hillin' up behind me. We had done planted 'bout a dozen rows when Ah looked back and seen de corn comin' up. Ah didn't want it to grow too fast 'cause it would make all fodder and no roastin' ears so Ah hollered to my brother to sit down on some of it to stunt de growth. So he did, and de next day he dropped me back a note—says: 'passed thru Heben yesterday at twelve o'clock sellin' roastin' ears to de angels'."

IDAHO POTATOES[210]

In the Snake River Valley lives an old-timer who is known as Old Jim. Old Jim comes to town now and then and boasts of the fertility of his land, but complains that he is unable to market the stuff. He grew pumpkins, but they were so large he could not get them on to a wagon, and then ventured into potatoes. When, two years ago, a CCC camp was established nearby, Old Jim was approached by a man who wanted to buy a hundred pounds of spuds. "Only a hundred pounds?" he asked, scratching his pate. "No, I can't do it. I wouldn't cut a spud in two for no one."

"DAT AIN'T NO LIE"[211]

I. "Dat Wasn't Hot"

. . . "It sho is gittin' hot. Ah'll be glad when we git to de lake so Ah kin find myself some shade."

"Man, youse two mile from dat lake yet, and otherwise it ain't hot today", said Joe Wiley. "He ain't seen it hot, is he, Will House?"

"Naw, Joe, when me and you was hoboing down in Texas it was so hot till we saw old stumps and logs crawlin' off in de shade."

Eugene Oliver said, "Aw dat wasn't hot. Ah seen it so hot till two cakes of ice left the ice house and went down the street and fainted."

Arthur Hopkins put in: "Ah knowed two men who went to Tampa all dressed up in new blue serge suits, and it was so hot dat when de train pulled into Tampa two blue suits got off de train. De men had done melted out of 'em."

Will House said, "Dat wasn't hot. Dat was chilly weather. Me and Joe Wiley went fishin' and it was so hot dat before we got to de water, we met de fish, coming swimming up de road in dust."

"Dat's a fact, too", added Joe Wiley. "Ah remember dat day well. It was so hot dat Ah struck a match to light my pipe and set de lake afire. Burnt half of it, den took de water dat was left and put out de fire."

Joe Willard said, "Hush! Don't Ah hear a noise?"

Eugene and Cliffert shouted together, "Yeah—went down to de river—

> Heard a mighty racket
> Nothing but de bull frog
> Pullin' off his jacket!"

II. Giant Insects

"Dat ain't what Ah hea'd", said Joe.

"Well, whut did you hear?"

"Ah see a chigger over in de fence corner wid a splinter in his foot and a seed tick is pickin' it out wid a fence rail and de chigger is hollerin', 'Lawd, have mercy.'"

"Dat brings me to de boll-weevil", said Larkins White. "A boll-weevil flew onto de steerin' wheel of a white man's car and says, 'Mister, lemme drive yo' car.'

"De white man says, 'You can't drive no car.'

"Boll-weevil says: 'Oh yeah, Ah kin. Ah drove in five thousand cars last year and Ah'm going to drive in ten thousand dis year.'

"A man told a tale on de boll-weevil agin. Says he heard a terrible racket and noise down in de field, went down to see whut it was and whut you reckon? It was Ole Man Boll-Weevil whippin' li' Willie Boll-Weevil 'cause he couldn't carry two rows at a time."

Will House said, "Ah know a lie on a black gnat. Me and my buddy Joe Wiley was ramshackin' Georgy over when we come to a loggin' camp. So bein' out of work we ast for a job. So de man puts us on and gives us some oxes to drive. Ah had a six-yoke team and Joe was drivin' a twelve-yoke team. As we was comin' thru de woods we heard somethin' hummin' and we didn't know what it was. So we got hungry and went in a place to eat and when we come out a gnat had done et up de six-yoke team and de twelve-yoke team, and was sittin' up on de wagon pickin' his teeth wid a ox-horn and cryin' for somethin' to eat."

"Yeah", put in Joe Wiley, "we seen a man tie his cow and calf out to pasture and a mosquito come along and et up de cow and was ringin' de bell for de calf."

"Dat wasn't no full-grown mosquito at dat", said Eugene Oliver. "Ah was travellin' in Texas and laid down and went to sleep. De skeeters bit me so hard till Ah seen a ole iron wash-pot, so Ah crawled under it and turned it down over me good so de skeeters couldn't git to me. But you know dem skeeters bored right thru dat iron pot. So I up wid a hatchet and bradded their bills into de pot. So they flew on off 'cross Galveston bay wid de wash-pot on their bills."

"Look", said Black Baby, "on de Indian River we went to bed and heard de mosquitoes singin' like bull alligators. So we got under four blankets. Shucks! dat wasn't nothin'. Dem mosquitoes just screwed off dem short bills, reached back in they hip-pocket and took out they long bills and screwed 'em on and come right on through dem blankets and got us."

"Is dat de biggest mosquito you all ever seen? Shucks! dey was li'l baby mosquitoes! One day my ole man took some men and went out into de woods to cut some fence posts. And a big rain come up so they went up under a great big ole tree. It was so big it would take six men to meet around it. De other men set down on de roots but my ole man stood up and leaned against de tree. Well, sir, a big old skeeter come up on de other side of dat tree and bored right thru it and got blood out of my ole man's back. Dat made him so mad till he up wid his ax and bradded dat mosquito's bill into dat tree. By dat time de rain stopped and they all went home.

"Next day when they come out, dat mosquito had done cleaned up ten acres dying. And two or three weeks after dat my ole man got enough bones from dat skeeter to fence in dat ten acres."

PAUL BUNYAN NATURAL HISTORY[212]

Inhabiting the big pine woods, the swamps, lakes and streams in the vicinity of Paul Bunyan's old-time logging camps were a considerable number of very wild animals. These differed considerably or greatly from the common bear, deer, wildcats and wolves of the timber lands. Most of them are now extinct or but rarely seen. Some were quite harmless, but most of them were of a very vicious or poisonous nature. Most were active only during the winter months, during the summer they hid in thickets or windfalls, hibernated in caves or hollow trees, or migrated to the North Pole. Tall tales of encounters with some of these mythical wild animals were often told in the lumber camp bunkhouses at night to create mirth or to impress and frighten the greenhorns. The information here collected concerning these Bunyan beasts, birds, reptiles and fish was obtained from various reliable, as well as unreliable and doubtful sources. The descriptions of these are arranged in alphabetical order for convenience of ready identification.

I. ANIMALS

AXEHANDLE HOUND. Like a dachshund in general appearance, with a hatchet-shaped head, a short handle-shaped body and short, stumpy legs. It prowled about the lumber camps at night looking for axe or peavy handles, this being the only kind of food it was known to touch. Whole cords of axe handles were eaten by these troublesome wild hounds.

ARGOPELTER. This hoary beast lived in the hollow trunks of trees. From this point of vantage it dropped or threw chunks or splinters of wood on its victims. It but seldom missed its aim and a considerable number of lumberjacks were annually maimed by its gunnery. No complete description of it has ever been obtained and its life history is unknown.

CAMP CHIPMUNK. Originally small animals, they ate the tons of prune stones discarded from Paul Bunyan's camp cook shanty and grew so big and fierce that they killed all of the bears and catamounts in the neighbourhood. Later Paul and his men shot them for tigers.

FLITTERICKS. The variety of flying squirrels which frequented the vicinity of the lumber camps were very dangerous because of the great rapidity of their flights. It was impossible to dodge them. One struck an ox between the eyes with such force as to kill the animal.

GUMBEROO. It lived in burned-over forests and was therefore easily avoided. It was very ferocious. It was "larger than a bear and had a round, leathery body that nothing could pierce. Bullets bounded off its tough hide. Often they struck the hunter on the rebound and killed him. The only thing that could kill a gumberoo was fire. Often at night the lumberjacks were awakened by loud explosions. These were caused by gumberoos blowing up in flames". A foolhardy photographer once took a picture of one but this also finally blew up.

GYASCUTUS. Also called the Stone-eating Gyascutus. This sordid beast has been described as "about the size of a white-tailed deer. Has ears like a rabbit and teeth like a mountain lion. It has telescopic legs which enable it to easily graze on hills. It has a long tail which it wraps around rocks when its legs fail to telescope together. It feeds on rocks and lichens, the rocks enabling it to digest the tough and leathery lichens. It is never seen except after a case of snake-bite."

HANGDOWN. Its Latin name is unknown. This utterly foolish animal lives in big woods "where it hangs down from the limbs of trees, either with its fore or hind paws, either head down or head on, either way making no difference to its digestion. It climbs along the bottom of a limb after the manner of a sloth. Its skin brings a high price. It is more easily hunted at night when a tub must be placed over it. It is then killed with an axe".

HIDEBEHIND. A very dangerous animal which undoubtedly accounted for many missing lumberjacks. It was always hiding behind something generally a tree trunk. Whichever way a man turned it was always behind him. From this position it sprang upon its human prey, dragged or carried the body to its lair and there feasted on it in solid comfort. Because of its elusive habits no satisfactory description of it has ever been obtained.

HODAG. The Black Hodag (Bovinus spiritualis) was discovered by E. S. "Gene" Shepard, a former well-known timber cruiser of Rhinelander, Wisconsin. Its haunts were in the dense swamps of that region. According to its discoverer, this fearful beast fed on mud turtles, water snakes and muskrats, but it did not disdain human flesh. Mr. Shepard found a cave where one of these hodags lived. With the aid of a few lumberjacks he blocked the entrance with large rocks. Through a small hole left in the barricade he inserted a long pole on the end of which he fastened a sponge soaked in chloroform. The hodag, thus rendered unconscious, was then securely tied and taken to Rhinelander, where a stout cage had been prepared for it. It was exhibited at the Oneida County fair. An admission fee was charged and a quite large sum of money earned. Later Mr. Shepard captured a female hodag with her thirteen eggs. All of these hatched. He taught the young hodags a series of tricks, hoping to exhibit the animals for profit.

This ferocious beast had horns on its head, large bulging eyes, terrible horns and claws. A line of large sharp spikes ran down the ridge of its back and long tail. Coloured photographs of it can be obtained at Rhinelander. The hodag never laid down. It slept leaning against the trunks of trees. It could only be captured by cutting deeply into the trunks of its favourite trees. It was a rare animal of limited distribution.

LUFERLANG. A curious animal with a dark blue stripe running down the length of its back. Its brushy tail was in the middle of the back. Its legs were triple-jointed and it could run equally fast in any direction. It attacked its prey without provocation and its bite was certain death. "It bites but once a year, so if one met one that had already bitten someone, one was perfectly safe."

ROPERITE. A very active animal as large as a pony. It had a rope-like beak with which it roped the swiftest rabbits. Sometimes it got a tenderfoot logger. It generally travelled in small herds. Probably now extinct.

RUMPTIFUSEL. A very ferocious animal of large size and great strength. When at rest it wraps its thin body about the trunk of a tree, a clever stratagem for securing its prey. A lumberjack mistakes it for a fur robe, approaches it and is thereafter missing.

SIDEHILL DODGER. It lived on the sides of hills only. It had two short legs on the up-hill side. It burrowed in hillsides, having a number of such burrows and was always dodging in and out of these. It was harmless but its very strange antics frightened many a lumberjack into fits.

SLIVER CAT. This fierce denizen of the pineries was a huge cat with tasselled ears. Its fiery red eyes were in vertical instead of horizontal eye slits. It had a very long tail with a ball-shaped knob at its end. The lower side of this knob was bare and hard, on its upper side were sharp spikes. The big cat would sit on a limb waiting for a victim. When one passed beneath it would knock him down with the hard side and then pick him up with the spikes. Paul Bunyan's crews suffered continual losses from the depredations of these big cats.

TEAKETTLER. A small animal which obtains its name from the noise which it made, resembling that of a boiling teakettle. Clouds of vapour issued from its nostrils. It walked backward from choice. But few woodsmen have ever seen one.

TOTE-ROAD SHAGAMAW. An animal enigma. Its hind legs have the hoofs of a moose and its fore legs the claws of a bear, making it very hard to track. When it tires of using one set of legs it travels on the other set. It prowls along the tote roads devouring any coats or other articles of lumberjacks' clothing which it finds hung on trees or logs. It is fierce in appearance but is shy and harmless.

TRIPODERO. It had tripod-legs. "Its beak is like the muzzle of a gun with a sight on the end. Going through the brush it raises and lowers itself to look for game. Upon seeing a bird or small animal it tilts itself to the rear, sights along its beak and lets fly a pellet of clay. A quantity of squids of this material it carries in its cheeks. It never misses a shot." This is more particularly an animal of the vicinity of the civil engineering and railroad construction than of the logging camps.

II. Birds

GOOFUS BIRD. One of the peculiar birds nesting near Paul Bunyan's old time camp on the Big Onion River. It was the opposite of most other birds—it always flew backwards instead of forwards. This curious habit an old lumberjack explained: "It doesn't give a darn where it's going, it only wants to know where it's been." It also built its nest upside down.

GILLYGALOO. This hillside plover nested on the slopes of Bunyan's famous Pyramid Forty. Living in such a locality it laid square eggs so that they could not roll down the steep incline. The lumberjacks hard-boiled these eggs and used them as dice.

PINNACLE GROUSE. This bird had only one wing. This enabled

it to fly in only one direction about the top of a conical hill. The colour of its plumage changed with the seasons and with the condition of the observer.

PHILLYLOO BIRD. It had a long beak like a stork and long legs. It had no feathers to spare. It flew upside down the better to keep warm and to avoid rheumatism in its long limbs. It laid Grade D eggs.

MOSKITTOS. The naturalist in Paul Bunyan's camp classified these as birds. When Paul was logging in the Chippewa River region the mosquitos were particularly troublesome. They were so big that they could straddle the stream and pick the passing lumberjacks off the log drive. Sometimes a logging crew would find one in this position, quickly tie his legs to convenient trees and use him for a bridge across the river. Paul imported from Texas a drove of fighting bumblebees to combat the mosquitos. They fought for a while, then made peace and intermarried. The result of this crossing made the situation worse than ever before for the loggers. The offspring had stingers at both ends.

III. Snakes

HOOP SNAKE. A very poisonous reptile. It could put its tail in its mouth and roll with lightning-like rapidity after its prey. The only way to avoid it was to quickly jump through its hoop as it approached. This so confused the large serpent that it rolled by and could not get back. Its sting was in its tail. A hoop snake once stung a peavy handle. This swelled to such great size that Paul Bunyan cut one thousand cords of wood out of it.

SNOW SNAKE. These reptiles came over from Siberia by frozen Bering Strait during the very cold year of the two winters. Being pure white in colour they were always more plentiful during the winter time. They were very poisonous and savage. Tanglefoot oil was the only remedy for their bite.

IV. Fish

COUGAR FISH. This savage fish, armed with sharp claws, lived in the Big Onion River. It was the cause of the disappearance and death of many river drivers, whom it clawed off the logs and beneath the water. Paul Bunyan offered a big reward for their capture and extermination, but the fish heard of it and stayed away. None were taken.

GIDDY FISH. They were small and very elastic, like indiarubber. They were caught through holes in the ice during the winter. The method pursued was to hit one on the head with a paddle. This fish would bounce up and down. Taking the cue from him the other fish would bounce also. Presently all would bounce themselves out of the water onto the ice. There they were easily gathered up.

GOOFANG. This curious fish always swam backward instead of forward. This was to keep the water out of its eyes. It was described as "about the size of a sunfish, only larger".

LOG GAR. These big fish had a snout so well armed with large saw teeth that they could saw right through a log to get at a juicy lumberjack. Once in the water they made mince meat of him.

UPLAND TROUT. These very adroit fish built their nests in trees and were very difficult to take. They flew well but never entered the water. They were fine pan fish. Tenderfeet were sent out into the woods to catch them.

WHIRLIGIG FISH. Related to the Giddy Fish. They always swam in circles. They were taken in the winter months through holes in the ice, like their relatives. The loggers smeared the edges of the holes with ham or bacon rind. Smelling this the fish would swim around the rims of the holes, faster and faster, until they whirled themselves out on the ice. Thousands were thus taken.

V. Bugs

Chiefly bed bugs and greybacks. The men soon got used to them and tolerated them. Wood ticks were in the brush but were out of date and inactive in the winter time.

FEARSOME CRITTERS[213]

I. The Cactus Cat
(*Cactifelinus inebrius*)

How many people have heard of the cactus cat? Thousands of people spend their winters in the great South-west—the land of desert and mountain, of fruitful valleys, of flat-topped mesas, of Pueblos, Navajos, and Apaches, of sunshine, and the ruins of ancient Cliff-dwellers. It is doubtful, however, if one in a hundred of these people ever heard of a cactus cat, to say nothing of seeing one sporting about among the cholla and palo verde. Only the old-timers know of the beast and its queer habits.

The cactus cat, as its name signifies, lives in the great cactus districts; and is particularly abundant between Prescott and Tucson. It has been reported, also, from the valley of the lower Yaqui, in Old Mexico, and the cholla-covered hills of Yucatan. The cactus cat has thorny hair, the thorns being especially long and rigid on its ears. Its tail is branched and upon the forearms above its front feet are sharp, knifelike blades of bone. With these blades it slashes the base of giant cactus trees, causing the sap to exude. This is done systematically, many trees being slashed in the course of several nights as the cat makes a big circuit. By the time it is back to the place of beginning the sap of the first cactus has fermented into a kind of mescal, sweet and very intoxicating. This is greedily lapped up by the thirsty beast, which soon becomes fiddling drunk, and goes waltzing off in the moonlight, rasping its bony forearms across each other and screaming with delight.

II. The Squonk
(Lacrimacorpus dissolvens)

The range of the squonk is very limited. Few people outside of Pennsylvania have ever heard of the quaint beast, which is said to be fairly common in the hemlock forests of that State. The squonk is of a very retiring disposition, generally travelling about at twilight and dusk. Because of its misfitting skin, which is covered with warts and moles, it is always unhappy; in fact it is said, by people who are best able to judge, to be the most morbid of beasts. Hunters who are good at tracking are able to follow a squonk by its tear-stained trail, for the animal weeps constantly. When cornered and escape seems impossible, or when surprised and frightened, it may even dissolve itself in tears. Squonk hunters are most successful on frosty moonlight nights, when tears are shed slowly and the animal dislikes moving about; it may then be heard weeping under the boughs of dark hemlock trees. Mr. J. P. Wentling, formerly of Pennsylvania, but now at St. Anthony Park, Minnesota, had a disappointing experience with a squonk near Mont Alto. He made a clever capture by mimicking the squonk and inducing it to hop into a sack, in which he was carrying it home, when suddenly the burden lightened and the weeping ceased. Wentling unslung the sack and looked in. There was nothing but tears and bubbles.

III. The Splinter Cat
(*Felynx arbordiffisus*)

A widely distributed and frightfully destructive animal is the splinter cat. It is found from the Great Lakes to the Gulf, and eastward to the Atlantic Ocean, but in the Rocky Mountains has been reported from only a few localities. Apparently the splinter cat inhabits that part of the country in which wild bees and raccoons abound. These are its natural food, and the animal puts in every dark and stormy night shattering trees in search of coons or honey. It doesn't use any judgment in selecting coon trees or bee trees, but just smashes one tree after another until a hollow one containing food is found. The method used by this animal in its destructive work is simple but effective. It climbs one tree, and from the uppermost branches bounds down and across toward the tree it wishes to destroy. Striking squarely with its hard face, the splinter cat passes right on, leaving the tree broken and shattered as though struck by lightning or snapped off by the wind. Appalling destruction has been wrought by this animal in the Gulf States, where its work in the shape of a wrecked forest is often ascribed to windstorms.

IV. The Billdad
(*Saltipiscator falcorostratus*)

If you have ever paddled around Boundary Pond, in north-west Maine, at night you have probably heard from out the black depths of a cove a spat like a paddle striking the water. It may have been a paddle, but the chances are ten to one that it was a billdad fishing. This animal occurs only on this one pond, in Hurricane Township. It is about the size of a beaver, but has long, kangaroo-like hind legs, short front legs, webbed feet, and a heavy, hawk-like bill. Its mode of fishing is to crouch on a grassy point overlooking the water, and when a trout rises for a bug, to leap with amazing swiftness just past the fish, bringing its heavy, flat tail down with a resounding smack over him. This stuns the fish, which is immediately picked up and eaten by the billdad. It has been reported that sixty yards is an average jump for an adult male.

Up to three years ago the opinion was current among lumber jacks that the billdad was fine eating, but since the beasts are exceedingly shy and hard to catch no one was able to remember having tasted the meat. That fall one was killed on Boundary Pond and brought into the

Great Northern Paper Company's camp on Hurricane Lake, where the cook made a most savoury slumgullion of it. The first (and only) man to taste it was Bill Murphy, a tote-road swamper from Ambegogis. After the first mouthful his body stiffened, his eyes glazed, and his hands clutched the table edge. With a wild yell he rushed out of the cook-house, down to the lake, and leaped clear out fifty yards, coming down in a sitting posture—exactly like a billdad catching a fish. Of course, he sank like a stone. Since then not a lumber jack in Maine will touch billdad meat, not even with a pike pole.

V. The Tripodero
(*Collapsofemuris geocatapeltes*)

The chaparral and foothill forests of California contain many queer freaks of one kind and another. One of the strangest and least known is the tripodero, an animal with two contractile or telescopic legs and a tail like a kangaroo's. This peculiarity in structure enables the animal to elevate itself at will, so that it may tower above the chaparral, or, if it chooses, to pull in its legs and present a compact form for crowding through the brush. The tripodero's body is not large but is solidly built, and its head is nearly all snout, the value of which is seen in the method by which food is obtained. As the animal travels through the brush-covered country it elongates its legs from time to time, thus shoving itself up above the brush for purposes of observation. If it sights game within a range of ten rods it takes aim with its snout and tilts itself until the right elevation is obtained, then with astounding force blows a sundried quid of clay, knocking its victim senseless. (A supply of these quids is always carried in the left jaw.) The tripodero then contracts its legs and bores its way through the brush to its victim, where it stays until the last bone is cracked and eaten.

PART FIVE

FOLK TALES AND LEGENDS

'Twas so much of a tale spun out to pass day-light.

—ROBERT L. MORRIS

Item. To my beloved grandnephew and name-sake, Matthew, I do bequeath and give (in addition to the lands devised and the stocks, bonds and moneys willed to him, as hereinabove specified) the two mahogany bookcases numbered 11 and 13, and the contents thereof, being volumes of fairy and folk tales of all nations, and dictionaries and other treatises upon demonology, witchcraft, mythology, magic and kindred subjects, to be his, his heirs, and his assigns, forever.

—EUGENE FIELD

Introduction to Part Five

ANIMAL TALES AND NURSERY TALES

> *Animals talk to each other, of course. There can be no question about that; but I suppose there are very few people who can understand them.*
>
> —MARK TWAIN

> *"You des got de idee in yo' min' dat when I set down fer ter tell you sump'n hit's bleedz ter be a tale. . . . "*
>
> —JOEL CHANDLER HARRIS

Next to hero tales and tall tales, animal tales are perhaps the most congenial to American folk story-tellers and their audiences. Animal tales proper, as distinct from mere tales about animals, are those in which animal characters talk and act like human beings. Originating in the primitive's sense of kinship with animals, animal tales have lent themselves to the purposes of allegory, satire, and children's "bed-time" stories. The fact that the best-known of our animal tales, the Uncle Remus stories, survive on the nursery level is another illustration of the "downward process" of tradition (also seen in games), by which children retain what was once the property of adults.

Historically, the social rôle of the Negro slave as story-teller to his master's children accounts for the large proportion of African survivals in Negro animal tales as compared with the predominance of white traits in other parts of his lore. At the same time, a good many of the plantation stereotypes linger in the nostalgic versions of Negro folk stories and storytellers by Joel Chandler Harris, Louise Clarke Pyrnelle, and Virginia Frazer Boyle.

Although Harris discounted the literary value of the "old darkey's poor little stories" and the art of his own retelling, his renditions of "fantasies as uncouth as the original man ever conceived of" are perhaps more properly literature than folklore. But whether quaint or stark, Negro animal tales project the "compensatory dreams of the subject races and serf-populations, expressed both in folk-tale and folk-ballad [which] delight in the victory of the weak over the strong and in the triumph of brains over brute strength".[214] The way in which the Negro, more peculiarly than any other minority group, has made this symbolism his own and a vehicle for his philosophy, constitutes one of his most important contributions to folk literature and wisdom.

Story-telling for children has kept alive not only folk tales but also the art of oral narration. For young and old 'alike the fairy tale is the most appealing of folk tale types. This is the story of the trials and ultimate success of an imaginary hero or heroine, involving elements of the supernatural or the marvellous. The nature of the fairy tale, as compared with other folk-tale types, is that it is told not to be believed but to be enjoyed and admired or wondered at. For, unlike the lying tale, which deceives, the fairy tale or wonder tale may inculcate a certain imaginative wisdom and even instruction. It is imaginatively true in the way that dreams are true—a projection of subconscious desires and a survival of primitive patterns of experience and faith. The appeal of the fairy tale lies not only in the ingeniousness of the incidents but also in its beauty of form and style. Here stock motifs, episodes, and plots play an important part. The effectiveness of repetition and especially cumulative iteration as a device of oral narration is demonstrated by its wide use in both fairy tales and ballads. Above all, the atmosphere of the fairy tale, as of the ballad, weaves a spell of far away and long ago and diffuses a light that never was on land or sea.

The most effective American folk tales employ homely vernacular or dialect and other oral devices. Certain tales, like "Tailypo", depend almost entirely upon the voice for their effect. Mark Twain gave this technique an amusing twist in his platform recital of a variant of "The Golden Arm". This is the tale in which the husband has stolen the coppers from the eyelids of his dead wife and is haunted by her ghost, which repeatedly appears wailing, "Who's got my money? I want my money." After working up his audience to an excruciating pitch, Mark Twain remained silent for a couple of seconds and, slowly advancing, with appropriate gestures, suddenly stamped and yelled "Boo!"[215]

WITCHES, DEVILS AND GHOSTS

Where folks believe in witches, witches air;
But when they don't believe, there are none
there.

"Why, I could tell ye a story'd make your har
rise on eend, only
I'm 'fraid of frightening boys when they're jist
going to bed."
—HARRIET BEECHER STOWE

"Here, take dis hot coal and g'wan off and
start you a hell uh yo' own."
—ZORA NEALE HURSTON

Stories of witches survive long after people have ceased to believe in witchcraft or take it seriously. The cult itself, allied to the black art, may linger in remnants of spells and charms or counter-charms, as in conjure or hoodoo, becoming mixed with beliefs in haunts and spirits generally. But present-day witch tales, like ghost and devil tales, are told either to thrill or to amuse.

On the eerie and blood-chilling side is the favourite motif of the witch prevented from re-entering her skin. This is based on the "slipskin" belief that a skinless person is invisible and that witches slip off their skin after midnight in order to perform their nefarious deeds unseen. In "De Witch-'ooman an' de Spinnin'-Wheel" this motif is combined with that of the witch-wife. The shape-shifting witchwoman may be discovered by a mutilated hand or foot or other part of the body, according to the notion that wounds inflicted on the animal shape persist in the human form.

On the prankish side, witches are tricksters who make a nuisance of themselves in all the ways known to playfully malevolent spirits. Their pranks range from milk-stealing to riding a person in his sleep. In one of the best of American legends of the supernatural, "The Bell Witch of Tennessee and Mississippi", the hag or disembodied spirit is both revenant and hobgoblin, combining the destructive persecution of the vampire with the obstreperous annoyance of the poltergeist or noisy ghost.

"Real" ghost stories or accounts of individual experiences with haunts and legends of haunted houses and other places belong to psychic research and local history rather than to folklore. To have fun with ghosts, as with witches, the story-teller must not take them too seriously. Fair game for such a story-teller are persons who accept a dare or a bet to spend the night in a haunted house, especially those who boast that they are not afraid of ghosts. Here practical jokes are a great temptation.

"The Half-Clad Ghost" is an amusing take-off on the ghost who returns for a missing object, already seen in "Tailypo". "High Walker and Bloody Bones" is a ghoulish dense macabre.

People who traffic with the Devil for their own gain or pleasure generally end up by disappearing in smoke or turning into a jack-o-lantern or an African monkey. Sometimes the poor Devil is the victim, duped or discomfited by superior brain or brawn. Slightly less familiar are the Devil's musical exploits. He not only loves singing but is a master of the violin, of which instrument of evil he is reputedly the inventor. By the same token he can give mastery of the violin, bartering infernal skill for the pupil's soul. These legends are related to the larger belief in the supernatural origin of musical skill and individual songs.

Ghostly and devilish adventures like those of Dowsabel Casselman and curious relations between people and animals as in the stories of "The Lobo Girl of Devil's River" carry over from folk tales to local legends. Many of the latter are adaptations of migratory legends. Thus "The Lobo Girl of Devil's River" relates to the world-wide legend of wolf-children.

Approaching fiction in the individuality of their characterization and setting, tales like these stand out above the lovers'-leap type of local legend; and yet for all their bizarreness they do not, like many a literary treatment of legend, smell of the lamp. Recalling the saga (e.g., Dick Whittington) type of folk tale, they lend enchantment to history.

Part Five

ANIMAL TALES AND NURSERY TALES

THE TAR BABY [WATER-WELL VERSION] [216]

Once upon a time there was a water famine, and the runs went dry and the creeks went dry and the rivers went dry, and there wasn't any water to be found anywhere, so all the animals in the forest met together to see what could be done about it. The lion and the bear and the wolf and the fox and the giraffe and the monkey and elephant, and even the rabbit—everybody who lived in the forest was there, and they all tried to think of some plan by which they could get water. At last they decided to dig a well, and everybody said he would help—all except the rabbit, who always was a lazy little bugger, and he said he wouldn't dig. So the animals all said, "Very well Mr. Rabbit, if you won't help dig this well, you shan't have one drop of water to drink." But the rabbit just laughed and said, as smart as you please, "Never mind, you dig the well and I'll get a drink all right."

Now the animals all worked very hard, all except the rabbit, and soon they had the well so deep that they struck water and they all got a drink and went away to their homes in the forest. But the very next morning what should they find but the rabbit's footprints in the mud at the mouth of the well, and they knew he had come in the night and stolen some water. So they all began to think how they could keep that lazy little rabbit from getting a drink, and they all talked and talked and talked, and after a while they decided that someone must watch the well, but no one seemed to want to stay up to do it. Finally, the bear said, "I'll watch the well the first night. You just go to bed, and I'll show old Mr. Rabbit that he won't get any water while I'm around."

So all the animals went away and left him, and the bear sat down by the well. By and by the rabbit came out of the thicket on the hillside and there he saw the old bear guarding the well. At first he didn't know what to do. Then he sat down and began to sing:

> "Cha ra ra, will you, will you, can you?
> Cha ra ra, will you, will you, can you?"

Presently the old bear lifted up his head and looked around. "Where's all that pretty music coming from?" he said. The rabbit kept on singing:

> "Cha ra ra, will you, will you, can you?
> Cha ra ra, will you, will you, can you?"

This time the bear got up on his hind feet. The rabbit kept on singing:

> "Cha ra ra, will you, will you, can you?
> Cha ra ra, will you, will you, can you?"

Then the bear began to dance, and after a while he danced so far away that the rabbit wasn't afraid of him any longer, and so he climbed down into the well and got a drink and ran away into the thicket.

Now when the animals came the next morning and found the rabbit's footprints in the mud, they made all kinds of fun of old Mr. Bear. They said, "Mr. Bear, you are a fine person to watch a well. Why, even Mr. Rabbit can outwit you." But the bear said, "The rabbit had nothing to do with it. I was sitting here wide-awake, when suddenly the most beautiful music came down out of the sky. At least I think it came down out of the sky, for when I went to look for it, I could not find it, and it must have been while I was gone that Mr. Rabbit stole the water." "Anyway", said the other animals, "we can't trust you any more. Mr. Monkey, you had better watch the well tonight, and mind you, you'd better be pretty careful or old Mr. Rabbit will fool you." "I'd like to see him do it", said the monkey. "Just let him try." So the animals set the monkey to watch the well.

Presently it grew dark, and all the stars came out; and then the rabbit slipped out of the thicket and peeped over in the direction of the well. There he saw the monkey. Then he sat down on the hillside and began to sing:

> "Cha ra ra, will you, will you, can you?
> Cha ra ra, will you, will you, can you?"

Then the monkey peered down into the well. "It isn't the water", said he. The rabbit kept on singing:

> "Cha ra ra, will you, will you, can you?
> Cha ra ra, will you, will you, can you?"

This time the monkey looked into the sky. "It isn't the stars", said he. The rabbit kept on singing.

This time the monkey looked toward the forest. "It must be the leaves," said he. "Anyway, it's too good music to let go to waste." So he began to dance, and after a while he danced so far away that the rabbit wasn't afraid, so he climbed down into the well and got a drink and ran off into the thicket.

Well, the next morning, when all the animals came down and found the footprints again, you should have heard them talk to that monkey. They said, "Mr. Monkey, you are no better than Mr. Bear; neither of you is of any account. You can't catch a rabbit." And the monkey said, "It wasn't old Mr. Rabbit's fault at all that I left the well. He had nothing to do with it. All at once the most beautiful music that you ever heard came out of the woods, and I went to see who was making it." But the animals only laughed at him. Then they tried to get some-one-else to watch the well that night. No one would do it. So they thought and thought and thought about what to do next. Finally the fox spoke up. "I'll tell you what let's do", said he. "Let's make a tar man and set him to watch the well." "Let's do", said all the other animals together. So they worked the whole day long building a tar man and set him to watch the well.

That night the rabbit crept out of the thicket, and there he saw the tar man. So he sat down on the hillside and began to sing:

> "Cha ra ra, will you, will you, can you?
> Cha ra ra, will you, will you, can you?"

But the man never heard. The rabbit kept on singing:

> "Cha ra ra, will you, will you, can you?
> Cha ra ra, will you, will you, can you?"

But the tar man never heard a word. The rabbit came a little closer:

> "Cha ra ra, will you, will you, can you?
> Cha ra ra, will you, will you, can you?"

The tar man never spoke. The rabbit came a little closer yet:

> "Cha ra ra, will you, will you, can you?
> Cha ra ra, will you, will you, can you?"

The tar man never spoke a word.

The rabbit came up close to the tar man. "Look here", he said, "you get out of my way and let me down into that well." The tar man never moved. "If you don't get out of my way, I'll hit you with my fist", said the rabbit. The tar man never moved a finger. Then the rabbit raised his fist and struck the tar man as hard as he could, and his right fist stuck tight in the tar. "Now you let go of my fist or I'll hit you with my other fist", said the rabbit. The tar man never budged. Then the rabbit struck him with his left fist, and his left fist stuck tight in the tar. "Now you let go of my fists or I'll kick you with my foot?", said the rabbit. The tar man never budged an inch. Then the rabbit kicked him with his right foot, and his right foot stuck tight in the tar. "Now you let go of my foot or I'll kick you with my other foot", said the rabbit. The tar man never stirred. Then the rabbit kicked him with his left foot, and his left foot stuck tight in the tar. "Now you let me go or I'll butt you with my head", said the rabbit. And he butted him with his head, and there he was; and there the other animals found him the next morning.

Well, you should have heard those animals laugh. "Oh, ho, Mr. Rabbit", they said. "Now we'll see whether you steal any more of our water or not. We're going to lay you across a log and cut your head off." "Oh, please do," said the rabbit. "I've always wanted to have my head cut off. I'd rather die that way than any other way I know." "Then we won't do it," said the other animals. "We are not going to kill you any way you like. We are going to shoot you." "That's better", said the rabbit. "If I had just stopped to think, I'd have asked you to do that in the first place. Please shoot me." "No, we'll not shoot you", said the other animals; and they had to think and think for a long time.

"I'll tell you what we'll do"' said the bear. "We'll put you into a cupboard and let you eat and eat and eat until you are as fat as butter, and then we'll throw you up into the air and let you come down and burst." "Oh, please don't!" said the rabbit. "I never wanted to die that way. Just do anything else, but please don't burst me." "Then that's exactly what we'll do", said all the other animals together.

So they put the rabbit into the cupboard and they fed him pie and cake and sugar, everything that was good; and by and by he got just as fat as butter. And then they took him out on the hillside and the lion took a paw, and the fox took a paw, and the bear took a paw, and the monkey took a paw; and then they swung him back and forth, and back and forth, saying: "One for the money, two for the show, three to make ready, and four to go." And up they tossed him into the air, and he came down and lit on his feet and said:

> "Yip, my name's Molly Cotton-tail;
> Catch me if you can."

And off he ran into the thicket.

SHEER CORPS[217]

Br'er Bear en Br'er Rabbit dey wuz farmers. Br'er Bear he has acres en acres uf good bottom land, en Br'er Rabbit has des' er small sandy-land farm. Br'er Bear wuz allus er "raisin' Cain" wid his neighbors, but Br'er Rabbit was er most engenerally raisin' chillun.

Arter while Br'er Rabbit's boys 'gun to git grown, en Br'er Rabbit 'lows he's gwine to have to git more land if he makes buckle en tongue meet.

So he goes ober to Br'er Bear's house, he did, en he say, sez he, "Morning, Br'er Bear. I craves ter rent yer bottom field nex' ye'r."

Br'er Bear he hum en he haw, en den he sez, "I don't spec I kin 'commodate yer, Br'er Rabbit, but I moughten consider hit, bein's hit is you."

"How does you rent yer land, Br'er Bear?"

"I kin onliest rent by der sheers."

"What is yer sheer, Br'er Bear?"

"Well", said Br'er Bear, "I takes der top of de crop fer my sheer, en you takes de rest fer yo' sheer."

Br'er Rabbit thinks erbout it rale hard, en he sez, "All right, Br'er Bear, I took it; we goes ter plowin' ober dare nex' week."

Den Br'er Bear goes back in der house des' er-laughin'. He sho is tickled ez to how he hez done put one by ole Br'er Rabbit dat time.

Well, 'long in May Br'er Rabbit done vent his oldest son to tell Br'er Bear to come down to de field to see erbout dat are sheer crop. Br'er Bear he comes er-pacin' down to de field en Br'er Rabbit wuz er-leanin' on de fence.

"Mo'nin', Br'er Bear. See what er fine crop we hez got. You is to hate de tops fer yer sheer. Whare is you gwine to put 'em? I wants ter git 'em off so I kin dig my 'taters."

Br'er Bear wuz sho hot. But he done made dat trade wid Br'er Rabbit, en he had to stick to hit. So he went off all huffed up, en didn't even tell Br'er Rabbit what to do wid de vines. But Br'er Rabbit perceeded to dig his 'taters.

'Long in de fall Br'er Rabbit 'lows he's gwine to see Br'er Bear ergin en try to rent der bottom field. So he goes down to Br'er Bear's house en after passin' de time of day en other pleasant sociabilities, he sez, sez he, "Br'er Bear, how erbout rentin' der bottom field nex' year? Is yer gwine ter rent hit to me ergin?"

Br'er Bear say, he did, "You cheat me out uf my eyes las' year, Br'er Rabbit. I don't think I let yer hate it dis ye'r."

Den Br'er Rabbit scratch his head er long time, en he say, "Oh, now, Br'er Bear, you know I ain't cheated yer. Yer just cheat yerself. Yer made de trade yerself en I done tuck yer at yer word. Yer sed yer wanted der tops fer yer sheer, en I gib um ter you, didn't I? Now you des' think hit all ober ergin en see if you can't make er new deal fer yerself."

Den Br'er Bear said, "Well, I rents to you only on dese perditions: dat yer hate all de tops fer yer sheer en I hate all de rest fer my sheer."

Br'er Rabbit he twis' en he turn en he sez, "All right, Br'er Bear, I'se got ter hate more land fer my boys. I'll tuck hit. We go to plowin' in dare right away."

Den Br'er Bear he amble back into de house. He wuz shore he'd made er good trade dat time.

Way 'long in nex' June Br'er Rabbit done vent his boy down to Br'er Bear's house ergin, to tell him to come down ter de field ter see erbout his rent. When he got dare, Br'er Rabbit say, he did:

"Mo'nin', Br'er Bear. See what er fine crap we hez got? I specks hit will make forty bushels to de acre. I'se gwine ter put my oats on der market. What duz yer want me ter do wid yer straw?"

Br'er Bear sho wuz mad, but hit wa'n't no use. He done saw whar Br'er Rabbit had 'im. So he lies low en 'lows to hisself how he's gwine to git eben wid Br'er Rabbit yit. So he smile en say, "Oh, der crop is all right, Br'er Rabbit. Jes' stack my straw enywheres eround dare. Dat's all right."

Den Br'er Bear smile en he say, "What erbout nex' year, Br'er Rabbit? Is you cravin' ter rent dis field ergin?"

"I ain't er doin' nothin' else but wantin' ter rent hit, Br'er Bear", said Br'er Rabbit.

"All right, all right, you kin rent her ergin. But dis time I'se gwine ter hate der tops fer my sheer, en I'se gwine ter hate de bottoms fer my sheer too."

Br'er Rabbit wuz stumped. He didn't know what ter do nex'. But he finally managed to ask, "Br'er Bear, ef yer gits der tops en der bottoms fer yer share, what will I git fer my sheer?"

Den old Br'er Bear laff en say, "Well, you would git de middles."

Br'er Rabbit he worry en he fret, he plead en he argy, but hit does no good.

Br'er Bear sez, "Take hit er leave hit", en jes' stands pat.

Br'er Rabbit took hit.

Way 'long nex' summer ole Br'er Bear 'cided he would go down to der bottom field en see erbout dat dare sheer crop he had wid Br'er Rabbit. While he wuz er-passin' through de woods on his way, he sez to himself, he did:

"De fust year I rents to de ole Rabbit, I makes de tops my sheer, en old Rabbit planted 'taters; so I gits nothin' but vines. Den I rents ergin, en der Rabbit is to hate de tops, en I de bottoms, en ole Rabbit plants oats; so I gits nothin' but straw. But I sho is got dat ole Rabbit dis time. I gits both de tops en de bottoms, en de ole Rabbit gits only de middles. I'se bound ter git 'im dis time."

Jes' den de old Bear come ter de field. He stopped. He look at hit. He shet up his fist. He cuss en he say, "Dat derned little scoundrel! He done went en planted dat fiel' in corn."

HOW SANDY GOT HIS MEAT—A NEGRO TALE FROM THE BRAZOS BOTTOMS[218]

Brer Rabbit an Brer Coon wuz fishermuns. Brer Rabbit fished fur fish an Brer Coon fished fur f-r-o-g-s.

Arter while de frogs all got so wile Brer Coon couldent ketch em, an he hadn't hab no meat to his house an de chilluns wuz hongry and de ole omen beat em ober de haid wid de broom.

Brer Coon felt mighty bad an he went off down de rode wid he haid down wundering what he gwine do. Des den ole Brer Rabbit wuz er skippin down he rode an he seed Brer Coon wuz worried an thronged up his years an say-ed:

"Mornin, Brer Coon."

"Mornin, Brer Rabbit."

"How is yer copperrosity segashuatin, Brer Coon?"

"Porely, Brer Rabbit, porely. De frogs haz all got so wile I cain't ketch em an I ain't got no meat to my house an de ole omen is mad an de chilluns hongry. Brer Rabbit, I'se got to hab help. Sumthin' haz got to be dun."

Old Brer Rabbit looked away cross de ruver long time; den he scratch his year wid his hind foot, an say:

"I'll tole ye whut we do, Brer Coon. We'll git eber one of dem frogs. You go down on de san bar an lie down an play des lack you wuz d-a-i-d. Don't yer mobe. Be jes as still, jest lack you wuz d-a-i-d."

Old Brer Coon mosied on down to de ruver. De frogs hear-ed em er comin an de ole big frog say-ed:

"Yer better look er roun. Yer better look er roun. Yer better look er roun."

Nother ole frog say-ed:

"Knee deep, knee deep, knee deep."

An "ker-chug" all de frogs went in de water.

But Ole Brer Coon lide down on de san an stretched out jest lack he wuz d-a-i-d. De flies got all ober em, but he never moobe. De sun shine hot, but he never moobe; he lie still jest lack he wuz d-a-i-d.

Directly Old Brer Rabbit cum er runnin tru de woods an out on de san bar an put his years up high an hollered out:

"Hay, de Ole Coon is d-a-i-d."

De ole big frog out in de ruver say-ed:

"I don't bleve it, I don't bleve it, I don't bleve it."

An all de littul frogs roun de edge say-ed:

"I don't bleve it, I don't bleve it, I don't bleve it."

But de ole coon play jes lack he's d-a-i-d an all de frogs cum up out of de ruver an set er roun where de ole coon lay.

Jes den Brer Rabbit wink his eye an say-ed:

"I'll tell you what I'de do, Brer Frogs. I'de berry Ole Sandy, berry em so deep he never could scratch out."

Den all de frogs gun to dig out de san, dig out de san from under de ole coon. When dey had dug er great deep hole wid de ole coon in de middle of it, de frogs all got tired an de ole frog say-ed:

"Deep er nough—deep er nough—deep er nough."

An all de littul frogs say-ed:

"Deep er nough—deep er nough—deep er nough."

Old Brer Rabbit was er takin er littul nap in der sun, an he woke up and say-ed:

"Kin you jump out?"

De ole big frog look up to de top of de hole an say-ed:

"Yes I kin. Yes I kin. Yes I kin."

An de littul frogs say-ed:

"Yes I kin. Yes I kin. Yes I kin."

Ole Brer Rabbit tole em:

"Dig it deeper."

Den all de frogs went to wuk an dug er great deep hole way down inside de san wid Ole Brer Coon right in de middle jest lack he wuz d-a-i-d. De frogs wuz er gittin putty tired an de ole big frog sung out loud:

"Deep er nough. Deep er nough. Deep er nough."

An all de littul frogs sung out too:

"Deep er nough. Deep er nough. Deep er nough."

An Old Brer Rabbit woke up er gin an exed em:

"I bleve I kin. I bleve I kin. I bleve I kin."

Old Brer Rabbit look down in de hole agin an say-ed:

"Dig dat hole deeper."

Den all de frogs gin to wuk throwin out san, throwin out san, clear till most sun down and dey had er great deep hole way, way down in de san, wid de ole coon layin right in de middle. De frogs wuz plum clean tired out and de ole big frog say-ed:

"Deep er nough. Deep er nough. Deep er nough."

An all de littul frogs say-ed:

"Deep er nough. Deep er nough; Deep er nough."

Ole Brer Rabbit peeped down in de hole an say:

"Kin yer jump out?"

An de ole frog say:

"No I cain't. No I cain't. No I cain't."

An all de littul frogs say:

"No I cain't. No I cain't. No I cain't."

Den ole Brer Rabbit jump up right quick an holler out:

"RISE UP SANDY AN GIT YOUR MEAT."

An Brer Coon had meat fer sepper dat nite.

OLE SIS GOOSE[219]

Ole sis goose wuz er sailin' on de lake, and old brer fox wus hid in de weeds. By um by ole sis goose swum up close to der bank and ole brer fox lept out and cotched her.

"O yes, ole sis goose, I'se get yer now, you'se been er sailin' on mer lake er long time, en I'se got yer now. I'se gwine to break yer neck en pick yer bones."

"Hole on der', brer fox, hole on, I'se get jes as much right to swim in der lake as you has ter lie in der weeds. Hit's des as much my lake as hit is yours, and we is gwine to take dis matter to der cotehouse and see if you has any right to break my neck and pick my bones."

And so dey went to cote, and when dey got dere, de sheriff, he wuz er fox, en de judge, he wuz er fox, and der tourneys, dey wuz foxes, en all de jurrymen, dey was foxes, too.

And dey tried ole sis goose, en dey 'victed her and dey 'scuted her, and dey picked her bones.

Now my chilluns, listen to me, when all de folks in de cotehouse is foxes, and you is jes er common goose, der ain't gwine to be much jestice for you pore nigger.

THE HAWK AND THE BUZZARD[220]

You know de hawk and de buzzard was settin' up in a pine tree one day, so de hawk says: "How you get yo' livin', Brer Buzzard?"

"Oh Ah'm makin' out pretty good, Brer Hawk. Ah waits on de salvation of de Lawd."

Hawk says, "Humph, Ah don't wait on de mercy of nobody. Ah takes mine."

"Ah bet Ah'll live to pick yo' bones, Brer Hawk."

"Aw naw, you won't, Brer Buzzard. Watch me git my livin'."

He seen a sparrer sittin' on a dead limb of a tree and he sailed off and dived down at dat sparrer. Du end of de limb was stickin' out and he run his breast right up on de sharp point and hung dere. De sparrer flew on off.

After while he got so weak he knowed he was gointer die. So de buzzard flew past just so—flyin' slow you know, and said, "Un hunh, Brer Hawk, Ah told you Ah was gointer live to pick yo' bones. Ah waits on de salvation of de Lawd."

And dat's de way it is wid some of you young colts.

TAILYPO[221]

Once upon a time, way down in de big woods ob Tennessee, dey lived a man all by hisself. His house didn't hab but one room in it, an' dat room was his pahlor, his settin' room, his bedroom, his dinin' room, an' his kitchen, too. In one end ob de room was a great, big, open fiahplace, an' dat's wha' de man cooked an' et his suppah. An' one night atter he had cooked an' et his suppah, dey crep' in troo de cracks ob de logs de curiestes creetur dat you ebber did see, an' it had a *great, big, long tail.*

Jis' as soon as dat man see dat varmint, he reached fur his hatchet, an' wid one lick, he cut dat thing's tail off. De creetur crep' out troo de cracks ob de logs an' run away, an' de man, fool like, he took an' cooked dat tail, he did, an' et it. Den he went ter bed, an' atter a while, he went ter sleep.

He hadn't been 'sleep berry long, till he waked up, an' heerd sumpin, climbin' up de side ob his cabin. It sounded jis' like a cat, an' he could heer it *scratch, scratch, scratch*, an' by-an'by, he heerd it say, " *Tailypo, tailypo; all I want's my tailypo.* "

Now dis yeer man had t'ree dogs: one wuz called Uno, an' one wuz called Ino, an' de udder one wuz called Cumptico-Calico. An' when he heerd dat thing he called his dawgs, *huh! huh! huh!* an' dem dawgs cum bilin' out from under de floo', an' dey chased dat thing way down in de big woods. An' de man went back ter bed an' went ter sleep.

Well, way long in de middle ob de night, he waked up an' he heerd sumpin' right above his cabin doo', tryin' ter git in. He listened, an' he could heer it *scratch, scratch, scratch*, an' den he heerd it say, "*Tailypo, tailypo; all I want's my tailypo.*" An' he sot up in bed and called his dawgs, *huh! huh! huh!* an' dem dawgs cum bustin' round de corner ob de house an' dey cotched up wid dat thing at de gate an' dey jis' tore de whole fence down, tryin' ter git at it. An' dat time, dey chased it way down in de big swamp. An' de man went back ter bed agin an' went ter sleep.

Way long toward mornin' he waked up, and he heerd sumpin' down in de big swamp. He listened, an' he heerd it say, " *You know, I know; all I want's my tailypo.*" An' dat man sot up in bed an' called his dawgs, *huh! huh! huh!* an' you know dat time dem dawgs didn' cum. Dat thing had carried 'em way off down in de big swamp an' killed 'em, or los' 'em. An' de man went back ter bed an' went ter sleep agin.

Well, jis' befo' daylight, he waked up an' he heerd sumpin' in his room, an' it sounded like a cat, climbin' up de civers at de foot ob his bed. He listened an' he could heer it *scratch, scratch, scratch,* an' he looked ober de foot ob his bed an' he saw two little pinted ears, an' in a minute, he saw two big, roun', fiery eyes lookin' at him. He wanted to call his dawgs, but he too skeered ter holler. Dat thing kep' creepin' up until by-an'-by it wuz right on top ob dat man, an' den it said in a low voice, *"Tailypo, tailypo; all I want's my tailypo."* An' all at once dat man got his voice an' he said, *"I hain't got yo' tailypo."* And dat thing said, *"Yes you has",* an' it jumped on dat man an' scratched him all to pieces. An' sum folks say he got his tailypo.

Now dey ain't nothin' lef' ob dat man's cabin way down in de big woods ob Tennessee, 'ceptin' the chimbley, an' folks w'at lib in de big valley say dat when de moon shines bright an' de win' blows down de valley you can heer sumpin' say, "Tailypo . . . ," an' den, die away in de distance.

THE SINGING GEESE[222]

A man went out one day to shoot something for dinner, and as he was going along, he heard a sound in the air above him and looking up saw a great flock of geese, and they were all singing.

"La-lee-lu, come quilla, come quilla, bung, bung, bung, quilla bung."

He up with his gun and shot one of the geese and it sang as it fell,

"La-lee-lu, come quilla, come quilla, bung, bung, bung, quilla bung."

He took it home and told his wife to cook it for dinner and each feather as she picked it, flew out of the window. She put the goose in the stove, but all the time it was cooking, she could hear in muffled tones from the stove,

"La-lee-lu, come quilla, come quilla, bung, bung, bung, quilla bung."

When the goose was cooked, she set it on the table, but as her husband picked up his knife and fork to carve it, it sang,

"La-lee-lu, come quilla, come quilla, bung, bung, bung, quilla bung."

When he was about to stick the fork in the goose, there came a tremendous noise, and a whole flock of geese flew through the window singing,

"La-lee-lu, come quilla, come quilla, bung, bung, bung, quilla bung."

And each one stuck a feather in the goose. Then they picked it up off the dish and all flew out of the window singing,

"La-lee-lu, come quilla, come quilla, bung, bung, bung, quilla bung."

THE GUNNY WOLF[223]

A man and his little daughter lived alone in a forest and there were wolves in the forest. So the man built a fence round the house and told his little daughter she must on no account go outside the gate while he was away. One morning when he had gone away the little girl was hunting for flowers and thought it would do no harm just to peep through the gate. She did so and saw a little flower so near that she stepped outside to pick it. Then she saw another a little farther off and went for that. Then she saw another and went for that and so she kept getting farther and farther away from home. As she picked the flowers she sang a little song. Suddenly she heard a noise and looked up and saw a great gunny wolf and he said,

"Sing that sweeten, gooden song again."

(This is said in a low, gruff voice.)

She sang, "Tray-bla, tray-bla, cum qua, kimo."

Pit-a-pat, pit-a-pat, pit-a-pat, pit-a-pat.

(This is said softly to represent the child's steps.)

She goes back. Presently she hears, pit-a-pat, pit-a-pat, pit-a-pat,

(coarse deep voice)

coming behind her and there was the wolf, an' 'e says:

"You move?" (Gruff voice.)

"O no my dear, what 'casion I move?" (In childish voice.)

"Sing that sweeten, gooden song again."

She sang, "Tray-bla, tray-bla, cum qua, kimo."

Wolf he gone.

Pit-a-pat, pit-a-pat, pit-a-pat.

She goes back some more. Presently she hears,

Pit-a-pat, pit-a-pat, pit-a-pat,

coming behind her, and there was the wolf, an' 'e says,

"You move."

"O no my dear, what 'casion I move?"

"Sing that sweeten, gooden song again."

She sang, "Tray-bla, tray-bla, tray-bla, cum qua, kimo."

Wolf, he gone.

Pit-a-pat, pit-a-pat, pit-a-pat coming behind her and there was the wolf, an' 'e say,

"You move."

"O no my dear, what 'casion I move?"

"Sing that sweeten, gooden song again."

She sang, "Tray-bla, tray-bla. cum qua, kimo."

Wolf he gone.

Pit-a-pat, pit-a-pat, pit-a-pat.

She goes back some more and this time when she hears pit-a-pat, pit-a-pat, pit-a-pat coming behind her, she slips inside the gate and shuts it and wolf, he can't get her.

WITCHES, DEVILS AND GHOSTS

DE WITCH-'OOMAN AN' DE SPINNIN'-WHEEL[224]

THE WITCH PREVENTED FROM RE-ENTERING HER SKIN:
A TALE FROM LOUISIANA.

One time dey wuz a man whar rid up at night ter a cabin in de eedge o' de swamp. He wuz dat hongry an' ti'd dat he say ter hissef: "Ef I kin git a hunk o' co'n-pone and a slice o' bakin', I doan kur what I pays!" On dat here come a yaller-'ooman spankin' out'n de cabin. She wuz spry on her foot ez a catbird, an' her eyes wuz sof' an' shiny. She ax de man fer ter light an' come in de cabin, an' git some supper. An' Lawd! how he mouf do water when he cotch a glimpst er de skillet on de coals! He luk it so well dat he stay; an' he sot eroun' in dat cabin ontwel he git so fat dat de grease fa'r run out'n he jaws when he look up at de sun. De yaller-'ooman she spen' her time cookie' fer him, an' waitin' on him wi' so much oberly, dat at las' de man, he up an' marry dat yaller-'ooman.

At fus' dey git erlong tollable well, but a'ter erwhile he gin ter notice dat sump'n curus 'bout dat yaller-'ooman. She ain' never in de cabin when he wake up in de night time! So, he mek up his min' fer ter spy on her. He lay down one night on de fo' pos' bed in de cornder, 'ten luk he sleep. De yaller-'ooman watch him out'n de een o' her eye, an' when she hear him gin a sno' (caze *cose* he 'ten luk he sno') she jump up an' pat a juba in de middle o' de flo'. Den she reach down a big gridi'on fum de wall, an' rake out some coals, an' haul de big spinnin'-wheel close ter de ha'th. Den, she sot herself down on dat gridi'on, an' soon ez it wuz red-hot she 'gin ter spin her skin off'n her body on de spinnin'-wheel. "Tu'n an' spin, come off skin, tu'n an' spin, come off skin." An' fo' de Lawd, de skin come off'n dat witch-'ooman's body, berginning at de top o' her head, ez slick es de shush come off de ear o' corn. An' when it wuz fa'r off, den she wuz a gret big yeller cat. Den, she tuk her skin an' chuck it onder de bed. "Lay dar, skin", she say, "wi' dat fool nigger sno'in' in de bed, ontwel I come back. I gwine ter ha' some fun, I is."

Wi' dat she jump out'n de winder an' lope off. Soon ez she wuz gone de man, he jump out'n de bed an' tuk out skin an' fill it plum full o' salt an' pepper, un' th'ow it back onder de bed. Den he crope out an' watch thro' de key-hole ontwel de witch-'ooman come home. She laugh whilse she wuz rakin' out de skin fum onder de bed, an' shakin' herse'f inter it. But when she feel de salt an' pepper, she laugh on de yether side her mouf. She moan an' groan so you kin hear her a mile! But she ain' able ter git out'n dat skin, an' de man watch her thoo de key-hole twel she fall down an' die on de flo'.

THE BELL WITCH OF TENNESSEE AND MISSISSIPPI[225]

A FOLK LEGEND

Back in the days before the War there lived somewhere in old North Carolina a man by the name of John Bell. Bell was a planter and was well fixed. He had a good-sized plantation and a dozen niggers of field-hand age, and mules and cows and hogs a-plenty. His family was made up of his wife, a daughter thirteen or fourteen years old they say was mighty pretty, and two or three young-uns that don't figure much in this story. Until he hired him an overseer, Bell got along fine.

The overseer was a Simon Legree sort of fellow, always at sixes and sevens with other folks, and especially with the niggers. He didn't even mind jawing with his boss. They say Mr. Bell was half a mind to fire the scoundrel and hire another one. But he tended to his business. He had a way with the women-folks. Some say he had an eye open for Mary, the daughter. And Mrs. Bell stood up for him. So he stayed on for a good while, and the longer he stayed the uppiter he got. Whenever he and Bell had a row—and their rows got bigger and bitterer—the overseer went out and blacksnaked three or four niggers, for they

were the only critters in the shape of man that he could abuse without
a come-back. He was the worst kind of a bully, and a man of high
temper, in fact, a regular overseer of the kind you hear about in Yankee stories.

Mr. Bell had a tall temper too, and the men did not spend a lot of
time patting each other on the back and bragging about each other's
good points. A stand-up fight was bound to come off.

It did. Some say it was about the way the overseer had beat up one
of the niggers. Some say it was about something Mr. Bell heard and
saw from behind a cotton-house one day when Mary rode through the
field where the overseer was working a gang of niggers. Bell went
away blowing smoke from his pistol barrel, and mumbling something
about white trash. The overseer didn't go away at all.

Of course Bell was brought into court, but he plead self-defence,
and the jury let him off. He went home, hired him another overseer,
and allowed that everything was settled. But the truth was that everything was now plumb unsettled.

That year and the next and the next the crops on the Bell place were
an out-and-out failure: bumblebee cotton and scraggly tobacco and
nubbin corn. His mules died of colic or some strange disease like it.
His cows and hogs got sick of something the horse-doctor couldn't
cure. He had to sell his niggers one by one, all except an old woman.
Finally he went broke. He got what he could for his land—lock, stock,
and barrel—and moved with his family to Tennessee. They say that
where he settled down the town of Bell, Tennessee, was named for
him. Anyway, he bought him a house and a patch of land near the
home of old Andy Jackson, who had knocked off from being President
and was living in a big house called the Hermitage.

Not long after the move to Tennessee, strange things began to happen in the Bell home. The children got into the habit of tumbling, or
being tumbled, out of bed at least once a week, and of waking up
every morning with every stitch of the bed-clothes snatched off and
their hair all tangled and mussed up. Now for young-uns to tumble out
of bed and to wake up in the morning with their heads uncombed is a
mighty strange thing, and the Bells realized it. The children couldn't
explain this carrying-on, for they were always asleep till they hit the
floor; and it was a peculiar fact that they were never tumbled out while
awake.

The old nigger woman told them it was the ha'nt of the overseer

Mr. Bell had killed that was pestering the children. She was as super-stitious as any other nigger, and she said she had always felt jubous about what the ha'nt of a man like the overseer would do. But she had spunk, and one day she allowed she would find out whether she was right by spending the night under the young-uns' bed. In the middle of the night Mr. and Mrs. Bell were fetched out of their bed by a squall like a pant'er's. When they lit a lamp and ran into the room, they found the old nigger woman sprawled in the middle of the floor, dripping cold sweat like an ash-hopper, her face grey-blue as sugar-cane peeling, and her eyes like saucers in a dish-pan. She was stiff-jointed and tongue-tied. When they got her sitting up and her tongue loosened, she screeched: "Hit's him! Hit's him! Fo' Gawd, hit's him! Hit peenched me all over, stuck pins in me, snatched de keenks outen ma haiuh, an' whup me, Lawd Gawd, how hit whup me, whup me limber and whup me stiff, whup me jes' lack *him*. Ain't gwine back dauh no mo', ain't gwine back dauh no mo'.'"

The Bells were so scared they told some of the neighbours. Old Andy Jackson heard about it and decided to ride over. He didn't take any stock in ha'nts, and as he rode through the gate he spoke his mind out loud about tarnation fools that believed nigger tales about them. He hadn't got the words out of his mouth before something whaled him over the head and skipped his hat twenty or thirty yards back down the road. Old Andy didn't say any more. He motioned his nigger boy to hand him his hat, and he went away from there.

It seems like the Witch could get hungry like folks, and was satis-fied with folks' grub. But it had to be the best. One day the old nigger woman came tearing into the front room where Mrs. Bell was quilting and said the Witch was back in the kitchen drinking up all the sweet milk.

Mrs. Bell was scared and said the old woman was lying.

"Come see fo' yo'se'f, missus. Come see fo' yo'se'f. Ah was back dauh a-mixin' up de biscuit, an' Ah retched ovah to git a cup o' miu'k, an' fo' Gawd, de cup was in de middle o' de auh, an' de miu'k was a-runnin' rat outen hit—an' hit wa'n't gwine nowheah, missus—hit wa'n't gwine nowheah. Jes' run outen de cup, an' den Ah couldn' see hit no mo'.'"

"You're just seeing things", said Mrs. Bell.

"Jes' whut Ah ain' doin'—ain' seein' de miu'k. Go on back in de kitchen efen you don' believe hit. Go on back dauh an' look fo' yo'se'f. . . . No, ma'am. Ah train' gwine back in dat place. No, ma'am, dat ha'nt kin guzzle an' bile up all de miu'k de cows evah give 'fo' Ah raise mah finger to stop hit."

Mrs. Bell went back into the kitchen and looked. There was a cup there that had had milk in it, and the milk was gone, sure as shootin'. She was now as scared as the old nigger woman, and sent right away for her husband to come out of the field.

They couldn't figure out how a ghost could drink milk, or what becomes of the milk if he does. Does the milk dry up into the ghost of itself? If not, where does it go when the ghost swallows it? Ghosts can't be seen. At least, this one couldn't. They could see through where it was. If they could see through it, why couldn't they see the milk as plain when it was inside the ghost as when it was outside? The old nigger woman said the milk was running out of the cup, but it "wa'n't gwine nowheah". An old Holy Roller preacher from down in Tallahatchie bottom who rode over to talk about it argued that if the old woman's tale was so milk must be of a higher class than folks. When it turns into the soul of itself, it leaves nothing behind; but folks leave behind a corpse that must be covered up with dirt right away. Folks argued about it on front galleries in the summer time and around the fire in winter—but they didn't argue about it on the Bells' front gallery or by the Bells' fire. And the preachers preached about it at camp meetings.

But the Witch didn't let up on the Bells' grub. No one ever saw it; but lots of times some member of the family would see something to eat dive out of the cupboard or pop out of the safe. The Witch's favourite was cream, and he got to skimming it from every pan in the spring-house. The Bells were never able to get any butter from the churning.

Mr. Bell might have stood for having his young-uns' rest disturbed and his old nigger woman all tore up this way, but he couldn't stand for letting the ghost eat him out of house and home. So he called the family together and allowed he would move again—this time to Mississippi, where land was rich and cheap. Mrs. Bell raised up.

"Pa", said she, "it seems like to me we have been gettin' along tolerable well here. I don't see any use moving away. What would be to keep the Witch from following us down there?"

"Nothing in the world", spoke up a hide-bottomed Chair from a corner of the room. "I'll follow you wherever you go," the Chair went on. "And I'll tell you what: if you stay on here, I won't bother you much; but if you go traipsing off to Mississippi—well, you'll wish you hadn't."

Mr. Bell was scared and bothered, but he studied a while and screwed up his courage enough to ask the Witch why he couldn't live where he pleased. But there was no answer. He asked some more questions. But the Chair had lapsed into the habit of silence that chairs have.

Mary, Mr. Bell's daughter, was now old enough to argue with the old folks about things. She was pretty as a spotted puppy, they say, and had lots of spunk and took after her pa. She sided with him. Girls always like to be moving. So when the family got over its scare about the Chair they argued back and forth. But finally Mrs. Bell and what they remembered about the Witch got the upper hand. Mr. Bell and Mary gave up the idea of moving to Mississippi—for a while anyway.

And for a while the Witch eased up on them. It even did some good turns. One day Mr. Bell was talking of visiting a family across the creek where he had heard everybody was sick. "I have just come from there", said a Voice from the eight-day clock, and went on to tell how well everybody was and what everybody was doing. Later Mr. Bell met up with a member of the family and learned that everything the Witch said was so.

Maybe because she had taken side with him in the argument about going to Mississippi, the Witch was partial to Mrs. Bell. The old nigger woman said the ha'nt sided with her because she had stood up for the overseer when Mr. Bell wanted to fire him in North Carolina. One Christmas time the family was invited to a taffy-pulling. Mrs. Bell was sick and couldn't go. They talked about whether they ought to go off and leave their mammy feeling poorly. Mr. Bell was invited too, and they needed him to do the driving; so Mary and the children begged him to take them. Mrs. Bell told them to go ahead, she didn't need them and could make out all right. So they all piled into the wagon and started.

But before they got far one of the wagon wheels flew off and let the axle down into the road with a bump. It looked like a common accident, and the old man climbed down and put the wheel back on the axle and stuck the linchpin in. He looked at all the other linchpins and saw they were on all right. Before long another wheel flew off. They looked on the ground for the linchpin but couldn't find it there. Mr. Bell whittled a new one, and when he went to put the wheel back on he found the old one in place. He fixed the wheel and drove off again, telling all of the children to watch all of the wheels. Soon they saw something like a streak of moonshine dart around the wagon, and all four wheels flew off, and the wagon dropped kersplash into a mud-hole. They put them back on, turned round, and drove back home, going quiet and easy, like sitting on eggs.

When they got there, they found their mammy sitting up by the Christmas tree eating a plate of fresh strawberries, and feeling lots better.

Other pranks were laid to the Witch. Often when the old man and the boys would go to the stable to catch the horses and mules for the day's plowing or a trip to town, the critters would back their ears and rare and kick and stomp like hornets or yellow-jackets were after them. Some morning they would be puny as chickens with the pip, and caked with sweat and mud, and their manes and tails tangled in witch-locks. The neighbours said that off end on they met an un-bridled and bare-backed horse, and the horse would stop, and some-thing on his back that they couldn't see would talk to them—but not long—they had business the other way.

Maybe because Mary had sided with her pa against her mammy and the Witch, the Witch was harder on her after the argument than any-body else. She would wake up in the middle of the night, screaming and crying that something cold and heavy had been sitting on her breast, sucking her breath and pressing the life out of her.

One time she was getting ready to go to a play-party. Some of the young sprouts were waiting for her in the front room. While she was combing her long, black hair, it suddenly was full of cuckleburs. She tugged and pulled and broke the comb to untangle it, and when she couldn't, she leaned on the bureau and cried.

"I put them in your hair", said the Witch from the looking-glass. "You've got no business going to the party. Stay here with me. I can say sweet things to you."

She screamed, and the young fellows rushed in the room, and when she told them about the Voice they shot at the glass with their pistols. But the glass didn't break. And the witch caught every bullet and pitched it into their vest pockets and laughed. So they called it a draw and went out of there. And Mary stayed at home.

Mary was now mighty near grown. She had turned out to be a beautiful woman. She had lots of beaux. But whenever one of them screwed himself up to the point of popping the question he always found that the words stuck in his throat and his face and ears burned. For young fellows these were strange signs. But it was always that way. And none of them seemed to be able to ask Mary the question. They laid it on the Witch, and finally quit hitching their horses to the Bell fence.

All but one. His name was Gardner. He was a catch for any girl, smart as a briar, good-looking, easy-going and open-hearted, and the owner of rich bottom land, a passel of niggers, and a home as big as the court-house, with columns as tall and white. He got all wrapped up in Mary, and they say Mary was leaning to him.

The way of the Witch with him was different, more businesslike. Maybe it was because the Witch realized this was the man Mary was setting her heart on. One night when Gardner was walking up the row of cedars in the Bell yard to see Mary, something he couldn't see reached out from a big cedar and touched him on the shoulder, and a voice said, "Wait a minute." Gardner was afraid to wait, but he was more afraid to run. So he waited.

"You might as well understand, here and now, that you are not going to have Mary Bell."

"Why not?" Gardner asked.

"You might have guessed from all that's happened round here. I'm in love with her myself. It's going to be hard to get her consent, and it may be harder to get the old man's. But she's not going to marry you. I'll see to that. If you open your mouth about it to-night, you'll be dead as a door-nail before morning."

Gardner studied a while and said, "If you'd only come out like a man."

The cedar tree stepped out and snatched his hat off and stomped it.

"Well, I reckon I'll have to lay off for a while", says Gardner. "But I do love her, and I'd go to the end of the world for . . . "

"Well, you don't have to go that far, and it wouldn't do you any good if you did, and if you love her the only way you can keep her out of hell is to get out yourself. If you keep on hanging round here, I'll make it hell for you. Now this is how far you go. Pack up your traps and get out of the country, hide and hair. Go any place you think the Bells won't hear tell of you—and go before breakfast. If you slip out quiet without raising any rookus I'll never pester you again. What's more, on the day you get married I'll give you a pair of new boots you'll be proud of all your life."

Gardner couldn't see why the Witch's promise of a pair of wedding boots was in the same class as the threat of death before breakfast, but he didn't split hairs, and he didn't argue any more. He picked up his hat, sneaked back to his horse, and rode off.

He never said or wrote a thing to the Bells about what had happened, part because he was scared, but more because he was ashamed of being scared. He left the neighbourhood before sun-up and moved to the western part of the state. He got somebody else to sell out for him. They say the town of Gardner, where he settled, was named after him when he got old and respected.

After he had been there a while he fell in love with a girl and got engaged to her. And they say that when he was dressing for the wedding he couldn't find his boots. He looked high and low, every place a pair of boots was liable to be and lots of places where they couldn't possibly be, but no boots could he find. He was about to give up and go to his wedding in his sock feet, when a Voice told him to crawl out from under the bed and look in the bed. And there between the sheets he found a pair of shiny new boots. He put them on and went his way rejoicing and thinking of how well a ghost kept his word, and wondering if the boots would ever wear out and if they were like the Seven-League boots he had read about in old McGuffey.

But they looked like natural boots. He told some of his friends how he had got them. They thought he was a liar. But they had to own up they were wrong. One day Gardner's house-boy made a mistake and carried them instead of another pair to a cobbler. The cobbler said they were in perfect shape, that they were not made by mortal hands, and that the soles were sewed on in a way that no man or man-made machine could have stitched them. And there is a lady in this neighbourhood who has seen the boots.

While Gardner's mind was getting mossed over about Mary, Mr. Bell decided again to move to Mississippi. It looked like his move from North Carolina was jumping from the frying pan into the fire, but he figured maybe the skillet wouldn't be any hotter. Gardner's break-up with Mary and Mary not marrying hung heavy on his mind. Mrs. Bell raised up again, telling him about rolling stones. And the Witch horned in. By this time the family got used to the Witch and would talk free with him, but respectful. Every time the question came up there was a row between Mr. Bell and Mary on one side and Mrs. Bell and the Witch on the other. The old nigger woman told Mr. Bell the ha'nt didn't want him to move because he was afraid of witch hunters in Mississippi. She said there were powerful ones down there.

And so one winter after the crops had petered out on him again, he sold his place dirt cheap. But the old nigger woman told him to wait till spring to start. She said Easter was early that year and there would be plenty of time to pitch a crop. Good Friday would be a good day to leave, she said, for the ha'nt would have to go back to his grave and stay three days under the ground and would be puny-like several days more. While he was in good working order he could be in two or three places at once and be in any of them in the bat of an eye, but then he would have to lie low, and that would give them plenty of start. So Mr. Bell early on Good Friday stacked his furniture and duds in a couple of wagons, climbed into the front one with Mary, put the old nigger woman and his biggest boy into the hind one, and told Mrs. Bell, "Git in with old Patsy if you're a-comin', and don't forgit the young-uns."

And that was the way the Bell family came to Mississippi. Mr. Bell bought him a little place in Panola County, ten miles east of Batesville on the Oxford Road. He was all ready to begin life over again without supernatural interference.

But the Witch made a quick come-back, not before the family got there, but before they moved into their new home.

When Mr. Bell first got to Batesville, or Panola as they called it then, he left the family there and went out to look at the land he aimed to buy. When he got a place that suited him, he went back to town for his family and stuff. There was some sort of hitch, and the wagons did not get started till late in the evening. As the wagons moved slowly out of town, dark clouds began to roll up in the south and west, and before they had gone three miles the storm broke. Dark came on earlier than usual, for the clouds hid the sun. The rain beat down on the wagon covers. Every now and then the lightning flashes lit up the swaying trees on each side of the road, the draggle-tailed horses, and the road itself—a long, muddy creek—and then it was dark as a stack of black cats. The folks all stopped talking. There was nothing to listen to but the beating rain and the thunder and the suck of the horses' feet and the wheels in the mud.

All at once the hind wagon, with the family in it, slid to the side of the road and sunk into the mud up to the bed. Mr. Bell saw it in a lightning flash and came back. It couldn't be moved; the horses had no foothold, and the wheels were in too deep. The fix they were in wasn't dangerous, but it was mighty uncomfortable.

And then the Witch took a hand.

"If you'll go back to your wagon and stop your cussin'", said the empty dark beside the wagon, "I'll get you out. Hump it back to your wagon now—light a shuck!"

Mr. Bell waded back and crawled in.

And then the horses and the wagon and the furniture and the family and the dog under the wagon and the calf tied behind and everything else but the mud on the wheels riz up about eight feet high and floated down the road till they were just behind the front wagon, and then they settled down easy and went on home without any trouble.

The family got settled down in their two-story double-loghouse amongst the cedars on the Oxford road.

A few nights later, the Witch spoke up from one of the andirons and told Mr. and Mrs. Bell he was in love with Mary. He said he wanted to marry her. Mr. Bell was shocked and surprised. He explained respectful but emphatic like, that he could never dream of letting a daughter of his marry a ghost, not even so noble a ghost like the one he was talking with.

"I got a claim on you, John Bell", said the Witch. "I got a claim on you and yours. I got a claim." And his voice was deep and hollowlike.

This was a point Mr. Bell maybe didn't want to hear any more about. So he said, "Have you spoken to Mary?"

"No, not spoken."

"Well, how do you know she would have you?"

"I don't. But I haven't got any reason to believe she wouldn't love me. She's never seen me. She doesn't know whether she would or not. Maybe she would consider it an honour to be married to a ghost. Not many girls are, you know. Why, it would make her famous."

"I don't want any daughter of mine getting famous that way. And besides, what if you were to have children? What in the world do you reckon they'd be like? Like you or her? Maybe half good human meat and bone, and the other half sight unseen. Or maybe they'd be the vanishin' kind and goin' round here and raisin' hell invisible. Do you think I want a passel of soap-suds young-uns floatin' round here and poppin' up into puffs of wind every time I p'inted to the stovewood pile or sprouts on a ditch bank? Not on your life. I reckon plain flesh and blood's good enough for Mary."

"But, John Bell, I love Mary. And remember. Remember."

"So do I, and that's why I'm not a-goin' to let you marry her. Why, when she got old and hard-favoured I reckon you'd quit her for some young hussy. You could do it easy enough. Mary'd have a hard time keepin' up with a stack of wind and a voice, and I'd have a hard time trackin' down and shootin' a low-down, no-count dust devil. When Mary marries, she marries a man that's solid and alive in body."

"I gather, John Bell, that you're opposed to me courting your daughter. But she's the one to say, and I'm going to talk to her about it. You'll be my father-in-law yet, or you'll be a-mourning, a-mourning."

"But what kind of wedding would it be like?" Mrs. Bell put in. "Think of it. Mary standing in front of the preacher and the preacher saying, 'Do you take this woman?' to a vase of flowers. And the ring floating down to Mary from the hanging-lamp maybe, or rising up from under a bench. I won't stand for it. I've stood for a lot of things, and you can't say I haven't been a friend to you. But I won't stand for Mary being a laughing-stock and disgrace to the family."

"If we're a-goin' to add to this family", Mr. Bell took up, "we're a-goin' to be able to see what we're addin'. I don't even know what shape you've got, if any."

"Oh, I can give you some idea what shape I have. I'll let you shake hands with me. But you must promise not to squeeze. We're very delicate, especially when we touch folks. Here, hold out your hand, and I'll put mine in it."

Mr. Bell held out his hand, felt something, and grabbed it. It was, he said later, the hand of a new-born baby—soft and crinkly and warm and just about the size of a new-born baby's hand.

"How big are you all over?" he asked.

"I can't tell you that."

"Well, there's one other thing I want to know. How do you get into this house any time you want to when every window and door is locked and barred? Do you ooze through the walls?"

"No. It's a lot easier than that. If you'll watch the corner of the ceiling up there, you'll see."

And all the rest of his life Mr. Bell swore to trustworthy witnesses that he saw the corner of the ceiling raised a good three feet and then let down again—all without the slightest racket.

"Do you mean to tell me that anything with a hand like that can h'ist the top off of the house that a-way?"

"Sure", came the answer. "But—about Mary. I'm going to talk to her right off."

"Don't", said Mr. Bell. "Do you want to drive her crazy?"

But the meeting was over, for there was no answer. And the fire had died down, and the andiron looked glum.

The story is kind of skimpy here. Nobody seems to know what the Witch said to Mary or what Mary said to the Witch.

But the family noticed next day that she was drooping and wasn't minding what was going on around her. For days she wandered about the house and up and down the yard under the gloomy old cedars, like somebody sleep-walking. And the colour left her face, and deep in her wide-open black eyes was a far-away look, like she was trying to see something that ought to be but wasn't there. Every day she got up later and went to bed earlier.

And finally there came a day when she didn't get up at all. In the evening a screech-owl hollered in a cedar right by the gallery.

That night her fever was high, and by midnight she was raving. "We've put off seein' a doctor too long", said Mrs. Bell.

"The roads like they are, it'll take me two hours goin' and him and me two hours comin'", said Mr. Bell. "It'll be might' nigh daylight before we get back. But I reckon you're right, and I'll go as quick as I can saddle a horse."

"No use", said a Voice. "All the doctors and medicines in the world won't cure her. But if you want one, I'll get him, and get him a lot quicker than you can."

The doctor got there just as the old eight-day clock struck one. "I heard somebody hollering at my window about midnight, telling me to come out here right away. When I got to the door, nobody was there; but I thought I'd better come anyway." He was a young doctor just starting out. "Say, what kind of road overseer and gang do you fellows have out this way? Last time I came over this road, about Christmas, it was the worst I ever saw. Why, I picked up a Stetson hat in the middle of a mud-hole near the four-mile board, and by George there was a man under it. 'You're in the middle of a bad fix, old man', I said. 'Hell', he said, 'that ain't nothin' to the fix this mule's in under me.' I had to lift up my feet half the way to keep them from dragging in the mud by the horse's belly. But to-night my horse skimmed over it in an hour. Well, who's sick out here?"

"It's her mind and nerves", he told them after he had questioned them and examined Mary. "I won't conceal from you, she's in pretty bad shape. And medicine won't do her any good. You've just got to be gentle and careful with her. Humour her and be patient with her. I'll give her something to put her to sleep when she gets like this. Watch her close and don't let her get lonesome. She's young and strong and ought to come round in time."

But she never did. For a month she lay there on the bed, looking at nothing and yet straining to see something. Something too far off. At night her pa and ma took turns sitting up. They didn't want the neighbours in. They called the doctor back a few times, but he shook his head and said he couldn't do any more. So they would watch and wait, wanting to do something, but helpless.

One night her ma was sitting there, holding Mary's hand and stroking the dark hair back from her forehead. Suddenly Mary pushed her mother away and sat up and looked across the foot of the bed, as if somebody was standing there.

"Mamma", she whispered, "Mamma . . . I see him . . . at last. . . . And I think . . . I think . . . I'm going . . . to love him."

And she died with the only expression of happiness they had seen on her face in months.

Some folks have tried to explain Mary's strange death. A few say the Witch tortured her continually and kept her in such constant terror that her mind was affected. Others have heard that a school teacher ventriloquist that was jealous of Gardner played tricks on her and the family, and then when she wouldn't have him tormented and frightened her to death. Some believe she was in love with the overseer from the first, and then when he was killed she was in love with the Witch and didn't want to live because she knew she would never be happy with him until she too became a ghost.

But she died, just the same. And they say that on the day of the funeral, when the coffin was carried from the house to a wagon a great black bird flew down from the sky and hung in the air just above the wagon. And around its neck was a bell that tolled in the mournfullest tone ever heard by the ear of man. And when the funeral procession began to move, the great bird floated just in front of it all the way to the graveyard and circled round and round the grave during the burial, the bell tolling all the while. And when the mound was rounded up, the bird swung high up in the air and flew away to the west and finally became just a little speck above the treetops and disappeared. But long after it was gone the mourning notes of the bell floated back to those who stood and watched.

THE HALF-CLAD GHOST[226]

"I knew a' ole man once that alluz wo' two paiah o' draw's. But when he died his wife didn' lay out but one paiah foh 'im. Well, after de fune'l, he kep' a-comin' back an' a-comin' back. Evah night he'd come right in dat front do' o' her house. So she moved from dat place, but he jes' kep' a-comin' jes de same. She moved fo' o' five times, an' he jes' kep' on a-comin' back evah night o' de worl'. Finely she talked to some o' her frien's. They asked 'er why she don' talk to 'im. She say 'cause she scared to. But they say foh 'er to say, 'What in de name o' de Lawd do you want?' So dat night he come ag'in.

"This time she walk' right up an' met 'im an' say, 'What in de name o' de Lawd do you want?'

"He looked at 'er right study foh a long time, but she nevah move, an' she jes' stan' theah; an' finely he say, 'Honey, gimme 'nother paiah o' draw's, please.'

"She say, 'Aw right, I'll give 'em to you'; an' from dat day to this he nevah has come back no mo', she say. An' dat's de way it is: When you ask 'em what in de name o' de Lawd they want, an' then tell 'em you'll give it to 'em, they'll go 'way an' leave you alone."

HIGH WALKER AND BLOODY BONES[227]

This wuz uh man. His name wuz High Walker. He walked into a boneyard with skull heads and other bones. So he would call them, "Rise up bloody bones and shake yo'self." And de bones would rise up and come together, and shake theirselves and part and lay back down. Then he would say to hisself, "High Walker", and de bones would say, "Be walkin'."

When he'd git off a little way he'd look back over his shoulder and shake hisself and say, "High Walker and bloodybones", and de bones would shake theirselves. Therefore he knowed he had power.

So uh man sold hisself to de high chief devil. He give 'im his whole soul and body tuh do ez he pleased wid it. He went out in uh drift uh woods and laid down flat on his back beyond all dese skull heads and bloody bones and said, "Go 'way Lawd, and come here Devil and do as you please wid me. Cause Ah want tuh do everything in de world dats wrong and never do nothing right."

And he dried up and died away on doin' wrong. His meat all left his bones and de bones all wuz separated.

And at dat time High Walker walked upon his skull head and kicked and kicked it on ahead of him a many and a many times and said tuh it, "Rise up and shake yo'self. High Walker is here."

Ole skull head wouldn't say nothin'. He looked back over his shoulder cause he heard some noises behind him and said, "Bloody bones you won't say nothin' yet. Rise tuh de power in de flesh."

Den de skull head said, "My mouf brought me here and if you don't mind, your'n will bring you here."

High Walker went on back to his white folks and told de white man dat a dry skull head wuz talkin' in de drift today. White man say he didn't believe it.

"Well, if you don't believe it, come go wid me and Ah'll prove it. And if it don't speak, you kin chop mah head off right where it at."

So de white man and High Walker went back in de drift tuh find dis ole skull head. So when he walked up tuh it, he begin tuh kick and kick de ole skull head, but it wouldn't say nothin'. High Walker looked at de white man and seen 'im whettin' his knife. Whettin' it hard and de sound of it said rick-de-rick, rick-de-rick! So High Walker kicked and kicked dat ole skull head and called it many and many uh time, but it never said nothin'. So de white man cut off High Walker's head.

And de ole dry skull head said, "See dat now! Ah told you dat mouf brought me here and if you don't mind out it'd bring you here."

So de bloody bones riz up and shook they selves seben times and de white man got skeered and said, "What you mean by dis?"

De bloody bones say, "We got High Walker and we all bloody bones now in de drift together."

BIG SIXTEEN AND THE DEVIL[228]

It was slavery time, Zora, when Big Sixteen was a man. They called 'im Sixteen 'cause dat was de number of de shoe he wore. He was big and strong and Ole Massa looked to him to do everything.

One day Old Massa said, "Big Sixteen, Ah b'lieve Ah want you to move dem sills Ah had hewed out down in de swamp."

"I yassuh, Massa."

Big Sixteen went down in de swamp and picked up dem 12 X 12's and brought 'em on up to de house and stack 'em. No one man ain't never toted a 12 X 12 befo' nor since.

So Ole Massa said one day, "Go fetch in de mules. Ah want to look 'em over."

Big Sixteen went on down to de pasture and caught dem mules by de bridle but they was contrary and balky and he tore de bridles to pieces pullin' on 'em, so he picked one of 'em up under each arm and brought 'em up to Ole Massa.

He says, "Big Sixteen, if you kin tote a pair of balky mules, you kin do anything. You kin ketch de Devil."

"Yassuh, Ah kin, if you git me a nine-pound hammer and a pick and shovel!"

Ole Massa got Sixteen de things he ast for and tole 'im to go ahead and bring him de Devil.

Big Sixteen went out in front of de house and went to diggin'. He was diggin' nearly a month befo' he got where he wanted. Then he took his hammer and went and knocked on de Devil's door. Devil answered de door hisself.

"Who dat out dere?"

"It's Big Sixteen."

"What you want?"

"Wanta have a word wid you for a minute."

Soon as de Devil poked his head out de door, Sixteen lammed him over de head wid dat hammer and picked 'im up and carried 'im back to Old Massa.

Old Massa looked at de deed Devil and hollered, "Take dat ugly thing 'way from here, quick! Ah didn't think you'd ketch de Devil sho 'nuff."

So Sixteen picked up de Devil and throwed 'im back down de hole.

'Way after while, Big Sixteen died and went up to Heben. But Peter looked at him and tole 'im to g'wan 'way from dere. He was too powerful. He might git outa order and there wouldn't be nobody to handle 'im. But he had to go somewhere so he went on to hell.

Soon as he got to de gate de Devil's children was playin' in de yard and they seen 'im and run to de house, says, "Mama, mama! Dat man's out dere dat kilt papa!"

So she called 'im in de house and shet de door. When Sixteen got dere she handed 'im a li'l piece of fire and said, "You ain't comin' in here. Here, take dis hot coal and g'wan off and start you a hell uh yo' own."

So when you see a Jack O'Lantern in de woods at night you know it's Big Sixteen wid his piece of fire lookin' for a place to go.

JACK-O-MY LANTERN: A MARYLAND VERSION[229]

One day wuz a man name Jack. He wuz a mighty weeked man, an' treat his wife an' chil'en like a dawg. He didn' do nuthin' but drink from mawin' tell night, an' twarn' no use to say nuthin' 'tall to 'im 'cause he wuz jus' es ambitious es a mad dawg. Well suh, he drink an' he drink tel whisky couldn' mek 'im drunk; but et las' hit bu'n 'im up inside, an' den de Debble come fur 'im. When Jack see the Debble, he wuz so skeart he leetle mo'n er drapt in de flo'. Den he bague de Debble to let 'im off jes' a leetle while, but de Debble say:

"Naw, Jack, I ain' gwine wait no longer; my wife, Abbie Sheens, is speckin' yo'." So de Debble start off pretty bris' an' Jack wuz bleeged to foller tell dey come to a grog shop. "Mr. Debble", said Jack, "don' yo' wan' a drink?" "Well", said de Debble, "I b'leeve I does, but ain' got no small change; we don' keep no change down dyah." "Tell you wotcher do, Mr. Debble", said Jack, "I got one ten cent en my pocket; yo' change yo' sef inter'nurr ten cent, and we kin git two drinks, and den yo' kin change yo' sef back again." So de Debble change hisse'f inter a ten cent, and Jack pick 'im put, but 'stid o' gwine de grog shop, Jack clap de ten cent inter he pocket-book dat he hadn't took outen he pocket befo', 'cause he didn' wan' de Debble to see dat de ketch wuz in de shape ob a cross. He shet it tight, an' dyah he had de Debble, an' twarn' no use for 'im to struggle, 'cause he couldn' git by dat cross. Well suh; fus he swar and threat'n Jack wid wet he wuz going to do to 'im and den he begun to bague, but Jack jes' t'an round an' start to go home. Den de Debble say:

"Jack, ef yo'll lemme out o' hyah, I'll let yo' off fur a whole year. I will, fur trufe. Lemme go, Jack, Jack, 'cause Abbie Sheens is too lazy to put the bresh on de fire, an' hit'll all go black out ef I ain' dyah fo' long ten' to it."

Den Jack say ter hisse'f, "I gret min' to let 'im go, 'cause in a whole year, I kin 'pent and git 'ligion, an' git shet in 'im dat er way."

Den he say, "Mr. Debble, I'll letcher out ef yo' 'clar fo' gracious yo' won't come after me fur tweel month."

Den de Debble promise befo' Jack undo de clasp, an' by de time Jack got the pocket-book open he wuz gone. Den Jack say to hisse'f, "Well, now I gwine to 'pent and git 'ligion sho'; but 'haint no use bein' in no hurry; de las' six mont' will be plenty o' time. Whar dat ten cent? Hyah it is. I gwine git me a drink." When de six mont' was gone, Jack 'lowed one mont' would be time 'nuff to 'pent, and when de las' mont' come, Jack 'lowed he gwine hate one mo' spree, and den he would have a week or ten days lef', and dat was plenty of time, 'cause 'e done hearn o' folks 'penting on dey death bade. Den he went on a spree for sho', and when de las' week come, Jack had 'lirium trimblins, and de fus' ting he knowed, dyah wuz de Debble at de do', and Jack had to git outen he bade and go 'long wid 'im. After a while dey pass a tree full o' gret big apples.

"Don' yo' want some apples, Mr. Debble?" said Jack.

"Yo' kin git some ef yo' wan' 'em", said de Debble and he stop and look up in de tree.

"How yo' 'spec' a man wid 'lirium trimblins to climb a tree?" said Jack. "Yo' catch hol' de bough, an' I'll push yer up in de crotch, an' den yo' kin git all yo' wants."

So Jack push 'im in de crotch, an' de Debble 'gin to feel de apples to git a meller one. While he wuz doin' dat, Jack, he whip he knife outen he pocket, an' cut a cross in de bark ob de tree jes' under de Debble, and de Debble holler, "Tzip! Sumpi' nurr heet me den. Wotcher doin' down dyah, Jack? I gwine cut yo' heart out."

But he couldn' git down while dat cross wuz dyah, an' Jack jes' sat down on de grass, an' watch 'im ragin' an' swarin' an' cussin'. Jack keep 'im dyah all night, tell 'twuz gret big day, an' de Debble change he chune an' he say:

"Jack, lemme git down hyah an' I'll gib yo' nurr year."

"Gimme nuttin'", said Jack, an' he stretch hisse'f out on de grass. After a while, 'bout sun up, de Debble say:

"Jack, cut dis ting offen hyah, an' lemme git down, an' I'll gib yo' ten year."

"Naw, surre", said Jack, "I won' letcher git down less yo' clar fo' gracious dat yo' won' never come arfter me no mo'."

When de Debble fin' Jack woz es hard as rock, he 'greed, an' 'clared fo' gracious dat he wouldn' never come fur Jack agin, an' Jack cut de cross offen the tree, an' de Debble lef' widout a word. Arfter dat Jack never thought no mo' 'bout 'pentin', 'cause he warn'd feared ob de Debble, an' he didn' wan' to go whar dey warn' no whiskey. Den he lib on tell he body war out, an he wuz bleeged to die. Fus' he went to de gate o' heaven but de angel jes' shake he hade. Den he went to de gate o' hell, but when it would come dat Jack wuz dyah, de Debble holler to de imps:

"Shet de do' an' don' let dat man come in hyah; he done treat me scan'lous. Tell 'im to go long back whar he come from."

Den Jack say:

"How I gwine fine my way back in de dark? Gimme a lantern."

Den de Debble tek a chunk outen de fire, an' say, "Hyah, tek dis, an' dontcher nuver come back hyah no mo'."

THE RIGHT HAND OF ROBBER LEWIS[230]

It was on a fine Monday morning in the early fall of 1820, and wash day. An old-time copper kettle on a spider was boiling water by the kitchen door of the tavern, which was on the side of the building on which was painted on the plastered wall the white horse of colossal proportions which gave the old inn its name. Rosanna Casselman, the innkeeper's bustling wife, was at work over the tubs on the side porch, and her young daughter Dowsabel was carrying buckets of water from the well to replenish the kettle. The girl, who was of amazing loveliness, was standing by the well box, and while the long pole with chain attached was dipped into the watery depths to replenish "the old oaken bucket", a horseman approached on the road which led from the south. The autumnal sun was clearing away the fogs and mist as he drew rein at the horse-trough which received the overflow from the fountain's copious source. The stranger was a young man of possibly thirty years of age, wearing a broad-brimmed black felt hat, in which was stuck the wing feather of a golden eagle, and pulled down over his eyes, almost hiding his regular features, and his handsome dark side-whiskers; he wore a cloak, or "Cardinal", as they were called in those days, which was loosened at the collar, as the exercise and growing warmth of the day had made it a trifle uncomfortable. He was mounted on a superb black horse, an entire, called Pulverhorn, said to be a son of old Topgallant, by a fugitive union with a Cumberland horse doctor's mare; the same Topgallant known as the "iron horse" which later won the great race against Whalebone at Baltimore, in three mile heats, when in his twenty-fourth year. Hiram Woodruff, the greatest of horse trainers, said of him: "His like was never seen before or since." Touching the brim of his hat, the rider asked the girl if she could hand him a can of water from the well, while his horse quenched his thirst at the trough, which was hewed from a solid log of original white pine. The girl looked at him boldly, and deciding to be polite, as she liked his appearance, she, after balancing the filled bucket on the coping of the well, ran to the water-bench on the porch to get a cup. Returning in a minute with a gourd, she filled it to the brim with the sparkling water, and handed it over the paling fence to the thirsty horseman, smiling at him in her pleasantest manner. This is how she impressed the stranger, who was a hardened citizen of the world, and a connoisseur of the fair sex.

Dowsabel Casselman was a Pennsylvania mountain beauty, typical of her medley of Continental ancestors, all except in the colouring, for her cropped curly hair, instead of being of raven blackness, was of coppery gold. It is strange that out of every thousand of the dark mountain girls of Pennsylvania there will be one or two red heads, and these will be of rarest loveliness. Her eyes, however, were dark, a hazel or amber, though her skin was fair, transparently white as alabaster. She was a little above the average height, smoothly and gracefully built, with a wonderful pair of legs, as her skirts, worn above the knees in the style of the Indian girls of those days, generously disclosed. Pleased with his reception, the promising to return shortly for a stay at the hotel, the handsome stranger resumed his way in the direction of Berlin, and Brunerstown, now called Somerset. Dowsabel, fascinated, day-dreamed watching after him, until her mother brought her back to earth by incessantly shouting, "Bring that water instanter, or I'll put a tin ear on you, you dulless slommach, standing out there grinning at that laddy-buck like a Cheshire cat." Several days later Dowsabel was again at the well drawing a bucket of water to fill the big pint Stiegel glasses which were placed on the table at dinner time, when outside the fence she noticed the small figure of an old, old man, whose head hardly came above the top of the horse-trough. The aged stranger wore a broad-brimmed soft black hat, adorned with an eagle's plume, and pulled down over his eyes, barely revealing his fine high nose and full blue eyes; the rest of his face was hidden by a huge beard, yellowish white and curly, which hung several inches below his waist. Naturally short, his big head seemed top-heavy even for his sturdy body to support, and seemed to rest on one of his shoulders. He wore a ragged great-coat that had once been brown. In one hand he carried a blackthorn cane with a branch curling around it like a grape-vine, and in the other hand a small charcoal brazier, which he used partly to warm himself in the cold sheds and outbuildings where he generally slept, and partly to heat glue, for he was a travelling furni-ture-mender by occupation. Tipping his crumpled hat with old world politeness, he said: "Milady, would you be so kind as to fetch me a can so that I may have a drink of your good water." The handsome girl gazed at him a moment, contempt appearing in her flawless features, and, at length, replied in cutting tones: "Who do you think I am, old codger, to get your kind a cup; besides, I haven't got one, and if you're dry, the trough's in front of you."

The hardened old wayfarer was taken aback, but replied with spirit: "Young missy, if I was your lover, you would not have spoken that way to me, and would have broken your neck to get me a drink." The girl's pale face coloured a little as she replied: "I have no lover, and you can see for yourself there is no cup." "Stuff and nonsense, Car-rots", said the old man, as he turned to walk away, "you have had a dozen lovers already, and a thirteenth is on the way, and when he is finished you will be ready to lead an ape in hell. Au revoir, for I am sure that we will probably meet again a couple of times."

Dowsabel said nothing more, but filled her bucket and carried it to the house, for again her mother had her "dander up". "You goosesap", she shouted, "I've a notion to give you the worst ferricadouzer of your young life, shilly-shallying out there with that old chuckle-head." But the old man's remarks made an ugly impression on the girl's mind, and she was silent and moody the rest of the day.

Several days went by again, and the handsome stranger returned from Somerset and made a stay of nearly a week at the tavern, ostensi-bly to condition his horse, which he said had a "sidebone". While the steed rested the young man was tireless in pressing his suit with the lovely Dowsabel. It was an easy conquest, as he had the youth, the good looks, the smooth ways of the big world, which were the at-tributes that girls of Dowsabel's type most admired. When he went away the beautiful girl was in tears and begged him to return soon. "Quit your blubbering, kid, I'll be back soon enough", he said, as he mounted Pulverhorn and rode away.

Several weeks elapsed, and the stranger was at the White Horse again for a longer stay. This time he was put in the great east room, which commanded a glorious view from its long windows, the room that William Makepeace Thackeray occupied on his second American tour, when he sat on the broad window sill and wrote his name with a diamond on one of the small "lights" of home-made glass, and penned his immortal descriptions of Pennsylvania mountain scenery. He was laying his plans carefully for the coup that he had been planning ever since he first set eyes on the incomparably lovely girl at the well earlier in the autumn. He soon found out that she wasn't happy at home. He slept in the next room, and could hear her mother punishing her almost every night, and her cries of agony and outraged pride.

When he at last told her that he was leaving and might not return for a long time, if at all, Dowsabel again begged tearfully to be taken along. The stranger knew that his time had come, and in the chance meetings they had in the hallways, on the porch, in the yard, and in the harness room at the barn, gradually made clear to her who and what he was. He told her that while his real name was David Pevreferry, he was known on the roads as "Young Lewis", so much were his deeds and characteristics like the famous "David Lewis, the Robber", who had died a few months before in Bellefonte jail, having been mortally wounded by a sheriff's posse on the Driftwood Branch of Sinnemahoning, and buried in the jail yard of said prison on the night of July 13, 1820.

"I will take you along if you'll stop your didoes and can prove to me that you have the guts to stay with a dabster like myself." Dowsabel protested that there was no test or ordeal she would not undergo to prove her worthiness and fitness to be the companion of a man of the highroads, and be like Dally Sanry, the loveliest friend of David Lewis. "From the first time I laid eyes on you I would have put on boy's clothing and followed you to the ends of the earth", she protested over and over again. Then he explained to her that to prove this fitness she must secure for him what he most wanted, David Lewis' right hand, to be cut off the corpse which was now resting in the grave in the jail yard at Bellefonte.

It was a well-founded tradition on the roads in Europe, as well as in Pennsylvania and Maryland, that anyone possessing the right hand of a successful marauder, done to death for his crimes, exercised a spell over those he came in contact with, was able to put entire households to sleep and ransack premises at his leisure, and have nothing to fear in the way of annoyance, interference, apprehension or arrest. At the time of the wholesale hanging of highwaymen at Harper's Ferry in

1816, the only man who escaped had the right hand of an Indian murderer in his pocket, and thus equipped his horse could outrun any posse of pursuers on the road. But how was the hand to be secured from its grave inside the jail yard, with Dowsabel on the outside and guiltless of any offence making her eligible to be inside? "Young Lewis" then stated that as a prerequisite of her worthiness to be a second Dally Sanry she must help him decamp with her father's hooded gig, which was the old taverner's holiday and Battalion Day Pride, also his best brass-mounted harness, and with these they would drive to the vicinity of Bellefonte, as far as Earlysburg. Then she must walk to Bellefonte, and put up at the Benner House, and wait there until bills announcing rewards for her capture as a runaway were posted at the hotel and she was recognized and taken up. These he would have printed at Lewistown while she was on her way to Bellefonte, and see that they were on view in every public house and every conspicuous post and pillar in the "village of the belles".

Dowsabel heard the plot with keen interest and could scarcely repress screaming with enthusiasm. On a dark night during the equinoctial rains "Young Lewis" drugged the girl's parents by putting the parings of finger nails in their wine, and made his departure with the gig and harness, driving off behind his black horse through a back lane to a point a mile down the Pike, where, under a clump of old white pines, Dowsabel awaited him, filled with loving excitement. She had slipped out of the house earlier in the evening and was not missed. The plucky steed, which had once been a lead horse in a stage-coach, was fit for the long drive ahead of him, carrying them at a break-neck pace through the muddy roads, on and on without stopping, over a succession of mountain ranges in the direction of Earlysburg. There were no telegraphs or other rapid means of communications, and only a few weekly newspapers in the back country in those days and news travelled slowly. By the time that John Caspar Peter Casselman recovered from his surprise and went to Brunerstown to advertise the loss of daughter, covered gig, brass-mounted harness and best whip with stock of mountain ash (to ward off highwaymen or evil eye), the wonderful-looking, copper-haired Dowsabel was comfortably ensconced at the spacious old Benner House at Bellefonte. There she was the object of admiration and consternation of the village sheiks who frequented the hostelry. Meanwhile the pseudo Lewis, Jr. had gotten bills struck off at Lewistown, which read approximately:

Disappeared from "The White Horse", in Somerset County, Pa., on night of September 14, 1820, girl answering name of Dowsabel Urckart Casselman: She is aged eighteen years coming November 19, will weigh 120 lbs., 5:5 1/2 inches tall, red gold hair worn Indian style, jasper eyes, white complexion, wore white linsey woolsey jersey, dark green velvet skirt, black cotton stockings, low-cut shoes. All are asked to take her up on sight and communicate with Col. J. C. P. Casselman, Wellersburg, Pa.

Coming to the hotel at dinner time, "Lewis" tacked the bill below the face of the grandfather clock in the lobby, unobserved by anyone. He had arranged with the trusting belle that if she should be seized by too zealous claimants for the reward and hurried in the direction of Brunerstown without the formality of consigning her to jail, he would adopt desperate measures and waylay and rescue her at the rock once frequented by the genuine David Lewis, on top of the Seven Brothers (this rock was blasted away only a few months ago by State Highway engineers while reconstructing the Earlysburg-Milroy road), and he whispered to her that it might even be said that "she had been captured and carried off by Robber Lewis' ghost". But it was most likely that she would first be put in jail and her family notified, and kept there until they arrived to divide the rewards among those who gave information, the sheriff and jailers.

But the hardest ordeal of all was that she must exhume the right arm of Lewis, break the hand off at the wrist, and climb to freedom over the twenty-foot jail wall. If she couldn't scale the wall, the stranger would have to wait until she started for Brunerstown with her captors, when he would waylay and capture her in the place and manner previously stated. The landlord at the Benner House quickly recognized the girl described on the bill so mysteriously tacked up on the clock as his guest. The broadside was worded in a way to arouse most anyone's cupidity, and, despite her tears and protests, the beautiful Dowsabel was marched off to the gloomy precincts of Bellefonte jail. There were several graves of unfortunates in the central court-yard of the jail, and the rows of "cells" looked out on this enclosure. Some of the cells intended for robbers or hardened criminals were equipped with a grille of iron bars, over which doors were closed at night, while the rest were like boxstalls at a race track with oaken panelled doors and no gratings. There were small barred windows at the backs of all the cells. Young Lewis had given the girl a tiny saw to sever the bars, which she kept in the corsage of her dress, as, not being accused of any crime except truancy, she was not likely to be searched before her committal. She was not put in a cell, but in one of the "stalls" with an oaken door, and heavy lock and key. The approximate location of Lewis' grave had been explained to her by the stranger, but Dowsabel quickly verified it from her fellow-inmates of the jail. But there was another complication. A big dog, part wolf, which today would be called a "German police dog", had the run of the jailyard at night. "Lewis, Jr." had given the girl some pills to put to sleep the little penny dog at the White Horse (called Wasser, which meant that no hechs could ever take hold of him) the night of their joint escape, in reality nux vomica, which killed the poor little faithful watcher despite his mystic name. She had some of this poison left to use on the magnificent half-wild beast of the Seven Mountains. But Dietz, the wolf-dog, took an uncanny fancy to her, and as she was allowed the freedom of the jailyard, he attached himself to her like a shadow.

It was arranged that she should make her getaway on the second night, but before she was locked in her "box" for the night, the dog became so friendly that Nick Pankaloss, the old Greek from Aaronsburg, who acted as warder, allowed the animal to sleep by her spool bed. There were only three other prisoners in the jail at the time, all decrepit old men, "in" for variations of the more or less technical charge of vagrancy and beneath the dignity of the dog to guard. One of them happened to be Gaston Ythorrotz, the old furniture-mender whose request for a cup of water at the White Horse she had so insolently refused, but he chose not to notice her, and she pretended that she had never seen him before. However, his presence again made her nervous and melancholy. At eight o'clock on the appointed night a game of French ruff was in progress in the sheriff's parlour facing the main street, participated in by the high sheriff himself, his deputy, the turnkey and the old Greek, who, in his way, was a regular levanter, or card sharper. Dowsabel, inspired by great love, which gave her added strength to return to the man of her choice, and anxiety to be away from the old furniture-mender, cleverly broke off the old, rusty lock, and with the big dog licking at her hands, calmly walked out into the jail-yard. The other cell doors were shut tight, and none could see her even if there had been any light. It had been arranged that she was to be arrested during the dark of the moon, and this was a dreary night, cold, and a few snowdrops drifting about. There was a pick and shovel standing against the stone wall in a corner of the yard, and Dowsabel was soon at work digging open David Lewis' grave in the half-frozen ground.

The erstwhile robber chief had been buried three feet deep, but the quicklime had already gotten in its work. The darkness saved the girl from a gruesome sight, but she soon had a grip on the crumbling right arm, and dragged it forth, deftly twisting off the hand at the wrist, which caused such an odour of lime to arise that her eyes smarted. She covered the body again with the lime and clay, while Dietz lay beside her, flopping his tail against the hard ground as if to register satisfaction. Then, almost before the dog could realize what she was doing, the girl walked to the door of the warden's house, through the hall, and out into the street, holding all the while the ghastly but precious relic of David Lewis, which would forever keep her lover out of the toils of the law and make his horse show his heels to the fleetest of his foes, and which acted as a charm to her.

At the end of the steep road which leads out of town below the present site of the Academy, "Lewis, Jr." was waiting with the covered gig and the black horse resplendent in the brass-mounted harness. And they made a second getaway into the night, into a snowstorm which came out of the east and grew in velocity as they sped down Penn's Valley and almost engulfed them when they reached the Narrows.

After Dowsabel had gone, the wolf-dog began to run about and howl dismally, but he was given to such spells of melancholy restlessness. Besides, the jailers were too intent on French ruff and too much under the influence of "shrub" to recall that Dietz had been locked up with the girl. In the morning Dowsabel's "box" was found open; the $200 golden bird had flown. Snow had mercifully covered Lewis' rifled grave, and there were no signs but that it was still inviolate. None of the prisoners could have seen her escape, and they were not questioned. Five days later, before the hue and cry was scarcely beyond the borders of Centre County—in fact, the local authorities did not want the news to spread, in the hopes that they might recapture the fair jail-breaker and save the rewards for themselves—a hooded gig, drawn by a great black horse, drew up in front of the old stone tavern on the edge of Millerstown. Until the day before "Young Lewis" and Dowsabel had been only a few miles outside of Centre County, quietly "stowed away" in a resort frequented by counterfeiters and gamblers, near the easterly outlet of the dark, wooded narrows between Motz's

Bank, now known as Woodward and Hartley Hall, now called Hartleton, in the shadow of Jones Mountain. The pattern of David Lewis ordered the girl, who was joyously glad to comply with his slightest wish, to go in the hotel to see if accommodation were to be had. As she hurried into the kitchen, the only room where there was any light, she noticed an old man seated on one of the courting blocks in the inglenook. When he saw her, he rose up, waving his heavy blackthorn staff and pointing at her, his eyes ablaze with surprise and rage. It was Gaston Ythorrotz, the old furniture-mender. "Bloody murder," he shouted, "here's that young huzzy that made the getaway from Bellefonte jail; there's reward of $100 in gold from her people in Somerset County, and $100 more gold from Centre County. Boys, oh, boys, take her up quick!"

His cries literally "brought the whole house to the kitchen", to use an old expression. Dowsabel turned to escape, but the old man was already at the door blocking the way with his cane. There she was caught red-handed; she didn't have a chance. In fact, her screams for assistance only served as a warning to "Young Lewis", knight of the road, outside in the covered gig, who fancied that his new-found possession of the grisly right hand of David Lewis was quickly beginning to prove his lucky talisman. He laid the long whip with its stock of "quicken tree" over the black horse's flanks, and was gone like a spectre into the night, leaving his sweetie and slave in hostile hands, a prisoner for cash rewards.

Soon the sturdy Dutch landlord and his boys, acting under the old furniture-mender's instructions, tied her hand and foot. "She's cute as a pet fox, and quick as chain lighting", he said. They tossed her on a sofa in an alcove in a cold, empty room to await the morning. After she was placed in that helpless position like a sack of buckwheat, and the captors made ready to leave the room, the old man came close to her, holding aloft his old brazier, like a lantern, saying: "Now, my beauty, the tables have turned. When I saw you in Bellefonte jail I thought to myself, 'I will say nothing, my time is the third time we meet', and I let you get away as neat as any hechs could have done it. Now I say, 'I am the law, the law of retribution'."

After a further consultation with the landlord it was suggested that with $200 in gold at stake, a gigantic sum in those poverty stricken days, when the whole country was "flat" from the effects of the War of 1812–1815, someone should watch her all night, lest "Young Lewis" return and stage another "Bellefonte jail delivery"; "That dressy off-scouring will not come back for her", said the old furniture-mender, "I've known him and his kind too well for more than fifty years. Yet I'll watch this tricky minx only too gladly, but I don't think she is overly anxious to go home." Then he drew a huge flint-lock pistol from his belt under his long coat, which he brandished in a menacing fashion. "All right, daddy, go at it, we know we're leaving her in good hands", said the landlord, as he left the room. The old man drew a deer horn stool out of the hall, and slouched down on it in a corner, with the smouldering brazier at his feet.

For a time he sat there, pistol in his lap, gazing at the gagged and helpless damsel in all the misery of her ignominious position. As soon as they were alone together, Dowsabel never allowed her dark Levantine eyes off his face, seeking to cast her glamour over him, as they say in the mountains. Gradually, under the effect of her dazzling beauty, as revealed to him by the red glow of the brazier, the old man began to review his past life, the man he might have been before the weight of human misery and injustice had borne him down, and he became less determined. Women had ill-used him in many lands, in war and in peace, and he had no kindly feeling for any of them except the one who gave him birth, yet he had never taken a mean advantage of any of them. Dowsabel's coppery beauty tantalized him as no other woman's had, cold as she was to him.

Looking at her with his squinty, bloodshot eyes that had beheld from afar many pulchritudinous women, he fancied that she must be fully as beautiful as that red-headed Dutch girl of Bruges, in honour of whom Duke Philip of Burgundy instituted the Order of the Golden Fleece. At last he whispered to her: "I am so very sorry that I let you into this mess, but my heart rebelled at the way you treated me at the 'White Horse'." Dowsabel did not answer; it was as if she had known what was coming, the usual tribute to the power of her matchless loveliness. Rising up from the stool, the old man fumbled in his belt, under his long coat, drawing forth from its shabby sheath a schlor, or Gypsy dagger, made out of a single piece of steel, and sharp and glistening as a misericorde. With it he cut the gag, and the ropes which bound her lovely wrists and ankles. "Go", he continued, "I don't care where, back home to your mother, who'll whallop the lights out of you, to your lover, who'll deceive the heart out of you, or to lead an ape in hell, it's all the same to me."

Dowsabel straightened herself up, and on tiptoes vanished from the room, uttering not a word, partly because she was naturally wayward and partly as she knew that her real days of suffering were close in front of her. The old man put his schlor back in sheath, his pistol in his belt, settled down on the stool, and began warming his hands at the almost extinguished flame of his rusty brazier. As he gazed at the empty couch his brooding thoughts began to picture, while his great head nodded, an ideal kingdom of life where the obstacles of age, poverty and physical imperfection were but a state of mind that vanished, and he had but to fix his fancy on a person for his love to be requited. But those moments of sublime introspection were as near to human happiness as he would ever reach in his long span of earthly existence. Just before the tall clock in a corner of the kitchen, which had painted on the dial that strange Biscayan proverb, "Every hour wounds, the last one kills", struck three, and the Creeley roosters had begun to crow, he pulled himself together and slipped out a side door, fading into the fog which precedes the dawn along the Juniata. When, half an hour later, the landlord and his family came downstairs, they felt as if the previous evening's happenings had been some fantastic dream.

THE LOBO GIRL OF DEVIL'S RIVER[231]

In the fall of 1830 John Dent and Will Marlo went in partners to trap fur along the headwaters of Chickamauga River in Georgia. Pelts were plentiful, and they got along harmoniously enough until the spring of 1833, when they fell out over a division of the winter's catch.

A woman was at the bottom of the quarrel. She was Mollie Pertul, daughter of a mountaineer. While trapping in the vicinity of the Pertul cabin, John Dent had fallen in love with her and the two had engaged to be married. In forming their partnership the two trappers had agreed to sell jointly all pelts they took and to divide the money equally. Through two seasons this agreement they had carried out, but now Dent insisted on taking half the hides and disposing of them in his own way. He had a notion that he could get more money, to start married life on, by selling his fur separately.

After a bitter quarrel the division was made as Dent wanted it. Immediately almost, Marlo began telling around that he had been cheated. The quarrel went on for about two weeks; then there was a fight in which Dent stabbed Marlo to death. Public opinion was against him, and there was nothing for him to do but skip the country. Before leaving, however, he managed to see his love and tell her that he was going to locate a place in which they could live together and that he would return and steal her away.

Months passed by and people began to lose interest in the matter. During all this time, presumably, Mollie Pertul heard nothing from her murderer lover. Then a little after sundown on April 13, 1834—just a year to the day after Marlo was stabbed—the mountaineer girl went to the cow lot to milk as was her daily custom. After she had been absent from the house an unusually long time, her parents decided to investigate and see if anything had gone wrong. They found the cows unmilked and in the empty milk pail a Bowie knife with dried blood caked about the hilt. It had a staghorn handle of peculiar design that made it easily identified, next day, as the knife with which Dent had killed Marlo.

In the darkness of the night the parents called and searched for Mollie, but in vain. As soon as daylight showed, a few mountaineers who had been summoned began looking for sign. They struck the tracks of a man and woman leading to the Chickamauga River. There they found in the bank a freshly driven stob to which, apparently, a small canoe had recently been moored. Mollie Pertul was gone without a word of explanation and without a moment's preparation. All she took with her were the clothes on her back.

Six months passed. Then old Mrs. Pertul received a letter postmarked Galveston, Texas. It read:

"Dear Mother,
   "The Devil has a river in Texas that is all his own and it is made only for those who are grown.
                         Yours with love—
                              Mollie."

In those days the people of Georgia were not familiar with the streams of Texas and their names. Indeed, very few people in Texas itself knew anything about Devil's River, far to the west of San Antonio, the outpost of all settlements, its inhabitants almost exclusively Spanish-speaking. Mrs. Pertul and her husband and neighbours merely considered that somewhere in Texas Dent had to himself a river on which to trap. They knew that Dent was a devil all right, though maybe they were a little surprised at Mollie's admitting it.

Now, one of the little known chapters in Texas history is of a small colony of English people who in 1834 settled on Devil's River, calling their settlement Dolores. It was short-lived. Indians killed most of the settlers. A few of them drifted into Mexico. The remainder, fourteen adults and three children, in attempting to get back east were attacked at Espantosa Lake, near what is now Carrizo Springs. After killing them all, the Comaches threw their bodies and the carts in which they were travelling into the lake. That is why to this day Mexicans consider the lake haunted, the name Espantosa meaning "frightful".

Dent and his bride had joined this English colony. Devil's River had plenty of beaver; so did the Rio Grande both above and below where Devil's River empties into it. We may be sure that Dent did not live in the group of Englishmen, but, like the lone wolf he was, off to one side. He, no doubt, had an agreement with the Indians. A considerable ride westward two or three Mexican families, more Indianized than anything else, raised a few goats on the Pecos Canyon.

About noon one day in May of the year 1835, a rider on a reeling horse drew up at one of these goat ranches. He told the Mexican *ranchero* and his wife that he was camped where Dry Creek runs into Devil's River. He said that his wife was giving birth to a baby and that they must have help. The Mexican woman agreed to go with her husband, who at once began saddling the horses. Meantime, one of those black electricity-charged clouds for which that part of the country is noted was coming up. A bolt of lightning struck the messenger dead.

This delayed the Mexicans considerably in getting off. From the description of his camp site given by the dead man the *ranchero* knew how to reach it, but night came on before he and his wife got over the divide to Devil's River. They did not find the camp until next morning. There, under an open brush arbour lay the woman dead, alone. Indications pointed to the fact that she had died while giving birth to a child. Yet no child was visible. No child could be found. No trace of it was evident anywhere. Tracks thick around the brush arbour made the *ranchero* suspect that lobo wolves had devoured the infant.

In the scantily furnished brush cabin the Mexicans found a letter, which they took along to show the first person they might encounter who could read English. This letter, as it later developed, had been written by Mollie Pertul Dent to her mother in Georgia several weeks before her death. It served to identify her and her husband. Thus their romance ended.

Ten years passed. A wagon road that had been laid out across the new Republic of Texas to El Paso went by San Felipe Springs (now Del Rio), where there were a few Mexicans, and on across Devil's River, only twelve miles beyond, and then across the Pecos. Occasionally armed travellers passed over the road. In the year 1845 a boy living at San Felipe Springs reported that he had seen a pack of lobo wolves attacking a herd of goats and with them a creature, long hair half covering its features, that looked like a naked girl. Some passing Americans who heard the story quizzed him. But they seemed more interested in getting his description of what a naked girl looked like than in getting information about the strange creature he reported. The story was ridiculed, but it spread back among the settlements.

Not more than a year after this a Mexican woman at San Felipe declared she had seen two big lobos and a naked girl devouring a freshly killed goat. She got close to them, she said, before they saw her. Then they all three ran. The naked girl ran at first on all-fours, but then rose up and ran on two feet, keeping in company with the wolves. The woman was positive of what she had seen. The few people in the Devil's River country began to keep a sharp lookout for the girl. They recalled the disappearance of the dead Mollie Dent's infant amid lobo tracks. Men of the camp told how female wolves carried their cubs by the scruff of the neck without injuring them. Perhaps, they said, some lobo wolf in whom the mother instinct was strong had carried the new-born to her den and raised it. Indians reported having noted in sandy places along the river barefoot tracks, sometimes accompanied by hand prints.

A hunt was organized to capture the Lobo, or Wolf, Girl of the Devil's River, as she had now come to be called. It was made up mostly of wild-riding Mexican vaqueros. These people had doubtless never heard anything of the story of the wolf-suckled Romulus and Remus who founded Rome or of wolf-nursed children in India like Kipling's Mowgli, but far out on this isolated, stark border they had been confronted with unmistakable evidence of a human being reared by and running wild with lobo wolves.

On the third day of the hunt two of the riders jumped the girl near a side canyon. She was with a big lobo that cut off from her when she dodged into a crevice. Here the vaqueros cornered her. She cowered at first like a rabbit. Then she spat and hissed like a wildcat. She fought too, clawing and biting. While the vaqueros were tying her she began to belch forth pitiful, frightful, unearthly sounds described as resembling both the scream of a woman and the howl of a lobo but being neither. As she was howling forth this awful scream, a monster he-wolf, presumably the one from whom she had become separated, suddenly appeared rushing at her captors. The fact that one of them saw it coming before it got close enough to use its powerful jaws probably saved their lives. He shot it dead with a pistol. At that the wild girl sank into a silent faint.

The captured creature was now securely tied and could be examined more carefully. She was excessively hairy, but breasts of beautiful curvature and other features showed that she was a normally formed human female. Her hands and arms were muscled in an extraordinary manner but not ill proportioned.

Having revived from her faint, she was placed on a horse and carried to the nearest ranch. There she was unbound and turned loose in an isolated room for the night. With gestures of kindness she was offered a covering for her body, food and water, but no eagle of the free air, no lion of the deep jungle, ever showed more distrust and fear of its captors than she. She backed into the darkest corner, and there she was left alone. The door to the room was closed. The only other opening was a little window across which a board had been nailed.

The ranch was but a two-roomed hovel, alone amid the desert wilderness. By dark four or five men were gathered at it, and now the wild and frantic being fastened up in the room began voicing forth the terrifying screamish howls. Through the log walls of many vents they carried far on the night air. Soon they were answered by the long drawn out, deep howls of lobos beyond. Lobos seemed to answer from all sides, and their dismal and far-carrying voices brought answers from farther and farther away. All the lobos of the western world seemed to be gathering. Rancheros who all their lives had heard lobos howl had never heard anything like this, either from such a number of wolves now assembling or in the sullen, doom-like quality of the long, deep howling. Nearer and more compactly the horde gathered. Now they would howl all in unison, a bass-throated chorus of ferocity and darkness and lost hopes such as no musician of the world ever dreamed of. Then they would be silent as if waiting for some answer, and the wild girl in the dark room there would answer back with her unearthly howling scream, a voice neither of woman nor of beast.

After a time the great pack made a rush for the corrals, attacking goats, milk cows and the saddle horses. The noises made by these domestic animals, especially the screams and neighs of the plunging kicking horses, brought the men to the rescue. Ordinarily no man at all familiar with lobo wolves would fear one. Now these rancheros kept together, shooting in the darkness and yelling as they advanced. The wolves retreated.

Meantime, in the pandemonium, the Lobo Girl somehow wrenched the cross plank from the window and got out. It was supposed that she immediately rejoined the wolves. Hardly another howl was heard that night, and the next day not a track of the girl could be found. For a long time the sight of a wolf in that particular region was very rare.

Nothing more was heard of the Wolf Girl of Devil's River for six years. Meantime, gold had been discovered in California and travel westward had greatly increased. Along in 1852 an exploring party of frontiersmen hunting a route to El Paso that would be better watered than the Chihuahua Trail, as the road used was called, rode down to the Rio Grande at a sharp bend far above the mouth of Devil's River.

They were almost upon the water before they saw it or could be seen from its edge. There, sitting on a sand bar, two young wolf whelps tugging at her full breasts, they at close range caught clear sight of a naked young woman. In an instant she was upon her feet, a whelp under each arm, dashing into the breaks at a rate no horse could follow. The creature could have been no other than the wild Lobo Girl of Devil's River.

So far as is known she was never glimpsed by man after this, though perhaps some of the old-time Apaches might have had a tale to tell could they have been asked. What the fate of the Lobo Girl—or woman—was, nobody probably will ever know. During the war of extermination that had been waged on lobos, the most predatory of animals that stockmen of America have known, in the border country, a wolf has occasionally been found with a marked human resemblance, and for many years now "human-faced" wolves, so called, have been considered the final culmination of a Georgia murder and elopement. If man can bear the "mark of the beast", why may not beast bear the mark of the man? Speaking only for myself, I will say that despite the fact that over a century has passed since the beginning of the incidents just related, yet during the past forty years I have in the western country met more than one wolf face strongly marked with human characteristics.

PART SIX

SONGS AND RHYMES

*There were games that everyone played; and
when there was music, everyone sang.*
—M. L. Wilson

Introduction to Part Six

RHYMES, CATCHES AND SONGS

> *Marezleetoats*
> *Dozeleetoats*
> *Dozeleetivytoo*
> *(Mares will eat oats; does'll eat oats; does'll eat ivy too.)*
>
> —OLD RIDDLE

> *These amusements came into existence because they were adapted to the conditions of early life; they pass away because those conditions are altered. The taste of other days sustained them; the taste of our day abandons them.*
> —W. W. NEWELL

One of the most fascinating fields for the student of beliefs and customs as these enter into the vernacular poetry of folk rhymes is the jingles and doggerels of childhood. The persistence and diffusion of such rhymes is infinite variety and yet in much the same form all over the world offers conclusive evidence of the twin aspects of tradition, especially the tradition of children—its inventiveness and its conservatism.

Like popular jests and sayings in general, play rhymes and catches have their local and contemporary sources or applications, illustrating the principle that "The happiness of a witticism or of a taunt hangs on its relationship at some sort of angle to the customs and notions prevalent in a country."[232] The 1944 version of the old counting-out rhyme has it, in Washington, D. C.:

Eenie, meenie, minie, mo,
Catch a Jap by the toe.
If he hollers, make him say:
"I surrender, U. S. A."

In 1938, in the shadow of war and hunger, New York City children
jingled this ironic bit of nonsense reminiscent of Old Dan Tucker:

Haile Selassie was a kind old man,
He lit the match to the frying pan.
When all the people tasted the beef,
They all trucked off to the home relief.

These "waifs and strays of folklore", remnants of ancient charms
and rituals, are both trivia and curiosa, eloquent with nostalgia for the
side-walks and back-yards of one's play-time. Recited or chanted as a
rhymed or rhythmic accompaniment to rope-skipping or ball-bounc-
ing, as a formula for counting out, as a nominy or set speech, as a
taunt, quip, or crank, they have social and poetic interest apart from
their game or pastime usage.

Salt, vinegar, mustard, pie and
    [cayenne] PEPPER!

Harvey, jarvey, jig, jig, jig,
Went to buy a pig, pig, pig.
Went to France to learn to dance,
Harvey, jarvey, jig, jig, jig.

————'s it
And caught [got] a fit,
And don't know how
To get out of [over] it!

Do you like jelly?
Punch in the belly!

Do you like gravy?
Punch in the navy [navel]!

Engine, engine, number nine,
Running on Chicago Line.
If it's polished, it will shine,
Engine, engine, number nine.

Knife and fork!
Bottle and cork!
That's the way to
Spell New York!

Do you like bananners?
Go play the planner!

Do you like cheese?
You big Japanese!

Do you know what?
What?
That's what!

In the field of the game and dance, two distinctive American developments from British sources are the square dance, quadrille, or cotil-
lion (as distinguished from the English contra-dance or longways dance,
which still persists in New England) and the play-party.

In the United States the term square dance has come to stand for old-time set dancing generally, whether of the square, longways, or circle formation. Although the guitar and the banjo are used to accompany the fiddle at dances, as well as to accompany the folk singer, the fiddle is the American folk musical instrument par excellence. Its portability and adaptability made it the musical voice of backwoods and frontier America and the country fiddler one of the most picturesque of pioneer folk characters. Another minstrel type is the square-dance caller or prompter, who, in a mixture of rhythmic prose and doggerel made up of "calls" interspersed with patter, intones and (in the Northeast and Southwest) sings or half-sings the directions.

Because of religious prejudice against dancing and especially the fiddle, as the instrument of the devil, the young people of rural America developed the play-party as an alternative form of amusement, which substituted singing for instrumental accompaniment. A cross between dancing and the traditional singing games of children, the play-party retains the best features of both. To the courtship and other dramatic devices of the game, such as choosing and stealing partners, the play-party adds certain square dance movements and figures, in which, however, partners are swung by the hands instead of by the waist. The leader combines the functions of caller and floor-manager; and like the caller he is something of a folk-poet, with the gift of improvisation.

A comparison of party games and singing games shows the former returning to the grown-up level from which the latter were originally descended. Whether or not singing games reflect, in their form and content, the traditional formations and formulae of ancient pagan ceremonials, they represent the survival, on the childhood level, of the rounds, reels, and carols of adults of an earlier day. In the process of "downward transmission", singing games have acquired many childish features, such as the "pleasures of motion" and "playing at work." Play-party games, on the other hand, have come of age, and make the most of realistic and satiric comment on the personalities of the players and incidents of the "swinging play" as well as on the customs, characters, objects, activities, and backgrounds of rural and frontier America.

These changes also illustrate the process of modernization and localization. Thus in an Oklahoma version of "Hog Drovers" (originally an Irish game played at wakes) cowboys and oil-drillers are among the rejected occupations.

BALLADS AND SONGS

> *It has often been pointed out that contemporary historians endeavour to chronicle the common man as well as the hero. . . . Similarly, the interest of literary historians and of students and readers has extended downward from the masterpiece till it embraces the humble and unrecorded literature of the folk.*
> —LOUISE POUND

Folk song should properly be regarded as an activity, A functional activity of the group singing or playing for self-gratification or for power, to attain the ends of social adjustment and human freedom, by lightening labour, filling leisure, recording events, voicing praise or protest. Certain "traditionalist" folk-song authorities like Cecil J. Sharp tend to stress the "heritage" rather than the "participation" aspects of folk song and the passive rather than the active role of the folk singer, making him out to be a carrier of national culture, who sings to "forget himself and everything that reminds him of his everyday life" and thus, by escaping into an "imaginary world", to "enter- into [his] racial inheritance".[233] The "functionalists", on the other hand, such as Alan Lomax, stress the role of folk song in America as "an expression of its democratic, interracial, international character, as a function of its inchoate and turbulent many-sided development". According to this view, people not only sing songs in their own way but make their own songs as they begin to "examine their problems self-consciously and comment on them with an objective vigour and irony".[234] Taking issue with Sharp, John and Alan Lomax fling down this challenge:

> The American singer has been concerned with themes close to his everday experience, with the emotions of ordinary men and women who are fighting for freedom and for a living in a violent new world.[235]

Accepting the latter interpretation, one comes to regard the difference between folk singers and art singers as not so much the difference between not having and having an audience as a difference in the relationship between the singer and his audience. In the case of folk singing, like folk story-telling, there is no sharp differentiation between performer and auditor. The rôles are interchangeable, and both participate in the performance as a shared experience, drawing upon the common stock of ideas and expressions and communicating chiefly by symbols, or signs which "bind value to value and man to man by bonds of common meaning and shared emotion".

Every folk song, of course, has an author; but his authorship is conceived in terms of the proverb's wit of one and wisdom of the many, and he is eventually forgotten as his song enters into the public domain. The folk singer, as truly as the professional singer, is an artist in his own right; but he is a people's artist, who sings from the heart and to the hearts of the people and whose distinguishing mark is a sense of the proper balance between remembering and inventing, between pattern and variation. In him the art of improvisation has been raised to high art. This is a matter not of "ad libbing" but of fitting new words to old tunes and old texts to changing circumstances. It is participation made spontaneous. It is rhythmic and poetic freedom akin to the freedom of interpolation and variation that belongs to the blues and jazz and the impromptu steps of the square dance.

The folk basis of the blues and jazz in Negro blues, work songs, hollers, and reels points to the existence of an urban as well as a rural folk music and to the fact that folk music is not a pure but a hybrid activity, which is a fusion of "folk", "art", and "popular" idioms and tastes. This very quality of mixed style and of a certain complex, plastic simplicity and collective individuality, rather than any other single trait, may be the hallmark of folk song as of all folk art. The exploitation of folk music for the purposes of commercial entertainment has resulted in cheapening and slicking up the product by means of hokam and "corn". But there is good "corn" as well as bad "corn", and even "hillbilly" has its place in the hierarchy of American folk styles.

The same mixed or hybrid character applies to types of folk song, and requires that we do not distinguish too sharply between them. For instance, the ballad, or story-telling song, has its lyric elements, as the folk-lyric has its narrative or dramatic elements. Although ballads are not something that we read in the newspapers, they deal with the same situations that make the headlines—wars, crimes, disasters, love tragedies, family feuds, and passion and violence generally. Just as ballad singers and hawkers of broadside ballads once performed a journalistic function, so spectacular and sensational events, such as wrecks, storms, floods, fires, and executions, still bring in their train the crude minstrelsy of local bards. Here the line between fact and fantasy, the timely and the timeless, is a shifting one. History passes into legend and legend into history.

In the same way written and unwritten tradition, the academic and the commercial, mingle in the creation and diffusion of ballads and folk songs. In addition to broadsides, songsters, manuscript collections, and scrap-books, the stage, travelling troupes of singers, medicine and minstrel shows, camp and political meetings, and the like have served to keep folk songs alive and afloat. To-day the phonograph, the radio, the folk song archive, and the folk festival tend to perform the same function in folk song survival or revival. But for all these external aids folk song is still distinguished from popular and art song by the predominance of word-of-mouth transmission.

Perhaps the best example of the transitional, evolving nature of folk song as the product of an interim or backward stage of culture or society is afforded by Negro folk song—slave songs, spirituals, work songs, reels, and blues. With the displacement of hand by machine labour, work songs of the choral type, such as shanties, field songs, chopping songs, steel-driving songs, etc., tend to disappear. The last refuge of gang or group-hand-labour songs in the United States has been the Southern prison, which until recently provided a "pocket" for primitive labour conditions that have passed out of existence elsewhere. Cultural isolation, as in the Southern mountains, has also fostered the survival of traditional ballads and social songs. With the exception of sea shanties and cowboy songs, our white occupational songs, including lumberjack, canaller, and miners' songs, are social songs to accompany leisure, rather than work, or songs of protest, akin to the "hard times" songs of the pioneer, or (more recently) industrial union songs.

Almost every phase or period of American life has left its record in the form of folk songs that describe, reflect, or evoke the time and the place, their conditions, customs, and characters. In this sense American folk song provides material for a social and cultural history of the United States which comes as near as anything we have to being a folk or people's history—a history. of, by, and for the people, in which for the first time the people speak and are allowed to tell their own story, in their own way.

Part Six

RHYMES, CATCHES AND SONGS

SIDEWALK RHYMES OF NEW YORK[236]

One, two, three a-lair-y, I spied Mis-sus Sa-ry, Sit-ting on a bum-ble-air-y, Just like a choc'-late fair-y

Roses are red,
Violets are blue,
I like pecans,
Nuts to you.

Roses are red,
Violets are blue,
Elephants are fat
And so are you.

Roses are red,
Violets are blue,
If I had your mug,
I'd join the zoo.

Roses are red,
Violets are blue,
Everybody stinks
And so do you.

Roses are red,
Violets are blue,
I use Lifebuoy.
Why don't you?

Looie, pooie,
You're full of hooey.

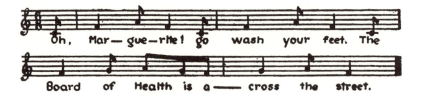

Marguerite,
Go wash your feet;
The Board of Health
Is 'cross the street.

Eight and eight are sixteen,
Stick your nose in kerosene,
Wipe it off with ice cream.

Tonight, tonight,
The pillow fight,
Tomorrow's the end of school;
Break the dishes, break the chairs,
Trip the teachers on the stairs.

Bouncy, bouncy ballie,
I lose the leg of my dollie;
My mother came out
And gave me a clout
That turned my petticoat
Inside out.

My mother, your mother, hanging out the clothes,
My mother gave your mother a punch in the nose.
What colour did it turn?
Red, yellow, blue, green, violet, orange, etc.

Your mother, my mother, live across the way;
Every night they have a fight,
And this is what they say:
"Your old man is a dirty old man,
'Cause he washes his face in the frying pan,
He combs his hair
With the leg of a chair;
Your old man is a dirty old man."

I should worry, I should care,
I should marry a millionaire;
He should die, I should cry,
I should marry another guy.

I had a little brother,
His name was Tiny Tim;
I put him in the bathtub
To teach him how to swim.
He drank up all the water,
He ate up all the soap;
He died last night
With a bubble in his throat.

Mother, Mother, I am sick;
Send for the doctor, quick, quick, quick.
Doctor, Doctor, shall I die?
Yes, my darling, do not cry.
How many coaches shall I have?
Ten, twenty, thirty, etc.
        (*Till the skipper misses.*)

Teddy on the railroad,
Picking up stones;
Along came an engine
And broke Teddy's bones.
"Oh", said Teddy,
"That's no fair!"
"Oh", said the engineer,
"I don't care."

Silence in the courtroom!
The judge wants to spit.

Mother, Mother, Mother, pin a rose on me.
Two little girls [or boys] are after me;
One is blind and the other can't see;
Mother, Mother, Mother, pin a rose on me.

Bless the meat,
Damn the skin,
Open your mouth
And cram it in.

Jesus, lover of my soul,
Lead me to the sugar bowl.
If the sugar bowl is empty,
Lead me to my mamma's pantry.

Up the river,
Down the lake;
The teacher's got
The bellyache.

Hot roasted peanuts,
Tell the teacher she's nuts;
If she asks you what's your name,
Tell the teacher she's a pain.

Up the ladder,
Down the tree,
You're a bigger
Fool than me.

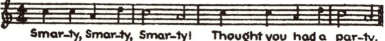

Smar-ty, Smar-ty, Smar-ty!   Thought you had a par-ty.

Smarty, smarty,
Had a party,
And nobody came
But an old fat darky.[237]

Mary's mad,
And I am glad,
And I know what will please her:
A bottle of wine
To make her shine,
And a sweet little boy to squeeze her.

Mary's mad,
And I am glad,
And I know what will please her:
A bottle of ink
To make her stink,
And a little nigger to squeeze her.

I went down to Grandpa's farm,
The billygoat chased me all around the barn,
Chased me up in the sycamore tree,
And this is the song he sang to me:
"I love coffee, I love tea,
I love the boys and the boys love me."

If you don't like my apples,
Then don't shake my tree;
I'm not after your boy friend,
He's after me.

Life is short,
Death will come;
Go it, Ruth,
While you're young.

When you get married,
And your husband gets cross,
Just pick up the broom
And ask who's boss.

May your life be strewn with roses,
And your children have pug noses.

First comes love,
Then comes marriage;
Then comes Edith
With a baby carriage.

Buck, buck, you lousy muck,
How many fists have I got up,
One, two, or none?

Inty minty tibblety fig,
Deema dime doma nig,
Howchy powchy domi nowchy,
Hom tom tout,
Olligo bolliga boo,
Out goes YOU.

One-ery two-ery ickery Ann,
Fillicy fallacy Nicholas John,

Queever quaver Irish Mary,
Stinclum stanclum buck.

Ibbety bibbety gibbety goat,
Ibbety bibbety canalboat,
Dictionary,
Down the ferry,
Out goes YOU.

Minnie and a minnie and a ha, ha, ha,
Kissed her fellow in a trolley car;
I told Ma, Ma told Pa,
Minnie got a licking and a ha, ha, ha.

I went downtown
To meet Mrs. Brown;
She gave me a nickel
To buy me a pickle;
The pickle was sour,
She gave me a flower;
The flower was dead,
She gave me a thread;
The thread was thin,
She gave me a pin;
The pin was sharp,
She gave me a harp;
The harp began to sing:
Minnie and a minnie and a ha, ha, ha.

Cinderella, dressed in yellow,
Gone downtown to buy an umbrella;
On the way she met her fellow.
How many kisses did she receive?
Five, ten, fifteen, twenty, etc.

Cinderella, dressed in red,
Went downtown to buy some thread.
Along came a fellow whose name was Red,
And shot her with a bullet that was made of lead.

Judge, judge, tell the judge
Mamma has a baby.

It's a boy, full of joy,
Papa's going crazy.
Wrap it up in tissue paper,
Send it down the elevator.
How many pounds did it weigh?
One, two, three, etc.

I won't go to Macy's any more, more, more,
There's a big fat policeman at the door, door, door,
He grab me by the collar and he make me pay a dollar,
So I won't go to Macy's any more, more, more.

Ivory soap,
See it float
Down the river
Like a boat.

Roll, roll, Tootsie Roll,
Roll, marble, in the hole.

Floor to let,
Inquire within;
Lady put out
For drinking gin.
If she promises to drink no more,
Here's the key to her back door.

When Buster Brown was one,
He used to suck his thumb,
Thumb me over, thumb me over,
A, B. C.
When Buster Brown was two,
He used to buckle his shoe.
Shoe me over, shoe me over,
A,B,C,etc.

Happy Hooligan, number nine,
Hung his breeches on the line;
When the line began to swing,
Happy Hooligan began to sing:
"On the mountain stands a lady,
Who she is I do not know;

All she wants is gold and silver,
And a nice young man with whom to go."
Come in, my sister————,
Go out, my sister————.

Toots and Casper went to town,
Tootsie bought an evening gown,
Casper bought a pair of shoes,
Buttercup bought the *Daily News*.
How many pages did he read?
Five, ten, fifteen, twenty, etc.

> Rin Tin Tin
> Swallowed a pin,
> He went to the doctor,
> And the doctor wasn't in.
> He went to the nurse,
> And she said a curse,
> And that was the end
> Of Rin Tin Tin.

> Rin Tin Tin
> Swallowed a pin,
> He went to the doctor,
> And the doctor wasn't in.
> He knocked on the door,
> And fell on the floor;
> Along came a nurse,
> And hit him on the jaw.

Charlie Chaplin sat on a pin;
How many inches did it go in?
One, two, three, etc.

Charlie Chaplin went to war;
He pulled the trigger,
And shot a nigger,
And that was the end of the war.

One, two, three, four,
Charlie Chaplin went to war.
He taught the nurses how to dance,
And this is what he taught them:
Heel, toe, over we go,

Heel, toe, over we go;
Salute to the king,
And bow to the queen,
And turn your back
On the Kaiserine.

> I scream,
> You scream,
> We all scream
> For ice cream.

> Annie bolanny,
> Tillie annie, go sanny,
> Tee-legged, tie-legged,
> Bow-legged Annie.

I asked my mother for fifty cents
To see the elephant jump the fence;
He jumped so high,
He reached the sky,
And never came back till the Fourth of July.

Yellow-belly, yellow-belly, come and take a swim;
Yes, by golly, when the tide comes in.

WALKING ON THE GREEN GRASS[238]

Walking on the green grass,
　Walking side by side,
Walking with a pretty girl,
　She shall be my bride.

And now we form a round ring,
　The girls are by our sides;
Dancing with the pretty girls
　Who shall be our brides.

And now the king upon the green
Shall choose a girl to be his queen;
　Shall lead her out his bride to be,
　And kiss her, one, two, three.
Now take her by the hand, this queen,
And swing her round and round the green.

Oh, now we'll go around the ring,
And ev'ry one we'll swing.
Oh, swing the king and swing the queen,
Oh, swing the king and swing the queen,
Oh, swing 'em round and round the green.
Oh, swing 'em round the green.

Walk-ing on the green grass, Walk-ing side by side,
Walk-ing with a pret-ty girl, She shall be my bride. And
now we form a round ring, The girls are by our sides;
Danc-ing with the pret-ty girls Who shall be our brides. And
now the king up-on the green, Shall choose a girl to be his queen; Shall
lead her out his bride to be, And kiss her one, two, three.
Now take her by the hand, this queen, And
swing her round and round the green. Oh, now we'll go a—
round the ring, And ev'—ry one we'll swing.
Oh, swing the king and swing the queen, Oh,
swing the king and swing the queen, Oh, swing 'em round and
round the green, Oh, swing 'em round the green.

This dance, belonging to young men and women as well as to children, is described by the recorder as follows:

The men select their partners as if for a dance, and, thus paired, promenade as in a school procession, singing the first verse, "Walking on the green grass". The procession then resolves itself into a ring, youths and maidens alternating, all singing: "And now we form a round ring." During the singing of this stanza the ring has kept moving. It is next broken into two lines, one of maidens, the other of youths, facing each other as for a reel. The song is resumed with the words, "And now the king upon the green", and each of the actions described in the verse is performed by the couple at the head of the lines. Having thus called out, saluted, and swung his partner, the man begins with the second woman, and thence down the line, swinging each of the women dancers in turn, the example being followed by his partner with the men, the song continuing, "Oh, now we'll go around the ring, and every one we'll swing." These words are sung over and over, if necessary, until all the dancers have been swung. Thereupon the king and queen take their places at the foot of the lines, and become the subjects of another couple, song and action beginning with the verse, "And now the king upon the green", etc. After all the couples have played at royalty, the promenade is resumed, and the game begun again, generally with change of partners.

This song is unrecorded in Great Britain; but its antiquity and status as a portion of a dance of which "Tread the Green Grass" is also a fragment seem to me sufficiently attested by correspondence with the third verse of the following rhyme, given by Mrs. Gomme:

> Here we come up the green grass,
>   Green grass, green grass,
> Here we come up the green grass,
>   Dusty, dusty, day.
>
> Fair maid, pretty maid,
>   Give your hand to me,
> I'll show you a blackbird,
>   A blackbird on the tree.
>
> We'll all go roving,
>   Roving side by side;
> I'll take my fairest———,
>   I'll take her for a bride.

SWINE-HERDERS (HOG DROVERS)[239]

"Hog— dri— vers, hog-dri—vers, hog— dri—vers we air, A-
cour—tin' yer dar—ter so sweet and fair, And
kin we git lodg——in' here, O here And
kin we git lodg———in' here?"

A.—"Hog-drivers, hog-drivers, hog-drivers we air,
    A-courtin' yer darter so sweet and fair;
    And kin we git lodgin' here, O here—
    And kin we git lodgin' here?"
    "Now this is my darter that sets by my side,
    And no hog-driver can get 'er fer a bride;
    And you kain't git lodgin' here, O here—
    And you kain't git lodgin' here."
    "Yer darter is pretty, yer ugly yerself,
    So we'll travel on further and seek better wealth,
    And we don't want lodgin' here, O here—
    And we don't want lodgin' here."
    "Now this is my darter that sets by my side,
    And Mr.—kin git 'er fer a bride,
    And he kin git lodgin' here, O here—
    And he kin git lodgin' here."

BALLADS AND SONGS

BONNY BARBARA ALLEN[240]

It was upon a high, high hill,
Two maidens chose their dwelling,
And one was known both far and wide,
Was known as Barb'ra Allen.

'Twas in the merry month of May,
All the flowers blooming,
A young man on his deathbed lay
For the love of Barbara Allen.
He sent a servant unto her
In the town where she was dwelling.
"Come, Miss, O Miss to my master dying
If your name be Barb'ra Allen!"

Slowly, slowly she got up,
And to his bedside going,
She drew the curtain to one side
And said, "Young man you're dying".

He stretched one pale hand to her
As though he would to touch her.
She hopped and skipped across the floor.

"Young man," says, "I won't have you."
"Remember, 'member in the town,
'Twas in the tavern drinking,
You drank a health to the ladies all
But you slighted Barb'ra Allen."

He turned his face toward the wall,
His back upon his darling.
"I know I shall see you no more,
So goodbye, Barb'ra Allen."

As she was going to her home,
She heard the church bell tolling.
She looked to the east and looked to the west,
And saw the corpse a-coming.

"O hand me down that corpse of clay
That I may look upon it.
I might have saved that young man's life,
If I had done my duty.

"O mother, mother, make my bed;
O make it long and narrow.
Sweet William died for me today,
I shall die for him tomorrow."

Sweet William died on a Saturday night,
And Barb'ra Allen on a Sunday.
The old lady died for the love of them both,
She died on Easter morning.

Sweet William was buried in one graveyard,
Barb'ra Allen in another;
A rose grew on Sweet William's grave
And a brier on Barb'ra Allen's.

They grew and they grew to the steeple top,
And there they grew no higher;
And there they tied in a true-lover knot,
The rose clung 'round the brier.

YOUNG CHARLOTTE [241]

Young Charlotte lived by the mountainside
In a lone and dreary spot.
No dwelling there, for five miles round,
Except her father's cot;
But yet on many a winter's eve
Young swains would gather there,
For her father kept a social board
And she was very fair.

Young Char-lotte lived by the moun-tain-side In a
lone and drear-y spot. No dwel—ling there, for
five miles round, Ex—cept her fa—ther's
cot; But yet on many a win—ter's eve Young
swains would ga—ther there, For her fa—ther kept a
so—cial board And she was ver—y fair.

Her father loved to see her dressed
Fine as a city belle,
For she was the only child he had,
And he loved his daughter well.
'Twas New Year's Eve.
The sun went down.
Wild looked her anxious eyes
Along the frosty window panes
To see the sleighs pass by.

At a village Inn, fifteen miles round,
There's a merry ball to-night.
The air is freezing cold above,
But the hearts are warm and light.
And while she looked with longing eyes,
Then a well-known voice she hears,
And dashing up to the cottage door
Young Charley's sleigh appears.

Her mother says, "My daughter dear,
This blanket around you fold,
For it is a dreadful night abroad,
You'll take your death of cold."
"Oh, no! oh, no!" young Charlotte said,
And she laughed like a gypsy queen,
"For to ride in blankets muffled up
I never could be seen.

"My silken cloak is quite enough.
'Tis lined, you know, throughout,
And then I have the silken scarf
To tie my face about."
Her gloves and bonnet being on,
She jumped into the sleigh
And away they ride o'er the mountainside
And o'er the hills away.

There's merry music in the bells
As o'er the hills they go,
For the creaking rake the runners make
As they bite the frozen snow.
Then o'er the hills and faster o'er
And by the cold starlight,
When Charles, in these few frozen words,
At last the silence broke:

"Such a night as this I never knew.
My reins I scarce can hold."
Young Charlotte said with a trembling voice,
"I am exceeding cold."
He cracked his whip which urged his steed

Much faster than before,
And then the other five miles round
In silence were rode o'er.

"How fast", says Charles, "the freezing ice
Is gathering on my brow."
Young Charlotte said with a feeble voice,
"I'm growing warmer now."
Then o'er the hills and faster o'er
And by the cold starlight
Until they reached the village inn
And the ballroom was in sight.

They reached the inn and Charles sprang out
And giving his hand to her,
"Why sit you like a monument
What has no power to stir?"
He called her once, he called her twice,
But yet she never stirred.
He called her name again and again,
But she answered not a word.

He took her hand in his. O God!
'Twas cold and hard as stone.
He tore the mantle from her brow
And the cold stars on her shone.
Then quickly to the lighted hall
Her lifeless form he bore,
For Charlotte was a frozen corpse
And a word spake never more.

He knelt himself down by her side
And bitter tears did flow,
For he said, "My young intended bride,
I never more shall know."
He flung his arms around her neck
And kissed her marble brow.
His thoughts went back to the place she said,
"I'm growing warmer now."

He bore her out into the sleigh
And with her he rode home,

And when they reached the cottage door
Oh, how her parents mourned!
They mourned for the loss of their daughter dead,
And Charles mourned o'er the gloom
When Charles' heart with grief did break,
They slumber in one tomb.

SONGS OF SAILORMEN AND RIVERMEN

GREENLAND FISHERY[242]

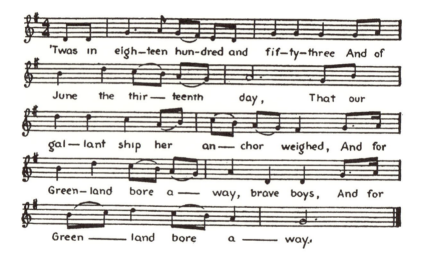

'Twas in eighteen hundred and fifty three
And of June the thirteenth day,
That our gallant ship her anchor weighed,
And for Greenland bore away, brave boys,
And for Greenland bore away.

The lookout in the crosstrees stood,
With his spyglass in his hand.
"There's a whale, there's a whale, there's a whalefish," he cried,
"And she blows at every span, brave boys,
And she blows at every span."

The captain stood on the quarter-deck,
And a fine little man was he.
"Overhaul! Overhaul! Let your davit-tackles fall,
And launch your boats for sea, brave boys,
And launch your boats for sea."

Now the boats were launched and the men aboard,
And the whale was in full view;
Resolv-ed was each seaman bold
To steer where the whalefish blew, brave boys,
To steer where the whalefish blew.

We struck that whale, the line paid out,
But she gave a flourish with her tail;
The boat capsized and four men were drowned,
And we never caught that whale, brave boys,
And we never caught that whale.

"To lose the whale," our captain said,
"It grieves my heart full sore;
But Oh! to lose four gallant men,
It grieves me ten times more, brave boys,
It grieves me ten times more."

"The winter star cloth now appear,
So, boys, we'll anchor weigh;
It's time to leave this cold country,
And homeward bear away, brave boys,
And homeward bear away."

Oh, Greenland is a dreadful place,
A land that's never green,
Where there's ice and snow, and the whalefishes blow,
And the daylight's seldom seen, brave boys,
And the daylight's seldom seen.

STORMALONG[243]

> *Solo*: Old Stormy was a fine old man,
> *Chorus*: To me way, O Stormalong!
> *Solo*: Old Stormy was a fine old man
> *Chorus*: Way, hay, hay, Mister Stormalong!
>
> Old Stormy he is dead and gone,
> Oh, poor old Stormy's dead and gone.
>
> We'll dig his grave with a silver spade (*twice*)
>
> And lower him down with a golden chain (*twice*)
>
> I wish I was old Stormy's son;
> I'd build me a ship of a thousand ton.
>
> I'd sail this wide world round and round;
> With plenty of money I'd be found.
>
> I'd fill her up with New England rum,
> And all my shellbacks they'd have some.
>
> Oh, Stormy's dead and gone to rest;
> Of all the sailors he was the best.

LUMBERJACK SONGS

GERRY'S ROCKS[244]

Come all ye true born shan-ty-boys, Who-ev—er that ye be, I would have you pay at — ten —tion and lis—ten un—to me, Con — cern—ing a young shan—ty—boy, so tall, gen-teel and brave, 'Twas on a jam on Ger—ry's Rocks he met a wa—t'ry grave.

Come, all ye true born shanty-boys, whoever that ye be,
I would have you pay attention and listen unto me,
Concerning a young shanty-boy so tall, genteel, and brave,
'Twas on a jam on Gerry's Rocks he met a wat'ry grave.

It happened on a Sunday morn as you shall quickly hear.
Our logs were piled up mountain high, there being no one to keep
them clear.
Our boss he cried, "Turn out, brave boys. Your hearts are void of fear.
We'll break that jam on Gerry's Rocks, and for Agonstown we'll
steer."

Some of them were willing enough, but others they hung back.
'Twas for to work on Sabbath they did not think 'twas right.
But six of our brave Canadian boys did volunteer to go
And break the jam on Gerry's Rocks with their foreman, young Mon-
roe.

They had not rolled off many logs when the boss to them did say,
"I'd have you be on your guard, brave boys. That jam will soon give
way."

But scarce the warning had he spoke when the jam did break and go,
And it carried away these six brave youths and their foreman, young
Monroe.

When the rest of the shanty-boys these sad tidings came to hear,
To search for their dead comrades to the river they did steer.
One of these a headless body found, to their sad grief and woe,
Lay cut and mangled on the beach the head of young Monroe.

They took him from the water and smoothed down his raven hair.
There was one fair form amongst them, her cries would rend the air.
There was one fair form amongst them, a maid from Saginaw town.
Her sighs and cries would rend the skies for her lover that was drowned.

They buried him quite decently, being on the seventh of May.
Come all the rest of you shanty-boys, for your dead comrade pray.
'Tis engraved on a little hemlock tree that at his head cloth grow,
The name, the date, and the drowning of this hero, young Monroe.

Miss Clara was a noble girl, likewise the raftsman's friend.
Her mother was a widow woman lived at the river's bend.
The wages of her own true love the boss to her did pay,
And a liberal subscription she received from the shanty-boys next day.

Miss Clara did not long survive her great misery and grief.
In less than three months afterwards death came to her relief.
In less than three months afterwards she was called to go,
And her last: request was granted—to be laid by young Monroe.

Come all the rest of ye shanty-men who would like to go and see,
On a little mound by the river's bank there stands a hemlock tree.
The shanty-boys cut the woods all around. These lovers they lie low.
Here lies Miss Clara Dennison and her shanty-boy, Monroe.

THE LITTLE BROWN BULLS[245]

Not a thing on the river McCluskey did fear
When he drew the stick o'er the big spotted steers.
They were young, quick, and sound, girting eight foot and three.
Says McCluskey the Scotchman, "They're the laddies for me."

Chorus:
Derry down, down, down derry down.

Bull Gordon, the Yankee, on skidding was full,
As he cried "Whoa-hush" to the little brown bulls.
Short-legged and soggy, girt six foot and nine.
Says McCluskey the Scotchman, "Too light for our pine."

It's three to the thousand our contract did call.
Our hauling was good and the timber was tall.
McCluskey he swore he'd make the day full
And skid two to one of the little brown bulls.

"Oh no", says Bull Gordon; "that you cannot do,
Though it's well do we know you've the pets of the crew.
And mark you, my boy, you would have your hands full,
If you skid one more log than the little brown bulls."

The day was appointed and soon it drew nigh,
For twenty-five dollars their fortunes to try.
Both eager and anxious that morning were found,
And scalers and judges appeared on the ground.

With a whoop and a yell came McCluskey in view,
With the big spotted steers, the pets of the crew,
Both chewing their cuds—"O boys, keep your jaws full,
For you easily can beat them, the little brown bulls."

Then out came Bull Gordon with a pipe in his jaw.
The little brown bulls with their cuds in their mouths;
And little we think, when we seen them come down,
That a hundred and forty could they jerk around.
Then up spoke McCluskey: "Come stripped to the skin.
We'll dig them a hole and tumble them in.
We'll learn the d—d Yankee to face the bold Scot.
We'll mix them a dose and feed it red hot."

Said Gordon to Stebbin, with blood in his eye,
"Today we must conquer McCluskey or die."
Then up spoke bold Kennebec, "Boy, never fear,
For you ne'er shall be beat by the big spotted steers."

The sun had gone down when the foreman did say,
"Turn out, boys, turn out; you've enough for the day.
We have scaled them and counted, each man to his team,
And it's well do we know now which one kicks the beam."

After supper was over McCluskey appeared
With the belt ready made for the big spotted steers.
To form it he'd torn up his best mackinaw.
He was bound he'd conduct it according to law.

Then up spoke the scaler, "Hold on, you, a while.
The big spotted steers are behind just one mile.
For you have a hundred and ten and no more,
And Gordon has beat you by ten and a score."

The shanty did ring and McCluskey did swear.
He tore out by handfuls his long yellow hair.
Says he to Bull Gordon, "My colours I'll pull.
So here, take the belt for the little brown bulls."

Here's health to Bull Gordon and Kennebec John;
The biggest day's work on the river they done.
So fill up your glasses and fill them up full;
We'll drink to the health of the little brown bulls.

COWBOY SONGS

THE OLD CHISHOLM TRAIL[246]

Come a-long boys and lis—ten to my tale, I'll
tell you of my trou-bles on the old Chis—holm trail, Come a
ti yi yip—pee, come a ti yi yea, Come a
ti yi yip—pee, come a ti yi yea.

Come along boys and listen to my tale,
I'll tell you of my troubles on the old Chisholm trail.

Refrain:
    Come a ti yi yippee, come a ti yi yea,
    Come a ti yi yippee, come a ti yi yea.

Oh, a ten-dollar hose and a forty-dollar saddle,
And I'm gain' to punchin Texas cattle.

I wake in the mornin' adore daylight
And afore I sleep the moon shines bright.
It's cloudy in the west, a-lookin' like rain,
And my durned old slicker's in the wagon again.

No chaps, no slicker, and it's pourin' down rain,
And I swear, by gosh, I'll never night-herd again.

Feet in the stirrups and seat in the saddle,
I hung and rattled with them long-horn cattle.

The wind commenced to blow, and the rain began to fall,
Hit looked, by grab, like we was gain' to lose 'em all.

I don't give a darn if they never do stop;
I'll ride as long as an eight-day clock.

We rounded 'em up and put 'em on the cars,
And that was the last of the old Two Bars.

Oh, it's bacon and beans most every day,
I'd as soon be a-eatin' prairie hay.

I went to the boss to draw my roll,
He had it figgered out I was nine dollars in the hole.

Goin' back to-town to draw my money,
Goin' back home to see my honey.

With my knees in the saddle and my seat in the sky,
I'll quit punchin' cows in the sweet by and by.

THE COWBOY'S LAMENT[247]

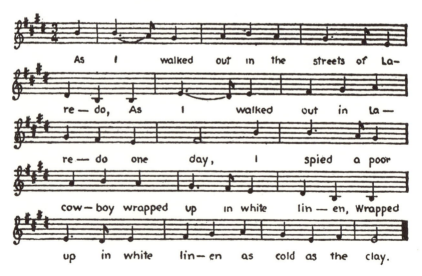

As I walked out in the streets of La-
re — do, As I walked out in la —
re — do one day, I spied a poor
cow — boy wrapped up in white lin — en, Wrapped
up in white lin — en as cold as the clay.

As I walked out in the streets of Laredo,
As I walked out in Laredo one day,
I spied a poor cowboy wrapped up in white linen,
Wrapped up in white linen as cold as the clay.

"Oh, beat the drum slowly and play the fife lowly,
Play the dead march as you carry me along;
Take me to the green valley, there lay the sod o'er me,
For I'm a young cowboy and I know I've done wrong.

"I see by your outfit that you are a cowboy"—
These words he did say as I boldly stepped by.
"Come sit down beside me and hear my sad story;
I am shot in the breast and I know I must die.

"Let sixteen gamblers come handle my coffin,
Let sixteen cowboys come sing me a song.
Take me to the graveyard and lay the sod o'er me,
For I'm a poor cowboy and I know I've done wrong.

"My friends and relations they live in the Nation,
They know not where their boy has gone.
He first came to Texas and hired to a ranchman,
Oh, I'm a young cowboy and I know I've done wrong.

"It was once in the saddle I used to go dashing,
It was once in the saddle I used to go gay;
First to the dram-house and then to the card-house;
Got shot in the breast and I am dying today.

"Get six jolly cowboys to carry my coffin;
Get six pretty maidens to bear up my pall.
Put bunches of roses all over my coffin,
Put roses to deaden the sods as they fall.

"Then swing your rope slowly and rattle your spurs lowly,
And give a wild whoop as you carry me along;
And in the grave throw me and roll the sod o'er me
For I'm a young cowboy and I know I've done wrong.

"Oh, bury beside me my knife and six-shooter,
My spurs on my heel, my rifle by my side,
And over my coffin put a bottle of brandy
That the cowboys may drink as they carry me along.

"Go bring me a cup, a cup of cold water,
To cool my parched lips", the cowboy then said;
Before I returned his soul had departed,
And gone to the round-up—the cowboy was dead.

We beat the drum slowly and played the fife lowly,
And bitterly wept as we bore him along;
For we all loved our comrade, so brave, young, and handsome,
We all loved our comrade although he'd done wrong.

MINERS' SONGS

SWEET BETSEY FROM PIKE[248]

Oh, don't you remember sweet Betsey from Pike,
Who crossed the big mountains with her lover Ike,
With two yoke of cattle, a large yellow dog,
A tall shanghai rooster and one spotted hog.

Chorus:
Singing tooral lal looral lal looral lal la,
Singing tooral lal looral lal looral lal la,
Sing tooral lal looral, sing tooral lal la,
Singing tooral lal looral lal looral lal la.

One evening quite early they camped on the Platte,
'Twas near by the road on a green shady flat,
Where Betsey, sore-footed, lay down to repose—
With wonder Ike gazed on that Pike County rose.

Their wagon broke down with a terrible crash,
And out on the prairie rolled all kinds of trash;
A few little baby clothes done up with care—
'Twas rather suspicious, though all on the *square*.

The shanghai ran off, and their cattle all died;
That morning the last piece of bacon was fried;
Poor Ike was discouraged, and Betsey got mad,
The dog dropped his tail and looked wondrously sad.

They stopped at Salt Lake to inquire the way,
When Brigham declared that sweet Betsey should stay;
But Betsey got frightened and ran like a deer,
While Brigham stood pawing the ground like a steer.

They soon reached the desert, where Betsey gave out,
And down in the sand she lay rolling about;
While Ike, half distracted, looked on with surprise,
Saying, "Betsey, get up, you'll get sand in your eyes."

Sweet Betsey got up in a great deal of pain,
Declared she'd go back to Pike County again;
But Ike gave a sigh, and they fondly embraced,
And they travelled along with his arm round her waist.

They suddenly stopped on a very high hill,
With wonder looked down upon old Placerville;
Ike sighed when he said, and he cast his eyes down,
"Sweet Betsey, my darling, we've got to Hangtown."

Long Ike and sweet Betsey attended a dance;
Ike wore a pair of his Pike County pants;
Sweet Betsey was covered with ribbons and rings;
Say Ike, "You're an angel, but where are your wings?"

A miner said, "Betsey, will you dance with me?"
"I will that, old hoss, if you don't make too free;
But don't dance me hard; do you want to know why?
Dog on you! I'm chock full of strong alkali!"

This Pike County couple got married of course,
And Ike became jealous—obtained a divorce;
Sweet Betsey, well satisfied, said with a shout,
"Good-by, you big lummox, I'm glad you've backed out!"

DOWN, DOWN, DOWN[249]

"Down, Down, Down", another barroom ballad, relates the experiences of a miner reporting for work with a hangover. But it is more than the record of a tipsy worker's muddled thoughts. Rather is it a reflection of the anthracite miner's buffetings which gives it added significance.

"The material for 'Down, Down, Down'," writes William Keating, its author, "was picked up between gangway roof falls, put together on a mine car bumper, pencilled with car sprays, punctuated with mule kicks, tuned to the thunder and vibration of underground blasts and muted to the solitude of the mines, while this mule driver rhymester worked between drunks travelling in and out of the Buck Mountain counter gangway on the third level of Oak Hill shaft at Buckley's Gap, Duncott."

"Down, Down, Down," for a long time an exclusively bar-room ballad, has become generally popular. Keating himself, with his resonant bass voice, is its best interpreter. The manner in which it was sung in the first years of its existence, and how he happened to compose it, are told by Keating as follows:

> In the days when I was hittin' the booze the drinks would come up, up, up when I sang "Down, Down, Down." She was too long to sing straight through, so I broke her up into groups of verses corresponding to levels in a mine. When I got through singing one level, the boys alongside the bar would yell, "Time out for drinks." Then the drinks would go round and Billy Keating would have a drink on the house or on whoever was payin' at the time. As the ballad has about forty verses, you can imagine in what condition the singer and the customers were by the time I got to the end. The barroom floor was me stage for thirty years and, be jabers, I done it up brown when I was at it. But I'm off the hard stuff for life. I've got it licked now.
>
> How did I happen to make up "Down, Down, Down"? Well, about twenty years ago I was drivin' a mule in the Oak Hill mine. Me and the mule were the only livin' things in the gangway unless you counts the rats. It got kind o' lonesome, me sittin' there on the bumper with the cars rattlin' along the dark gangways and headin's. To break the loneliness and at the same time show Jerry, me mule, that I wasn't such a bad egg after all, I used to make up ditties out o' me head and sing them as we rode along. One of them was "Down, Down, Down."

"Down, Down, Down" circulated a long time by word of mouth before being set down on paper. Keating was unable to write until he was thirty-two years old and even after he had learned to write, putting things down on paper was too irksome for him. It was so much easier to make up a ballad out of his head and just sing it.

The incentive finally to write out "Down, Down, Down", came to him in the fall of 1927 under the following circumstances: He sang the ballad at a picnic of Oak Hill colliery employees at Duncott, Schuylkill County, and when he had finished, a mine boss named McGee, from the western part of the county, offered him five dollars for a copy of the ballad. This embarrassed Keating as there were no copies in existence, and he promised to make one. However, when he realized the momentous task ahead of him, he promptly forgot the promise.

Then, three weeks later, came a memorable after pay-day spree at Duncott in which the balladist and several butties indulged. Keating had bartered a ham for a quart of moonshine, and after the bottle had made the rounds it became empty. Powerful stuff, the moonshine knocked them out. Stretched out on the grass, they lay moaning and groaning and, even in their stupor, trying to find a way to obtain a refill of the bottle. Finally an idea emerged from the party.

"Say Bill", said one of the boys. "Did you ever write that copy of 'Down, Down, Down,' for that mine boss from the West End—remember, at the Oak Hill picnic he told you he'd give you five bucks for it?"

Keating was in no condition to do any writing, but slowly it penetrated his befogged mind that this was an opportunity to earn enough cash with which to purchase more moonshine.

"We'll go over to my place", he replied at length. "My woman'll raise hell with the whole of us, but I'll write that song, even if it takes me until midnight."

Keating describes the next scene as follows: "We went to my house. I borrowed several sheets of writing-paper from my nearest neighbour and, seated around our middle-room table, with the rest of the fellows helping me with the 'spelling' (while my wife RAVED!), I wrote 'Down, Down, Down'. After several hours' (awful!) efforts, we finished a shamefully 'scribbled!' but possibly readable, copy of my song."

The next problem was to find the boss whose address Keating knew only vaguely as somewhere in the West End. The four booze-thirsty

musketeers then got into a rickety automobile and rode to the West
End looking for a McGee where the woods could not be seen for
McGees. "Finally, after miles of back-tracking, after hootin', and tootin'
the flivver's horn through nearly every town, village and 'Patch' in the
western end of Schuykill County without finding 'our' McGee", writes
Keating, "we gave up, or rather, we took a different 'tack'."

They stopped in front of a pool room speakeasy which made them
feel at home. The sage behind the bar knew plenty of McGees but not
the one the boys were hunting. While Keating poured out his story, the
bartender kept his Irish blue eyes glued to the scribbled copy of "Down,
Down, Down", smiling as he read. Presently he said, "Say, Butty, is
this the only copy ye have of this song?" To which Keating replied, "It
is, and it's only through the Mercy of God that I had strength enough
in me hand to write that one this evenin'."

"Well", said the bartender, "ye needn't hunt any farther for any
McGees. I'll give ye five dollars fer this song, and call your butties in.
I'll give ye all a drink and thin ye'll sing this song till I learn the
'chune' av it if it takes from now till mornin'."

"The show was on", Keating adds. "We drank' I sang. We drank
again, and I sang again—this song without end. Amen!"

With your kind at — ten—tion, a song I will
trill, All ye who must toil with the
pick and the drill, And sweat for your
bread in that hole in Oak Hill, That goes
down, down, down.

With your kind attention, a song I will trill,
All ye who must toil with the pick and the drill,
And sweat for your bread in that hole in Oak Hill,
That goes down, down, down.

When I was a boy says my daddy to me:
"Stay out of Oak Hill, take my warning", says he,
"Or with dust you'll be choked and a pauper you'll be,
Broken down, down, down."

But I went to Oak Hill and I asked for a job,
A mule for to drive or a gangway to rob.
The boss said, "Come out, Bill, and follow the mob
That goes down, down, down."

On the strength of the job and the tune of this rhyme,
I strolled into Tim's an' drank twenty-five shines;
Reported next morning, half dead but on time
To go down down, down.

Says Pete McAvoy, "Here's Bill Keatin' the scamp."
Just back, Pete supposed, from a million-mile tramp.
Pete showed me the "windie"[250] where I'd get a lamp
To go down, down, down.

The lamp man he squints through the window at me,
"What's your name? What's your age? What's your number?" says he.
"Bill Keatin', I'm thirty, number twenty-three,
Mark that down, down, down."

With a frown of disfavour, my joke it was met,
For an argument plainly, the lamp man was set.
He told me that civil a lamp would I get
To go down, down, down.

Says I, "Mr. Lamp Man, now don't l'ave us fight;
Can't ye see be me eyes I was boozin' all night?
Sure the mines will be dark and I'll have to have light
While I'm down, down, down."

With an old greasy apron, Jim polished his specks,
Declarin' the lamp house rules would be wrecked,

If he'd give out his lantherns 'thout gettin' brass checks
From us Clowns! Clowns! Clowns!

I found the supply clerk, of him I inquired
If he had any checks of the sort Jim desired.
He said: "Here's a check, if you lose it, you're fired,
Mark that down, down, down."

I had the precious lamp check that would pacify Jim,
Flip, into his window, I flung it to him
Sayin', "Now quit your grumbling, an' give me a glim
To go down, down, down."

A contraption Jim gave me, a hose on a box,
'Twas so heavy I thought it was loaded with rocks.
If a car jumped the track, you could use it for blocks
While you're down, down, down.

The box breaks the bones in the small of your back,
Wears the hide off your hips where it hangs be a strap;
Oh! the gawk that transported such lamps to the Gap
May go down, down, down.

When you ask for a lamp you commit an offence,
You'd imagine the lamp man stood all the expense;
While for lamps that won't light we pay sixty-five cents
While we're down, down, down.

We wait at Jim's window while winter winds stab,
While the lamp man unravels a lot of crank gab.
Did ye e'er meet a lamp man that wasn't a crab
In your rounds? Aren't they hounds?

Crabbed lamp lords, ye'll cringe for your cranks whin ye die,
For the way that ye bulldozed me butties[251] and I;
Me and Tracy'll be twanging this ballad on high
While you're down, down, down.

Then into the office I sauntered to Boss Sam.
With a cheery "Good mornin'," says I, "here I am,
With booze in me bottle and beer in me can
To go down, down, down."

"Well, Billy, me bucko, how are you today?"

"Outside of a headache", says I, "I'm O.K.
I've been samplin' the soda in every cafe
In the town, town, town.

"Sam, where is my job at?" I wanted to know.
"Was it in the new drift?" Sam shook his head, no.
"When you hit the fifth lift you'll have one more to go
So get down, down, down."

I asked Sam what tools would I need in the place.
"Very few", said the boss with a grin on his face.
"One seven-size scoop in a coop-stoopy space
Away down, down, down."

With a note from the boss to the shaft I made haste,
Saluted the top-man and in line took me place
Sayin' "Gi' me a cage, for I've no time to waste,
Let me down, down, down."

"All aboard for the bottom!" the top-man did yell,
We stepped on the cage, he ding-donged a bell;
Through that hole in Oak Hill, like a bat out o' hell
We went down, down, down.

In wet or dry weather that shaft always rains,
There's a trembling of timbers and clanking of chains.
Just off of a spree, it flip-flopped me few brains
Going down, down, down.

It happened that something was wrong with the pump,
The water was up—we struck a wet bump.
But the cage kept descending and into the sump[252]
We went down, down, down.

I've been on the outside and inside before,
I fell into oceans and rivers galore,
But that dip in that deep dirty sump made me sore
Away down, down, down.

The fireboss he flagged me, fool questions to ask.
Was I married, or single and where I worked last.
Says I, "Lind me you pencil, me present and past
I'll write down, down, down."

Between the sump bath and headache I felt like a dope,
Going down in the gloom of the underground slope,
On a tricky man-truck and a rotten old rope,
Going down, down, down.

She was blocked from the dish to the knuckle with smoke,
The dust was so thick that I thought I would choke.
Says I to meself I guess here's where I croak
Away down, down, down.

Groped into the gangway they gave me a scoop,
The cut was just fired, muck heaped to the roof.
I stooped an' I scooped till me back looped-the-loop
Stoopin' down, down, down.

That first car we loaded held five tons I swore
And that Buck Mountain coal has the weight of iron ore.
We scooped seven cars but when they brought us one more
I laid down, down, down.

She was heaved on the bottom and cracked on the top
Ne'er a pole, ne'er a slab, ne'er a laggin', nor prop
Pretty soon I expect that Gap Mountain will drop
And come down, down, down.

That journey each morning it near breaks me heart,
The steps in the mule-way is ten feet apart,
You must watch your brogans, for if you get a start
You'll roll down, down, down.

The Oak Hill officials are foxy galoots,
With company-store tyrants they're all in cahoots,
With the gangways a river, you're bound to buy boots,
While you're down, down, down.

On pay days I rave, Rube Tracy oft swore,
In fact 'twas enough to make both of us sore,
When our wives drag our wages all out in the store
While we're down, down, down.

But yet I'm in right, for I'm on the ground floor,
In deep in the wet and in deep in the store,
If they sink Oak Hill shaft six or seven lifts more
I'll go down, down, down.

It's a most cruel fate, but continue we must,
Delvin' deep for black diamonds, beneath the earth's crust,
Moil for mush and molasses and eating coal dust
Away down, down, down.

All I drew for a year was a dollar or three,
Those company-store thieves made a pauper of me,
But for ballads like this, I'd have starved for a spree
In the town, town, town.

Toil, you put early-grey on my poor daddy's head,
While he slaved in Oak Hill to provide us with bread,
How I wish I had heeded the warning he plead:
"Don't go down, down, down."

Now my back is toil-bent, my feet work-worn, slow.
Soon the hair on my head will be white as the snow.
Then I fear I'll be shipped to the Pogie below—
Broken down, a pauperized clown.

SONGS OF THE FARMER

THE DODGER[253]

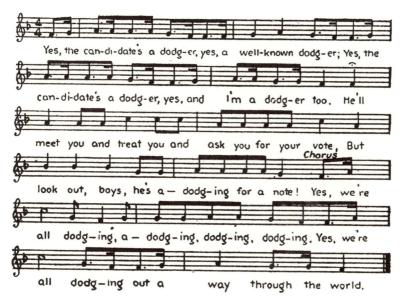

Yes, the can-di-date's a dodg-er, yes, a well-known dodg-er; Yes, the
can-di-date's a dodg-er, yes, and I'm a dodg-er too. He'll
meet you and treat you and ask you for your vote, But
look out, boys, he's a — dodg-ing for a note! Yes, we're
Chorus
all dodg-ing, a — dodg-ing, dodg-ing, dodg-ing. Yes, we're
all dodg-ing out a way through the world.

Yes, the candidate's a dodger, yes, a well-known dodger;
Yes, the candidate's a dodger, yes, and I'm a dodger too.
He'll meet you and treat you and ask you for your vote,
But look out, boys, he's a-dodging for a note!

Chorus:
  Yes, we're all dodging, a-dodging, dodging, dodging,
  Yes, we're all dodging out a way through the world.

Yes, the lawyer he's a dodger, yes, a well-known dodger;
Yes, the lawyer he's a dodger, yes, and I'm a dodger too.
He'll plead you a case and claim you as a friend,
But look out, boys, he's easy for to bend!

Yes, the doctor he's a dodger, yes, a well-known dodger;
Yes, the doctor he's a dodger, yes, and I'm a dodger too.
He'll doctor you and cure you for half you possess,
But look out, boys, he's a-dodging for the rest!

Yes, the preacher he's a dodger, yes, a well-known dodger;
Yes, the preacher he's a dodger, yes, and I'm a dodger too.
He'll preach you a gospel and tell you of your crimes,
But look out, boys, he's a-dodging for your dimes!

Yes, the merchant he's a dodger, yes, a well-known dodger;
Yes, the merchant he's a dodger, yes, and I'm a dodger too.
He'll sell you the goods at double the price,
But when you go to pay him, you'll have to pay him twice!

Yes, the farmer he's a dodger, yes, a well-known dodger.
Yes, the farmer he's a dodger, yes, and I'm a dodger too.
He'll plow his cotton, he'll plow his corn,
He'll make a living just as sure as you're born!

Yes, the lover he's a dodger, yes, a well-known dodger;
Yes, the lover he's a dodger, yes, and I'm a dodger, too.
He'll hug you and kiss you and call you his bride,
But look out, girls, he's telling you a lie!

THE FARMER COMES TO TOWN[254]

When the farmer comes to town,
With his wagon broken down,
Oh, the farmer is the man who feeds them all.
If you'll only look and see,
I am sure you will agree
That the farmer is the man who feeds them all.

Chorus:
    The farmer is the man,
    The farmer is the man,
    Lives on credit till the fall;
    Then they take him by the hand

And they lead him from the land,
And the middleman's the man who gets it all.

When the lawyer hangs around,
While the butcher cuts a pound,
Oh, the farmer is the man who feeds them all.
And the preacher and the cook
Go a-strolling by the brook,
Oh, the farmer is the man who feeds them all.

Chorus:
The farmer is the man,
The farmer is the man,
Lives on credit till the fall;
With the int'rest rate so high,
It's a wonder he don't die,
For the mortgage man's the man who gets it all.

When the banker says he's broke,
And the merchant's up in smoke,
They forget that it's the farmer feeds them all.
It would put them to the test
If the farmer took a rest;
Then they'd know that it's the farmer feeds them all.

Chorus:
The farmer is the man,
The farmer is the man,
Lives on credit till the fall;
And his pants are wearing thin,
His condition it's a sin;
He's forgot that he's the man who feeds them all.

HOBO AND JAILHOUSE SONGS

THE BIG ROCK CANDY MOUNTAINS[255]

One ev'ning as the sun went down
And the jungle fire was burning,
Down the track came a hobo, hamming[256]
And he said, "Boys, I'm not turning.
I'm headed for a land that's far away,
Beside the crystal fountains.
I'll see you all this coming fall
In the Big Rock Candy Mountains.

Refrain:
"In the Big Rock Candy Mountains,
There's a land that's fair and bright,
Where the handouts grow on bushes
And you sleep out ev'ry night,
Where the boxcars all are empty
And the sun shines ev'ry day—
Oh, the birds and the bees and the cigaret trees,
The rock-and-rye springs where the whangdoodle sings,
In the Big Rock Candy Mountains."

Refrain

Big Rock Can-dy Moun-tains. In the Big Rock Can-dy Moun-tains, There's a land that's fair and bright, Where the hand-outs grow on bush-es And you sleep out ev'-ry night, Where the box-cars all are emp-ty .And the sun shines ev'-ry day— Oh, the birds and the bees and the cig-a-ret trees, The rock-and-rye springs where the whang-dood-le sings, In the Big Rock Can-dy Moun-tains."

In the Big Rock Candy Mountains,
All the cops have wooden legs,
And the bulldogs all have rubber teeth,
And the hens lay softboiled eggs.
The farmers' trees are full of fruit,
And the barns are full of hay.
Oh, I'm bound to go where there ain't no snow,
Where the sleet don't fall and the wind don't blow,
In the big Rock Candy Mountains.

"In the Big Rock Candy Mountains,
You never change your socks,
And the little streams of alkyhol
Come trickling down the rocks.
The shacks all have to tip their hats
And the railroad bulls are blind,
There's a lake of stew and of whisky, too,
You can paddle all around in a big canoe,
In the Big Rock Candy Mountains.

"In the Big Rock Mountains,
The jails are made of tin,
And you can bust right out again
As soon as they put you in.
There ain't no shorthandled shovels,
No axes, saws or picks—
I'm a-going to stay where you sleep all day—
Oh, they boiled in oil the inventor of toil
In the Big Rock Candy Mountains.

"Oh, come with me, and we'll go see
The Big Rock Candy Mountains."

PIE IN THE SKY[257]

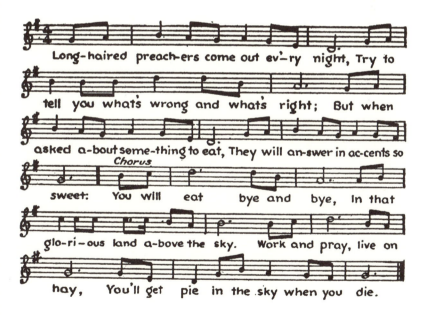

Long-haired preachers come out ev'ry night,
Try to tell you what's wrong and what's right;
But when asked about something to eat,
They will answer in accents so sweet:

Chorus:
You will eat bye and bye,
In that glorious land above the sky.
                    (way up high)
Work and pray, live on hay,
You'll get pie in the sky when you die.
                    (that's no lie!)

And the starvation army they play,
And they sing and they clap and they pray,
Till they get all your coin on the drum,
Then they'll tell you when you're on the bum:

Holy rollers and jumpers come out,
And they holler and jump and they shout,
But when eating time comes around they will say,
"You will eat on that glorious day."

MOUNTAIN SONGS

SOURWOOD MOUNTAIN[258]

I got a girl in the head of the hollow,
Hey, diddledum dey. She won't come and I won't call 'er,
Hey, diddledum dey,
Hey, diddledum dey,
Hey, diddledum dey.
She won't come and I won't call 'er,
Hey, diddledum dey.

She sits up with ole Si Hall,
Hey, diddledum dey.
Me and Jeff can't go there a-tall,
Hey, diddledum dey,
Hey, diddledum dey,
Hey, diddledum dey.
Me and Jeff can't go there a-tall,
Hey, diddledum dey.

Some-a these days before very long,
Hey, diddledum dey,
I'll get that gal and a-home I'll run,
Hey, diddledum dey,
Hey, diddledum dey,
Hey, diddledum dey.
I'll get that gal and a-home I'll run,
Hey, diddledum dey.

CINDY[259]

I wish I was an apple,
A-hangin' in the tree,
And ev'ry time my sweetheart passed,
She'd take a bite of me.
She told me that she loved me,
She called me sugar plum,
She throwed 'er arms around me—
I thought my time had come.

Chorus:
> Git along home, Cindy, Cindy,
> Git along home, Cindy, Cindy,
> Git along home, Cindy, Cindy,
> I'll marry you some time.

She took me to the parlour,
She cooled me with her fan,
She swore that I's the purtiest thing
In the shape of mortal man.
Oh where did you git your liquor,
Oh where did you git your dram,
I got it from a nigger
Away down in Rockingham.

Cindy got religion,
She had it once before,
When she heard my old banjo
She 'uz the first un on the floor.
I wish I had a needle,
As fine as I could sew,
I'd sew the girls to my coat tail,
And down the road I'd go.

DOWN IN THE VALLEY[260]

Down in the valley, valley so low,
Hang your head over, hear the wind blow.
Hear the wind blow, dear, hear the wind blow;
Hang your head over, hear the wind blow.

If you don't love me, love whom you please;
Throw your arms round me, give my heart ease.
Give my heart ease, dear, give my heart ease;
Throw your arms round me, give my heart ease.

Write me a letter, send it by mail;
And back it in care of Birmingham Jail.
Birmingham Jail, dear, Birmingham Jail,
And back it in care of Birmingham Jail.

Writing this letter, containing three lines,
Answer my question, "Will you be mine?"
Will you be mine, dear, will you be mine?
Answer my question, "Will you be mine?"

Go build me a castle, forty feet high,
So I can see her as she goes by.
As she goes by, dear, as she goes by,
So I can see her as she goes by.

Roses love sunshine, violets love dew;
Angels in heaven know I love you.
Know I love you, dear, know I love you,
Angels in heaven know I love you.

AFRICAN-AMERICAN SONGS

MASSA HAD A YALLER GAL[261]

Massa had a yaller gal,
He brought her from de South;
Her hair it curled so very tight
She couldn't shut her mouth.

Chorus :
Oh, I ain't got time to tarry,
Oh, I ain't got time to tarry,
An' I ain't got time to tarry, boys,
For I'se gwine away.

He took her to de tailor,
To have her mouth made small.
She swallowed up the tailor,
Tailorshop and all.

Massa had no hooks nor nails
Nor anything like that;
So on this darky's nose he used
To hang his coat and hat.

I'M GWINE TO ALABAMY[262]

I'm gwine to Alabamy,—Oh,
For to see my mammy,—Ah.

She went from Ole Virginy,—Oh,
And I'm her pickaninny,—Ah.

She lives on the Tombigbee,—Oh,
I wish I had her wid me,—Ah.

Now I'm a good big nigger,—Oh,
I reckon I won't git bigger,—Ah.

But I'd like to see my mammy,—Oh,
Who lives in Alabamy,—Ah.

CHARLESTON GALS[263]

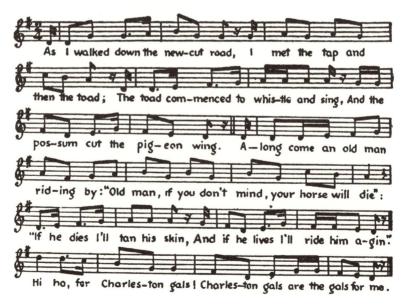

As I walked down the new-cut road,
I met the tap and then the toad;
The toad commenced to whistle and sing,
And the possum cut the pigeon wing.

Along come an old man riding by:
"Old man, if you don't mind, your horse will die";
"If he dies I'll tan his skin,
And if he lives I'll ride him agin."

Hi, ho, for Charleston gals!
Charleston gals are the gals for me.

As I went a-walking down the street,
Up steps Charleston gals to take a walk with me.
I kep' a-walking and they kep' a-talking,
I danced with a gal with a hole in her stocking.

SHOCK ALONG, JOHN[264]

Shock along, John, shock along.
Shock along, John, shock along.

RUN NIGGER, RUN![265]

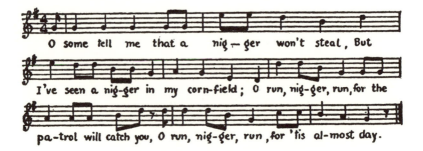

O some tell me that a nigger won't steal,
But I've seen a nigger in my cornfield;
O run, nigger, run, for the patrol will catch you,
O run, nigger, run, for 'tis almost day.

THE GREY GOOSE[266]

Well, las' Monday mornin',
    Lawd, Lawd, Lawd!
Well, las' Monday mornin',
    Lawd, Lawd, Lawd!

My daddy went a-hunting.

Well, he carried along his zulu.

Well, along come a grey goose.

Well, he thronged it to his shoulder.

Well, he reared his hammer 'way back.

Well, he pulled on his trigger.

Well, a-down he come windin'.
He was six weeks a-fallin'.
We was six weeks a-findin'.
And we put him on his wagon.
And we taken him to the white house.
He was six weeks a-pickin'.
Lordy, your wife and my wife.
Gonna give a feather-pickin'.
And we put him on to parboil.
He was six months a-parboil'.
And we put him on the table.
Now the forks couldn't stick him.
And the knife couldn't cut him.
And we thronged him in the hog-pen.
And he broke the belly's[267] jawbone.
And we taken him to the sawmill.
And he broke the saw's teeth out.
And the last time I seen him.
Well, he's flyin' across the ocean.
With a long string o' goslin's.
And he's goin' "Quank quink-quank!"

THE MIDNIGHT SPECIAL[268]

Well, you wake up in the mornin', hear the ding dong ring,
You go a-marchin' to the table, see the same damn thing.
Well, it's on-a one table, knife-a, fork, an' a pan,
An' if you say anything about it, you're in trouble with the man.

Chorus :
    Let the Midnight Special shine its light on me,
    Let the Midnight Special shine its ever-lovin' light on me.

If you go to Houston, you better walk right;
You better not stagger, you better not fight,
Or Sheriff Benson will arrest you, he will carry you down.
If the jury finds you guilty, you'll be penitentiary-bound.

Yonder comes li'l Rosie. How in the worl' do you know?
I can tell her by her apron and the dress she wo',
Umberella on her shoulder, piece o' paper in her han'.
Well, I heard her tell the captain: "I want my man."

I'm gwine away to leave you, an' my time ain't long.
The man is gonna call me an' I'm a-goin' home.
Then I'll be done all my grievin', whoopin', holl'in', an' a-cryin',
Then I'll be done all my studyin' 'bout my great long time.

Well, the biscuits on the table, just as hard as any rock.
If you try to swallow them, break a convict's heart.
My sister wrote a letter, my mother wrote a card—
"If you want to come an' see us, you'll have to ride the rods."

PO' LAZ'US (POOR LAZARUS)[269]

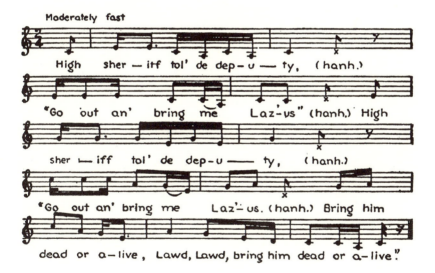

High sheriff tol' de deputy (*hanh*.) "Go out an' bring me Laz'us."
    (*hanh*.)
High sheriff tol' de deputy (*hanh*.) "Go out an' bring me Laz'us."
    (*hanh*.)
Bring him dead or alive, Lawd, Lawd, bring him dead or alive."

Oh, bad man Laz'us done broke in de commissary winder,
Oh, bad man Laz'us done broke in de commissary winder.
He been paid off, Lawd, Lawd, he been paid off.

Oh, de deputy 'gin to wonder, where in de worl' he could fin' him.
Oh, de deputy 'gin to wonder, where in de worl' he could fin' him.
Well, I don' know, Lawd, Lawd, I jes' don' know.

Oh, dey foun' po' Laz'us way out between two mountains,
Oh, dey foun' po' Laz'us way out between two mountains,
An' dey blowed him down, Lawd, Lawd, an' dey blowed him down.

Ol' Laz'us tol' de deputy he had never been arrested,
Ol' Laz'us tol' de deputy he had never been arrested,
By no one man, Lawd, Lawd, by no one man.

So dey shot po' Laz'us, shot him wid a great big number,
Dey shot po' Laz'us, shot him wid a great big number.
Number 45, Lawd, Lawd, number 45.

An' dey taken po' Laz'us an' dey laid him on de commissary county.
Dey taken po' Laz'us an' dey laid him on de commissary county,
An' dey walked away, Lawd, Lawd, an' dey walked away.

Laz'us tol' de deputy, "Please gimme a cool drink o' water."
Laz'us tol' de deputy, "Please gimme a cool drink o' water,
Jes' befo' I die, Lawd, Lawd, jes' befo' I die."

Laz'us' sister run an' tol' her mother,
Laz'us' sister run an' tol' her mother,
Dat po' Laz'us dead, Lawd, Lawd, po' Laz'us dead.

Laz'us' mother, she laid down her sewin',
Laz'us' mother, she laid down her sewin',
'Bout de trouble, Lawd, Lawd, she had wid Laz'us.

Laz'us' mother she come a-screamin' an' a-cryin',
Laz'us' mother she come a-screamin' an' a-cryin',
"Dat's my only son, Lawd, Lawd, dat's my only son."

DELIA HOLMES[270]

De-lia, De-lia, Why did'nt you run? -See dat des-per-a-do, Had a
for-ty-fo' smoke-less gun, Cryin', "All I had done gone."

Chorus

All I had done gone ! All I had done gone !

Good-by, Moth-er, friends and all; All I had done gone!

Delia, Delia,
Why didn't you run?
See dat desperado,
Had a forty-fo' smokeless gun,
Cryin', "All I had done gone."

Chorus:
All I had done gone!
All I had done gone!
Good-by, Mother, friends and all;
All I had done gone!

Now Coonie an' his little sweet-
heart
Settin' down talkie' low;
Axed her would she marry him,
She said, "Why sho'."

When the time come for marriage
She refuse' to go.
"If you don't marry me
You cannot live no mo'."

Shot her with a pistol,
Number forty-fo'.
"You did not marry me,
You cannot live no mo'."

Turned po' Delia over
On her side very slow.
She was cryin', "Coonie,
Please don't shoot no mo'."

Death had proceeded,
It wasn't so very long
Till her mother come runnin'
With a bucket on her arm.

"Tell me, my darlin',
What have you done wrong,
Cause Coonie to shoot you
With that forty-fo' smokeless
gun?"

"Some give a nickel
Some give a dime,
Help to bury
This body of mine."
Threw down his pistol
An' tried to get away.
Officers picked him up
In just a few days.

Placed him in the jail
Till his trial should come.
"Tell me now, officer,
What have I done?"

They axed him did he remember
    this
"A girl that you were in love,
An' spoken things unto her
That instantly taken her nerve?"

"She moved closely beside of me
An' threw her arms around."
"Do you remember little Delia
    Holmes
And which you shot down?"

"Have I now any bond,
Or can I get one,
For the crime that I am charged,
I plead guilty I have done?"

The judge that tried him,
Handsome with the time,
Say, "Coonie, if I don't hang you
I'll give you ninety-nine."

Coonie went to Atlanta,
Drinkin' from a silver cup.
Po' li'l Delia's in the cemetery,
I hope to never wake up.

Delia's mother
Taken a trip out west,

Just to keep from hearin' the talk
Of po' li'l Delia's death.

Everywhere the train would stop
You could hear the people moan,
Singin' dat lonesome song,
"Po' Delia's dead an' gone."

Rubber tire' buggy,
Rubber tire' hack,
Take you to de cemetery,
Don't never bring you back.

Coonie wrote to the Governor,
Asked him, "Pardon me,
I was charged with murder
In the first degree.

"The judge was liberal
In givin' me my time;
Happened that he didn't hang me,
But he give me ninety-nine.

"I am now a murderer,
Servin' a long, long time;
And if you will pardon me,
I'll not be guilty of another crime.

"This is Coonie in Atlanta,
Workin' 'mong the stone.
Have been here for forty-five
    years,
And I'm now needed at home."

TAKE THIS HAMMER[271]

Take this ham-mer, (huh!) car-ry it to the cap—tain, (huh!) Take this ham-mer, (huh!) car-ry it to the cap—tain, (huh!) Take this ham-mer, (huh!) car-ry it to the cap—tain, (huh!) Tell him I'm gone, (huh!) tell him I'm gone. (huh!)

Take this hammer, (*huh!*) carry it to the captain,(*huh!*)
Take this hammer, (*huh!*) carry it to the captain, (*huh!*)
Take this hammer, (huh!) carry it to the captain, (huh!)
Tell him I'm gone, (*huh!*) tell him I'm gone. (*huh!*)

Take this hammer, (*huh!*) carry it to the captain, (*huh!*)
Take this hammer, (*huh!*) carry it to the captain, (*huh!*)
Take this hammer, (*huh!*) carry it to the captain, (*huh!*)
Tell him I'm gone, (*huh!*) tell him I'm gone. (*huh!*)

If he ask you (*huh!*) was I runnin', (*huh!*)
Tell him I's flyin', (*huh!*) tell him I's flyin'. (*huh!*)

If he ask you (*huh!*) was I laughin', (*huh!*)
Tell him I's cryin', (*huh!*) tell him I's cryin'. (*huh!*)

Cap'n called me, (*huh!*) called me "a nappy-headed devil", (*huh!*)
That ain't my name, (*huh!*) that ain't my name. (*huh!*)

I don't want no (*huh!*) peas, cornbread, neither molasses, (*huh!*)
They hurt my pride, (*huh!*) they hurt my pride. (*huh!*)

I don't want no (*huh!*) cold iron shackles (*huh!*)
Around my leg, (*huh!*) around my leg. (*huh!*)

Cap'n got a big gun, (*huh!*) an' he try to play bad. (*huh!*)
Go'n' take it in the mornin' (*huh!*) if he make me mad. (*huh!*)

I'm go'n' make these (*huh!*) few days I started, (*huh!*)
Then I'm goin' home, (*huh!*) then I'm goin' home, (*huh!*)

LITTLE BLACK TRAIN IS A-COMIN'[272]

God tole Hezykiah
In a message from on high:
Go set yo' house in ordah,
For thou shalt sholy die.
He turned to the wall an' a-weepin',
Oh! see the King in tears;
He got his bus'ness fixed all right,
God spared him fifteen years.

Chorus:
Little black train is a-comin',
Get all yo' bus'ness right;
Go set yo' house in ordah,
For the train may be here tonight.

Go tell that ball room lady,
All filled with worldly pride,
That little black train is a-comin',
Prepare to take a ride.
That little black train and engine
An' a little baggage car,
With idle thoughts and wicked deeds,
Must stop at the judgment bar.

There was a po' young man in darkness,
Cared not for the gospel light,
Suddenly a whistle blew
From a little black train in sight.
"Oh, death, will you not spare me?
I'm just in my wicked plight.
Have mercy, Lord, do hear me,
Pray come an' set me right."
But death had fixed his shackles
About his soul so tight,
Just befo' he got his bus'ness fixed,
The train rolled in that night.

LORD, REMEMBER ME[273]

Oh, Deat' he is a lit-tle man, And he goes from do' to do. He kill some souls and he wound-ed some, And he lef' some souls to pray. Oh, Lord, re-mem-ber me, Do, Lord, re-mem-ber me; Re-mem-ber me as the year roll round, Lord, re-mem-ber me

Oh, Deat' he is a little man,
    And he goes from do' to do'.
He kill some souls and he wounded some,
    And he lef' some souls to pray.

Oh[274], Lord, remember me,
    Do, Lord, remember me;
Remember me[275] as de year roll round,
    Lord, remember me.

I want to die like-a Jesus die,
    And he die wid a free good will,
I lay out in de grave and I stretchee out e arms,
    Do, Lord, remember me.

BOLL WEEVIL SONG[276]

Oh, de boll weevil am a little black bug,
    Come from Mexico, dey say,
Come all de way to Texas, jus' a-lookin' foh a place to stay,
    Jus' a-lookin' foh a home, jus' a-lookin' foh a home.

De first time I seen de boll weevil,
    He was a-settin' on de square.
De next time I seen de boll weevil, he had all of his family dere,
    Jus' a-lookin' foh a home, jus' a-lookin' foh a home.

De first time I seen de boll weevil,
  He was a-settin' on de square.
De next time I seen de boll weevil, he had all of his family dere,
  Jus' a-lookin' foh a home, jus' a-lookin' foh a home.

De farmer say to de weevil:
  "What make yo' head so red?"
De weevil say to de farmer, "It's a wondah I ain't dead,
  A-lookin' foh a home, jus' a-lookin' foh a home."

De farmer take de boll weevil,
  An' he put him in de hot san'.
De weevil say: "Dis is mighty hot, but I'll stan' it like a man,
  Dis'll be my home, it'll be my home."

De farmer take de boll weevil,
  An' he put him in a lump of ice;
De boll weevil say to de farmer: "Dis is mighty cool an' nice
  It'll be my home, dis'll be my home."

De farmer take de bold weevil,
  An' he put him in de fire.
De boll weevil say to de farmer: "Here I are, here I are,
  Dis'll be my home, dis'll be my home."

De boll weevil say to de farmer:
  "You better leave me alone;
I done eat all yo' cotton, now I'm goin' to start on yo' corn,
  I'll have a home, I'll have a home."

De merchant got half de cotton,
  De boll weevil got de res'.
Didn't leave de farmer's wife but one old cotton dress,
  An' it's full of holes, it's full of holes.

De farmer say to de merchant:
  "We's in an awful fix;
De boll weevil et all de cotton up an' lef' us only sticks,
  We's got no home, we's got no home."

De farmer say to de merchant:
  "We ain't made but only one bale,
And befoh we'll give yo' dat one we'll fight an' go to jail,
  We'll have a home, we'll have a home."

De cap'n say to de missus:
    "What d' you t'ink o' dat?
De boll weevil done make a nes' in my bes' Sunday hat,
    Goin' to have a home, goin' to have a home."

And if anybody should ax you
    Who it was dat make dis song,
Jus' tell 'em 'twas a big buck niggah wid a paih o' blue duckin's on.
    Ain' got no home, ain's got no home.

Notes

1. *A History of New York*, by Diedrich Knickerbocker (1809), Book VI, Chapter III.
2. Wildfire was not Paulding's only attempt to portray backwoods character, for in Ambrose Bushfield, in *Westward Ho!* (1832), he created a burlesque Natty Bumppo.
3. It has been suggested that the original of Wildfire may have been Florida's Governor William Pope Duval (father of John C. Duval), who supplied material for several stories by Washington Irving, Paulding's collaborator in the *Salmagundi* papers.
4. *Literary Life of James K. Paulding,* by William I. Paulding (1867), pp. 218–219.
5. See the plate facing page 504 in *Annals of the New York Stage*, by George C. D. Odell, Vol. III
6. *Ben Hardin, His Times and Contemporaries*, by Lucius P. Little (1887) p. viii.
7. *Life of Colonel David Crockett* (1860), p. 140n.
8. "A Neglected Epic", *Essays on Authorship* (1902)
9. *Sketches and Eccentricities of Col. David Crockett, of West Tennessee* (1833), pp. 77, 78.
10. Speech on the Fortification Bill, *Register of Debates in Congress*, Part IV of Vol. X, June 19, 1834, p. 4,586.
11. For ten "Crockett" tall tales of hunting and shooting, see Vance *Randolph's Ozark Mountain Folks* (1932)
12. *Underground, or Life Below the Surface*, by Thomas W. Knox (1873), pp. 630–684.
13. *A-Rafting on the Mississip'*, by Charles Edward Russell (1928), pp. 189-190.
14. *Short Grass Country*, by Stanley Vestal (1941), p. 26.
15. "Justice in Early Iowa", by George F. Robeson, *The Palimpsest*, Vol. 5. (March, 1924), No 3, p. 105.
16. *The Bad Man of the West*, by George D. Hendricks (1941), p. 96.
17. *Belle Starr*, by Burton Rascoe (1941), pp. 9–10.
18. *A Vaquero of the Brush Country*, by J. Frank Dobie (1929), p. 174n.
19. *Law West of the Pecos*, The Story of Roy Bean, by Everett Lloyd (1936), pp. 74–75. 66–67.
20. *The Making of Buffalo Bill*. A Study in Heroics, by Richard J. Walsh, in collaboration with Milton S. Salsbury (1928), p.v.
21. *Paul Bunyan*, by James Stevens (1925), p. 1.
22. See his letter to Louise Pound in her article on "Nebraska Strong Men", *Southern Folklore Quarterly*, Vol. VII (September, 1943), No. 3, pp. 133-143. For Paul Bunyan bibliography see "Paul Bunyan Twenty-Five Years After", by Gladys J. Haney, *The Journal of American Folklore*, LV (July-September, 1942), No. 217, pp. 155–168.

23. In a note on "Paul Bunyan—Myth or Hoax?", in *Minnesota History*, Vol. XXI (March, 1940) No. 1, pp. 55–58, Carleton C. Ames places the burden of proof on "those who are presenting Paul Bunyan as a native product of the imagination of the shanty boy, and who are making him, in a sense the patron saint of the old-time logger". On the basis of the negative evidence that Paul Bunyan was unknown to old-timers in Wisconsin and Minnesota and of certain anachronisms in Esther Shephard's version, he reaches the "tentative conclusion" that "Paul Bunyan as the legendary hero of the shanty boy, as true folklore, is spurious. He may have appeared in the camps of a later day possibly about the turn of the century, when the true shanty boy had all but vanished. He may exist among the lumberjacks of the Pacific Coast, where logging is a far different operation than the Minnesota and Wisconsin jack ever knew, but he was a stranger to the loggers of the Middle West when logging was at its height".

24. *Men and Steel*, by Mary Heaton Vorse (1920), p. 20.

25. From *American Ballads and Folk Songs*, collected and compiled by John A. Lomax and Alan Lomax, pp. 251–253. Copyright, 1934, by The Macmillan Company. New York. Adapted from "The Ballad of Davy Crockett", by Julia Beazley, in *Texas and Southwestern Lore*, Publications of the Texas Folk-Lore Society, Number VI (1927), edited by J. Frank Dobie, pp. 205–206.

26. "Davy Crockett" is an interesting example of a folklorized negro minstrel song. "Pompey Smash" was a popular song on the minstrel stage before the middle of the nineteenth century. It is included in *The Negro Singer's Own Book* (Philadelphia, n. d.) and in Lloyd's *Ethiopian Song Book* (London, 1847). It has been twice before reported as a transformed folk song: in H. M. Belden's *A Partial List of Song Ballads and Other Popular Poetry Known in Missouri*, No. 59; and in J. H. Cox's *Folk-Songs of the South*. No. 177. But neither of these versions is as complete as the one reported here by Miss Beazley, nor has any folk tune, so far as I know, been heretofore recorded.—L. W. Payne, Jr.

   Nearly a generation ago, before the advent of motor-cars and motor-boats, I heard some sailors on the Texas coast singing "Davy Crockett". They were old time sailor men, and the ruggedness of the meter of the song in nowise hampered their gusto in singing it. For the music of the song I am indebted to Mrs. Tom C. Rowe, of Houston, who transcribed it, and to Mrs. Melton, who sang it. The words as sung by Mrs. Melton are slightly different from those originally learned by me, but the meter is the same.—J. B.

27. *From Twenty-Five Cents Worth of Nonsense; or The Treasure Box of Unconsidered Trifles* Philadelphia New York, and Boston: Fisher & Brothers. [184– ?]

28. From *Mince Pie for the Million*. Philadelphia and New York: Turner & Fisher. 1846.

29. *Ibid.*

30. *Ibid.*

31. From *David Crockett, American Comic Legend*, selected and edited by Richard M. Dorson, pp. 16–17. Copyright, 1939, by Rockland Editions. New York. Reprinted from the 1854 Crockett Almanac (New York, Cozans).

32. From "The Disgraced Scalp-Lock, or, Incidents on the Western Waters", in *The Mysteries of the Backwoods, or, Sketches of the Southwest: including Character, Scenery, and Rural Sports*, by T.B. Thorpe, pp. 119–136. Philadelphia: Carey & Hart. 1846. Also published as "The Flat-boatmen of the West . . . " in *Cincinnati Miscellany, or Antiquities of the West:* and Pioneer History and General and Local Statistics, Compiled from the Western General Advertiser, from April 1, 1845 to April 1, 1846, by Charles Cist, Vol. II, pp. 332–334, 342–344. Cincinnati: Robinson & Jones. 1846.

33. From *The Drama in Pokerville; The Bench and Bar of Jurytown, and Other Stories*, by "Everpoint" (J. M. Field, Esq., of the *St. Louis Reveille*), pp. 177–183. Philadelphia: Carey and Hart. 1847. Reprinted from the *St. Louis Reveille*, October, 21, 1844.
34. *St. Louis Reveille.*.—J. M. F
35. *From Sketches and Eccentricities of Col. David Crockett, of West Tennessee*, p. 164. New York: Printed and Published by J. & J. Harper. 1833.
36. From *Mike Fink, King of Mississippi Keelboatmen*, by Walter Blair and Franklin J. Meine, pp. 105–106. Copyright, 1933, by Henry Holt & Company, Inc. New York.
37. From *Cowboy Songs and Other Frontier Ballads*, collected by John A. Lomax and Alan Lomax, pp. 135-136. Revised and Enlarged. Copyright, 1910, 1916, 1938, by The Macmillan Company 1938 by John A. Lomax. New York.
    Cf.:
    Raised in a canebrake and suckled by a lion,
    Head like a bombshell and teeth made out of iron;
    Nine rows of jaw teeth and holes punched for more.
    I come from ourang-a-tang where the bullfrogs jump
    from north to south.
    —*Cowboy Songs and Other Frontier Ballads*, collected by John A. Lomax and Alan Lomax, p. 63.
38. From *American Ballads and Folk Songs*, collected and compiled by John A. Lomax and Alan Lomax; pp. 382–383. Copyright, 1934, by The Macmillan Company. New York.
39. From *American Ballads and Folk Songs*, collected and compiled by John A. Lomax and Alan Lomax, pp. 381–382. Copyright, 1934, by The Macmillan Company. New York.
40. As told by Walter R. Smith, St. Louis, Oklahoma. From "Tall Talk and Tall Tales of the Southwest", by B. A. Botkin, *The New Mexico Candle*, New Mexico Normal University, Las Vegas, New Mexico, June 28, 1933.
41. By Onah L. Spencer. From *Direction*, Vol. IV (Summer, 1941), No. 5, pp. 14–17. Copyright, 1941, by Direction, Inc.
    Edna Ferber named a steamboat in *Showboat* after Stackalee. I am also told that policy players in American Black Bottoms highly prize luck charms bearing his name, that such charms, or (in Black Bottom vernacular) mojoes, sell from one dollar up.—O. L. S.
42. Cf. "Po' Laz'us" in Part Six.
43. Cf. "The Farmer's Curst Wife" (Child, No. 278).
44. From *Vinegarroon*, The Saga of Judge Roy Bean, "Law West of the Pecos", by Ruel McDaniel pp. 83–89. Copyright, 1936, by Ruel McDaniel. Kingsport, Tenn.: Southern Publishers.
45. This rhetorical or mock-rhetorical address to a condemned prisoner has been attributed to other Western jurists, notably, Judge Parker ("The Hanging Judge") of Fort Smith and Judge Benedict of Santa Fe.
46. From copyright deposit typescript in the Library of Congress, dated June 1, 1885. Entered according to Act of Congress, by W. P. Cody, at Washington, D.C., on the 22nd Day of December, 1883. All Rights Reserved.
47. By Acel Garland. From *Foller de Drinkin' Gou'd*, Publications of the Texas Folk-Lore Society Number VII, edited by J. Frank Dobie, pp. 55–61. Copyright, 1928, by the Texas Folk-Lore Society. Austin.
48. The reader may take his choice of spellings: "tower" or "tour". The word is

pronounced "tower", and means a shift of men. The drilling crews work in two towers of twelve hours each, from twelve o'clock to twelve. The tower that goes on at midnight is the "graveyard tower", the one that goes on at noon is the "gravy tower".—A. G.

49. From *Erie Railroad Magazine*. Vol. 24 (April, 1928), No. 2, pp. 13, 44.
50. From *Erie Railroad Magazine*, Vol. 28 (April, 1932), No. 3, pp. 12, 46.
51. *Erie Railroad Magazine*, Vol. 28 (April 1932), No. 2, p. 12. The present text (*ibid.*, Vol. 24 April, 1928, No. 2, p. 12), like the tune, is traditional, differing from the popular song version principally in the absence of the chorus. Copyright 1909 by Newton & Seibert. Copyright renewed. By permission of Shapiro, Bernstein & Co., Inc.
52. By Owen Francis. From *Scribner's Magazine*, Vol. XC (November, 1931), No. 5, pp. 505–511. Copyright, 1931, by Charles Scribner's Sons.
53. From *Popeye starring in Choose Your Weppins*. A creation of E. C. Segar. Adaptation by Charles T. Clinton from the Max Fleischer Cartoon. A Paramount Picture. Copyright, 1935, 1936, by King Features Syndicate, Inc., New York. Akron, Ohio, and New York: The Saalfield Publishing Company.
54. By W. D. Haley. From *Harper's New Monthly Magazine*, Vol. XLIII (November, 1871), No. CCLVIII, pp. 830–836.
55. Cf. "The Histrionic West," by Stanley Vestal, *Space*, Vol. 1 (June, 1934), No. 2, pp. 13–16.
56. Mr. Cathcart, of Indiana, in the House of Representatives, February 6, 1846. Cited by Thornton in *An American Glossary* (1912), Vol. II, p. 985.
57. Cf. the similar nicknames of cities: The City Beautiful, the City of Magic, the City of Opportunities, the City of Prosperity, the Crown City, the Queen City.
58. *A Dictionary of American English on Historical Principles*, edited by Sir William A. Craigie and James R. Hulbert, Vol. II (1940), p. 646.

   The idea of a country "under God's care" or "that God remembers" is encountered frequently in the West, especially in the language of boosters: "Colorado is a land whereon the Creator has stamped his eternal monogram" (the Colorado Association), "Out in Arizona where God is all the time" (the Hon. David Kincheloe, of Kentucky, in the *Congressional Record*). See "Rocky Mountain Metaphysics", by Thomas Horneby Ferril, *Folk-Say, A Regional Miscellany: 1930*, edited by B. A. Botkin, pp. 305–316.
59. "Kentucky", *The Southern Guide*, Vol. I (January, 1878), No. 1, p. 59.
60. *The Resources and Attractions of Colorado for the Home Seeker, Capitalist and Tourist* (Union Pacific Railway, Omaha, 1888), pp. 61–62.
61. *California for the Settler*, by Andrew Jackson Wells (Southern Pacific Company, San Francisco, 1915), p. 62.
62. See *The Facts of Life in Popular Song* (1934), by Sigmund Spaeth.
63. "I saw a cowboy in California once who was a hundred if he was a day. It's astonishing how old these greasers get to be. I have travelled a great deal in Mexico, and it don't occur to me just now where I ever saw a graveyard. There's the Tombstone district in Arizona, and I know there isn't a tombstone in it. The people just dry up and blow away, and maybe you think it don't blow down there sometimes." . . . *Ten Wise Men and Some More*, by William Lightfoot Visscher (1909), p. 89.
64. Told by B. A. Trussell, of Miami, Florida, in *Tall Stories*, by Lowell Thomas (1931), pp. 236–237.
65. *Tall Stories*, by Lowell Thomas (1931), pp. 212–235.
66. *North America*, by J. Trussell Smith and M. Ogden Phillips (1942), p. 349.

67. *Thomas W. Jackson with all the "Funny Ones"*, by Thomas W. Jackson (1938, p. 79.

68. *Report of the Commissioner of Patents for the Year* 1851, Part II, Agriculture (1852), pp. 3–7.

69. Although the author of this anonymous satire on land frauds maintains that "never could there be experienced just such another confounded take-in" Major Wilkey's misfortunes in "Edensburgh" may have furnished suggestions to Dickens (even to the name of the place) for the somewhat similar experiences of Martin Ghuzzlewit in the city of "Eden", published four years later.

70. *The Grapes of Wrath*, by John Steinbeck (1939), p. 257.

71. *Pioneer Life in Nebraska*, Pamphlet One, *We Settled the Plains*, Series One, compiled by Workers of the WPA Writers Programme of the Work Projects Administration in the State of Nebraska (Oct. 1941), p. 3.

72. "Legends of Febold Feboldson", by Paul R. Beath, in *Nebraska Folklore Pamphlets*, Number Eight, p. 7. Lincoln: Federal Writers' Project in Nebraska. Sept. 15, 1937.

73. For the proverbial aspects of local witticisms—the French *blason populaire* and the German *ortsneckereien*—see *The Proverb*, by Archer Taylor (1931), pp. 97-105.

74. *Beyond the Mississippi: From the Great River to the Great Ocean*, Life and Adventure on the Prairies, Mountains, and Pacific Coast.... 1857–1867, by Albert D. Richardson (1867), p. 132.

"Puke" has also been interpreted as a corruption of "Pike", from Pike County Missouri. The Pike County dialect—a generalized South-western speech (largely "low colloquial") made popular by the writings of John Hay and Bret Harte—is identified with the "poor white" character described by Bayard Taylor: "A pike in the California dialect is a native of Missouri, Arkansas, Northern Texas, or Southern Illinois. The first emigrants that came over the plains were men from Pike County, Missouri, but the phrase, 'Pike County Man'.... was soon abbreviated into 'A Pike'. He is the Anglo-Saxon relapsed into semi-barbarism. He is long, lathy, and sallow; he expectorates vehemently; he takes naturally to whisky, he has 'the shakes' his life long at home, though he generally manages to get rid of them in California, he has little respect for the rights of others he distrusts man in 'store clothes', but venerates the memory of Andrew Jackson."

For a full-length portrait of "squatter types", see *Mark Twain's America*, by Bernard DeVoto (1932), pp. 54–62.

75. See Part Four.

76. *The Great Plains* (1931), p. 9.

77. For a discussion of the cycle, see "Hell in Texas" by George E. Hastings, *Southwestern Lore* (Publications of the Texas Folk-Lore Society, Number IX, 1931), edited by J. Frank Dobie, pp. 175–182. For a Texas-Mexican legend on a similar theme, see "The Devil on the Border", by Jovita Gonzáles, Publications of the Texas Folk-Lore Society, Number VIII, 1930, pp. 106–109.

78. *The Truth about Arkansas*, by William H. Edmonds (1895), pp. 6, 15

For an exhaustive investigation of the "comic notoriety" of Arkansas, see *Tall Tales of Arkansaw*, by James R. Masterson (1943).

79. For discussions of Hall, see *Arizona, A State Guide*, compiled by Workers of the Writers' Programme of the Work Projects Administration in the State of Arizona (1940) and *Desert Country*, by Edwin Corle (1941).

80. Cf. "Whimsical Dialogue between an Irish Innkeeper and an Englishman", *Wit and Wisdom Or The World's Jest-Book* . . . (London Thomas Allman . . . 1853),

pp. 28–29; "A Musical Tennessee Landlord", by "Dresbach", *Spirit of the Times*, XVI (February 13, 1847), p. 603.

81. See "The Inquisitive Yankee Descendants in Arkansas", by Walter Blair, *American Speech*, XIV (February, 1939), 11–22, where Blair points out that whereas in the East the native is usually the questioner and the traveller the questioned, the roles have been reversed in the West, *The Arkansas Traveller* being a case in point. Cf. " 'Old Sense' of Arkansas", Part Three.

82. Cf. *The Southern Poor-White from Lubberland to Tobacco Road*, by Shields McIlwaine (1939).

83. See *The Arkansas Traveller*, by Thomas Wilson (1900).

84. *The Arkansas Traveller's Songster, Containing the Celebrated Story of the Arkansas Traveller with the Music for Violin or Piano, and Also an Extensive and Choice Collection of New and Popular Comic and Sentimental Songs* (New York: Dick & Fitzgerald, copyright 1863), which reprints, on pages 5–9, the Blodgen & Bradford version (Buffalo, ca. 1850) ascribed to Mose Case. Of the several newspapers of this name (see F. W. Allsopp's *History of the Arkansas Press*, 1922), the most famous is that founded and edited by the Arkansas humorist, Opie Read. The first weekly issue (June 6 1882) reprinted Faulkner's *Arkansas Traveller*, together with the tune and the two Washbourne paintings.

85. *The Arkansas Traveller and Rackinsac Waltz*, arranged by William Cumming (Louisville: Peters & Webster, Cincinnati: Peters & Field, copyright, 1847).

The authorship of the tune has been assigned variously to Sandford C. Faulkner of Little Rock, Joseph Tasso of Cincinnati, and Mose Case of Buffalo, who, together with Edward P. Washbourne, claim the authorship of the dialogue. For an account of these disputed and unsettled claims see James R. Masterson, *Tall Tales of Arkansas* (1943), pp. 220–232; and for the several versions, *ibid*, pp. 186–219; also Catherine Marshall Vineyard, 'The Arkansas Traveller", *Backwoods to Border*, edited by Mody C. Boatright and Donald Day, Texas Folk-Lore Society Publications No. XVIII (1943), pp. 11–60.

86. For a discussion of "slow train" humour, see James R. Masterson, *op. cit.*, pp. 269–280.

87. From *Westward Ho!* by James K. Paulding (1837).

88. From *Mike Fink: A Legend of the Ohio*, by Emerson Bennett (1848).

89. From "Fight with a Puke", in *Mince Pie for the Million.*

90. See "Speech of Colonel Crockett in Congress."

91. From *Col. Crockett's Exploits and Adventures in Texas*, Written by Himself (1836), p. 129.

92. From Paulding's *Westward Ho!*

93. From Bird's *Nick of the Woods.*

94. From *Travels on an Inland Voyage*, by Christian Schulz, Jr., Volume II, pp. 145–146. New York: Printed by Isaac Riley. 1810.

95. ". . . . 'specimen of eloquence' from an authentic speech made by General Buncombe, in the House of Representatives, in the days of 'Fifty-four Forty or Fight'," *Knickerbocker Magazine*, XLVI (August, 1855), No. 2, p. 212. New York: Samuel Hueston.

96. From "Speech of Hon. S. C. Pomeroy, of Kansas, on the Homestead Bill", delivered in the Senate of the United States, May 5, 1862.

97. From an advertisement of C. F. Simmons, San Antonio, Texas, "How to Secure a River Farm and Home in Town for $120", in *Bob Taylor's Magazine*, November, 1906. Copyright, 1906, by the Taylor Publishing Company. Nashville, Tennessee.

98. From *Going to God's Country*, by Martha L. Smith, with an introduction by Dr. Clara B. Krefting. Copyright, 1941, by the Christopher Publishing House. Boston.

99. From *Iowa: The Home for Immigrants*, prepared by Secretary A. R. Fulton of the Iowa Board of Immigration, in 1870. Cited in *The Palimpsest*. XVIII (July 1937), pp. 226–242.

100. From *The Iowa Handbook for* 1857, by Nathan H. Parker. Boston: J. P. Jewett and Company.

101. From *The American Songbag*, by Carl Sandburg, pp. 278–279. Copyright, 1927, by Harcourt, Brace and Company, Inc. New York.

102. The phrase "out of sight" in the late 1880's was slang indicating excellence or superfine quality—C. S.

103. Moses P. Kinkaid, Congressman from the Sixth District; 1903–1919, introduced a bill for 640-acre homesteads and was hailed as a benefactor of the sand hill region.—C. S.

104. From *Cowboy Songs and Other Frontier Ballads*, collected by John A. Lomax and Alan Lomax, Revised and Enlarged, pp. 424–426. Copyright, 1910, 1916, 1938, by The Macmillan Company. Copyright, 1938, by John A. Lomax.

   Oscar J. Fox, San Antonio, Texas, published an arrangement of this song after it had remained unnoticed for many years in *Cowboy Songs*. For a time "Home on the Range" was the most popular song on the air. A suit for a half-million dollars was brought on copyright—probably the largest sum ever asked for one song. A Negro saloon keeper in San Antonio gave me the music to "Home on the Range" as herein reprinted. The words were also identical with the version of *Cowboy Songs*, 1910. They were assembled from several sources and have since often been pirated.—J. A. L. and A. L.

105. From *Struggles and Triumphs: or The Life of P. T. Barnum*, Written by Himself edited with an introduction, by George S. Bryan, Volume I, pp. 168–169. Copyright, 1927, by Alfred A. Knopf, Inc. New York and London.

   Cf. Barnum's account of Hawley: "We reached Montgomery Ala., February 28th, 1837. Here we met a legerdemain performer by the name of Henry Hawley. He was about forty-five years of age, but being prematurely grey, he had the appearance of a venerable gentleman of seventy. He purchased one half of my exhibition. . . .

   "After the performances in country places, Hawley usually sat in the village bar-room, and a knot of astonished and credulous persons would gather about him. They were also attracted by the marvellous stories in which he indulged. His grey head, grave countenance, and serious manner, carried conviction in the more probable narratives—the barely possible were swallowed, though with occasional signs of choking—but when he enlarged in his Munchausen vein, some of his auditors would forget his venerable presence, and cry out, 'That's a lie, by thunder!' Hawley would laugh heartily and reply, 'It is as true as anything I have yet told you.'

   "He had a singularly lively imagination, and his inventive faculty regarded neither rhyme nor reason. Had he lived in the times of the Arabian Nights' Entertainments, he would have been celebrated, as I think a few specimens of his bar-room stories will show." Op. cit., pp. 163, 165.

106. From *Forty-Niners, the Chronicle of the California Trail*, by Archer Butler Hulbert, pp. 20–21. Copyright, 1931, by Archer Butler Hulbert. Boston: Little, Brown & Company.

107. This tale, although oft repeated by Forty-Niners, was originally published by E. Bryant in 1848. Is it not the first California "booster" story?—A. B. H.

108. From *A Kansas Farm, or the Promised Land*, by Fannie McCormick, pp. 76–79. Copyright, 1891, by Fannie McCormick. New York: John B. Alden, Publisher.
109. From *Short Grass Country*, by Stanley Vestal, pp. 205–206, 208. *American Folkways*, edited by Erskine Caldwell, Copyright, 1941, by Stanley Vestal. New York: Duell, Sloan & Pearce.
110. From *The American Songbag*, by Carl Sandburg, p. 280. Copyright, 1927, by Harcourt, Brace & Company. New York. As "Nebraska Land" this is sung to "Maryland, My Maryland" or "Sweet Genevieve".
111. From *The American Songbag*, by Carl Sandburg, pp. 120–122. Tune: "The Irish Washerwoman". From *Folk-Dance Music*, selected and compiled by Elizabeth Burchenal and C. Ward Crampton (n.d.), p. 22.
112. From *Folk Music of the United States*, Album VII, edited by B. A. Botkin. Washington, D. C.: Archive of American Folk Song, Library of Congress. 1943. Sung by I. F. Greer, Thomasville N. C. Recorded by Fletcher Collins. Transcribed by Charles Seeger.
113. From *Put's Golden Songster*, Containing the Largest and Most Popular Collection of California Songs Ever Published, by the Author of "Put's Original California Songster", pp. 63–64. Entered according to Act of Congress, in the year 1858, by John A. Stone, in the Clerk's Office of the District Court of the United States for the Northern District of California. San Francisco: D. E. Appleton & Co.
114. From *Our Southern Highlanders*, by Horace Kephart, pp. 301, 302, 304. Copyright, 1913, by Outing Publishing Company, and 1922, by the Macmillan Company.
115. From *Dictionary of Americanisms*, by John Russell Bartlett, pp. 180–181. New York: Bartlett and Welford, 1848.
116. From *Americanisms; The English of the New World*, by M. Schele de Vere, p. 659. Copyright, 1871, by Charles Scribner & Co., New York.
117. From *Dictionary of Americanisms*, by John Russell Bartlett, p. 343. New York: Bartlett and Welford, 1848.
118. From *An Account of Col. Crockett's Tour to the North and Down East* . . . Written by Himself, p. go. Philadelphia: E. L. Carey and A. Hart. 1835.
119. From "Vive la Bagatelle!" in *The Southern Literary Messenger*, Vol. VI (June, 1840), No. 6, p. 416.
120. From *Yankee Notions, or The American Joe Miller*, by Sam Slick, Junr., p. 47. London: Ball, Arnold & Co., Edinburgh Fraser and Crawford; Glasgow: John Robertson. 1839.
121. From *The Great Plains*, by Walter Prescott Webb, pp. 22, 320. Copyright, 1931, by Walter Prescott Webb. Boston: Ginn and Company.
122. That is, climb the windmill tower to turn the wheel by hand, and dig mesquite roots.—W. P. W.
     Cf. T. Frank Dobie, *The Flavor of Texas* (1936), p. 15: "Texas is where 'a man has to dig (mesquite roots) for wood and climb (go up gravely canyons) for water'."
123. Opening stanza of a poem written by Leona Mae Austin, a fourteen-year-old high-school girl, who had lived in Childress, Texas. From *Cowboy Songs and Other Frontier Ballads*, collected by John A. Lomax and Alan Lomax, pp. 413–414. Revised and Enlarged. Copyright, 1910, 1916, 1938, by The Macmillan Company; 1938, by John A. Lomax.
     Cf. J. Frank Dobie, *The Flavor of Texas*, p. 15: "Texas has more rivers and less water, more climate and less rain, more earth and less dirt, more cows and

less milk, more preachers and less religion, more hot days and more cold nights, etc.—than any other place on earth."

124. From *Salome Sun*, Vol. I, Nos. 2 and 4, February and April, 1921. Dick Wick Hall, Editor and Miner. Salome, Arizona.

125. From *The Arkansas Traveller*, B. S. Alford, Photographer, Little Rock, Arkansas. Entered according to Act of Congress, in the Year 1876, by B. S. ALFORD, LITTLE ROCK, ARK., in the Office of the Librarian of Congress, Washington, D. C.

COL. SANDY FAULKNER, the original "Arkansaw Traveller", was born in Georgetown, Scott county Kentucky, March 3, 1803. He came to Arkansas in 1829, and settled in Chicot county on the Mississippi river, as a cotton planter. In 1839, Col. Faulkner (with his father, the late Nicholas Faulkner, a Virginian by birth) took up his residence in Little Rock where he died August 4, 1874, at the age of seventy-one years.

It is well known throughout the Northwest that Col. Faulkner was the original personator of the "Arkansaw Traveller"; it was his pride to be known as such. The story, it is said, was founded on a little incident which occurred in the campaign of 1840, when he made the tour of the state in company with the Hon. A. H. Sevier, Gov. Fulton, Chester Ashley and Gov. Yell. One day in the Boston mountains, the party approached a squatter's for information of the route, and Col. "Sandy" was made spokesman of the company, and it was upon his witty responses the tune and story were founded. On return to Little Rock, a grand banquet was given in the famous "bar room" which used to stand near the Anthony house, and Col. "Sandy" was called upon to play the tune and tell the story. Afterward it grew into popularity. When he subsequently went to New Orleans, the fame of the "Arkansas Traveller" had gone ahead of him, and at a banquet, amid clinking glasses and brilliant toasts, he was handed a violin by the then governor of Louisiana, and requested to favour them with the favourite Arkansas tune. At the old St. Charles hotel a special room was devoted to his use, bearing in gilt letters over the door, Arkansas Traveller.—B. S. A.

According to James R. Masterson, in *Tall Tales of Arkansas* (1943), p. 359, the Alford version, "in all except a few phrases, is identical with that dated between 1858 and 1860 [now unavailable]. Colonel Faulkner's connection with the earlier version we do not know. He may have given Washbourne a manuscript; he may have dictated to him; or Washbourne may have written down the dialogue from memory after hearing it recited (whether by Faulkner or by someone else). We do know that Colonel Faulkner was popularly regarded as the composer of the dialogue, and hence we can hardly doubt that he would have obtained a copy of the early printed version, even if Washbourne had published without his permission. In this copy he doubtless made marginal changes, or he may have embodied the changes in a separate manuscript, prepared with the printed copy before him. From one source or the other, we may presume, the version of 1876 was published".

126. Sassafras tea.

127. From *Folklore of Romantic Arkansas*, by Fred W. Allsopp, Volume II, pp. 87–90. Copyright, 1931, by the Grolier Society.

128. There is a tradition that away back yonder—about the time when the Arkansaw Traveller story came into being—it was proposed to change the name of Arkansas by legislative enactment. Some say the question was actually introduced at a session of the Legislature, and that a member delivered a fiery speech on the subject "Change the name of Arkansas? Hell, No!" he is supposed to have

declared. The writer has been requested many times for a copy of that speech. Investigation fails to reveal any official record of such a deliverance, but it seems certain that there was some discussion of the matter, in or out of halls of state, and the speech may have been delivered sub rosa at a committee meeting, or, more likely, in a bar-room. It has frequently been referred to at banquets and on other convivial occasions, always being described as a wickedly lurid gem. As often rehearsed by George Williams, a member of the Arkansas Legislature from Pulaski County, some 25 years ago, it went something like this barring its unprintable profanity and obscenity—F. W. A.

129. Here is another version of what is supposed to have been the speech, delivered by Cassius M. Johnson, as printed in a pamphlet at Cleveland, Ohio. Printed by J. H. Philips, Cleveland, Ohio, no date.—F. W. A.

130. See *Thomas Chandler Haliburton*, by V. L. O. Chittick (1924).

131. *Here We Are Again*, by Robert Edmund Sherwood (1926), p. 191.

132. In addition to such April Fool stunts as tying a string to a pocketbook left lying on the sidewalk and jerking it away from the victim who tries to pick it up, there are such time-honoured gags as telephoning the zoo to ask for Mr. Wolf or Mr. Fox.

133. According to G. W. Orians, *Peck's Bad Boy* was inspired by Thomas Bailey Aldrich's *The Story of a Bad Boy*. It will be observed, however, that Tom Bailey was a "good bad boy".

134. See the stories of Ring Lardner, George Milburn, and Erskine Caldwell.

135. *A Song of the Pipeline*, by Daniel M. Garrison, *Folk-Say, A Regional Miscellany:* 1930, edited by B. A. Botkin, p. 110. See "Mirages" Part Four.

136. *Abraham Lincoln, The Prairie Years*, by Carl Sandburg (1926), Vol. II, p. 81.

137. See "Tricks and Catches", Part Six.

138. "Range Lore", by W. W. Adney, San Angelo, Texas. Manuscripts of Federal Writers' Project for the Works Progress Administration in the State of Texas.

139. *The Cowboy*, by Philip Ashton Rollins (1922), p. 184. For an example of a conversational sell, "in the way of a string of plausibly worded sentences that didn't mean anything under the sun", see "First Interview with Artemus Ward", in *Mark Twain's Sketches New and Old*, pp. 283–286.

140. *Hoaxes*, by Curtis D. MacDougall (1940), p. vi. Among the folkloric hoaxes treated by MacDougall are mythical monsters (the hodak), historical myths (Parson Weems' cherry tree myth) tall stories and legendary heroes (Johnny Appleseed).

141. The backwoods Lincoln has often been compared to Davy Crockett as a stump-speech storyteller. With Crockett, however, as has been pointed out above, the funny story was, like the treat chiefly a vote-getting expedient.

142. For a classification of "fool" motifs, see *Motif-Index of Folk-Literature*, by Stith Thompson, under "The Wise and the Foolish".

143. "High John de Conquer", by Zora Neale Hurston, *The American Mercury*, Vol. LVII (October, 1943), No. 238, pp. 450–458.

144. By Cornelia Chambers. From *Straight Texas*, Publications of the Texas Folk-Lore Society Number XIII, 1937, edited by J. Frank Dobie and Mody C. Boatright, pp. 106–110. Copyright 1937, by the Texas Folk-Lore Society. Austin.

145. From *The Hell-Roarin' Forty-Niners*, by Robert Welles Ritchie, pp. 233–237. Copyright 1928, by J. H. Sears & Co., Incorporated. New York.

146. From "Anecdotes from the Brazos Bottoms", by A. W. Eddins, *Straight Texas*, Publications of the Texas Folk-Lore Society, Number XIII, 1937, edited by J. Frank Dobie and Mody C Boatright, p. 94. Copyright, 1937, by the Texas Folk-Lore Society. Austin.

147. *Ibid.*, pp. 88–89.
148. *Ibid.*, p. 90.
149. *Ibid.*, p. 98.
150. *Ibid,*. p. 98.
151. *Ibid.*, p 99–100.
152. From *Backwoods America*, by Charles Morrow Wilson, pp. 15–26. Copyright, 1934, by the University of North Carolina Press. Chapel Hill.
153. From *Uncle Remus and His Friends, Old Plantation Stories, Songs, and Ballads with Sketches of Negro Character*, by Joel Chandler Harris, pp. 147–153. Copyright, 1892, by Joel Chandler Harris Boston and New York: Houghton, Mifflin and Company.
154. From *Mules and Men*, by Zora Neale Hurston, pp. 217–218. Copyright, 1935, by Zora Neale Hurston. Philadelphia and London: J. B. Lippincott Company.
155. Panting.—Z. N. H.
156. From *Nigger to Nigger*, by E. C. L. Adams, pp. 136–138. Copyright, 1928, by Charles Scribner's Sons.
157. From *Mules and Men*, by Zora Neale Hurston, pp. 96–99. Copyright, 1935, by Zora Neale Hurston. Philadelphia and London: J. B. Lippincott Company.
158. *Ibid.*, pp. 117–119.
159. *Ibid*, pp. 111–112.
160. *Ibid.*, pp. 100–101.
161. From *Nigger to Nigger*, by E. C. L. Adams, pp. 223–224. Copyright, 1928, by Charles Scribner's Sons. New York.
162. From "Little Moron' Stories", by Ernest W. Baughman, *Hoosier Folklore Bulletin*, edited by Herbert Halpert, Vol. II (June, 1943), No. I, pp. 17–18.

These stories were heard by my sister, Ruth Baughman, from students on the campus of Ball State Teachers College, Muncie, Indiana, during the past year. Since then I have heard them in many localities. Such jokes seem to circulate orally among city people, office workers and college people in particular. Most of these stories would probably be classified by Professor Stith Thompson in his Motif-Index under *Absurd Misunderstandings*. Some of the people I have heard seem to make a speciality of telling stories of this type which depend on gestures for their effectiveness. I have not included any of this type.—E. W. B.

Cf. *Little Moron*, by Abbott ("Heck") Hoecker and Clydene ("Ilda") Oliver (1943).
163. From "The Demise of the Little Moron", by Rudolph Umland, *Esquire*, The Magazine for Men, Vol. XX (September, 1943), No. 3, pp. 32–33, 154–155. Copyright, 1943, by Esquire, Inc.
164. From *Yankee Notions; or The American Joe Miller*, by Sam Slick, Junr., p. 20, 28, 33, 39. London: Ball, Arnold & Co. Edinburgh: Fraser and Crawford. Glasgow; John Robertson. 1889.
165. From *Mules and Men*, by Zora Neale Hurston, p. 47. Copyright, 1935, by Zora Neale Hurston. Philadelphia and London: J. B. Lippincott Company.
166. *Ibid.*, p. 94.
167. "Blue Baby" was so black he looked blue.—Z. N. H.
168. From *Mules and Men*, by Zora Neale Hurston, pp. 95–96. Copyright, 1935, by Zora Neale Hurston. Philadelphia and London: J. B. Lippincott Company.
169. From *Idaho Lore*, prepared by the Federal Writers' Project of the Work Projects Administration, Vardis Fisher, State Director, American Guide Series, pp. 119–120, 132. Copyright, 1939, by George H. Curtis, Secretary of State for the State of Idaho. Caldwell, Idaho: The Caxton Printers Ltd.

170. From *I Blew in from Arkansaw,* A Trip of Fun through Hoosierdom, by Geo. D. Beason, pp. 48–49. Copyright, 1908, by Geo. D. Beason. Chicago: Geo. D. Beason Publisher.

171. From *Library of Wit and Humour by Mark Twain and Others, with the Philosophy of Wit and Humour,* by Melville D. Landon, A. M. (Eli Perkins), n. 98. Copyright, 1883, by L. W. Yaggy and, 1898, by Star Publishing Co. Chicago: Thompson and Thomas.

172. From *Choice Slang,* by High Jinks Junior [Harold Poe Swartwood], pp. 74–75. Copyright, 1915, by The Coronodo Company.

173. *Ibid.,* pp. 64–67.

174. *Ibid.,* pp. 105–106.

175. From *Stuff That Travels,* by William G. Bradshaw, pp. 37, 51. Copyright, 1921, by William G. Bradshaw. Saratoga Springs, New York.

176. From *Laughter for the Millions,* The Drollest Wit, The Funniest Gags, The Gayest Laughs, The Merriest Humour, The Greatest Hilarity, edited by Louis Shomer, p. 117. Copyright, 1935, by Louis Shomer. New York: Louellen Publishing Co.

177. From *Knock Knock,* Featuring Enoch Knox, by Bob Dunn. Copyright, 1936, by Whitman Publishing Co., Racine, Wisconsin. Published by Dell Publishing Company, Inc., New York.

178. From *Small Town Humour,* by Robert Peery, Little Blue Book No. 1397, edited by E. Haldeman-Julius, pp. 7–8. Copyright, 1929 by Haldeman-Julius Company, Girard, Kansas.

179. From "Phrases of the People", recorded by Harris Dickson, Vicksburg, Mississippi, in *American Stuff,* An Anthology of Prose and Verse by Members of the Federal Writers Project, pp. 149–152. Copyright, 1937, by The Guilds' Committee for Federal Writers' Publications, Inc. The Viking Press. New York.

180. *Humour of the Old Deep South,* by Arthur Palmer Hudson (1936), pp. 16–17.

181. *The Complete Works of Charles P. Browne,* better known as "Artemus Ward", (London: John Camden Hotten), pp. 316–317.

182. "South-western Slang," by Socrates Hyacinth, *The Overland Monthly,* Vol. III (August, 1869), p. 125.

183. "An eastern visitor once wrote in a bread-and-butter letter to a Roundup newspaper editor: 'Out there every prairie dog hole is a gold mine; every hill a mountain; every creek a river; and everybody you meet is a liar'."—*Montana, A State Guide Book* (1939), p. 258.

184. The "deacon's seat" was the lumberjack's name for the place on the "liars' bench" occupied successfully by the bunkhouse story-tellers at the evening session of yarning. See *The Hodag, and Other Tales of the Logging Camps,* by Lake Shore Kearney (Wausau, Wisconsin, 1928).

185. *Hoosier Tall Stories* (Federal Writers' Project in Indiana, 1937), pp. 1–2.

186. The *Sazerac Lying Club,* a Nevada Book, by Fred. W. Hart (Henry Keller & Co., San Francisco, 1878).

187. *Tall Stories,* the Rise and Triumph of the Great American Whopper, by Lowell Thomas (1931).

188. *The 25 Best Lies of 1933* (Burlington, Wisconsin, 1934), p. 1.

189. By Jack Conroy. From "Chicago Industrial Folklore". Manuscripts of the Federal Writers' Project of the Works Progress Administration for the State of Illinois.

190. *Ibid.* The demon bricksetter's place of residence varies with localities. For example, on a Missouri job he was represented as hailing from Harrison, Arkansas.—J. C.

191. That is, the nails bruised until they turn black or purple.—J. C.
192. By Jack Conroy. From "Chicago Industrial Folklore". Manuscripts of the Federal Writers' Project of the Works Progress Administration for the State of Illinois.
193. Five dollar bill.—J. C.
194. Rule forbidding excessive over time.—J. C.
195. By Jack Conroy. From "Chicago Industrial Folklore". Manuscripts of the Federal Writers' Project of the Works Progress Administration for the State of Illinois.

> I have no idea how general the legend of Slappy Hooper is among sign painters, since I have not encountered so very many of these craftsmen. There were quite a number of the incidents telling the results of Slappy's realism on billboards, and I have chosen only two representative ones.
> The attitude of the craftsman toward the helper is characteristic of most occupations.—J. C.

196. Slantwise, or crooked.—J. C.
197. Perforated outline or stencil for painters unable to do freehand work efficiently. Derived from the bag of chalk, or pounce, used to pat the stencil on to the billboard or sign. Sometimes the outline is transferred by blowing powdered chalk against the pounce.—J. C.
198. It is the pride of many independent craftsmen and boomers that they have never been chained to a job on "public works", i.e., in a large factory where a time clock is punched and the routine is deadening. To the freelancing artisans, going on "public works" is a fate worse than death.—J. C.
199. Boiling of clothing to kill body lice.—J. C.
200. Satchel, resembling a rigid suitcase, in which itinerant sign painters keep their work materials and often their clothing as well.—J. C.
201. From *Life in the Far West*, by George Frederic Ruxton, pp. 14–18. New York: Harper & Brothers 1949.
202. Among the few famous raconteurs of the genuine tall tale type of frontier adventure story to whom the North-west has some right to lay claim is one Moses ("Black" or "Major") Harris, who guided the Gilliam and Ford emigrants into Oregon in 1844, and is said to have conducted Marcus Whitman on his first journey into the same country. Harris also rendered valuable service in helping to discover a feasible trail across the Cascade mountains. In 1847 he trapped and fur-traded east to Missouri, in which section of the union he had originally begun his wanderings, and died there. It had been his intention to return west, to either Oregon or California. According to another account of his death he was shot for his traps and tobacco while on a hunting expedition in the Rockies.—V. L. O. Chittick, *The Frontier*, Vol. XII (January, 1932), Number 2, p. 173.
203. Meaning—if that's what you mean. The "stick" is tied to the beaver trap by a string, and, floating on the water, points out its position, should a beaver have carried it away.—G. F. R.
204. Scalped.—G. F. R.
205. Soles made of buffalo hide.—G. F. R.
206. From *Fisher's River (North Carolina) Scenes and Characters*, pp. 149–151, *by* "Skits" (H. F. Teliaferro). N.Y.: Harper & Bros. 1859.
207. From *Mules and Men*, by Zora Neale Hurston, pp. 135–136. Copyright, 1935, by Zora Neale Hurston. Philadelphia and London: J. B. Lippincott Company.
208. Stake.—Z. N. H
209. Commercial fertiliser.—Z. N. H.

210. From *Idaho Lore*, prepared by the Federal Writers' Project of the Work Projects Administration Vardis Fisher, State Director, American Guide Series, p. 139. Copyright, 1939, by George H. Curtis Secretary of State for the State of Idaho. Caldwell, Idaho: The Caxton Printers Ltd.

211. From *Mules and Men*, by Zora Neale Hurston, pp. 132–137, 149–151. Copyright, 1935, by Zora Neale Hurston. Philadelphia and London: J. B. Lippincott Company.

212. *Paul Bunyan Natural History*. Describing the Wild Animals, Birds, Reptiles and Fish of the Big Woods about Paul Bunyan's Old Time Logging Camps, Habitat and Habits of the Flitterick, Gumberoo, Hangdown, Hidebehind, Hodag, Luferlang, Rumptifusel, Sliver Cat, Shagamaw, Goofus Bird, Hoop Snake, Whirligig Fish and Others, by Charles Edward Brown. Madison, Wisconsin: C. E. Brown. 1935.

213. From *Fearsome Creatures of the Lumberwoods, With a Few Desert and Mountain Beasts*, by William T. Cox, pp. 27, 31, 37, 43, 45. Copyright, 1911, by William T. Cox. Washington, D.C.: Press of Judd & Detweiler, Inc., 1910.

214. *Rumours and Hoaxes, Classic Tales of Fraud and Deception*, collected and arranged with an introduction by Peter Haworth (1928), p. xviii.

215. "Mark Twain's Ghost Story", by E. P. Pabody, *Minnesota History*, Vol. 18 (March, 1937), No. 1, pp. 28–35.

216. From *Negro Tales from West Virginia*, by John Harrington Cox, *The Journal of American Folklore* Vol. XLVII (October-December, 1934), No. CLXXXVI, pp. 344-347.

     "The Rabbit That Wouldn't Help Dig A Well." Contributed by Miss Dora Lee Newman to a book, *Marion County in the Making*, Fairmont, Marion County, West Virginia, 1918. Privately printed. Learned from her father, who, in turn, learned it when a child from "our Old Sukey and black Canada. . . ."—J. H. C.

217. From "Brazos Bottom Philosophy", by A. W. Eddins, *Southwestern Lore*, Publications of the Texas Folk-Lore Society, Number IX, 1931, edited by J. Frank Dobie, pp. 153–156. Copyright 1931 by the Texas Folk-Lore Society. Dallas: The Southwest Press.

218. By A. W. Eddins. From *Publications of the Folk-Lore Society of Texas, No. I*, edited by Stith Thompson, pp. 47–49. Copyright, 1916, by the Folk-Lore Society of Texas. Austin.

219. From "Brazos Bottom Philosophy", by A. W. Eddins; Publications of the Texas Folk-Lore Society, No. II, 1923, edited by J. Frank Dobie, pp. 50–51. Copyright, 1923, by the Texas Folk-Lore Society. Austin.

220. From *Mules and Men*, by Zora Neale Hurston, pp. 153–154. Copyright, 1935, by Zora Neale Hurston. Philadelphia and London: J. B. Lippincott Company.

221. From *Negro Tales from West Virginia*, by John Harrington Cox, *The Journal of American Folk-Lore* Vol. XLVII (October-December, 1934), No. CLXXXVI, pp. 341–342. New York.

     Learned by the Editor from Mr. Richard Wyche, Honorary President of The Story-Tellers' League, Washington, D. C. Printed by his permission. A quite different version of this story is printed in Harris, *Uncle Remus Returns*, pp. 52–78.—J. H. C.

222. From Folk-Lore from Maryland, collected by Annie Weston Whitney and Caroline Canfield Bullock, Memoirs of the American Folk-Lore Society, Volume XVIII, 1925, p. 179. New York.

223. *Ibid.*, pp. 178–179.

224. By Mrs. M. E. M. Davis, New Orleans, La. From *The Journal of American*

Folk-Lore, Vol. XVIII (July-September, 1905), No. LXX, pp. 251–252. Copyright, 1905, by the American Folk-Lore Society. Boston and New York: Houghton, Mifflin & Company.

225. By Arthur Palmer Hudson and Pete Kyle McCarter. From *The Journal of American Folk-Lore*, Vol. XLVII (January-March, 1934), No. CLXXXIII, pp. 45–63.

The legend of the Bell Witch recounts the misfortunes of a family named Bell who moved from North Carolina to the midlands of Tennessee in the early 1800's and then, in one branch, to northern Mississippi, about forty years later. It is well known to oral tradition in the designated sections of the two latter states. The Tennessee versions of it have been made the subject of at least two obscurely published books. In 1894, at Clarksville, Tennessee, appeared M. V. Ingram's *An Authenticated History of the Famous Bell Witch. The Wonder of the 19th Century, and Unexplained Phenomenon of the Christian Era. The Mysterious Talking Goblin that Terrorized the West End of Robertson County, Tennessee, Tormenting John Bell to his Death. The Story of Betsy Bell, Her Lover and the Haunting Sphinx.* This book professes "to record events of historical fact, sustained by a powerful array of incontrovertible evidence. . . . The author only assumes to compile data, formally presenting the history of this greatest of all mysteries, just as the matter is furnished to hand, written by Williams Bell, a member of the family some fifty-six years ago, together with corroborative testimony by men and women of irreproachable character and unquestioned veracity". Ingram's book is now rare and hard to get. Drawing on much the same sources and telling much the same story is Harriett Parks Miller's *The Bell Witch of Middle Tennessee* (Clarksville, 1930). This pamphlet and letters from residents of Middle Tennessee attest the independent oral survival of the legend in that region. As late as 1910 it was still told, "under the most appropriate surroundings—country parties, hayrides, and fireside gatherings".

In northern Mississippi, where descendants of the original family concerned still live, the legend survives in somewhat fragmentary but independent, orally traditional form. Of the considerable number of people who told it, or parts of it, to us, a few said that they had seen "the book" (Ingram's) a long time ago, and most of the others had heard of the book, but we were unable to find a copy in Mississippi.

Our following version of the legend has been recovered exclusively from oral tradition in Mississippi, and was put together before we ever saw a printed version. Most of our sources know the main outlines but remember especially some particular episodes or motives. A few tell the whole substantially as we reproduce it. But there is great diversity in the details and motives. We have taken the main outline on which all agree and have sketched in, as consistently as possible, the minutiae from numerous Mississippi sources. The dialect used, the few simple figures of speech, and the folk locutions are genuine and are true to the speech of our informants.—A. P. H. and P. K. M.

226. From "Dyin' Easy", by Martha Emmons, *Tone the Bell Easy*, Publications of the Texas Folk-Lore Society, edited by J. Frank Dobie, Number X, p. 59. Copyright, 1932, by the Texas Folk-Lore Society. Austin.

Elmira Johnson, of Waco, Texas, who gave the story to me, is a bright, vivacious Negro woman of some fifty or sixty years. She has a slight tendency to lisp, and a pronounced tendency to see the humour of things—even in ghost tales. Though very active and fairly supple, Elmira scorns dancing because "it's sinful". But she admits that sometimes "de Lawd jes' gits in my feet". Such must have been the case the morning she sang for us the song which is at the close of this paper. For she danced and skipped as she sang of being "done crossed over".—M. E.

227. From *Mules and Men*, by Zora Neale Hurston, pp. 219–220. Copyright, 1935, by Zora Neale Hurston. Philadelphia and London: J. B. Lippincott Company.

228. *Ibid.*, pp. 207–208.

229. From *Folk-Lore from Maryland*, collected by Annie Weston Whitney and Caroline Canfield Bullock, Memoirs of the American Folk-Lore Society, Volume XVIII, 1925, pp. 181–183. New York.

230. From *Two Pennsylvania Mountain Legends*, collected by Henry W Shoemaker, pp. 2–11, Publications of The Pennsylvania Folk-Lore Society, Volume I, Number 4. Published by The Reading Eagle Press, Reading, Pa. 1928.

    This is a story that an old lady; Mrs. Elmira Atkinson, born in 1828, and still living in her cabin in the foothills of the Alleghenies, in Clinton County, told to this writer. . . . The first scene of the story takes place at the White Horse Tavern, in Somerset County.—H. W. S.

231. By L. D. Bertillion. From *Straight Texas,* Publications of the Texas Folk-Lore Society, Number XIII, edited by J. Frank Dobie and Mody C. Boatright, pp. 79–85. Copyright, 1937, by the Texas Folk-Lore Society.

232. *Studies in Jocular Literature*, by W. C. Hazlitt (1890), p. 26.

233. *English Folk Songs from the Southern Appalachians*, collected by Cecil J. Sharp, edited by Maud Karpeles (1932), Vol. I, 'Introduction to the First Edition, 1917'.

234. "Songs of the American Folk", *Modern Music*. Vol. XVIII (January-February, 1941), No. 2, p. 138.

235. *Our Singing Country*, collected and compiled by John A. Lomax and Alan Lomax (1941), p, xiii.

236. From "Songs of Innocence", by Dorothy Mills and Morris Bishop, *The New Yorker*, Vol. XII (November 13, 1937), No. 39, pp. 32–42. Copyright, 1937, by the F-R Publishing Corporation, New York City. Tunes transcribed by Charles Seeger.

237. Tune transcribed by Charles Seeger.

238. From *Games and Songs of American Children*, collected and compared by William Wells Newell pp. 227–229. Copyright, 1883, 1903, by Harper & Brothers, New York and London.

239. *Ibid.*, pp. 232–233.

240. From *American Anthology of Old-World Ballads*, compiled and edited by Reed Smith, settings by Hilton Rufty, pp. 32–34. Copyright, 1937, by J. Fischer & Brother. New York.

    Of all the ballads in America "Barbara Allen" has more texts, more tunes, and wider geographical spread than any other. It is found all over the United States. Virginia, alone, for example, affords ninety-two variant texts and a dozen tunes. Six different tunes have been recorded in New England. Its wide American prevalence is not entirely due to oral tradition, for it has appeared in many old song books, first in *The American Songster* issued at Baltimore in 1830 and repeated since.

    In. Great Britain it was first printed in Allan Ramsay's *Tea-Table Miscellany*, 1740, and next in Percy's *Reliques*, 1765.—R. S.

241. From *Vermont Folk-Songs and Ballads*, Edited by Helen Hartness Flanders and George Brown pp. 35–38. The Green Mountain Series. Copyright, 1932, by Arthur Wallace Peach as Trustee for Committee on Vermont Traditions and Ideals. Brattleboro: Stephen Daye Press.

"Young Charlotte" was written by Seba Smith, best known as the author of the *Jack Downing Letters*. It was published by him in *The Rover* (1884), II, 225. He tells us it was based on an actual event reported in the papers; we have found the record in the *New York Observer*, February 8, 1840. . . . Accordingly, the place of William Lorenzo Carter, the blind Homer of Benson, Vermont, in the composition and diffusion of this ballad must now be reinvestigated. . . . The frequent occurrence of the ballad in the vicinity of early Mormon settlements in the West, where he is known to have been since he was a Mormon himself . . . indicates that he must have had much to do with the early diffusion of it in the West. It is probable, though it cannot be proved, that Carter wrote the additional stanzas of the ballad. . . . Moreover, it seems safe to infer that it was Carter who associated the text with the *Western tune*, a set of the air to "The False-Hearted Knight", Child 4. . . . The Eastern or woods tune is the exceedingly popular "Fainne Geal an Lae" (The Bright Dawn of Day, or The Dawning of the Day). . . . —Phillips Barry, *The New Green Mountain Songster*, Traditional Folk Songs of Vermont, collected, transcribed, and edited by Helen Hartness Flanders, Elizabeth Flanders Ballard, George Brown, and Phillips Barry (1939), pp. 112–113.

242. *Front Songs of American Sailormen*, by Joanna C. Colcord, pp. 151–152. Copyright, 1938, by W. W. Norton & Company. New York.

A forcastle song. Joanna Colcord notes: "'Greenland Fishery' or 'The Whale' was not more popular on whaling ships than in the ships of the merchant marine. It arose in the British, not the American whaling trade, probably in the latter part of the eighteenth century, and in the earlier British versions, the ship's name, the *Lion*, and the captain's, Speedicutt, are both preserved."

243. *Ibid.*, pp. 88–89. This and the next two songs are windlass or capstan shanties.

Bullen says . . . "It embodies all the admiration that a sailor used to feel for a great seaman; gives it expression as it were, though I have never been able to learn who the antitype or Stormalong could have been. I suspect that he was just the embodiment of all the prime seamen the sailor had ever known, and in the song he voiced his heart's admiration."—J. C.

244. From *Ballads and Songs of the Shanty-Boy*, collected and edited by Franz Rickaby, pp. 11–14. Copyright 1926, by Harvard University Press. Cambridge.

This ballad, one of several celebrating death by that most spectacular of all hazards in lumbering, the log jam, was easily the most widely current of all lumber woods songs. Some of the old fellows have told me that anyone starting Gerry's Rocks in the shanties was summarily shut off because the song was sung to death; others vow that of all songs it was ever and always the most welcome.

* * * * *

One of the most interesting elements in the story, one which appears in all versions, and happily one reflecting a well-authenticated shanty-boy habit, is the subscription presented to the bereaved sweetheart. In actual life this contribution was sent the wife or other dependent; but the practice was common.—F. R.

245. *Ibid.*, pp. 65–68.

This is an old Wisconsin classic, dating from the days when oxen were used in the woods almost entirely. It resounds with that valorous spirit of the days when supremacy among men and animals was measured in terms of ability to do work, to stand physical exertion. Competition between camps, teams and even individual men, was a tremendous driving force. . . . One cannot help regretting the ballad "leap" between stanzas 9 and 10; for, although one gets from the ballad as it is a considerable reflection of the spirit in which the contest was waged, there is no word of the battle itself, which must have had its Homeric aspects.

According to Mr. Fred Bainter, the singer . . . , the ballad was composed in Mart Douglas's camp in northwestern Wisconsin in 1872 or 1873. It was in this camp and at this date. he said, that the contest between the big spotted steers and the little brown bulls was waged.—F. R.

246. From *American Songs for American Children* [edited by Alan Lomax, Charles Seeger, and Ruth Crawford Seeger], pp. 8–9. Chicago: Music Educators National Conference. 1942.

The Chisholm Trail once wound all the way from San Antonio to Montana, and old-time punchers say that if you laid all the stanzas of this ballad end to end, they would stretch all the way to the Canadian line.

This song is the cowboy folk-song par excellence, completely improvised and casual, and every man who ever sang it added his own verses. In fact, it's still growing to-day. Into it the cowboys poured the account of every movement, every accident of the day's work. If the foreman of an outfit drove his men too hard, he was sure to be made the butt of some satiric stanza of this cowboy epic When a cowboy dashed away after an unruly steer to turn him back into the herd, he might shout out a new stanza to the rhythm of his galloping horse as he rode.

There are almost as many versions of the ballad as there are singers, but the tunes are all basically kin. All end with the "ti-yi-youpy" or the "ki-yi-yippy" refrain, which may be an imitation of an Indian war-cry, for the Indians taught the Mexicans how to tame and ride the Western pony and the Mexican vaqueros taught the Texas cowboys. My father, John A. Lomax, says that this version is the one that was sung to the easy-pace gait of the cowpony—the gentle, rocking pace that devours miles and does not bore the rider.—A. L.

247. From *Cowboy Songs and Other Frontier Ballads*, collected by John A. Lomax and Alan Lomax, Revised and Enlarged, pp. 417–420. Copyright, 1910, 1916, 1938, by The Macmillan Company. New York. Copyright, 1938, by John A. Lomax.

248. From *Put's Golden Songster*, Containing the Largest and Most Popular Collection of California Songs Ever Published, by the Author of "Put's Original California Songster", pp. 50–52. Copyright, 1858, by John A. Stone. San Francisco: D. E. Appleton & Co.

The tune ("Villikins and His Dinah") and chorus are given as sung by John McCready at Groveland Tuolumne Co., California, recorded by Sidney Robertson for the Archive of California Folk Music at the University of California, and published in *The Gold Rush Song Book*, compiled by Eleanora Black and Sidney Robertson (1940), pp. 10–11.

249. From *Minstrels of the Mine Patch*, Songs and Stories of the Anthracite Industry, by George Korson, pp. 38–41, 48–53. Copyright, 1938, by the University of Pennsylvania Press. Philadelphia.

250. Window.—G. K.

251. Fellow miners, especially one who works abreast in partnership with another miner. A term used in English mining for two hundred years, and by soldiers in the World War under its other form "buddy".—G. K.

252. A basin at the bottom of a slope or shaft where water is collected to be pumped out.—G. K.

253. From Resettlement Song Sheets [edited by Charles Seeger]. Washington, D. C.:

Special Skills Division of the Resettlement Administration. [1936–1937.]

Mrs. Emma Dusenbury, of Mena, Arkansas, sings "The Dodger" in this way. She learned it in the 1880's when a farmer could still make a living, "just as sure as he was born".—C. S.

254. From Resettlement Song Sheets [edited by Charles Seeger]. "Number 1 in a series of American songs rarely found in popular collections." Washington, D. C.: Special Skills Division of the Resettlement Administration. [1936–1937.]

In his *American Songbag*, Carl Sandburg says that he heard fragments of this song in Illinois in the early 1890's. "S. K. Barlow", he says, "a Galesburg milkman, who used to be a fiddler at dances near Galva, sang it for me as we washed eight- and two-gallon delivery cans and quart-measure cups on winter afternoons. W. W. Delaney said, 'As near as I can remember, that song came out in the 1860's just after the war.'"—C. S.

255. From *The Hobo's Hornbook*, A Repertory for a Gutter Jongleur, collected and annotated by George Milburn, pp. 86–88. Copyright, 1930, by George Milburn. New York: Ives Washburn.

256. *Ham*, to walk across country. From the traditional ham actor whose company gets stranded on the road, and who is forced to walk back to the city.—G. M.

257. From *The Hobo's Hornbook*, A Repertory for a Gutter Jongleur, collected and annotated by George Milburn, pp. 83–85. New York: Ives Washburn.

At the missions where the hobo sometimes applies for food and shelter he hears and becomes familiarized with religious tunes. This, in part, accounts for the amazing popularity, among hoboes, of Joe Hill's parodies. One of the best known is "Pie in the Sky", which Hill adapted to the tune of "In the Sweet Bye and Bye". Its spirit is indicative of the hobo's resentful attitude toward organized religion and, very possibly, is a more genuine expression than the mission stiff's testimonials.—G. M.

258. From *30 and 1 Folksongs* (From the Southern Mountains), Compiled and Arranged by Bascom Lamar Lunsford and Lamar Stringfield, pp. 24–25. Copyright, 1929, by Carl Fischer, Inc. New York. International Copyright secured.

This song, which is also used as a fiddle tune, has many stanzas in addition to those given above. It is sung and played in the Carolinas, East Tennessee, and Kentucky.—B. L. L.

259. *Ibid.*, pp. 42–43.

A "crackerjack" party tune, with countless stanzas.—B. L. L.

260. From Resettlement Song Sheets [edited by Charles Seeger]. "Number 5 of a series of American songs to supplement popular collections." Washington, D. C.: Special Skills Division of the Resettlement Administration. [1936–1937.]

This song is also widely known as "Birmingham Jail"; but the names of other cities are found in its stead, with, of course, a countless variety of verses: as "Barbourville Jail", in Kentucky; "Powder Mill Jail", in Tennessee, etc. Upon the San Francisco Bridge in 1935, it was sung as "We're building bridges, bridges so low, Hang yourself over, feel the wind blow." Then there are the verses called "Little Willie":

Tree on the mountain, tree in full bloom;
Oh, Willie my darling, I've loved you too soon.
Your parents don't like me, so well do I know
They say I'm not worthy to knock at your door.—C. S.

261. From *On the Trail of Negro Folk-Songs*, by Dorothy Scarborough, assisted by Ola Lee Gulledge p. 68. Copyright, 1925, by Harvard University Press. Cambridge. From Louise Laurens, of Shelbyville, Kentucky.

262. From *Slave Songs of the United States*, by William Francis Allen, Charles Pickard Ware, Lucy McKim Garrison, p. 89. Copyright, 1867. Reprinted 1929. New York: Peter Smith.

   A very good specimen, so far as notes can give one, of the strange barbaric songs that one hears upon the Western steamboats.—W. F. A., C. P. W., L. McK. G.

263. *Ibid.*, p. 88.

264. From *Slave Songs of the United States*, by William Francis Allen, Charles Pickard Ware, Lucy McKim Garrison p. 67. Copyright, 1867. Reprinted 1929. New York: Peter Smith.

   A corn-song, of which only the burden is remembered.—W. F. A., C. P. W., L. McK. G.

265. *Ibid.*, p. 89.

266. As sung by Alan Lomax. Transcribed by Charles Seeger. The design for the song is the African leader-chorus form, and this version is used on the Texas prison farms for hoeing—a whole gang moving forward together, their hoes flashing together in the sun, across an irrigation ditch, thus:

   Well, *las'* Monday *mornin'*
   Lawd, Lawd, *Lawd!*
   —A. L.

267. The sow's.—A. L.

268. As sung by Huddie ("Lead Belly") Ledbetter. Transcribed by Peter Seeger.

269. From *American Ballads and Folk Songs*, collected and compiled by John A. Lomax and Alan Lomax, pp. 91–93. Copyright, 1934, by The Macmillan Company. New York.

   Some of the verses of this ballad work song we have taken from *Negro Workaday Songs*. The rest of the words and the tune were recorded in Southern Prison camps.—J. A. L. and A. L.

270. From "Delia Holmes—A Neglected Negro Ballad", by Chapman J. Milling, *Southern Folklore Quarterly,* Vol I (December, 1937), No. 4., pp. 3–7.

   . . . Will Win [is] a most interesting coloured troubadour who has wandered all over the South and West, carrying a battered guitar and earning his meals and lodging by his song. Although bearing many outward indications of an unsheltered life, Will possesses a personality and natural born showmanship. He states that "Delia" originated following a murder in Georgia, having been composed about 1900 by a white minstrel of Dallas, Texas, known as "Whistlin' Bill Ruff". The song, however, seems too typically Negroid to admit of this explanation.

   Careful search among the most promising collections has failed to reveal anything approaching the story as rendered in Will's version. The tune could not be found at all. White, in *American Negro Folk Songs* (Cambridge, 1928), gives two brief variants of "Delia", one a mere fragment. Both of these are regarded by the compiler as variants of "Frankie and Johnny". The only other place I have been able to find the song is in Odum and Johnson's *The Negro and His Songs* (Chapel Hill, 1925). The authors here note that it is called "Pauly", "Frankie" or "Lilly", and list their version under the last name. It differs so little from "Frankie and Johnny" that I am forced to regard their variant as belonging to the latter, and better known, song.

   I am deeply indebted to Mr. H.J. Martin, Columbia, S. C., for transcribing the music in connection with this article. The refrain line is repeated at the end of each stanza. The chorus is sung after every six or eight stanzas.—C. J. M.

271. As sung by the Almanac Singers. Transcribed by Ruth Crawford Seeger.

272. From *The Negro Sings a New Heaven*, by Mary Allen Grissom, pp. 10–11. Copyright. 1930, by the University of North Carolina Press. Chapel Hill.
273. From *Slave Songs of the United States*, by William Francis Allen, Charles Pickard Ware, Lucy McKim Garrison, p. 12. Copyright, 1867. Reprinted, 1929. New York: Peter Smith.
274. Do.—W. F. A., C. P. W., L. McK. G.
275. I pray(cry) to de Lord.—W. F. A., C. P. W., L. McK. G.
276. From *The American Songbag*, by Carl Sandburg, pp. 8–10. Copyright, 1927, by Harcourt, Brace & Company. New York.

As you increase the farm products you increase the insects that destroy them. You will pretty soon find out what my old Latin teacher told me about the meaning of ad infinitum. He said, "As you have learned in your entomology, you will find big bugs have little bugs on their backs to bite 'em, and the little bugs have smaller bugs and so ad infinitum." I fail to quote it accurately but you have the idea. . . .

My friends, the cotton boll weevil awakes in the spring, and by the first of September the generations coming from one pair will amount to 154,000,000, equal to the population of the Chinese Empire. What a blessing it would have been if a lark had been there to catch that pair in the beginning. (Laughter).— *Speeches of William Henry Murray*, Governor of Oklahoma (1931), pp. 65–66.